Sources of
World Societies

VOLUME II: SINCE 1500

Sources of
World Societies

VOLUME II: SINCE 1500

Denis Gainty

GEORGIA STATE UNIVERSITY

Debra Michals

MERRIMACK COLLEGE

BEDFORD/ST. MARTIN'S   BOSTON ◆ NEW YORK

For Bedford/St. Martin's

Publisher for History: Mary Dougherty
Director of Development for History: Jane Knetzger
Executive Editor for History: Traci Mueller
Associate Editor for History: Lynn Sternberger
Assistant Production Manager: Joe Ford
Production Supervisor: Samuel Jones
Executive Marketing Manager: Jenna Bookin Barry
Project Management: DeMasi Design and Publishing Service
Cover Design: Sara Gates
Cover Art: Portrait of Yintang, Prince Yi, Looking through a Window. China, Qing dynasty, 18th century. Hanging scroll. Ink and color on silk. Arthur M. Sackler Gallery, Smithsonian Institution, Washington, D.C. Purchase from Smithsonian Collections Acquisition Program, and partial gift of Richard G. Pritzlaff, S1991.64. Emile Bernard (1868–1941), detail from *Study of a Mulatto Woman,* 1895. Oil on canvas. Musée Municipal, Boulogne-Billancourt, France, The Bridgeman Art Library. Copyright 2008 Estate of Emile Bernard/Artists Rights Society (ARS), NY.
Composition: Jeff Miller Book Design
Printing and Binding: RR Donnelley & Sons Company

President: Joan E. Feinberg
Editorial Director: Denise B. Wydra
Director of Marketing: Karen R. Soeltz
Director of Editing, Design, and Production: Marcia Cohen
Assistant Director of Editing, Design, and Production: Elise S. Kaiser
Manager, Publishing Services: Emily Berleth

Manufactured in the United States of America.

4 3 2 1 0
f e d c b

For information, write: Bedford/St. Martin's, 75 Arlington Street, Boston, MA 02116 (617-399-4000)

ISBN-10: 0-312-68858-X
ISBN-13: 978-0-312-68858-5

Acknowledgments
Acknowledgments and copyrights are continued at the back of the book on pages 409–413, which constitute an extension of the copyright page.

S*ources of World Societies* is a compilation of primary sources recorded
by those who shaped and experienced the cultural evolutions and
interactions that comprise the world's history from ancient times to the
present — among them rulers and subjects alike, men and women, philosophers, revolutionaries, economists, and laborers. With a parallel chapter
structure and documents hand-picked to further illustrate elements of the
text, this reader is designed to complement A *History of World Societies*,
eighth edition. *Sources of World Societies* aspires to animate the past for
students, providing resonant accounts of the people and events that changed
the face of world history, from myths of creation to tallies of the spoils and
fatalities of war.

While a good textbook creates a clear framework of major historical
figures and movements, *Sources* evokes the experiences of historical moments as they were lived and creates a dynamic connection for students
that bridges the events of the past with their own understandings of power
and its abuses, of the ripple effects of human agency, and of the material
conditions of life. For example, Chapter 15 of the textbook provides a personal history of Zheng He, commander of the Chinese Emperor Yongle's
massive treasure fleet, and describes the political and commercial impact
of his seven voyages. In *Sources*, Zheng He's own words convey the majesty
of his expeditions as no other narrative can. Of the fleet and its missions
he inscribes, "We have traversed more than one hundred thousand li of
immense water spaces and have beheld in the ocean huge waves like
mountains rising sky-high . . . traversing those savage waves as if we were
treading a public thoroughfare."

With input from the textbook authors, as well as from current instruc-
tors of the world history survey course, we have compiled these documents
with one goal foremost in mind: to make history's most classic and compelling voices accessible to students, from the most well-known thinkers
and documentarians of their times to the galvanized or introspective com-
moners. In Chapter 28, for example, official government documents,
newspaper editorials, and a personal letter depict in sharp relief numerous

nationalist movements fermenting in Asia in the early twentieth century. Students can follow the evolutionary course of the British government's 1917 Balfour Declaration supporting the creation of a Jewish homeland, then contrast their conception of British imperial power with feminist nationalist Sarojini Naidu's outrage over the violence of British troops in India just two years later.

We have stepped back from drawing conclusions and instead provide just enough background to enable students' own analysis of the sources at hand. Chapter-opening paragraphs briefly review the major events of the time and place the documents that follow within the framework of the corresponding textbook chapter. A concise headnote for each document provides context about the author and the circumstances surrounding the document's creation, while gloss notes supply clarification to aid comprehension of unfamiliar terms and references. Each document is followed by Reading and Discussion Questions that spur deep student analysis of the material, while chapter-concluding Comparative Questions encourage students to contemplate the harmony and discord among the sources within and, when called for, between the chapters. The excerpts range widely in length to allow for a variety of class assignments.

Acknowledgments

For their availability and insight, many thanks to *History of World Societies* authors John P. McKay, John Buckler, Clare Crowston, Patricia Ebrey, and Roger Beck, who went above and beyond to help us select and gather these sources despite full teaching and research schedules. Editor Shannon Hunt gave her time and expertise throughout, and this book would not have reached fruition without her hard work. Thanks to Lynn Sternberger for her wonderful insights and razor-sharp editor's pencil, and to Jane Knetzger and Heidi Hood for their support and encouragement. Sara Wise shepherded this project along from its very early stages. Emily Berleth of Bedford St. Martin's and Linda DeMasi of DeMasi Design made production of this book possible with remarkable finesse. Thanks also to C. Melissa Anderson for her thoughtful comments on wording and content.

CONTENTS

Sources of
World Societies

VOLUME II: SINCE 1500

CHAPTER 15

The Acceleration of Global Contact

Although long-standing trade routes meant that many of the world's civilizations were in contact with one another before 1500, this interaction accelerated drastically in the sixteenth century when Europe became a much larger player in world trade. Europe began establishing trade routes to the newly discovered Americas and sent Christian missionaries to all corners of the globe. The sources in this chapter examine the impact of Europe's entrance into the global community and address the continued importance of the civilizations that had established earlier trade routes in the Indian Ocean.

DOCUMENT 15-1

BARTOLOMÉ DE LAS CASAS
From Brief Account of the Devastation of the Indies
1542

Bartolomé de Las Casas (1484–1566) was one of the most vocal opponents of the Spaniards' treatment of the native people of the West Indies. In particular, the Dominican missionary criticized the encomienda *system, which allowed Spanish colonists to force local peoples to work the colonists' land or mines — often under deplorable conditions. In his* Brief Account, *Las Casas discusses the detrimental impact that the arrival of the Europeans had on the West Indies. He pays significant attention to the steep depopulation of*

Bartolomé de Las Casas, *The Devastation of the Indies: A Brief Account*, translated by Herma Briffault (New York: A Continuum Book from Seabury Press, 1974), 37–44, 51–52.

1

the islands of the Caribbean, one of the most dramatic events associated with the colonization of the West Indies.

The [West] Indies were discovered in the year one thousand four hundred and ninety-two. In the following year a great many Spaniards went there with the intention of settling the land. Thus, forty-nine years have passed since the first settlers penetrated the land, the first so-claimed being the large and most happy isle called Hispaniola, which is six hundred leagues in circumference. Around it in all directions are many other islands, some very big, others very small, and all of them were, as we saw with our own eyes, densely populated with native peoples called Indians. This large island was perhaps the most densely populated place in the world. There must be close to two hundred leagues of land on this island, and the sea-coast has been explored for more than ten thousand leagues, and each day more of it is being explored. And all the land so far discovered is a beehive of people; it is as though God had crowded into these lands the great majority of mankind.

And of all the infinite universe of humanity, these people are the most guileless, the most devoid of wickedness and duplicity, the most obedient and faithful to their native masters and to the Spanish Christians whom they serve. They are by nature the most humble, patient, and peaceable, holding no grudges, free from embroilments, neither excitable nor quarrelsome. These people are the most devoid of rancors, hatreds, or desire for vengeance of any people in the world. And because they are so weak and complaisant, they are less able to endure heavy labor and soon die of no matter what malady. The sons of nobles among us, brought up in the enjoyments of life's refinements, are no more delicate than are these Indians, even those among them who are of the lowest rank of laborers. They are also poor people, for they not only possess little but have no desire to possess worldly goods. For this reason they are not arrogant, embittered, or greedy. Their repasts are such that the food of the holy fathers in the desert can scarcely be more parsimonious, scanty, and poor. As to their dress, they are generally naked, with only their pudenda covered somewhat. And when they cover their shoulders it is with a square cloth no more than two varas [approximately 33 inches] in size. They have no beds, but sleep on a kind of matting or else in a kind of suspended net called hamacas. They are very clean in their persons, with alert, intelligent minds, docile and open to doctrine, very apt to receive our holy Catholic faith, to be endowed with virtuous customs, and to behave in a godly fashion. And once they begin to hear the tidings of the Faith, they are so insistent on knowing more and on taking the sacraments of the Church and on observing the divine cult that, truly, the missionaries who are here need to be endowed by God with great patience in order to cope with such eagerness. Some of the secular Spaniards who have been here for many years say that the goodness of the Indians is undeniable and that if this gifted people could be brought to know the one true God they would be the most fortunate people in the world.

Yet into this sheepfold, into this land of meek outcasts there came some Spaniards who immediately behaved like ravening wild beasts, wolves, tigers, or lions that had been starved for many days. And Spaniards have behaved in no other way during the past forty years, down to the present time, for they are still acting like ravening beasts, killing, terrorizing, afflicting, torturing, and destroying the native peoples, doing all this with the strangest and most varied new methods of cruelty, never seen or heard of before, and to such a degree that this Island of Hispaniola once so populous (having a population that I estimated to be more than three millions), has now a population of barely two hundred persons.

The island of Cuba is nearly as long as the distance between Valladolid and Rome; it is now almost completely depopulated. San Juan [Puerto Rico] and Jamaica are two of the largest, most productive and attractive islands; both are now deserted and devastated. On the northern side of Cuba and Hispaniola lie the neighboring Lucayos comprising more than sixty islands including those called Gigantes, beside numerous other islands, some small some large. The least felicitous of them were more fertile and beautiful than the gardens of the King of Seville. They have the healthiest lands in the world, where lived more than five hundred thousand souls; they are now deserted, inhabited by not a single living creature. All the people were slain or died after being taken into captivity and brought to the Island of Hispaniola to be sold as slaves. When the Spaniards saw that some of these had escaped, they sent a ship to find them, and it voyaged for three years among the islands searching for those who had escaped being slaughtered, for a good Christian had helped them escape, taking pity on them and had won them over to Christ; of these there were eleven persons and these I saw. . . .

As for the vast mainland, which is ten times larger than all Spain, even including Aragon and Portugal, containing more land than the distance between Seville and Jerusalem, or more than two thousand leagues, we are sure that our Spaniards, with their cruel and abominable acts, have devastated the land and exterminated the rational people who fully inhabited it.

We can estimate very surely and truthfully that in the forty years that have passed, with the infernal actions of the Christians, there have been unjustly slain more than twelve million men, women, and children. In truth, I believe without trying to deceive myself that the number of the slain is more like fifteen million.

The common ways mainly employed by the Spaniards who call themselves Christian and who have gone there to extirpate those pitiful nations and wipe them off the earth is by unjustly waging cruel and bloody wars. Then, when they have slain all those who fought for their lives or to escape the tortures they would have to endure, that is to say, when they have slain all the native rulers and young men (since the Spaniards usually spare only the women and children, who are subjected to the hardest and bitterest servitude ever suffered by man or beast), they enslave any survivors. With these infernal methods of tyranny they debase and weaken countless numbers of those pitiful Indian nations.

Their reason for killing and destroying such an infinite number of souls is that the Christians have an ultimate aim, which is to acquire gold, and to swell themselves with riches in a very brief time and thus rise to a high estate disproportionate to their merits. It should be kept in mind that their insatiable greed and ambition, the greatest ever seen in the world, is the cause of their villainies. And also, those lands are so rich and felicitous, the native peoples so meek and patient, so easy to subject, that our Spaniards have no more consideration for them than beasts. And I say this from my own knowledge of the acts I witnessed. But I should not say "than beasts" for, thanks be to God, they have treated beasts with some respect; I should say instead like excrement on the public squares. And thus they have deprived the Indians of their lives and souls, for the millions I mentioned have died without the Faith and without the benefit of the sacraments. This is a well known and proven fact which even the tyrant Governors, themselves killers, know and admit. And never have the Indians in all the Indies committed any act against the Spanish Christians, until those Christians have first and many times committed countless cruel aggressions against them or against neighboring nations. For in the beginning the Indians regarded the Spaniards as angels from Heaven. Only after the Spaniards had used violence against them, killing, robbing, torturing, did the Indians ever rise up against them. On the Island Hispaniola was where the Spaniards first landed, as I have said. Here those Christians perpetrated their first ravages and oppressions against the native peoples. This was the first land in the New World to be destroyed and depopulated by the Christians, and here they began their subjection of the women and children, taking them away from the Indians to use them and ill use them, eating the food they provided with their sweat and toil. The Spaniards did not content themselves with what the Indians gave them of their own free will, according to their ability, which was always too little to satisfy enormous appetites, for a Christian eats and consumes in one day an amount of food that would suffice to feed three houses inhabited by ten Indians for one month. And they committed other acts of force and violence and oppression which made the Indians realize that these men had not come from Heaven. And some of the Indians concealed their foods while others concealed their wives and children and still others fled to the mountains to avoid the terrible transactions of the Christians.

And the Christians attacked them with buffets and beatings, until finally they laid hands on the nobles of the villages. Then they behaved with such temerity and shamelessness that the most powerful ruler of the islands had to see his own wife raped by a Christian officer.

From that time onward the Indians began to seek ways to throw the Christians out of their lands. They took up arms, but their weapons were very weak and of little service in offense and still less in defense. (Because of this, the wars of the Indians against each other are little more than games played by children.) And the Christians, with their horses and swords and pikes began to carry out massacres and strange cruelties against them. They attacked the towns and spared neither the children nor the aged nor pregnant women nor women in childbed, not only stabbing them and dismembering them but cutting them to pieces as if dealing with sheep in the slaughter house. They laid bets as to who, with one stroke of the sword, could split a man in two or could cut off his head or spill out his entrails with a single stroke of the pike. They took infants from their mothers' breasts, snatching them by the legs and pitching them head-first against the crags or snatched them by the arms and threw them into the rivers, roaring with laughter and saying as the babies fell into the water, "Boil there, you offspring of the devil!" Other infants they put to the sword along with their mothers and anyone else who happened to be nearby. They made some low wide gallows on which the hanged victim's feet almost touched the ground, stringing up their victims in lots of thirteen, in memory of Our Redeemer and His twelve Apostles, then set burning wood at their feet and thus burned them alive. To others they attached straw or wrapped their whole bodies in straw and set them afire. With still others, all those they wanted to capture alive, they cut off their hands and hung them round the victim's neck, saying, "Go now, carry the message," meaning, Take the news to the Indians who have fled to the mountains. They usually dealt with the chieftains and nobles in the following way: they made a grid of rods which they placed on forked sticks, then lashed the victims to the grid and lighted a smoldering fire underneath, so that little by little, as those captives screamed in despair and torment, their souls would leave them. . . .

After the wars and the killings had ended, when usually there survived only some boys, some women, and children, these survivors were distributed among the Christians to be slaves. The repartimiento or distribution was made according to the rank and importance of the Christian to whom the Indians were allocated, one of them being given thirty, another forty, still another, one or two hundred, and besides the rank of the Christian there was also to be considered in what favor he stood with the tyrant they called Governor. The pretext was that these allocated Indians were to be instructed in the articles of the Christian Faith. As if those Christians who were as a rule foolish and cruel and greedy and vicious could be caretakers of souls! And the care they took was to send the men to the mines to dig for gold, which is intolerable labor, and to send the women into the fields of the big ranches to hoe and till the land, work suitable for strong men. Nor to either the men or the women did they give any food except herbs and legumes, things of little substance. The milk in the breasts of the women with infants dried up and thus in a short while the infants perished. And since men and women were separated, there could be no marital relations. And the men died in the mines and the women died on the ranches from the same causes, exhaustion and hunger. And thus was depopulated that island which had been densely populated.

READING AND DISCUSSION QUESTIONS

1. According to Las Casas, what motivated the Spaniards to settle the West Indies? What did they hope to gain?

2. Why did the West Indies experience a rapid depopulation when the Europeans arrived? According to Las Casas, how was this depopulation avoidable?

3. How does Las Casas suggest that the Christian mission to the New World had failed?

DOCUMENT 15-2

ZHENG HE

Stele Inscription

1431

Before the Europeans crossed the Atlantic and began exploring the New World, the Indian Ocean was the center of the world's sea trading routes and China dominated much of the trading activity. Zheng He (1371–1433) was an admiral during the Ming Dynasty who led seven naval expeditions to locations such as the Arabian peninsula, East Africa, India, and Southeast Asia. Compared to the three ships comprising Columbus's initial expedition, Zheng He's earlier fleet was massive, somewhere between 200 and 300 ships carrying around 28,000 men. Zheng He's inscription is a stele, or large rock monument, that describes his expeditions.

Record of the miraculous answer (to prayer) of the goddess the Celestial Spouse.[1]

The Imperial Ming Dynasty unifying seas and continents, surpassing the three dynasties even goes beyond the Han and Tang dynasties. The countries beyond the horizon and from the ends of the earth have all become subjects and to the most western of the western or the most northern of the northern countries, however far they may be, the distance and the routes may be calculated. Thus the barbarians from beyond the seas, though their countries are truly distant, "with double translation" have come to audience bearing precious objects and presents.

The Emperor, approving of their loyalty and sincerity, has ordered us (Zheng) He and others at the head of several tens of thousands of officers and flag-troops to ascend more than one hundred large ships to go and confer presents on them in order to make manifest the transforming power of the (imperial) virtue and to treat distant people with kindness. From the

---

Teobaldo Filesi, *China and Africa in the Middle Ages*, trans. David Morison (London: Frank Cass, 1972), 57–61.

[1] **the goddess the Celestial Spouse**: While in human form during the Song Dynasty, the goddess Tian Fei, or Mazu, was believed to have miraculously saved her merchant brothers during a storm at sea. As such, she was a natural choice for the explorer Zheng He to direct his prayers.

third year of Yongle[2] (1405) till now we have seven times received the commission of ambassadors to countries of the western ocean. The barbarian countries which we have visited are: by way of Zhancheng, Zhaowa, Sanfoqi, and Xianlo crossing straight over to Xilanshan in South India, Guli, and Kezhi, we have gone to the western regions Hulumosi, Adan, Mugudushu, altogether more than thirty countries large and small.[3] We have traversed more than one hundred thousand li[4] of immense water spaces and have beheld in the ocean huge waves like mountains rising sky-high, and we have set eyes on barbarian regions far away hidden in a blue transparency of light vapors, while our sails loftily unfurled like clouds day and night continued their course (rapid like that) of a star, traversing those savage waves as if we were treading a public thoroughfare. Truly this was due to the majesty and the good fortune of the Court and moreover we owe it to the protecting virtue of the divine Celestial Spouse.

The power of the goddess having indeed been manifested in previous times has been abundantly revealed in the present generation. In the midst of the rushing waters it happened that, when there was a hurricane, suddenly there was a divine lantern shining in the mast, and as soon as this miraculous light appeared the danger was appeased, so that even in the danger of capsizing one felt reassured that there was no cause for fear. When we arrived in the distant countries we captured alive those of the native kings who were not respectful and exterminated those barbarian robbers who were engaged in piracy, so that consequently the sea route was cleansed and pacified and the natives put their trust in it. All this is due to the favors of the goddess.

It is not easy to enumerate completely all the cases where the goddess has answered (prayers). Previously in a memorial to the Court we have requested that her virtue be registered in the Court of Sacrificial Worship and a temple be built at Nanking on the bank of the dragon river where regular sacrifices should be transmitted for ever. We have respectfully received an Imperial commemorative composition exalting the miraculous favors, which is the highest recompense and praise indeed. However, the miraculous power of the goddess resides wherever one goes. As for the

---

[2] **Yongle**: He was Emperor during most of Zheng He's expeditions.
[3] **by way of Zhancheng . . . small**: The journey that Zheng He describes routes around present-day Indonesia, south below India, and into the eastern coast of Africa.
[4] **one hundred thousand li**: One li is roughly a third of a mile, so they have sailed over 33,000 miles.

temporary palace on the southern mountain at Changle, I have, at the head of the fleet, frequently resided there awaiting the [favorable] wind to set sail for the ocean.

We, Zheng He and others, on the one hand have received the high favor of a gracious commission of our Sacred Lord, and on the other hand carry to the distant barbarians the benefits of respect and good faith (on their part). Commanding the multitudes on the fleet and (being responsible for) a quantity of money and valuables in the face of the violence of the winds and the nights our one fear is not to be able to succeed; how should we then dare not to serve our dynasty with exertion of all our loyalty and the gods with the utmost sincerity? How would it be possible not to realize what is the source of the tranquillity of the fleet and the troops and the salvation on the voyage both going and returning? Therefore we have made manifest the virtue of the goddess on stone and have moreover recorded the years and months of the voyages to the barbarian countries and the return in order to leave (the memory) for ever.

I.   In the third year of Yongle (1405) commanding the fleet we went to Guli and other countries. At that time the pirate Chen Zuyi had gathered his followers in the country of Sanfoqi, where he plundered the native merchants. When he also advanced to resist our fleet, supernatural soldiers secretly came to the rescue so that after one beating of the drum he was annihilated. In the fifth year (1407) we returned.

II. In the fifth year of Yongle (1407) commanding the fleet we went to Zhaowa, Guli, Kezhi, and Xianle. The kings of these countries all sent as tribute precious objects, precious birds and rare animals. In the seventh year (1409) we returned.

III. In the seventh year of Yongle (1409) commanding the fleet we went to the countries (visited) before and took our route by the country of Xilanshan. Its king Yaliekunaier [King of Sri Lanka] was guilty of a gross lack of respect and plotted against the fleet. Owing to the manifest answer to prayer of the goddess (the plot) was discovered and thereupon that king was captured alive. In the ninth year (1411) on our return the king was presented (to the throne) (as a prisoner); subsequently he received the Imperial favor of returning to his own country.

IV. In the eleventh year of Yongle (1413) commanding the fleet we went to Hulumosi [Ormuz] and other countries. In the country of

Sumendala [Samudra] there was a false king Suganla[5] who was marauding and invading his country. Its king Cainu-liabiding had sent an envoy to the Palace Gates in order to lodge a complaint. We went thither with the official troups [troops] under our command and exterminated some and arrested (other rebels), and owing to the silent aid of the goddess we captured the false king alive. In the thirteenth year (1415) on our return he was presented (to the Emperor as a prisoner). In that year the king of the country of Manlajia [Malacca] came in person with his wife and son to present tribute.

V. In the fifteenth year of Yongle (1417) commanding the fleet we visited the western regions. The country of Hulumosi presented lions, leopards with gold spots, and large western horses. The country of Adan presented qilin of which the native name is culafa [a giraffe] as well as the long-horned animal maha [oryx antelope]. The country of Mugudushu presented huafu lu [zebras] as well as lions. The country of Bulawa [Brava] presented camels which run one thousand li as well as camel-birds [ostriches]. The countries of Zhaowa and Guli presented the animal miligao. They all vied in presenting the marvellous objects preserved in the mountains or hidden in the seas and the beautiful treasures buried in the sand or deposited on the shores. Some sent a maternal uncle of the king, others a paternal uncle or a younger brother of the king in order to present a letter of homage written on gold leaf as well as tribute.

VI. In the nineteenth year of Yongle (1421) commanding the fleet we conducted the ambassadors from Hulumosi and the other countries who had been in attendance at the capital for a long time back to their countries. The kings of all these countries prepared even more tribute than previously.

VII. In the sixth year of Xuande (1431) once more commanding the fleet we have left for the barbarian countries in order to read to them (an Imperial edict) and to confer presents.

We have anchored in this port awaiting a north wind to take the sea, and recalling how previously we have on several occasions received the benefits of the protection of the divine intelligence we have thus recorded an inscription in stone.

---

[5] **false king Suganla**: Sekandar, who usurped the throne from the rightful ruler Zain Al'-Abidin. He is referred to as Cainu-liabiding in the next sentence.

READING AND DISCUSSION QUESTIONS

1. What does the inscription suggest about the importance of overseas exploration to the Ming Dynasty?

2. Describe the relationship between the Chinese explorers and the local populations that they encountered. How did the Chinese treat these populations? How did these people respond to the Chinese presence?

DOCUMENT 15-3

KING FERDINAND AND QUEEN ISABELLA

Agreements with Columbus

1492

An Italian of modest birth, Christopher Columbus (1451–1506) was an experienced seafarer when he approached King Ferdinand and Queen Isabella of Spain. He sought their funding for an expedition across the Atlantic, which Columbus mistakenly believed was a shorter route to Asia than the journey east that Europeans typically made. In the end, Columbus did not reach Asia, but rather discovered two continents previously unknown to medieval Europeans. As his initial agreements with the Spanish monarchs made clear, the trip westward was a dangerous but potentially profitable one for the Italian explorer.

Agreement of April 17, 1492

The things supplicated and which your Highnesses give and declare to Christopher Columbus in some satisfaction . . . for the voyage which now, with the aid of God, he is about to make therein, in the service of your Highnesses, are as follows:

King Ferdinand and Queen Isabella, "Agreements with Columbus of April 17 and April 30, 1492," in J. B. Thatcher, *Christopher Columbus, His Life and Work*, 3 vols. (New York and London: Putnam's Sons, 1903), 2:442–451.

Firstly, that your Highnesses as Lords that are of the said oceans, make from this time the said Don Christopher Columbus your Admiral in all those islands and mainlands which by his hand and industry shall be discovered or acquired in the said oceans, during his life, and after his death, his heirs and successors, from one to another perpetually, with all the preeminences and prerogatives belonging to the said office. . . .

Likewise, that your Highnesses make the said Don Christopher your Viceroy and Governor General in all the said islands and mainlands and islands which as has been said, he may discover or acquire in the said seas; and that for the government of each one and of any one of them, he may make selection of three persons for each office, and that your Highnesses may choose and select the one who shall be most serviceable to you, and thus the lands which our Lord shall permit him to discover and acquire will be better governed, in the service of your Highnesses. . . .

Item, that all and whatever merchandise, whether it be pearls, precious stones, gold, silver, spices, and other things whatsoever, and merchandise of whatever kind, name, and manner it may be, which may be bought, bartered, discovered, acquired, or obtained within the limits of the said Admiralty, your Highnesses grant henceforth to the said Don Christopher, and will that he may have and take for himself, the tenth part of all of them, deducting all the expenses which may be incurred therein; so that of what shall remain free and clear, he may have and take the tenth part for himself, and do with it as he wills, the other nine parts remaining for your Highnesses. . . .

Item, that in all the vessels which may be equipped for the said traffic and negotiation each time and whenever and as often as they may be equipped, the said Admiral Don Christopher Columbus may, if he wishes, contribute and pay the eighth part of all that may be expended in the equipment. And also that he may have and take of the profit, the eighth part of all which may result from such equipment. . . .

These are executed and despatched with the responses of your Highnesses at the end of each article in the town of Santa Fe de la Vega de Granada, on the seventeenth day of April in the year of the nativity of our Savior Jesus Christ one thousand four hundred and ninety-two.

AGREEMENT OF APRIL 30, 1492

Forasmuch as you, Christopher Columbus, are going by our command, with some of our ships and with our subjects, to discover and acquire certain islands and mainland in the ocean, and it is hoped that, by the help of God, some of the said islands and mainland in the said ocean will be discovered and acquired by your pains and industry; and therefore it is a just and reasonable thing that since you incur the said danger for our service you should be rewarded for it . . . it is our will and pleasure that you, the said Christopher Columbus, after you have discovered and acquired the said islands and mainland in the said ocean, or any of them whatsoever, shall be our Admiral of the said islands and mainland and Viceroy and Governor therein, and shall be empowered from that time forward to call and entitle yourself Don Christopher Columbus, and that your sons and successors in the said office and charge may likewise entitle and call themselves Don, and Admiral and Viceroy and Governor thereof; and that you may have power to use and exercise the said office of Admiral, together with the said office of Viceroy and Governor of the said islands and mainland . . . and to hear and determine all the suits and causes civil and criminal appertaining to the said office of Admiralty, Viceroy, and Governor according as you shall find by law, . . . and may have power to punish and chastise delinquents, and exercise the said offices . . . in all that concerns and appertains to the said offices . . . and that you shall have and levy the fees and salaries annexed, belonging and appertaining to the said offices and to each of them, according as our High Admiral in the Admiralty of our kingdoms levies and is accustomed to levy them.

READING AND DISCUSSION QUESTIONS

1. According to the agreements, what rewards could Columbus expect if his venture was successful? What reason is given for offering these rewards to Columbus?

2. What motivated King Ferdinand and Queen Isabella to fund Columbus's expedition?

DOCUMENT 15-4

BERNARDINO DE SAHAGÚN

From General History of the Things of New Spain

ca. 1545–1578

A member of the Franciscan order, the Spaniard Bernardino de Sahagún (1499–1590) was one of the earliest missionaries to arrive in Mexico. Although committed to converting the native population of Mexico to Christianity, Sahagún learned the Aztec language of Nahuatl and wrote an extensive study of Aztec culture and religious beliefs. This study raised concern among Sahagún's superiors for its sympathetic portrayal of the Aztec people. The controversial General History of the Things of New Spain *remained in manuscript form in a Spanish convent until its eventual publication in the nineteenth century. In the excerpt below, Sahagún describes the Spanish conquest of Mexico, led by Hernando Cortés (1485–1547).*

And after the dying in Cholula, the Spaniards set off on their way to Mexico,[6] coming gathered and bunched, raising dust. . . .

Thereupon Moteucçoma[7] named and sent noblemen and a great many other agents of his . . . to go meet [Cortés] . . . at Quauhtechcac. They gave [the Spaniards] golden banners of precious feathers, and golden necklaces.

And when they had given the things to them, they seemed to smile, to rejoice and to be very happy. Like monkeys they grabbed the gold. It was as though their hearts were put to rest, brightened, freshened. For gold was what they greatly thirsted for; they were gluttonous for it, starved for it, piggishly wanting it. They came lifting up the golden banners, waving them

---

James Lockhart, ed. and trans., *We People Here: Nahuatl Accounts of the Conquest of Mexico* (Berkeley: University of California Press, 1993), 96, 98, 100, 106, 108, 110, 112, 132, 134, 136, 180, 182, 186, 188, 210, 216, 218, 238, 240, 242.

[6] **Mexico**: Sahagún uses the term *Mexico* to refer to Tenochtitlán, the capital of the Aztec Empire. *Mexica* refers to the people living in Tenochtitlán and its suburbs.

[7] **Moteucçoma**: Sometimes spelled Montezuma, Moteucçoma (1466–1520) was the Aztec emperor at the time of the Spanish conquest.

from side to side, showing them to each other. They seemed to babble; what they said to each other was in a babbling tongue. . . .

(Cortés and his entourage continue their march.)

Then they set out in this direction, about to enter Mexico here. Then they all dressed and equipped themselves for war. They girded themselves, tying their battle gear tightly on themselves and then on their horses. Then they arranged themselves in rows, files, ranks.

Four horsemen came ahead going first, staying ahead, leading. . . .

Also the dogs, their dogs [bred for combat], came ahead, sniffing at things and constantly panting.

By himself came marching ahead, all alone, the one who bore the standard on his shoulder. He came waving it about, making it spin, tossing it here and there. . . .

Following him came those with iron swords. Their iron swords came bare and gleaming. On their shoulders they bore their shields, of wood or leather.

The second contingent and file were horses carrying people, each with his cotton cuirass [chest armor], his leather shield, his iron lance, and his iron sword hanging down from the horse's neck. They came with bells on, jingling or rattling. The horses, the deer [horses], neighed, there was much neighing, and they would sweat a great deal; water seemed to fall from them. And their flecks of foam splatted on the ground, like soapsuds splatting. . . .

The third file were those with iron crossbows, the crossbowmen. Their quivers went hanging at their sides, passed under their armpits, well filled, packed with arrows, with iron bolts. . . .

The fourth file were likewise horsemen; their outfits were the same as has been said.

The fifth group were those with harquebuses,[8] the harquebusiers, shouldering their harquebuses; some held them [level]. And when they went into the great palace, the residence of the ruler, they repeatedly shot off their harquebuses. They exploded, sputtered, discharged, thundered, disgorged. Smoke spread, it grew dark with smoke, everyplace filled with smoke. The fetid smell made people dizzy and faint.

Then all those from the various altepetl [sovereign territories] on the other side of the mountains, the Tlaxcalans, the people of Tliliuhquitepec, of Huexotzinco, came following behind. They came outfitted for war with their cotton upper armor, shields, and bows, their quivers full and packed

---

[8] **harquebuses**: The guns of the Spanish conquerors.

with feathered arrows, some barbed, some blunted, some with obsidian [glass] points. They went crouching, hitting their mouths with their hands yelling, singing, . . . whistling, shaking their heads. . . .

(Cortés and his army entered Tenochtitlán in November 1519 and were amicably received by Moctezuma, who was nonetheless taken captive by the Spaniards. Cortés's army was allowed to remain in a palace compound, but tensions grew the following spring. Pedro de Alvarado, in command while Cortés left to deal with a threat to his authority from the governor of Cuba, became increasingly concerned for the Spaniards' safety as the people of Tenochtitlán prepared to celebrate the annual festival in honor of Huitzilopochtli, the warrior god of the sun.)

And when it had dawned and was already the day of his festivity, very early in the morning those who had made vows to him [i.e., Huitzilopochtli, the sun god] unveiled his face. Forming a single row before him they offered him incense; each in his place laid down before him offerings of food for fasting and rolled amaranth dough. And it was as though all the youthful warriors had gathered together and had hit on the idea of holding and observing the festivity in order to show the Spaniards something, to make them marvel and instruct them. . . .

When it was time, when the moment had come for the Spaniards to do the killing, they came out equipped for battle. They came and closed off each of the places where people went in and out. . . . And when they had closed these exits, they stationed themselves in each, and no one could come out any more. . . . Then they surrounded those who were dancing, going among the cylindrical drums. They struck a drummer's arms; both of his hands were severed. Then they struck his neck; his head landed far away. Then they stabbed everyone with iron lances and struck them with iron swords. They struck some in the belly, and then their entrails came spilling out. They split open the heads of some, they really cut their skulls to pieces, their skulls were cut up into little bits. And if someone still tried to run it was useless; he just dragged his intestines along. There was a stench as if of sulfur. Those who tried to escape could go nowhere. When anyone tried to go out, at the entryways they struck and stabbed him.

And when it became known what was happening, everyone cried out, "Mexica warriors, come running, get outfitted with devices, shields, and arrows, hurry, come running, the warriors are dying; they have died, perished, been annihilated, O Mexica warriors!" Thereupon there were war cries, shouting, and beating of hands against lips. The warriors quickly came outfitted, bunched together, carrying arrows and shields. Then the fighting began; they shot at them with barbed darts, spears, and tridents, and they hurled darts with broad obsidian points at them. . . .

The fighting that ensued drove the Spaniards and their allies back to the palace enclave. Without a reliable supply of food and water, in July 1520, Cortés, who had returned with his power intact, led his followers on a desperate nocturnal escape from the city, but they were discovered and suffered heavy losses as they fled. They retreated to the other side of the lake, and the Aztecs believed the Spanish threat had passed.

Before the Spanish appeared to us, first an epidemic broke out, a sickness of pustules [smallpox]. . . . Large bumps spread on people; some were entirely covered. They spread everywhere, on the face, the head, the chest, etc. The disease brought great desolation; a great many died of it. They could no longer walk about, but lay in their dwellings and sleeping places, no longer able to move or stir. They were unable to change position, to stretch out on their sides or face down, or raise their heads. And when they made a motion, they called out loudly. The pustules that covered people caused great desolation; very many people died of them, and many just starved to death; starvation reigned, and no one took care of others any longer. . . .

This disease of pustules lasted a full sixty days; after sixty days it abated and ended. When people were convalescing and reviving, the pustules disease began to move in the direction of Chalco. And many were disabled or paralyzed by it, but they were not disabled forever. . . . The Mexica warriors were greatly weakened by it.

And when things were in this state, the Spaniards came, moving toward us from Tetzcoco. . . .

(Having resupplied his Spanish/Tlaxcalan army and having constructed a dozen cannon-carrying brigantines for use on the lake, Cortés resumed his offensive late in 1520. In April 1521 he reached Tenochtitlán and placed the city under a blockade.)

When their twelve boats had come from Tetzcoco, at first they were all assembled at Acachinanco, and then the Marqués [Cortés] moved to Acachinanco. He went about searching where the boats could enter, where the canals were straight, whether they were deep or not, so that they would not be grounded somewhere. But the canals were winding and bent back and forth, and they could not get them in. They did get two boats in; they forced them down the road coming straight from Xoloco. . . .

And the two boats came gradually, keeping on one side. On the other side no boats came, because there were houses there. They came ahead, fighting as they came; there were deaths on both sides, and on both sides captives were taken. When the Tenochca who lived in Çoquipan saw this, they fled, fled in fear. . . . They took nothing at all with them, they just left all their poor property in fear, they just scattered everything in their haste. And our enemies[9] went snatching things up, taking whatever they came upon. Whatever they hit on they carried away, whether cloaks, lengths of cotton cloth, warrior's devices, log drums, or cylindrical drums.

The Tlatelolca fought in Çoquipan, in war boats. And in Xoloco the Spaniards came to a place where there was a wall in the middle of the road, blocking it. They fired the big guns at it.

At the first shot it did not give way, but the second time it began to crumble. The third time, at last parts of it fell to the ground, and the fourth time finally the wall went to the ground once and for all. . . .

Once they got two of their boats into the canal at Xocotitlan. When they had beached them, then they went looking into the house sites of the people of Xocotitlan. But Tzilacatzin and some other warriors who saw the Spaniards immediately came out to face them; they came running after them, throwing stones at them, and they scattered the Spaniards into the water. . . .

When they got to Tlilhuacan, the warriors crouched far down and hid themselves, hugging the ground, waiting for the war cry, when there would be shouting and cries of encouragement. When the cry went up, "O Mexica, up and at them!" the Tlappanecatl Ecatzin, a warrior of Otomi rank,[10] faced the Spaniards and threw himself at them, saying, "O Tlatelolca warriors, up and at them, who are these barbarians? Come running!" Then he went and threw a Spaniard down, knocking him to the ground; the one he threw down was the one who came first, who came leading them. And when he had thrown him down, he dragged the Spaniard off.

And at this point they let loose with all the warriors who had been crouching there; they came out and chased the Spaniards in the passage-ways, and when the Spaniards saw it they, the Mexica, seemed to be intoxicated. Then captives were taken. Many Tlaxcalans, and people of Acolhuacan, Chalco, Xochimilco, etc. [i.e., allies of the Spaniards], were captured. A great abundance were captured and killed. . . .

Then they took the captives to Yacacolco, hurrying them along, going along herding their captives together. Some went weeping, some singing, some went shouting while hitting their hands against their mouths. When

---

[9] **our enemies**: The American Indian tribes that were allies of the Spaniards.
[10] **warrior of Otomi rank**: Warriors who swore an oath never to retreat.

they got them to Yacacolco, they lined them all up. Each one went to the altar platform where the sacrifice was performed. The Spaniards went first, going in the lead; the people of the different altepetl just followed, coming last. And when the sacrifice was over, they strung the Spaniards' heads on poles on skull racks; they also strung up the horses' heads. They placed them below, and the Spaniards' heads were above them, strung up facing east. . . .

(Despite this victory, the Aztecs could not overcome the problems of shortages of food, water, and warriors. In mid July 1521 the Spaniards and their allies resumed their assault, and in early August the Aztecs decided to send into battle a quetzal-owl [sacred bird] warrior, whose success or failure, it was believed, would reveal if the gods wished the Aztecs to continue the war.)

And all the common people suffered greatly. There was famine; many died of hunger. They no longer drank good, pure water, but the water they drank was salty. Many people died of it, and because of it many got dysentery and died. Everything was eaten: lizards, swallows, maize straw, grass that grows on salt flats. And they chewed at . . . wood, glue flowers, plaster, leather, and deerskin, which they roasted, baked, and toasted so that they could eat them, and they ground up medicinal herbs and adobe bricks. There had never been the like of such suffering. The siege was frightening, and great numbers died of hunger. And bit by bit they came pressing us back against the wall, herding us together. . . . There was no place to go; people shoved, pressed and trampled one another; many died in the press. But one woman came to very close quarters with our enemies, throwing water at them, throwing water in their faces, making it stream down their faces.

And when the ruler Quauhtemoctzin[11] and the warriors Coyohuehuetzin, Temilotzin, Topantemoctzin, the Mixcoatlailotlac Ahuelitoctzin, Tlacotzin, and Petlauhtzin took a great warrior named Tlapaltecatl opochtzin . . . and outfitted him, dressing him in a quetzal-owl costume. . . . "Let him wear it, let him die in it. Let him dazzle people with it, let him show them something; let our enemies see and admire it." When they put it on him he looked very frightening and splendid. And they ordered four [others] to come helping him, to accompany him. They gave him the darts of the devil,[12] darts of wooden rods with flint tips. And the

---

[11] **Quauhtemoctzin**: The Aztec emperor after Moteucçoma died while in Spanish captivity.

[12] **darts of the devil**: The battle darts of the god Huitzilopochtli.

reason they did this was that it was as though the fate of the rulers of the Mexica were being determined.

When our enemies saw him, it was as though a mountain had fallen. Every one of the Spaniards was frightened; he intimidated them, they seemed to respect him a great deal. Then the quetzal-owl climbed up on the roof. But when some of our enemies had taken a good look at him they rose and turned him back, pursuing him. Then the quetzal-owl turned them again and pursued them. Then he snatched up the precious feathers and gold and dropped down off the roof. He did not die, and our enemies did not carry him off. Also three of our enemies were captured. At that the war stopped for good. There was silence, nothing more happened. Then our enemies went away. It was silent and nothing more happened until it got dark.

And the next day nothing more happened at all, no one made a sound. The common people just lay collapsed. The Spaniards did nothing more either, but lay still, looking at the people. Nothing was going on, they just lay still. . . .

(Two weeks passed before the Aztecs surrendered on August 13, 1521, after a siege of over three months' duration.)

READING AND DISCUSSION QUESTIONS

1. What hardships did the Aztecs experience with the arrival of the Spaniards?

2. What were Cortés and his men seeking?

3. What different strategies of attack did the Spanish use against the Aztecs? How, ultimately, were they able to defeat the Aztecs?

4. What is Sahagún's attitude toward the Spaniards? What is his attitude toward the Aztecs? With whom does he identify?

MATTEO RICCI

From China in the Sixteenth Century

ca. 1607

Matteo Ricci (1552–1610) was an Italian Jesuit missionary to China. An exceptional scientist and mathematician, Ricci impressed China's scholars and eventually received an invitation from the emperor to visit the palace in Beijing. Ricci was an admirer of Chinese culture, who learned the language and studied Confucian texts as part of his missionary work. He hoped to convert the Chinese by demonstrating the ultimate compatibility between the Christian and Chinese traditions. This reading comes from the journal that he wrote in for twenty-seven years. Published after his death, Ricci's journals were a major source of information about China for Europeans.

During 1606 and the year following, the progress of Christianity in Nancian[13] was in no wise retarded. . . . The number of neophytes [converts] increased by more than two hundred, all of whom manifested an extraordinary piety in their religious devotions. As a result, the reputation of the Christian religion became known throughout the length and breadth of this metropolitan city. . . .

Through the efforts of Father Emanuele Dias another and a larger house was purchased, in August of 1607, at a price of a thousand gold pieces. This change was necessary, because the house he had was too small for his needs and was situated in a flood area. Just as the community was about to change from one house to the other, a sudden uprising broke out against them. . . .

At the beginning of each month, the Magistrates hold a public assembly . . . in the temple of their great Philosopher [Confucius]. When the rites of the new-moon were completed in the temple, and these are civil

---

From Matthew Ricci, *China in the Sixteenth Century*, trans. Louis J. Gallagher, S. J., copyright 1942, 1953, and renewed 1970 by Louis J. Gallagher, S. J. (New York: Random House, 1970).

[13] **Nancian:** Nanchang; a city in southeastern China founded during the Han Dynasty.

rather than religious rites,[14] one of those present took advantage of the occasion to speak on behalf of the others, and to address the highest Magistrate present. . . . "We wish to warn you," he said, "that there are certain foreign priests in this royal city, who are preaching a law, hitherto unheard of in this kingdom, and who are holding large gatherings of people in their house." Having said this, he referred them to their local Magistrate, . . . and he in turn ordered the plaintiffs to present their case in writing, assuring them that he would support it with all his authority, in an effort to have the foreign priests expelled. The complaint was written out that same day and signed with twenty-seven signatures. . . . The content of the document was somewhat as follows.

Matthew Ricci, Giovanni Soerio, Emanuele Dias, and certain other foreigners from western kingdoms, men who are guilty of high treason against the throne, are scattered amongst us, in five different provinces. They are continually communicating with each other and are here and there practicing brigandage on the rivers, collecting money, and then distributing it to the people, in order to curry favor with the multitudes. They are frequently visited by the Magistrates, by the high nobility and by the Military Prefects, with whom they have entered into a secret pact, binding unto death.

These men teach that we should pay no respect to the images of our ancestors, a doctrine which is destined to extinguish the love of future generations for their forebears. Some of them break up the idols, leaving the temples empty and the gods to be pitied, without any patronage. In the beginning they lived in small houses, but by this time they have bought up large and magnificent residences. The doctrine they teach is something infernal. It attracts the ignorant into its fraudulent meshes, and great crowds of this class are continually assembled at their houses. Their doctrine gets beyond the city walls and spreads itself through the neighboring towns and villages and into the open country, and the people become so wrapt up in its falsity, that students are not following their course, laborers are neglecting their work, farmers are not cultivating their acres, and even the women have no interest in their housework. The whole city has become disturbed, and, whereas in the beginning there were only a hundred or so professing their faith, now there are more than twenty thousand. These priests distribute pictures of some Tartar or Saracen,[15] who they say is God, who came down from Heaven to redeem and to instruct all of

---

[14] **civil rather than religious rites**: The Jesuits maintained that Confucian ceremonies were purely civil rather than religious in nature.

[15] **some Tartar or Saracen**: A reference to Jesus Christ.

humanity, and who alone, according to their doctrine, can give wealth and happiness; a doctrine by which the simple people are very easily deceived. These men are an abomination on the face of the Earth, and there is just ground for fear that once they have erected their own temples, they will start a rebellion. . . . Wherefore, moved by their interest in the maintenance of the public good, in the conservation of the realm, and in the preservation, whole and entire, of their ancient laws, the petitioners are presenting this complaint and demanding, in the name of the entire province, that a rescript of it be forwarded to the King, asking that these foreigners be sentenced to death, or banished from the realm, to some deserted island in the sea. . . .

Each of the Magistrates to whom the indictment was presented asserted that the spread of Christianity should be prohibited, and that the foreign priests should be expelled from the city, if the Mayor saw fit, after hearing the case, and notifying the foreigners. . . . But the Fathers [Jesuit priests], themselves, were not too greatly disturbed, placing their confidence in Divine Providence, which had always been present to assist them on other such dangerous occasions.

[Father Emanuele is summoned before the Chief Justice.]

Father Emanuele, in his own defense, . . . gave a brief outline of the Christian doctrine. Then he showed that according to the divine law, the first to be honored, after God, were a man's parents. But the judge had no mind to hear or to accept any of this and he made it known that he thought it was all false. After that repulse, with things going from bad to worse, it looked as if they were on the verge of desperation, so much so, indeed, that they increased their prayers, their sacrifices, and their bodily penances, in petition for a favorable solution of their difficulty. Their adversaries appeared to be triumphantly victorious. They were already wrangling about the division of the furniture of the Mission residences, and to make results doubly certain, they stirred up the flames anew with added accusations and indictments. . . .

The Mayor, who was somewhat friendly with the Fathers, realizing that there was much in the accusation that was patently false, asked the Magistrate Director of the Schools,[16] if he knew whether or not this man Emanuele was a companion of Matthew Ricci, who was so highly respected at the royal court, and who was granted a subsidy from the royal treasury, because of the gifts he had presented to the King. Did he realize that the Fathers had lived in Nankin [Nanjing] for twelve years, and that

---

[16]**Magistrate Director of the Schools**: The local Confucian academy. In this case, the director of the local academy was opposed to the Jesuit presence.

no true complaint had ever been entered against them for having violated the laws. Then he asked him if he had really given full consideration as to what was to be proven in the present indictment. To this the Director of the Schools replied that he wished the Mayor to make a detailed investigation of the case and then to confer with him. The Chief Justice then ordered the same thing to be done. Fortunately, it was this same Justice who was in charge of city affairs when Father Ricci first arrived in Nancian. It was he who first gave the Fathers permission, with the authority of the Viceroy, to open a house there. . . .

After the Mayor had examined the charges of the plaintiffs and the reply of the defendants, he subjected the quasi-literati[17] to an examination in open court, and taking the Fathers under his patronage, he took it upon himself to refute the calumnies of their accusers. He said he was fully convinced that these strangers were honest men, and that he knew that there were only two of them in their local residence and not twenty, as had been asserted. To this they replied that the Chinese were becoming their disciples. To which the Justice in turn replied: "What of it? Why should we be afraid of our own people? Perhaps you are unaware of the fact that Matthew Ricci's company is cultivated by everyone in Pekin [Beijing], and that he is being subsidized by the royal treasury. How dare the Magistrates who are living outside of the royal city expel men who have permission to live at the royal court? These men here have lived peacefully in Nankin for twelve years. I command," he added, "that they buy no more large houses, and that the people are not to follow their law." . . .

A few days later, the court decision was pronounced and written out . . . and was then posted at the city gates as a public edict. The following is a summary of their declaration. Having examined the cause of Father Emanuele and his companions, it was found that these men had come here from the West because they had heard so much about the fame of the great Chinese Empire, and that they had already been living in the realm for some years, without any display of ill-will. Father Emanuele should be permitted to practice his own religion, but it was not considered to be the right thing for the common people, who are attracted by novelties, to adore the God of Heaven. For them to go over to the religion of foreigners would indeed be most unbecoming. . . . It would therefore seem to be . . . [in] . . . the best interests of the Kingdom, to . . . [warn] . . . everyone in a public edict not to abandon the sacrifices of their ancient religion

---

[17] **quasi-literati**: The local scholars who criticized Ricci and the Jesuits. Most of these scholars had only passed the first of the three Confucian civil service exams.

by accepting the cult of foreigners. Such a movement might, indeed, result in calling together certain gatherings, detrimental to the public welfare, and harmful also to the foreigner, himself. Wherefore, the Governor of this district, by order of the high Magistrates, admonishes the said Father Emanuele to refrain from perverting the people, by inducing them to accept a foreign religion. The man who sold him the larger house is to restore his money and Emanuele is to buy a smaller place, sufficient for his needs, and to live there peaceably, as he has done, up to the present. Emanuele, himself, has agreed to these terms and the Military Prefects of the district have been ordered to make a search of the houses there and to confiscate the pictures of the God they speak of, wherever they find them. It is not permitted for any of the native people to go over to the religion of the foreigners, nor is it permitted to gather together for prayer meetings. Whoever does contrary to these prescriptions will be severely punished, and if the Military Prefects are remiss in enforcing them, they will be held to be guilty of the same crimes. To his part of the edict, the Director of the Schools added, that the common people were forbidden to accept the law of the foreigners, and that a sign should be posted above the door of the Father's residence, notifying the public that these men were forbidden to have frequent contact with the people.

The Fathers were not too disturbed by this pronouncement, because they were afraid that it was going to be much worse. In fact, everyone thought it was rather favorable, and that the injunction launched against the spread of the faith was a perfunctory order to make it appear that the literati were not wholly overlooked, since the Fathers were not banished from the city, as the literati had demanded. Moreover it was not considered a grave misdemeanor for the Chinese to change their religion, and it was not customary to inflict a serious punishment on those violating such an order. The neophytes, themselves, proved this when they continued, as formerly, to attend Mass.

READING AND DISCUSSION QUESTIONS

1. What were the concerns of the officials in Nanchang regarding the Jesuit missionaries?

2. How did Father Emanuele try to convince the Chinese authorities that Christianity and the Jesuits did not pose a threat? What reasons did he give for the continued work of the missionaries?

3. Aside from their roles as missionaries, what other roles did the Jesuits play in China, as implied by this account?

COMPARATIVE QUESTIONS

1. Compare Zheng He's inscription and Columbus's agreements with the Spanish rulers. What do these sources suggest about the role that exploration played in strengthening the Spanish and Chinese governments?

2. According to Las Casas and Sahagún, how did the Spaniards treat the native populations that they encountered? According to Zheng He's inscription, how did the Chinese treat local populations?

3. Compare Zheng He's inscription and the journals of Matteo Ricci. In what ways did the explorers and missionaries of this time feel that their actions were divinely compelled? What proof did they provide of divine favor?

4. Taking all the documents into consideration, what motivated the explorers of both the Western and Eastern worlds? What impact did this exploration have on the areas that they visited?

CHAPTER 16

Absolutism and Constitutionalism in Europe

ca. 1589–1725

The seventeenth century was a time of deep crisis for Europe. The commercial and agricultural sectors suffered from prolonged economic stagnation, and many nations found themselves locked in expensive and devastating internal and external wars. Despite these difficulties, as the century came to a close, Europe's governments experienced significant growth with increased control over taxation, the military, and the state bureaucracy. The following documents reveal the reactions of European governments to the difficulties of the seventeenth century. As the sources illustrate, Europe was divided in its response. Some countries, such as England, took the path of constitutionalism, while others — including France and Eastern European states — chose absolutism. Regardless of these differing paths, each country answered the challenges of the century by establishing centralized states that asserted sovereignty over their people.

DOCUMENT 16-1

LOUIS XIV

From Mémoires for the Instruction of the Dauphin

ca. 1666–1670

Louis XIV (r. 1643–1715) was a few months shy of his fifth birthday when he ascended to the French throne. At the time, France faced daunting challenges,

Louis XIV, *Mémoires for the Instruction of the Dauphin*, trans. and ed. Paul Sonnino (New York: Free Press, 1970), 21–26, 28–33, 35, 37–38, 40–44, 53–58, 68, 78.

including an increasingly disgruntled nobility and involvement in the Thirty Years' War. During the course of his seventy-two-year reign, Louis worked tirelessly to neutralize threats to his authority, claiming ultimately to have absolute power over his kingdom and its subjects. To ensure his legacy, Louis wrote the following instructions for his son to offer guidance to his heir. As it turned out, Louis outlived his son, as well as his grandsons. At his death in 1715, his five-year-old great-grandson inherited the throne and France's tradition of absolutism.

My son, many excellent reasons have prompted me to go to a considerable effort in the midst of my greatest occupations in order to leave you these memoirs of my reign and of my principal actions. I have never believed that kings, feeling as they do all the paternal affections and attachments in themselves, were dispensed from the common and natural obligation of fathers to instruct their children by example and by counsel. . . .

I have considered, moreover, what I have so often experienced myself: the crowd of people who will press around you, each with his own design; the difficulty that you will have in obtaining sincere advice from them; the entire assurance that you will be able to take in that of a father who will have had no interest but your own, nor any passion except for your greatness. . . .

Disorder reigned everywhere. My court, in general, was still quite far removed from the sentiments in which I hope that you will find it. People of quality accustomed to continual bargaining with a minister who did not mind it, and who had sometimes found it necessary, were always inventing an imaginary right to whatever was to their fancy; no governor of a stronghold who was not difficult to govern; no request that was not mingled with some reproach over the past, or with some veiled threat of future dissatisfaction. Graces [favors] exacted and torn rather than awaited, and extorted in consequence of each other, no longer really obligated anyone, merely serving to offend those to whom they were refused.

The finances, which move and activate the whole great body of the monarchy, were so exhausted that there hardly seemed to be any recourse left. Many of the most necessary and imperative expenses for my household and for my own person were either shamefully postponed or were supported solely through credit, to be made up for later. Affluence prevailed, meanwhile, among the financiers who, on the one hand, covered their irregularities by all kinds of artifices while they uncovered them, on the other, by insolent and brazen luxury, as if they were afraid to leave me ignorant of them.

The Church aside from its usual troubles, after long disputes over scholastic matters that were admittedly unnecessary for salvation — differences mounting each day with the excitement and the obstinacy of tempers and even mingling constantly with new human interest — was finally threatened openly with a schism [Jansenism] by people all the more dangerous since they could have been very useful, of great merit had they been less convinced of it. It was no longer merely a question of some individual theologians in hiding, but of bishops established in their see, capable of drawing the populace after them, of high reputation, of piety indeed worthy of reverence as long as it were accompanied by submission to the opinions of the Church, by mildness, by moderation, and by charity. . . .

The least of the defects in the order of the nobility was the infinite number of usurpers in its midst, without any title or having a title acquired by purchase rather than by service. The tyranny that it exercised over its vassals and over its neighbors in some of my provinces could neither be tolerated nor could it be suppressed without examples of severity and of rigor. The fury of duels, somewhat mitigated since my strict and inflexible enforcement of the latest regulations, already showed through the well-advanced recovery from such a deep-rooted evil that none was beyond remedy.

Justice, which was responsible for reforming all the rest, seemed itself to me as the most difficult to reform. An infinite number of things contributed to this: offices filled by chance and by money rather than by choice and by merit; lack of experience among the judges, even less learning; the ordinances of my predecessors on age and on service circumvented almost everywhere. . . . Even my council, instead of regulating the other jurisdictions, all too often confused them through an incredible number of conflicting decisions all given in my name as if coming from me, which made the disorder even more shameful.

All these evils, or rather, their consequences and their effects, fell primarily upon the lower class, burdened, moreover, with taxes and pressed by extreme poverty in many areas, disturbed in others by their own idleness since the peace, and especially in need of relief and of employment. . . .

All was calm everywhere. Not the slightest hint of any movement within the kingdom that could interrupt or oppose my plans. There was peace with my neighbors, apparently for as long as I would want it myself, owing to the circumstances in which they found themselves. . . .

It would undoubtedly have been a waste of such perfect and such rare tranquillity not to put it to good use, although my youth and the pleasure of leading my armies would have made me wish for a few more external affairs. . . .

Two things were necessary for me, undoubtedly: a great deal of work on my part; a careful choice of the persons who were to support me and relieve me in it.

As to work, my son, it may be that you will begin to read these memoirs at an age when it is far more customary to fear it than to enjoy it, delighted to have escaped from subjection to teachers and to masters, and to have no more set hours nor long and fixed concentration.

Here I shall not merely tell you that this is nonetheless how one reigns, why one reigns, and that there is ingratitude and temerity toward God as well as injustice and tyranny toward men in wanting one without the other, that these demands of royalty which may sometimes seem harsh and unpleasant to you from such a lofty post would appear delightful and pleasant to you if it were a question of attaining them! . . .

I made it a rule to work regularly twice a day for two to three hours at a time with various persons, aside from the hours that I worked alone or that I might devote extraordinarily to extraordinary affairs if any arose, there being no moment when it was not permitted to discuss with me anything that was pressing, except for foreign envoys, who sometimes use the familiarity that they are permitted in order to obtain something or to pry, and who must not be heard without preparation.

I cannot tell you what fruits I immediately gathered from this decision. I could almost feel my spirits and my courage rising. I was a different person. I discovered something new about myself and joyfully wondered how I could have ignored it for so long. That first shyness, which always comes with good sense and which was especially disturbing when I had to speak at some length in public, vanished in less than no time. I knew then that I was king, and born for it. I experienced, finally, an indescribable delight that you will simply have to discover for yourself. . . . The function of kings consists primarily of using good sense, which always comes naturally and easily. . . . Everything that is most necessary to this effort is at the same time pleasant. For it consists, in short, my son, of keeping an eye on the whole earth, of constantly learning the news of all the provinces and of all the nations, the secret of all the courts, the dispositions and the weaknesses of all the foreign princes and of all their ministers; of being informed of an infinite number of things that we are presumed to ignore; of seeing around us what is hidden from us with the greatest care; of discovering the most remote ideas and the most hidden interests of our courtiers coming to us through conflicting interests; and I don't know, finally, what other pleasures we would not abandon for this one, for the sake of curiosity alone. . . .

I commanded the four secretaries of state not to sign anything at all any longer without discussing it with me, the superintendent likewise, and for nothing to be transacted at the finances without being registered in a little book that was to remain with me, where I could always see at a glance, briefly summarized, the current balance and the expenditures made or pending. . . .

I announced that all requests for graces [favors] of any type had to be made directly to me, and I granted to all my subjects without distinction the privilege of appealing to me at any time, in person or by petitions. The petitions were initially very numerous, which did not discourage me, however. The disorder into which my affairs had fallen produced many of them; the idle or unjustified hopes which were raised by this novelty hardly stimulated a lesser number. I was given a great many [petitions] about lawsuits, which I saw no reason for withdrawing arbitrarily from the ordinary jurisdictions for trial before me. But even in these apparently useless things I discovered much that was useful. I learned thereby many details about the condition of my people. They saw that I was concerned about them, and nothing did so much to win me their hearts. . . .

As to the persons who were to support me in my work, I resolved above all not to have a prime minister, and if you and all your successors take my advice, my son, the name will forever be abolished in France, there being nothing more shameful than to see on the one hand all the functions and on the other the mere title of king.

For this purpose, it was absolutely necessary to divide my confidence and the execution of my orders without entirely entrusting it to anyone, assigning these various persons to various functions in keeping with their various talents, which is perhaps the first and foremost talent of princes. . . .

And as for this art of knowing men, which will be so important to you not merely on this but also on every other occasion of your life, I shall tell you, my son, that it can be learned but that it cannot be taught.

Indeed, it is only reasonable to attribute a great deal to a general and established reputation, because the public is impartial and is difficult to deceive over a long period. It is wise to listen to everyone, and not to believe entirely those around us, except for the good that they are compelled to admit in their enemies and for the bad that they try to excuse in their friends; still wiser is it to test of oneself in little things those whom one wants to employ in greater ones. But the summary of these precepts for properly identifying the talents, the inclinations, and the potential of each one is to work at it and to take pleasure in it. For, in general, from the smallest things to the greatest, you will never master a single one unless you derive pleasure and enjoyment from them. . . .

But to be perfectly honest with you, it was not in my interest to select individuals of greater eminence. It was above all necessary to establish my own reputation and to make the public realize by the very rank of those whom I selected, that it was not my intention to share my authority with them. It was important for they themselves not to conceive any greater hopes than I would please to give them, which is difficult for persons of high birth: and even with all these precautions, it took the world a rather long time to get to know me.

Many were convinced that before long some one around me would gain control over my mind and over my affairs. Most regarded my diligence as enthusiasm that must soon slacken, and those who wanted to judge it more favorably waited to decide later. . . .

I have believed it necessary to indicate this [seizure of personal power] to you, my son, lest from excessively good intentions in your early youth and from the very ardor that these mémoires will perhaps inspire in you, you might confuse two entirely different things; I mean ruling personally and not listening to any counsel, which would be an extreme as dangerous as that of being governed.

The most able private individuals procure the advice of other able persons about their petty interests. What then of kings who hold the public interest in their hands and whose decisions make for the misery or well-being of the whole earth? None [no decisions] should ever be reached of such importance without [our] having summoned, if it were possible, all the enlightenment, wisdom, and good sense of our subjects. . . .

But when, on important occasions, they have reported to us on all the sides and on all the conflicting arguments, on all that is done elsewhere in such and such a case, it is for us, my son, to decide what must actually be done. And as to this decision, I shall venture to tell you that if few lack neither sense nor courage, another never makes it as well as we. For decision requires the spirit of a master, and it is infinitely easier to be oneself than to imitate someone else. . . .

It was necessary for a thousand reasons, including the urgently needed reform of justice, to diminish the excessive authority of the principal courts, which, under the pretext that their judgments were without appeal, or as they say, sovereign and of the last instance, had gradually assumed the name of sovereign courts and considered themselves as so many separate and independent sovereignties. I announced that I would not tolerate their schemes any longer and to set an example, the Court of Excises of Paris having been the first to depart slightly from its duty, I exiled some of its officials, believing that a strong dose of this remedy initially would dispense me from having to use it often later, which has succeeded for me. . . .

I prohibited them all in general, by this decision, from ever rendering any [decisions] contrary to those of my council under any pretext whatsoever, whether of their jurisdiction or of the right of private individuals, and I ordered them, whenever they might believe that either one of them had been disturbed, to complain about it to me and to have recourse to my authority, that which I had entrusted to them being only for rendering justice to my subjects and not for procuring it for themselves, which is a part of sovereignty so essentially royal and so proper to the king alone that it cannot be transmitted to anyone else. . . .

In all these things, my son, and in some others that you will see subsequently which have undoubtedly humiliated my judicial officials, I don't want you to attribute to me, as those who know me less well may have done, motives of fear, hatred, and vengeance for what had transpired during the Fronde, when it cannot be denied that these courts often forgot themselves to the point of amazing excesses.

But in the first place, this resentment which appears initially so just might not perhaps fare so well on closer scrutiny. They have returned by themselves and without constraint to their duty. The good servants have recalled the bad. Why impute to the entire body the faults of a few, rather than the services which have prevailed in the end? . . .

It is usual for mature minds, which have received their first disposition for piety at an early age, to turn directly toward God in the midst of good fortune, although, as a major consequence of our weakness, a long sequence of successes, which we then regard as being naturally and properly due us, will customarily make us forget Him. I confess that in these beginnings, seeing my reputation growing each day, everything succeeding for me and becoming easy for me, I was as deeply struck as I have ever been by the desire to serve Him and to please Him. . . .

I revived, by a new ordinance, the rigor of the old edicts against swearing and blasphemy and wanted some examples to be made immediately; and I can say in this regard that my cares and the aversion that I have displayed toward this scandalous disorder have not been useless, my court being, God be thanked, more exempt from it than it long has been under the kings my predecessors. . . .

I dedicated myself to destroying Jansenism and to breaking up the communities where this spirit of novelty was developing, well-intentioned, perhaps, but which seemed to want to ignore the dangerous consequences that it could have. . . .

And as to my great number of subjects of the supposedly reformed religion [Huguenots], which was an evil that I had always regarded, and still regard, with sorrow, I devised at that time the plan of my entire policy toward them, which I have no grounds for regretting, since God has blessed it and still blesses it every day with a great number of conversions.

It seemed to me, my son, that those who wanted to employ violent remedies did not know the nature of this disease, caused in part by the excitement of tempers: which must be allowed to pass and to die gradually instead of rekindling it with equally strong contradictions, always useless, moreover, when the corruption is not limited to a clearly defined number, but spread throughout the state.

As far as I have been able to understand, the ignorance of the clergy in previous centuries, their luxury, their debaucheries, the bad examples that they set, those that they were obliged to tolerate for that very reason, the excesses, finally, that they condoned in the conduct of individuals contrary to the public rules and sentiments of the Church gave rise, more than anything else, to those grave wounds that it has received from schism and from heresy [the Protestant Reformation]. The new reformers obviously spoke the truth on many matters of fact and of this nature, which they decried with both justice and bitterness. They were presumptuous in regard to belief, and people cannot possibly distinguish a well-disguised error when it lies hidden, moreover, among many evident truths. It all began with some minor differences which I have learned that the Protestants of Germany and the Huguenots of France hardly consider any more today. These produced greater ones, primarily because too much pressure was put upon a violent and bold man [Martin Luther] who, seeing no other honorable retreat for himself, pushed ahead into the fray and, abandoning himself to his own reasoning, took the liberty of examining everything that he had accepted, promised the world an easy and shortened path to salvation, a means very suitable for flattering human reasoning and for drawing the populace. Love of novelty seduced many of them. The interests of various princes mingled in this quarrel. . . .

From this general knowledge, I believed, my son, that the best means to reduce gradually the number of Huguenots in my kingdom was, in the first place, not to press them at all by any new rigor against them, to implement what they had obtained from my predecessors but to grant them nothing further, and even to restrict its execution within the narrowest limits that justice and propriety would permit. . . .

But as to the graces [favors] that depended solely on me, I resolved, and I have rather scrupulously observed it since, not to grant them any, and this out of kindness rather than out of bitterness, so as to oblige them thereby to consider from time to time, by themselves and without constraint, if they had some good reason for depriving themselves voluntarily of the advantages that they could share with all my other subjects.

However, to profit from their greater willingness to be disabused of their errors, I also resolved to attract, even to reward, those who might be receptive; to do all I could to inspire the bishops to work at their instruction and to eliminate the scandals that sometimes separated them from us; to place, finally, in these highest posts and in all those to which I appoint for any reason whatsoever, only persons of piety, of dedication, of learning, capable of repairing, by an entirely different conduct, the disorders that their predecessors had primarily produced in the Church. . . .

[Louis warns against the practice of religion for purely selfish reasons.]

For indeed, my son, we must consider the good of our subjects far more than our own. They are almost a part of ourselves, since we are the head of a body and they are its members. It is only for their own advantage that we must give them laws, and our power over them must only be used by us in order to work more effectively for their happiness. It is wonderful to deserve from them the name of father along with that of master, and if the one belongs to us by right of birth, the other must be the sweetest object of our ambition. I am well aware that such a wonderful title is not obtained without a great deal of effort, but in praiseworthy undertakings one must not be stopped by the idea of difficulty. Work only dismays weak souls, and when a plan is advantageous and just, it is weakness not to execute it. . . .

I hope that I shall leave you with still more power and more greatness than I possess, and I want to believe that you will make still better use of it than I. But when everything that will surround you will conspire to fill you with nothing but yourself, don't compare yourself, my son, to lesser princes than you or to those who have borne or who may still unworthily bear the title of king. It is no great advantage to be a little better; think rather about all those who have furnished the greatest cause for esteem in past times, who from a private station or with very limited power have managed by the sole force of their merit to found great empires, have passed like comets from one part of the world to another, charmed the whole earth by their great qualities, and left, after so many centuries, a long and lasting memory of themselves that seems, instead of fading, to intensify and to gain strength with every passing day. If this does not suffice, be still more fair to yourself and consider for how many things you will be praised that you will perhaps owe entirely to fortune or to those whom it has itself placed in your service. Get down to some serious consideration of your own weaknesses, for even though you may imagine that all men, and even the greatest, have similar ones, nevertheless since you would find this harder to imagine and to believe of them than of yourself, it would undoubtedly diminish your conceit, which is the usual pitfall of brilliance and of fame.

Thereby, my son, and in this respect you will be humble. But when it will be a question, as on the occasion that I have just described to you, of your rank in the world, of the rights of your crown, of the king, finally, and not of the private individual, boldly assume as much loftiness of heart and of spirit as you can, and do not betray the glory of your predecessors nor the interest of your successors, whose trustee you are. . . .

READING AND DISCUSSION QUESTIONS

1. Two of the biggest threats to Louis' authority were the strength of the nobility and the dissension of French Protestants. How did Louis address these threats?

2. How would you summarize Louis' approach to governing?

3. What advice does Louis give to his son regarding his personal relationship with God? How does it differ from the advice he gives him regarding the church?

4. What, if any, missteps does Louis admit to making during his reign to this point?

JACQUES-BENIGNE BOSSUET

On Divine Right

ca. 1675–1680

French Absolutism developed in the seventeenth-century as a response to a number of crises, including the French Wars of Religion (ca. 1562–1598) and a civil war known as the Fronde (1648–1653). A bishop in the French Catholic church and tutor to the son of Louis XIV, Jacques-Benigne Bossuet (1627–1704) was an important architect of French absolutism. Drawing from biblical sources, Bossuet argued in his treatises that the monarch received his authority directly from God. This concept of the divine right of kings implied that any challenge to the authority of the king was tantamount to questioning God's divine plan.

We have already seen that all power is of God. The ruler, adds St. Paul, "is the minister of God to thee for good. But if thou do that which is evil, be afraid; for he beareth not the sword in vain: for he is the minister of God, a revenger to execute wrath upon him that doeth evil" [Rom. 13:1–7]. Rulers then act as the ministers of God and as his lieutenants on earth. It is through them that God exercises his empire. Think ye "to withstand the kingdom of the Lord in the hand of the sons of David" [Chron. 13:8]? Consequently, as we have seen, the royal throne is not the throne of a man, but the throne of God himself. . . .

Moreover, that no one may assume that the Israelites were peculiar in having kings over them who were established by God, note what is said in Ecclesiasticus: "God has given to every people its ruler, and Israel is manifestly reserved to him" [Eccl. 17:14–15]. He therefore governs all peoples and gives them their kings, although he governed Israel in a more intimate and obvious manner.

It appears from all this that the person of the king is sacred, and that to attack him in any way is sacrilege. God has the kings anointed by his prophets with the holy unction in like manner as he has bishops and altars anointed. But even without the external application in thus being anointed,

J. H. Robinson, ed., *Readings in European History*, 2 vols. (Boston: Ginn, 1906), 2:273–277.

they are by their very office the representatives of the divine majesty deputed by Providence for the execution of his purposes. . . . Kings should be guarded as holy things, and whosoever neglects to protect them is worthy of death. . . .

But kings, although their power comes from on high, as has been said, should not regard themselves as masters of that power to use it at their pleasure; . . . they must employ it with fear and self-restraint, as a thing coming from God and of which God will demand an account. "Hear, O kings, and take heed, understand, judges of the earth, lend your ears, ye who hold the peoples under your sway, and delight to see the multitude that surround you. It is God who gives you the power. Your strength comes from the Most High, who will question your works and penetrate the depths of your thoughts, for, being ministers of his kingdom, ye have not given righteous judgments nor have ye walked according to his will. He will straightway appear to you in a terrible manner, for to those who command is the heaviest punishment reserved. The humble and the weak shall receive mercy, but the mighty shall be mightily tormented. For God fears not the power of any one, because he made both great and small and he has care for both" [Ws 6:2]. . . .

Kings should tremble then as they use the power God has granted them; and let them think how horrible is the sacrilege if they use for evil a power which comes from God. We behold kings seated upon the throne of the Lord, bearing in their hand the sword which God himself has given them. What profanation, what arrogance, for the unjust king to sit on God's throne to render decrees contrary to his laws and to use the sword which God has put in his hand for deeds of violence and to slay his children! . . .

The royal power is absolute. With the aim of making this truth hateful and insufferable, many writers have tried to confound absolute government with arbitrary government. But no two things could be more unlike, as we shall show when we come to speak of justice.

The prince need render account of his acts to no one. "I counsel thee to keep the king's commandment, and that in regard of the oath of God. Be not hasty to go out of his sight: stand not on an evil thing for he doeth whatsoever pleaseth him. Where the word of a king is, there is power: and who may say unto him, What doest thou? Whoso keepeth the commandment shall feel no evil thing" [Eccles. 8:2–5]. Without this absolute authority the king could neither do good nor repress evil. It is necessary that his power be such that no one can hope to escape him, and, finally, the only protection of individuals against the public authority should be their innocence. This conforms with the teaching of St. Paul: "Wilt thou then not be afraid of the power? do that which is good" [Rom. 13:3].

I do not call majesty that pomp which surrounds kings or that exterior magnificence which dazzles the vulgar. That is but the reflection of majesty and not majesty itself. Majesty is the image of the grandeur of God in the prince.

God is infinite, God is all. The prince, as prince, is not regarded as a private person: he is a public personage, all the state is in him; the will of all the people is included in his. As all perfection and all strength are united in God, so all the power of individuals is united in the person of the prince. What grandeur that a single man should embody so much!

The power of God makes itself felt in a moment from one extremity of the earth to another. Royal power works at the same time throughout all the realm. It holds all the realm in position, as God holds the earth. Should God withdraw his hand, the earth would fall to pieces; should the king's authority cease in the realm, all would be in confusion.

Look at the prince in his cabinet. Thence go out the orders which cause the magistrates and the captains, the citizens and the soldiers, the provinces and the armies on land and on sea, to work in concert. He is the image of God, who, seated on his throne high in the heavens, makes all nature move. . . .

Finally, let us put together the things so great and so august which we have said about royal authority. Behold an immense people united in a single person; behold this holy power, paternal and absolute; behold the secret cause which governs the whole body of the state, contained in a single head: you see the image of God in the king, and you have the idea of royal majesty. God is holiness itself, goodness itself, and power itself. In these things lies the majesty of God. In the image of these things lies the majesty of the prince.

So great is this majesty that it cannot reside in the prince as in its source; it is borrowed from God, who gives it to him for the good of the people, for whom it is good to be checked by a superior force. Something of divinity itself is attached to princes and inspires fear in the people. The king should not forget this. "I have said," — it is God who speaks, — "I have said, Ye are gods; and all of you are children of the Most High. But ye shall die like men, and fall like one of the princes" [Ps. 82:6–7]. "I have said, Ye are gods"; that is to say, you have in your authority, and you bear on your forehead, a divine imprint. "You are the children of the Most High"; it is he who has established your power for the good of mankind. But, O gods of flesh and blood, gods of clay and dust, "ye shall die like men, and fall like princes." Grandeur separates men for a little time, but a common fall makes them all equal at the end.

O kings, exercise your power then boldly, for it is divine and salutary for human kind, but exercise it with humility. You are endowed with it from without. At bottom it leaves you feeble, it leaves you mortal, it leaves you sinners, and charges you before God with a very heavy account.

READING AND DISCUSSION QUESTIONS

1.   According to Bossuet, what is the nature of monarchical authority? What are its sources and purposes?

2.   Why must a prince wield his absolute power carefully?

3.   To whom does the author seem to be addressing this treatise? What gives you that impression?

DOCUMENT 16-3

JOHN LOCKE

From Two Treatises of Government: "Of the Ends of Political Society and Government"

1690

John Locke (1632–1704) provided a theoretical foundation for the development of constitutionalism in England. Locke was a physician, philosopher, and teacher who had ties to the pro-parliamentary faction of the English government. While in exile in the Dutch Republic during the early 1680s, Locke worked on his Two Treatises of Government. *The second of these documents, excerpted below, helped to justify the Glorious Revolution of 1688. Locke began the treatise by imagining the time before the establishment of government when humans lived in a state of nature. He then speculated on*

John Locke, *Two Treatises of Government*, A. Millnar et al. (London, 1764).

*the circumstances surrounding the formation of government in an effort to
determine the origins and nature of political power.*

Sec. 123. If man in the state of nature be so free, as has been said; if he be
absolute lord of his own person and possessions, equal to the greatest, and
subject to no body, why will he part with his freedom? Why will he give up
this empire, and subject himself to the dominion and control of any other
power? To which it is obvious to answer, that though in the state of nature
he hath such a right, yet the enjoyment of it is very uncertain, and constantly exposed to the invasion of others: for all being kings as much as he,
every man his equal, and the greater part no strict observers of equity and
justice, the enjoyment of the property he has in this state is very unsafe,
very unsecure. This makes him willing to quit a condition, which, however free, is full of fears and continual dangers: and it is not without reason,
that he seeks out, and is willing to join in society with others, who are
already united, or have a mind to unite, for the mutual preservation of their
lives, liberties, and estates, which I call by the general name, property.

Sec. 124. The great and chief end, therefore, of men's uniting into
commonwealths, and putting themselves under government, is the preservation of their property. To which in the state of nature there are many
things wanting.

First, There wants an established, settled, known law, received and
allowed by common consent to be the standard of right and wrong, and
the common measure to decide all controversies between them: for though
the law of nature be plain and intelligible to all rational creatures; yet men
being biassed by their interest, as well as ignorant for want of study of it, are
not apt to allow of it as a law binding to them in the application of it to their
particular cases.

Sec. 125. Secondly, In the state of nature there wants a known and
indifferent judge, with authority to determine all differences according to
the established law: for every one in that state being both judge and exe-
cutioner of the law of nature, men being partial to themselves, passion and
revenge is very apt to carry them too far, and with too much heat, in their
own cases; as well as negligence, and unconcernedness, to make them too
remiss in other men's.

Sec. 126. Thirdly, In the state of nature there often wants power to
back and support the sentence when right, and to give it due execution,
They who by any injustice offended, will seldom fail, where they are able,
by force to make good their injustice; such resistance many times makes

the punishment dangerous, and frequently destructive, to those who attempt it.

Sec. 127. Thus mankind, notwithstanding all the privileges of the state of nature, being but in an ill condition, while they remain in it, are quickly driven into society. Hence it comes to pass, that we seldom find any number of men live any time together in this state. The inconveniencies that they are therein exposed to, by the irregular and uncertain exercise of the power every man has of punishing the transgressions of others, make them take sanctuary under the established laws of government, and therein seek the preservation of their property. It is this makes them so willingly give up every one his single power of punishing, to be exercised by such alone, as shall be appointed to it amongst them; and by such rules as the community, or those authorized by them to that purpose, shall agree on. And in this we have the original right and rise of both the legislative and executive power, as well as of the governments and societies themselves.

Sec. 128. For in the state of nature, to omit the liberty he has of innocent delights, a man has two powers.

The first is to do whatsoever he thinks fit for the preservation of himself, and others within the permission of the law of nature: by which law, common to them all, he and all the rest of mankind are one community, make up one society, distinct from all other creatures. And were it not for the corruption and vitiousness of degenerate men, there would be no need of any other; no necessity that men should separate from this great and natural community, and by positive agreements combine into smaller and divided associations.

The other power a man has in the state of nature, is the power to punish the crimes committed against that law. Both these he gives up, when he joins in a private, if I may so call it, or particular politic society, and incorporates into any commonwealth, separate from the rest of mankind.

Sec. 129. The first power, viz. of doing whatsoever he thought for the preservation of himself, and the rest of mankind, he gives up to be regulated by laws made by the society, so far forth as the preservation of himself, and the rest of that society shall require; which laws of the society in many things confine the liberty he had by the law of nature.

Sec. 130. Secondly, The power of punishing he wholly gives up, and engages his natural force, (which he might before employ in the execution of the law of nature, by his own single authority, as he thought fit) to assist the executive power of the society, as the law thereof shall require: for being now in a new state, wherein he is to enjoy many conveniencies, from the labor, assistance, and society of others in the same community, as well as protection from its whole strength; he is to part also with as much of his natural liberty, in providing for himself, as the good, prosperity, and safety of the society shall require; which is not only necessary, but just, since the other members of the society do the like.

Sec. 131. But though men, when they enter into society, give up the equality, liberty, and executive power they had in the state of nature, into the hands of the society, to be so far disposed of by the legislative, as the good of the society shall require; yet it being only with an intention in every one the better to preserve himself, his liberty and property; (for no rational creature can be supposed to change his condition with an intention to be worse) the power of the society, or legislative constituted by them, can never be supposed to extend farther, than the common good; but is obliged to secure every one's property, by providing against those three defects above mentioned, that made the state of nature so unsafe and uneasy. And so whoever has the legislative or supreme power of any commonwealth, is bound to govern by established standing laws, promulgated and known to the people, and not by extemporary decrees; by indifferent and upright judges, who are to decide controversies by those laws; and to employ the force of the community at home, only in the execution of such laws, or abroad to prevent or redress foreign injuries, and secure the community from inroads and invasion. And all this to be directed to no other end, but the peace, safety, and public good of the people.

READING AND DISCUSSION QUESTIONS

1. According to Locke, what powers do individuals have in the state of nature? What are some of the inevitable difficulties that arise when living in the state of nature?

2. Once individuals agree to form a government, what powers does the government have? What are its primary obligations?

3. In what ways does the treatise challenge the absolutist tendencies of seventeenth-century English monarchs?

PETER THE GREAT

Edicts and Decrees: Imposing Western Style on the Russians

ca. 1699–1723

While all of seventeenth-century Europe struggled, Russia had unique eco-nomic and political challenges to address as a result of two hundred years of Mongol rule. When the tsar Peter the Great (r. 1682–1725) came to power, his predecessors had already broken free from the so-called Mongol Yoke and had significantly strengthened the Russian monarchy. To destroy any re-maining cultural legacy of the Mongols, Peter turned to Western Europe as a model for reforming the customs of the Russian people. He also looked to the West for guidance on his extensive economic reforms.

DECREE ON THE NEW CALENDAR, 1699

It is known to His Majesty that not only many European Christian lands, but also Slavic nations which are in total accord with our Eastern Ortho-dox Church . . . agree to count their years from the eighth day after the birth of Christ, that is from the first day of January, and not from the cre-ation of the world,[1] because of the many difficulties and discrepancies of this reckoning. It is now the year 1699 from the birth of Christ, and from the first of January will begin both the new year 1700 and a new century; and so His Majesty has ordered, as a good and useful measure, that from now on time will be reckoned in government offices and dates be noted on documents and property deeds, starting from the first of January 1700. And to celebrate this good undertaking and the new century . . . in the sover-eign city of Moscow . . . let the reputable citizens arrange decorations of pine, fir, and juniper trees and boughs along the busiest main streets and by the houses of eminent church and lay persons of rank. . . . Poorer per-

---

L. Jay Oliva, *Peter the Great* (Englewood Cliffs, NJ: Prentice-Hall, 1970).

[1] **agree to count their years . . . world**: Before January 1, 1700 Russians began the year on September 1, which they believed corresponded to the creation of the world.

sons should place at least one shrub or bough on their gates or on their house. . . . Also . . . as a sign of rejoicing, wishes for the new year and century will be exchanged, and the following will be organized: when fireworks are lit and guns fired on the great Red Square, let the boyars [nobility], the Lords of the Palace, of the Chamber, and the Council, and the eminent personages of Court, Army, and Merchant ranks, each in his own grounds, fire three times from small guns, if they have any, or from muskets and other small arms, and shoot some rockets into the air.

DECREE ON THE INVITATION OF FOREIGNERS, 1702

Since our accession to the throne all our efforts and intentions have tended to govern this realm in such a way that all of our subjects should, through our care for the general good, become more and more prosperous. For this end we have always tried to maintain internal order, to defend the state against invasion, and in every possible way to improve and to extend trade. With this purpose we have been compelled to make some necessary and salutary changes in the administration, in order that our subjects might more easily gain a knowledge of matters of which they were before ignorant, and become more skillful in their commercial relations. We have therefore given orders, made dispositions, and founded institutions indispensable for increasing our trade with foreigners, and shall do the same in the future. Nevertheless we fear that matters are not in such a good condition as we desire, and that our subjects cannot in perfect quietness enjoy the fruits of our labors, and we have therefore considered still other means to protect our frontier from the invasion of the enemy, and to preserve the rights and privileges of our State, and the general peace of all Christians. . . .

To attain these worthy aims, we have endeavored to improve our military forces, which are the protection of our State, so that our troops may consist of well-drilled men, maintained in perfect order and discipline. In order to obtain greater improvement in this respect, and to encourage foreigners, who are able to assist us in this way, as well as artisans profitable to the State, to come in numbers to our country, we have issued this manifesto, and have ordered printed copies of it to be sent throughout Europe. . . . And as in our residence of Moscow, the free exercise of religion of all other sects, although not agreeing with our church, is already allowed, so shall this be hereby confirmed anew in such manner that we, by the power granted to us by the Almighty, shall exercise no compulsion over the consciences of men, and shall gladly allow every Christian to care for his own salvation at his own risk.

An Instruction to Russian Students Abroad Studying Navigation, 1714

1. Learn how to draw plans and charts and how to use the compass and other naval indicators.
2. Learn how to navigate a vessel in battle as well as in a simple maneuver, and learn how to use all appropriate tools and instruments; namely, sails, ropes, and oars, and the like matters, on row boats and other vessels.
3. Discover . . . how to put ships to sea during a naval battle. . . . Obtain from foreign naval officers written statements, bearing their signatures and seals, of how adequately you are prepared for naval duties.
4. If, upon his return, anyone wishes to receive from the Tsar greater favors, he should learn, in addition to the above enumerated instructions, how to construct those vessels [aboard] which he would like to demonstrate his skills.
5. Upon his return to Moscow, every foreign-trained Russian should bring with him at his own expense, for which he will later be reimbursed, at least two experienced masters of naval science. They the returnees will be assigned soldiers, one soldier per returnee, to teach them what they have learned abroad. . . .

Decree on Western Dress, 1701

Western dress shall be worn by all the boyars, members of our councils and of our court . . . gentry of Moscow, secretaries, . . . provincial gentry, gosti,[2] government officials, streltsy,[3] members of the guilds purveying for our household, citizens of Moscow of all ranks, and residents of provincial cities . . . excepting the clergy and peasant tillers of the soil. The upper dress shall be of French or Saxon cut, and the lower dress . . . — waistcoat, trousers, boots, shoes, and hats — shall be of the German type. They shall also ride German saddles. Likewise the womenfolk of all ranks, including the priests', deacons', and church attendants' wives, the wives of the dragoons, the soldiers, and the streltsy, and their children, shall wear Western dresses, hats, jackets, and underwear — undervests and petticoats — and shoes. From now on no one of the abovementioned is to wear Russian dress or Circassian[4] coats, sheepskin coats, or Russian peasant coats,

---

[2] **gosti**: Merchants in the employ of the tsar.
[3] **streltsy**: The imperial guard in Moscow.
[4] **Circassian**: The Russian territory Circassia was located between the Caspian and Black Seas.

trousers, boots, and shoes. It is also forbidden to ride Russian saddles, and the craftsmen shall not manufacture them or sell them at the market-places.

Decree on Shaving, 1705

Henceforth, in accordance with this, His Majesty's decree, all court attendants . . . provincial service men, government officials of all ranks, military men, all the gosti, members of the wholesale merchants' guild, and members of the guilds purveying for our household must shave their beards and moustaches. But, if it happens that some of them do not wish to shave their beards and moustaches, let a yearly tax be collected from such persons; from court attendants. . . . Special badges shall be issued to them from the Administrator of Land Affairs of Public Order . . . which they must wear. . . . As for the peasants, let a toll of two half-copecks[5] per beard be collected at the town gates each time they enter or leave a town; and do not let the peasants pass the town gates, into or out of town, without paying this toll.

Decree on Promotion to Officer's Rank, 1714

Since there are many who promote to officer rank their relatives and friends — young men who do not know the fundamentals of soldiering, not having served in the lower ranks — and since even those who serve [in the ranks] do so for a few weeks or months only, as a formality; there-fore . . . let a decree be promulgated that henceforth there shall be no promotion [to officer rank] of men of noble extraction or of any others who have not first served as privates in the Guards. This decree does not apply to soldiers of lowly origin who, after long service in the ranks, have received their commissions through honest service or to those who are promoted on the basis of merit, now or in the future. . . .

Statute for the College of Manufactures, 1723

His Imperial Majesty is diligently striving to establish and develop in the Russian Empire such manufacturing plants and factories as are found in other states, for the general welfare and prosperity of his subjects. He [therefore] most graciously charges the College of Manufactures to exert itself in devising the means to introduce, with the least expense, and to

---

[5] **half-copecks**: A half-copeck was equivalent to one-twentieth of a ruble, the basic currency unit of Russia.

spread in the Russian Empire these and other ingenious arts, and especially those for which materials can be found within the empire. . . .

His Imperial Majesty gives permission to everyone, without distinction of rank or condition, to open factories wherever he may find suitable. . . .

Factory owners must be closely supervised, in order that they have at their plants good and experienced [foreign] master craftsmen, who are able to train Russians in such a way that these, in turn, may themselves become masters, so that their produce may bring glory to the Russian manufactures. . . .

By the former decrees of His Majesty commercial people were forbidden to buy villages [i.e., to own serfs], the reason being that they were not engaged in any other activity beneficial for the state save commerce; but since it is now clear to all that many of them have started to found manufacturing establishments and build plants, . . . which tend to increase the welfare of the state . . . therefore permission is granted both to the gentry and to men of commerce to acquire villages for these factories without hindrance. . . .

In order to stimulate voluntary immigration of various craftsmen from other countries into the Russian Empire, and to encourage them to establish factories and manufacturing plants freely and at their own expense, the College of Manufactures must send appropriate announcements to the Russian envoys accredited at foreign courts. The envoys should then, in an appropriate way, bring these announcements to the attention of men of various professions, urge them to come to settle in Russia, and help them to move.

READING AND DISCUSSION QUESTIONS

1. Peter the Great looked westward for models for reforming and improving Russia. What specific policies did he institute to increase contact between Russia and Western Europe?

2. What reforms did Peter introduce to stimulate the Russian economy and encourage commercial growth?

3. How did Peter address the lingering Mongol traditions in Russian society? How did he expect the social groups within his kingdom to respond to his reform of Russian customs?

COMPARATIVE QUESTIONS

1. Locke's treatise on constitutionalism in England and Louis XIV's letter to his son extolling French absolutism both address the nature of political authority. According to these two theories, what is the source of political authority? What are the obligations of the institutions or people who exercise political authority? What are the limits to political authority?

2. How might Locke have interpreted Bossuet's political treatise on divine right? Is there room for religion in Locke's state of nature?

3. Before the seventeenth century, the nobility wielded a significant amount of power in Europe. In what ways did the absolutist monarchs Louis XIV and Peter the Great attempt to weaken the nobility? How did these monarchs work with the nobility in order to secure sovereignty over their respective territories?

CHAPTER 17

Toward a New Worldview in the West

1540–1789

B eginning in the sixteenth century, Western Europe saw its religion-based notions of the natural and social worlds countered by arguments grounded in reason and observation. Leaders of the scientific revolution (ca. 1540–1690) drew on earlier European, Greek, and Arab insights to support their theories and challenge the church-dominated wisdom of the time. Advances in astronomy, physics, mathematics, and other fields were supported and promoted by the huge profits and increasing technological demands of growing European trade. Intellectuals in Europe and the United States next turned a critical eye toward society and politics. Those active in the period known as the Enlightenment, which stretched from the late seventeenth to the late eighteenth century, insisted on rational approaches to human relations, drawing on scientific arguments and existing critiques of organized religion in their calls for the reform of societies and governments.

DOCUMENT 17-1

GALILEO GALILEI

From a Letter to the Grand Duchess Christina

1615

Perhaps the best-known thinker of early modern Europe, Galileo Galilei (1564–1642) is most famous for arguing that the sun, not the earth, is at the center of the solar system, which contradicted contemporary Catholic doctrine.

Galileo Galilei, *Discoveries and Opinions of Galileo*, trans. Stillman Drake (New York: Random House, 1957).

In this letter to the grand duchess of Tuscany, distributed in manuscript form in 1615, Galileo defends his beliefs and his interpretation of the Christian Bible. In 1633, Galileo was found guilty of heresy and forced to recant his views, but his works continued to find an audience; this letter was published formally in 1636. Although historians point to political and personal motives for Galileo's conviction, the legend of Galileo as champion of reason over faith remains strong.

Some years ago, as Your Serene Highness well knows,[1] I discovered in the heavens many things that had not been seen before our own age. The novelty of these things, as well as some consequences which followed from them in contradiction to the physical notions commonly held among academic philosophers, stirred up against me no small number of professors — as if I had placed these things in the sky with my own hands in order to upset nature and overturn the sciences. They seemed to forget that the increase of known truths stimulates the investigation, establishment, and growth of the arts; not their diminution or destruction.

Showing a greater fondness for their own opinions than for truth, they sought to deny and disprove the new things which, if they had cared to look for themselves, their own senses would have demonstrated to them. To this end they hurled various charges and published numerous writings filled with vain arguments, and they made the grave mistake of sprinkling these with passages taken from places in the Bible which they had failed to understand properly, and which were ill suited to their purposes.

Persisting in their original resolve to destroy me and everything mine by any means they can think of, these men are aware of my views in astronomy and philosophy. They know that as to the arrangement of the parts of the universe, I hold the sun to be situated motionless in the center of the revolution of the celestial orbs while the earth rotates on its axis and revolves about the sun. They know also that I support this position not only by refuting the arguments of Ptolemy[2] and Aristotle, but by producing many counterarguments; in particular, some which relate to physical effects whose causes can perhaps be assigned in no other way. In addition

---

[1] **as your Serene Highness well knows**: Christina (1565–1637) was a member of the Medici family with whom Galileo had a good relationship. Galileo had tutored her son Cosimo in mathematics.

[2] **Ptolemy**: Greek astronomer who spent most of his life (ca. 100–170 c.e.) in Alexandria, Egypt, and who advanced the idea that all planets revolved around the earth.

there are astronomical arguments derived from many things in my new celestial discoveries that plainly confute the Ptolemaic system while admirably agreeing with and confirming the contrary hypothesis. Possibly because they are disturbed by the known truth of other propositions of mine which differ from those commonly held, and therefore mistrusting their defense so long as they confine themselves to the field of philosophy, these men have resolved to fabricate a shield for their fallacies out of the mantle of pretended religion and the authority of the Bible. These they apply, with little judgment, to the refutation of arguments that they do not understand and have not even listened to.

First they have endeavored to spread the opinion that such propositions in general are contrary to the Bible and are consequently damnable and heretical. . . . Next, becoming bolder, . . . they began scattering rumors among the people that before long this doctrine would be condemned by the supreme authority [the pope]. They know, too, that official condemnation would not only suppress the two propositions which I have mentioned, but would render damnable all other astronomical and physical statements and observations that have any necessary relation or connection with these. . . .

To this end they make a shield of their hypocritical zeal for religion. They go about invoking the Bible, which they would have minister to their deceitful purposes. Contrary to the sense of the Bible and the intention of the holy Fathers, if I am not mistaken, they would extend such authorities until even in purely physical matters — where faith is not involved — they would have us altogether abandon reason and the evidence of our senses in favor of some biblical passage, though under the surface meaning of its words this passage may contain a different sense. . . .

The reason produced for condemning the opinion that the earth moves and the sun stands still is that in many places in the Bible one may read that the sun moves and the earth stands still. Since the Bible cannot err, it follows as a necessary consequence that anyone takes an erroneous and heretical position who maintains that the sun is inherently motionless and the earth movable.

With regard to this argument, I think in the first place that it is very pious to say and prudent to affirm that the holy Bible can never speak untruth — whenever its true meaning is understood. But I believe nobody will deny that it is often very abstruse, and may say things which are quite different from what its bare words signify. Hence in expounding the Bible if one were always to confine oneself to the unadorned grammatical meaning, one might fall into error. Not only contradictions and propositions far from true might thus be made to appear in the Bible, but even grave here-sies and follies. Thus it would be necessary to assign to God feet, hands, and eyes, as well as corporeal and human affections, such as anger, re-pentance, hatred, and sometimes even the forgetting of things past and ignorance of those to come. These propositions uttered by the Holy Ghost were set down in that manner by the sacred scribes[3] in order to accommo-date them to the capacities of the common people, who are rude and unlearned. . . .

This being granted, I think that in discussions of physical problems we ought to begin not from the authority of scriptural passages but from sense-experiences and necessary demonstrations; for the holy Bible and the phe-nomena of nature proceed alike from the divine Word, the former as the dictate of the Holy Ghost and the latter as the observant executrix of God's commands. It is necessary for the Bible, in order to be accommodated to the understanding of every man, to speak many things which appear to differ from the absolute truth so far as the bare meaning of the words is concerned. But Nature, on the other hand, is inexorable and immutable; she never transgresses the laws imposed upon her, or cares a whit whether her abstruse reasons and methods of operation are understandable to men. For that reason it appears that nothing physical which sense-experience sets before our eyes, or which necessary demonstrations prove to us, ought to be called in question (much less condemned) upon the testimony of biblical passages which may have some different meaning beneath their words. For the Bible is not chained in every expression to conditions as strict as those which govern all physical effects; nor is God any less excel-lently revealed in Nature's actions than in the sacred statements of the Bible.

READING AND DISCUSSION QUESTIONS

1. Why does Galileo believe some people are opposed to his ideas? What actions have they taken against him?

2. What is Galileo's position on the "truth" of biblical text?

3. What does Galileo suggest is the relationship between the Bible and nature?

---

[3] **These propositions . . . sacred scribes**: The Holy Ghost is part of the Holy Trinity, along with the Father and the Son. Christians believe the Holy Ghost wrote through the authors of the Bible.

DOCUMENT 17-2

ISAAC NEWTON

On the Mathematical Principles of Natural Philosophy

1687

Isaac Newton (1643–1727) is best remembered for his important work in physics and mathematics. After graduating from Cambridge University, Newton studied independently in the English countryside, away from the plague that ravaged England's population from 1665 to 1666. There he began to develop his ideas of gravity, universal laws of motion, and mathematics. Newton synthesized the work of Nicolaus Copernicus (1473–1543), Johannes Kepler (1571–1630), and Galileo into his universal law of gravitation, which prevailed in scientific thought until the twentieth century. The document excerpted here, published in 1687 and republished twice before Newton's death, presents his arguments on gravity, mechanics, and the scientific method.

RULE I

We are to admit no more causes of natural things, than such as are both true and sufficient to explain their appearances.

To this purpose the philosophers say, that Nature does nothing in vain, and more is in vain, when less will serve; for Nature is pleased with simplicity, and affects not the pomp of superfluous causes.

RULE II

Therefore to the same natural effects we must, as far as possible, assign the same causes.

As to respiration in a man, and in a beast; the descent of stones in Europe and in America; the light of our culinary fire and of the sun; the reflection of light in the earth, and in the planets.

Isaac Newton, *The Mathematical Principles of Natural Philosophy*, trans. A. Motte (London, 1729).

Rule III

The qualities of bodies, which admit neither intension nor remission of degrees, and which are found to belong to all bodies within reach of our experiments, are to be esteemed the universal qualities of all bodies whatsoever.

For since the qualities of bodies are only known to us by experiments, we are to hold for universal, all such as universally agree with experiments; and such as are not liable to diminution, can never be quite taken away. We are certainly not to relinquish the evidence of experiments for the sake of dreams and vain fictions of our own devising; nor are we to recede from the analogy of Nature, which is wont to be simple, and always consonant to itself. We no other way know the extension of bodies, than by our senses, nor do these reach it in all bodies; but because we perceive extension in all that are sensible, therefore we ascribe it universally to all others, also. That abundance of bodies are hard we learn by experience. And because the hardness of the whole arises from the hardness of the parts, we therefore justly infer the hardness of the undivided particles not only of the bodies we feel but of all others. That all bodies are impenetrable we gather not from reason, but from sensation. The bodies which we handle we find impenetrables and thence conclude impenetrability to be a universal property of all bodies whatsoever. That all bodies are moveable, and endowed with certain powers (which we call the forces of inertia) or persevering in their motion or in their rest, we only infer from the like properties observed in the bodies which we have seen. The extension, hardness, impenetrability, mobility, and force of inertia of the whole result from the extension, hardness, impenetrability, mobility, and forces of inertia of the parts: and thence we conclude that the least particles of all bodies to be also all extended, and hard, and impenetrable, and moveable, and endowed with their proper forces of inertia. And this is the foundation of all philosophy. Moreover, that the divided but contiguous particles of bodies may be separated from one another, is a matter of observation; and, in the particles that remain undivided, our minds are able to distinguish yet lesser parts, as is mathematically demonstrated. But whether the parts so distinguished, and not yet divided, may, by the powers of nature, be actually divided and separated from one another, we cannot certainly determine. Yet had we the proof of but one experiment, that any undivided particle, in breaking a hard and solid body, suffered a division, we might by virtue of this rule, conclude, that the undivided as well as the divided particles, may be divided and actually separated into infinity.

Lastly, if it universally appears, by experiments and astronomical observations, that all bodies about the earth, gravitate toward the earth;

and that in proportion to the quantity of matter which they severally contain; that the moon likewise, according to the quantity of its matter, gravitates toward the earth; that on the other hand our sea gravitates toward the moon; and all the planets mutually one toward another; and the comets in like manner towards the sun; we must, in consequence of this rule, universally allow, that all bodies whatsoever are endowed with a principle of mutual gravitation. For the argument from the appearances concludes with more force for the universal gravitation of all bodies, than for their impenetrability, of which among those in the celestial regions, we have no experiments, nor any manner of observation. Not that I affirm gravity to be essential to all bodies. By their inherent force I mean nothing but their force of inertia. This is immutable. Their gravity is diminished as they recede from the earth.

RULE IV

In experimental philosophy we are to look upon propositions collected by general induction from phenomena as accurately or very nearly true, notwithstanding any contrary hypotheses that may be imagined, till such time as other phenomena occur, by which they may either be made more accurate, or liable to exceptions.

This rule we must follow that the argument of induction may not be evaded by hypotheses.

READING AND DISCUSSION QUESTIONS

1. How would you restate each of Newton's four rules in your own words?

2. Newton describes the use of specific experiences to generate universal ideas. In what instance is Newton careful to avoid generalizations? Why might he do so?

JEAN-JACQUES ROUSSEAU

From The Social Contract: *On Popular Sovereignty and the General Will*

1762

Jean-Jacques Rousseau (1712–1778) was a leading figure in the French Enlightenment. A writer of both fiction and social commentary, he addressed topics from education and nationalism to civilization and political theory. Rousseau's major work The Social Contract, *from which this excerpt is taken, argued that humans must each submit to a collective "general will" in order to safeguard the interests of the individual. It represents a shift in Rousseau's philosophy, as he had previously stated that the inequalities, pride, and greed inherent in most modern societies corrupted the natural state of man.*

Since no man has any natural authority over his fellowmen, and since force is not the source of right, conventions remain as the basis of all lawful authority among men. . . .

Now, as men cannot create any new forces, but only combine and direct those that exist, they have no other means of self-preservation than to form by aggregation a sum of forces which may overcome the resistance, to put them in action by a single motive power, and to make them work in concert.

This sum of forces can be produced only by the combination of many; but the strength and freedom of each man being the chief instruments of his preservation, how can he pledge them without injuring himself, and without neglecting the cares which he owes to himself? This difficulty, applied to my subject, may be expressed in these terms.

"To find a form of association which may defend and protect with the whole force of the community the person and property of every associate, and by means of which each, coalescing with all, may nevertheless obey

Jean-Jacques Rousseau, *The Social Contract*, in *Translations and Reprints from the Original Sources of European History* (Philadelphia: University of Pennsylvania Press, 1902), 1(6):14–16.

only himself, and remain as free as before." Such is the fundamental problem of which the social contract furnishes the solution. . . .

If then we set aside what is not of the essence of the social contract, we shall find that it is reducible to the following terms: "Each of us puts in common his person and his whole power under the supreme direction of the general will, and in return we receive every member as an indivisible part of the whole." . . .

But the body politic or sovereign, deriving its existence only from the contract, can never bind itself, even to others, in anything that derogates from the original act, such as alienation of some portion of itself, or submission to another sovereign. To violate the act by which it exists would be to annihilate itself, and what is nothing produces nothing. [Book I, Chapter 7].

It follows from what precedes, that the general will is always right and always tends to the public advantage; but it does not follow that the resolutions of the people have always the same rectitude. Men always desire their own good, but do not always discern it; the people are never corrupted, though often deceived, and it is only then that they seem to will what is evil. . . .

The public force, then, requires a suitable agent to concentrate it and put it in action according to the directions of the general will, to serve as a means of communication between the state and the sovereign, to effect in some manner in the public person what the union of soul and body effects in a man. This is, in the State, the function of government, improperly confounded with the sovereign of which it is only the minister.

What, then, is the government? An intermediate body established between the subjects and the sovereign for their mutual correspondence, charged with the execution of the laws and with the maintenance of liberty both civil and political. . . .

It is not sufficient that the assembled people should have once fixed the constitution of the state by giving their sanction to a body of laws; it is not sufficient that they should have established a perpetual government, or that they should have once for all provided for the election of magistrates. Besides the extraordinary assemblies which unforeseen events may require, it is necessary that there should be fixed and periodical ones which nothing can abolish or prorogue [postpone]; so that, on the appointed day, the people are rightfully convoked by the law, without needing for that purpose any formal summons. . . .

So soon as the people are lawfully assembled as a sovereign body, the whole jurisdiction of the government ceases, the executive power is suspended, and the person of the meanest citizen is as sacred and inviolable as that of the first magistrate, because where the represented are, there is no longer any representative. . . .

These assemblies, which have as their object the maintenance of the social treaty, ought always to be opened with two propositions, which no one should be able to suppress, and which should pass separately by vote. The first: "Whether it pleases the sovereign to maintain the present form of government." The second: "Whether it pleases the people to leave the administration to those at present entrusted with it."

I presuppose here what I believe I have proved, viz., that there is in the State no fundamental law which cannot be revoked, not even this social compact; for if all the citizens assembled in order to break the compact by a solemn agreement, no one can doubt that it could be quite legitimately broken. . . .

READING AND DISCUSSION QUESTIONS

1. What problem does Rousseau attempt to solve with his call for popular sovereignty and the general will? Restate Rousseau's explanation in your own words.

2. What is the relationship between sovereignty and government in Rousseau's model?

3. Rousseau suggests two propositions with which every political assembly should begin. How sensible do they seem to you? How effective would they be in today's society?

4. What parallels do you see between Rousseau's ideas and present-day politics on a local or national level?

DOCUMENT 17-4

VOLTAIRE

From Treatise on Toleration

1763

A major figure of the Enlightenment, Voltaire (1694–1778) was a literary genius with a keen sense of social responsibility. His writings were immensely popular during his lifetime, although his satirical voice often earned him enemies among France's religious and political elite. This excerpt is part of a larger work meant to call attention to the role of religious intolerance in the 1762 arrest, torture, and execution of Protestant merchant Jean Calas by Catholic French authorities. While his customary wit is evident in the earlier part of the work, the latter part reveals Voltaire's more direct and earnest side.

Of Universal Tolerance

No great art or studied eloquence is needed to prove that Christians should tolerate one another. I go even further and declare that we must look upon all men as our brothers. But the Turk, my brother? the Chinese, the Jew, the Siamese? Yes, of course; are we not all the children of one father and creatures of the same God?

But these people despise us; they call us idolators! Then I'll tell them they are quite wrong. I think I could at least shock the proud obstinacy of an imam [Muslim prayer leader] if I said to them something like this:

> This little globe, nothing more than a point, rolls in space like so many other globes; we are lost in this immensity. Man, some five feet tall, is surely a very small part of the universe. One of these imperceptible beings says to some of his neighbors in Arabia or Africa: "Listen to me, for the God of all these worlds has enlightened me: there are nine hundred million little ants like us on the earth, but only my anthill is beloved of God; He will hold all others in horror through all eternity; only mine will be blessed, the others will be eternally wretched."

Les Philosophes, ed. and trans. Norman L. Torrey (New York: Penguin, 1960).

At that, they would cut me short and ask what fool made that stupid remark. I would be obliged to reply, "You yourselves." Then I would try to mollify them; but that would not be easy.

I would speak now to the Christians and dare say, for example, to a Dominican Inquisitor,[4] "My brother, you know that every province in Italy has its dialect, and people in Venice and Bergamo speak differently from those in Florence. The Academy della Crusca[5] has standardized the language; its dictionary is an inescapable authority, and Buonmattei's grammar[6] is an absolute and infallible guide; but do you believe that the head of the Academy and in his absence, Buonmattei, would have been able in all good conscience to cut out the tongues of all those from Venice and Bergamo who persisted in using their own dialect?"

The Inquisitor replies: "There is a great difference; here it's a question of your salvation. It's for your own good the Director of the Inquisition orders that you be seized on the testimony of a single person, no matter how infamous or criminal he may be; that you have no lawyer to defend you; that the very name of your accuser be unknown to you; that the Inquisitor promise you grace and then condemn you; that you undergo five different degrees of torture and then be whipped or sent to the galleys, or ceremoniously burned at the stake. . . ."

I would take the liberty of replying: "My brother, perhaps you are right: I am convinced that you wish me well, but couldn't I be saved without all that?"

To be sure, these horrible absurdities do not soil the face of the earth every day, but they are frequent enough, and a whole volume could easily be written about them much longer than the Gospels which condemn them. Not only is it very cruel to persecute in this brief existence of ours those who differ from us in opinion, but I am afraid it is being bold indeed to pronounce their eternal damnation. It hardly seems fitting for us atoms of the moment, for that is all we are, to presume to know in advance the decrees of our own Creator. . . .

Oh, sectarians of a merciful God, if you had a cruel heart, if, while adoring Him whose only law consists in the words: "Love God and thy neighbor as thyself" (Luke X, 27), you had overloaded this pure and holy law with sophisms and incomprehensible disputations; if you had lighted

---

[4] **Dominican Inquisitor**: Catholic official responsible for punishing heretical beliefs.
[5] **Academy della Crusca**: Florentine Academy of Letters.
[6] **Buonmattei's grammar**: Benedetto Buonmattei; a seventeenth-century Italian grammarian whose book on the subject was widely used.

the torch of discord either over a new word or a single letter of the alphabet; if you had made eternal punishment the penalty for the omission of a few words or ceremonies which other nations could not know about, I would say to you, as I wept in compassion for mankind: "Transport yourselves with me to the day when all men will be judged and when God will do unto each man according to his works."

"I see all the dead of all centuries, past and present, appear before His presence. Are you quite sure that our Creator and Father will say to the wise and virtuous Confucius, to Solon the law-giver, to Pythagoras, Zaleucus, Socrates, and Plato, to the divine Antoninus, good Trajan, and Titus, the flowering of mankind, to Epictetus and so many other model men:[7] "Go, you monsters; go and suffer punishment, limitless in time and intensity, eternal as I am eternal. And you, my beloved, Jean Chatel, Ravaillac, Damiens, Cartouche,[8] etc., who died according to the prescribed formulas, share forever at my right hand my empire and my felicity."

You draw back in horror from these words, and since they escaped me, I have no more to say.

Prayer to God

I no longer address myself to men, but to thee, God of all beings, all worlds, and all ages. If indeed it is allowable for feeble creatures, lost in immensity and imperceptible to the rest of the universe, to dare ask anything of Thee who hast given all things, whose decrees are as immutable as they are eternal, deign to look with compassion upon the failings inherent in our nature, and grant that these failings lead us not into calamity.

Thou didst not give us hearts that we should hate each other or hands that we should cut each other's throats. Grant that we may help each other bear the burden of our painful and brief lives; that the slight difference in the clothing with which we cover our puny bodies, in our inadequate tongues, in all our ridiculous customs, in all our imperfect laws, in all our insensate opinions, in all our stations in life so disproportionate in our eyes but so equal in Thy sight, that all these little variations that differentiate the atoms called man, may not be the signals for hatred and persecution. . . .

May all men remember that they are brothers; may they hold in horror tyranny that is exercised over souls, just as they hold in execration the

---

[7] **to the wise . . . and so many other model men**: Pre-Christian moralists, enlightened political leaders, and philosophers.
[8] **Jean Chatel . . . Cartouche**: Notorious criminals of the day.

brigandage that snatches away by force the fruits of labor and peaceful industry. If the scourge of war is inevitable, let us not hate each other, let us not tear each other apart in the lap of peace; but let us use the brief moment of our existence in blessing in a thousand different tongues, from Siam to California, Thy goodness which has bestowed this moment upon us.

READING AND DISCUSSION QUESTIONS

1. Voltaire opens his treatise on tolerance by mentioning non-Christian groups. What is the effect of this wider focus?

2. Does Voltaire seem like a religious man? Why or why not?

3. What impact does Voltaire's mention of great pre-Christian men have on his argument?

DOCUMENT 17-5

IMMANUEL KANT

"What Is Enlightenment?"

1784

The Prussian professor Immanuel Kant (1724–1804) was perhaps the most influential philosopher of the Enlightenment. In Critique of Pure Reason *(1781), his best-known work, Kant sought to define what we can know and how we know it, thereby reconciling the previous schools of rationalist and empiricist thought and inspiring philosophical trends to this day. The following excerpt is taken from his "Answer to the Question: What Is Enlightenment?" published in 1784 in a monthly periodical. The short work, more accessible than his 800-page* Critique, *marked his renewed status as a public thinker and spoke to his beliefs about intellectual freedom.*

Immanuel Kant, "What is Enlightenment?" trans. Peter Gay, *Introduction to Contemporary Civilization in the West* (New York: Columbia University Press, 1954), 1071–1076. As printed in Margaret C. Jacob, *The Enlightenment* (Boston: Bedford/St. Martin's, 2001), 203–208.

Enlightenment is man's emergence from his self-imposed nonage. Nonage is the inability to use one's understanding without another's guidance. This nonage is self-imposed if its cause lies not in lack of understanding but in indecision and lack of courage to use one's own mind without another's guidance. *Dare to know! (Sapere aude.)* "Have the courage to use your own understanding," is therefore the motto of the enlightenment.

Laziness and cowardice are the reasons why such a large part of mankind gladly remain minors all their lives, long after nature has freed them from external guidance. They are the reasons why it is so easy for others to set themselves up as guardians. It is so comfortable to be a minor. If I have a book that thinks for me, a pastor who acts as my conscience, a physician who prescribes my diet, and so on — then I have no need to exert myself. I have no need to think, if only I can pay; others will take care of that disagreeable business for me. The guardians who have kindly taken supervision upon themselves see to it that the overwhelming majority of mankind — among them the entire fair sex — should consider the step to maturity not only as hard, but as extremely dangerous. First, these guardians make their domestic cattle stupid and carefully prevent the docile creatures from taking a single step without the leading-strings to which they have fastened them. Then they show them the danger that would threaten them if they should try to walk by themselves. Now, this danger is really not very great; after stumbling a few times they would, at last, learn to walk. However, examples of such failures intimidate and generally discourage all further attempts.

Thus it is very difficult for the individual to work himself out of the nonage which has become almost second nature to him. He has even grown to like it and is at first really incapable of using his own understanding, because he has never been permitted to try it. Dogmas and formulas, these mechanical tools designed for reasonable use — or rather abuse — of his natural gifts, are the fetters of an everlasting nonage. The man who casts them off would make an uncertain leap over the narrowest ditch, because he is not used to such free movement. That is why there are only a few men who walk firmly, and who have emerged from nonage by cultivating their own minds.

It is more nearly possible, however, for the public to enlighten itself; indeed, if it is only given freedom, enlightenment is almost inevitable. There will always be a few independent thinkers, even among the self-appointed guardians of the multitude. Once such men have thrown off the yoke of nonage, they will spread about them the spirit of a reasonable appreciation of man's value and of his duty to think for himself. It is especially to be noted that the public which was earlier brought under the yoke by these men afterward forces these very guardians to remain in submission, if it is so incited by some of its guardians who are themselves incapable of any enlightenment. That shows how pernicious it is to implant prejudices: they will eventually revenge themselves upon their authors or their authors' descendants. Therefore, a public can achieve enlightenment only slowly. A revolution may bring about the end of a personal despotism or of avaricious and tyrannical oppression, but never a true reform of modes of thought. New prejudices will serve, in place of the old, as guidelines for the unthinking multitude.

This enlightenment requires nothing but *freedom* — and the most innocent of all that may be called "freedom": freedom to make public use of one's reason in all matters. Now I hear the cry from all sides: "Do not argue!" The officer says: "Do not argue — drill!" The tax collector: "Do not argue — pay!" The pastor: "Do not argue — believe!" Only one ruler in the world says: "Argue as much as you please, and about what you please, but obey!" We find restrictions on freedom everywhere. But which restriction is harmful to enlightenment? Which restriction is innocent, and which advances enlightenment? I reply: the public use of one's reason must be free at all times, and this alone can bring enlightenment to mankind.

On the other hand, the private use of reason may frequently be narrowly restricted without especially hindering the progress of enlightenment. By "public use of one's reason" I mean that use which a man, as *scholar*, makes of it before the reading public. I call "private use" that use which a man makes of his reason in a civic post that has been entrusted to him. In some affairs affecting the interest of the community a certain [governmental] mechanism is necessary in which some members of the community remain passive. This creates an artificial unanimity which will serve the fulfillment of public objectives, or at least keep these objectives from being destroyed. Here arguing is not permitted: one must obey. Insofar as a part of this machine considers himself at the same time a member of a universal community — a world society of citizens — (let us say that he thinks of himself as a scholar rationally addressing his public through his writings) he may indeed argue, and the affairs with which he is associated in part as a passive member will not suffer. Thus, it would be very unfortunate if an officer on duty and under orders from his superiors should want to criticize the appropriateness or utility of his orders. He must obey. But as a scholar he could not rightfully be prevented from taking notice of the mistakes in the military service and from submitting his views to his public for its judgment. The citizen cannot refuse to pay the taxes levied upon him; indeed, impertinent censure of such taxes could be punished as a scandal that might cause general disobedience. Nevertheless, this man does not violate the duties of a citizen if, as a scholar, he publicly expresses his objections to the impropriety or possible injustice of such levies. A pastor too is bound to preach to his congregation in accord with the doctrines of the church which he serves, for he was ordained on that condition. But as a scholar he has full freedom, indeed the obligation, to communicate to his public all his carefully examined and constructive thoughts concerning errors in that doctrine and his proposals concerning improvement of religious dogma and church institutions. This is nothing that could burden his conscience. For what he teaches in pursuance of his office as representative of the church, he represents as something which he is not free to teach as he sees it. He speaks as one who is employed to speak in the name and under the orders of another. He will say: "Our church teaches this or that; these are the proofs which it employs." Thus he will benefit his congregation as much as possible by presenting doctrines to which he may not subscribe with full conviction. He can commit himself to teach them because it is not completely impossible that they may contain hidden truth. In any event, he has found nothing in the doctrines that contradicts the heart of religion. For if he believed that such contradictions existed he would not be able to administer his office with a clear conscience. He would have to resign it. Therefore the use which a scholar makes of his reason before the congregation that employs him is only a private use, for, no matter how sizable, this is only a domestic audience. In view of this he, as preacher, is not free and ought not to be free, since he is carrying out the orders of others. On the other hand, as the scholar who speaks to his own public (the world) through his writings, the minister in the public use of his reason enjoys unlimited freedom to use his own reason and to speak for himself. That the spiritual guardians of the people should themselves be treated as minors is an absurdity which would result in perpetuating absurdities.

But should a society of ministers, say a Church Council, . . . have the right to commit itself by oath to a certain unalterable doctrine, in order to secure perpetual guardianship over all its members and through them over the people? I say that this is quite impossible. Such a contract, concluded to keep all further enlightenment from humanity, is simply null and void even if it should be confirmed by the sovereign power, by parliaments, and by the most solemn treaties. An epoch cannot conclude a pact that will commit succeeding ages, prevent them from increasing their significant insights, purging themselves of errors, and generally progressing in enlightenment. That would be a crime against human nature, whose proper destiny lies precisely in such progress. Therefore, succeeding ages are fully entitled to repudiate such decisions as unauthorized and outrageous. The touchstone of all those decisions that may be made into law for a people lies in this question: Could a people impose such a law upon itself? Now, it might be possible to introduce a certain order for a definite short period of time in expectation of a better order. But while this provisional order continues, each citizen (above all, each pastor acting as a scholar) should be left free to publish his criticisms of the faults of existing institutions. This should continue until public understanding of these matters has gone so far that, by uniting the voices of many (although not necessarily all) scholars, reform proposals could be brought before the sovereign to protect those congregations which had decided according to their best lights upon an altered religious order, without, however, hindering those who want to remain true to the old institutions. But to agree to a perpetual religious constitution which is not to be publicly questioned by anyone would be, as it were, to annihilate a period of time in the progress of man's improvement. This must be absolutely forbidden.

A man may postpone his own enlightenment, but only for a limited period of time. And to give up enlightenment altogether, either for oneself or one's descendants, is to violate and to trample upon the sacred rights of man. What a people may not decide for itself may even less be decided for it by a monarch, for his reputation as a ruler consists precisely in the way in which he unites the will of the whole people within his own. If he only sees to it that all true or supposed [religious] improvement remains in step with the civic order, he can for the rest leave his subjects alone to do what they find necessary for the salvation of their souls. Salvation is none of his business; it *is* his business to prevent one man from forcibly keeping another from determining and promoting his salvation to the best of his ability. Indeed, it would be prejudicial to his majesty if he meddled in these matters and supervised the writings in which his subjects seek to bring their [religious] views into the open, even when he does this from his own highest insight, because then he exposes himself to the reproach: *Caesar non est supra grammaticos.*[9] It is worse when he debases his sovereign power so far as to support the spiritual despotism of a few tyrants in his state over the rest of his subjects.

When we ask, Are we now living in an enlightened age? the answer is, No, but we live in an age of enlightenment. As matters now stand it is still far from true that men are already capable of using their own reason in religious matters confidently and correctly without external guidance. Still, we have some obvious indications that the field of working toward the goal [of religious truth] is now being opened. What is more, the hindrances

---

[9] *Caesar non est supra grammaticos*: Latin for "Caesar is not above the grammarians."

against general enlightenment or the emergence from self-imposed non-age are gradually diminishing. In this respect this is the age of the enlightenment and the century of Frederick.[10]

A prince ought not to deem it beneath his dignity to state that he considers it his duty not to dictate anything to his subjects in religious matters, but to leave them complete freedom. If he repudiates the arrogant word *tolerant*, he is himself enlightened; he deserves to be praised by a grateful world and posterity as the man who was the first to liberate mankind from dependence, at least on the government, and let everybody use his own reason in matters of conscience. Under his reign, honorable pastors, acting as scholars and regardless of the duties of their office, can freely and openly publish their ideas to the world for inspection, although they deviate here and there from accepted doctrine. This is even more true of every other person not restrained by any oath of office. This spirit of freedom is spreading beyond the boundaries [of Prussia], even where it has to struggle against the external hindrances established by a government that fails to grasp its true interest. [Frederick's Prussia] is a shining example that freedom need not cause the least worry concerning public order or the unity of the community. When one does not deliberately attempt to keep men in barbarism, they will gradually work out of that condition by themselves.

I have emphasized the main point of the enlightenment — man's emergence from his self-imposed nonage — primarily in religious matters, because our rulers have no interest in playing the guardian to their subjects in the arts and sciences. Above all, nonage in religion is not only the most harmful but the most dishonorable. But the disposition of a sovereign ruler who favors freedom in the arts and sciences goes even further: he knows that there is no danger in permitting his subjects to make public use of their reason and to publish their ideas concerning a better constitution, as well as candid criticism of existing basic laws. We already have a striking example [of such freedom], and no monarch can match the one whom we venerate.

But only the man who is himself enlightened, who is not afraid of shadows, and who commands at the same time a well-disciplined and numerous army as guarantor of public peace — only he can say what [the sovereign of] a free state cannot dare to say: "Argue as much as you like, and about what you like, but obey!" Thus we observe here as elsewhere in human affairs, in which almost everything is paradoxical, a surprising and

---

[10] **the century of Frederick**: In the eighteenth century Prussia was ruled by three Fredericks: Frederick I (r. 1701–1713), Frederick William I (r. 1713–1740), and Frederick II (r. 1740–1786).

unexpected course of events: a large degree of civic freedom appears to be of advantage to the intellectual freedom of the people, yet at the same time it establishes insurmountable barriers. A lesser degree of civic freedom, however, creates room to let that free spirit expand to the limits of its capacity. Nature, then, has carefully cultivated the seed within the hard core — namely, the urge for and the vocation of free thought. And this free thought gradually reacts back on the modes of thought of the people, and men become more and more capable of acting in freedom. At last free thought acts even on the fundamentals of government, and the state finds it agreeable to treat man, who is now more than a machine, in accord with his dignity.

READING AND DISCUSSION QUESTIONS

1. Briefly summarize Kant's definition of *enlightenment*. Why is it so difficult for people to achieve enlightenment?
2. According to Kant, who is responsible for enlightening the populace?
3. What is the difference between "public" and "private" freedoms? What examples does Kant give of each?
4. How is Kant's definition limited to his time and place? How is it universally applicable?

COMPARATIVE QUESTIONS

1. How do the documents in this chapter reflect the tension between individual thought and social order? Which author seems the least concerned with those issues, and why?
2. Religion and spirituality play a role in the arguments of Galileo and Voltaire. How do they use religion to further their cases?
3. How do Galileo and Newton present nature in their explanations of scientific ideas?
4. Compare Rousseau's and Kant's views on the role of law and power in society. On what do they agree? On what do they differ?

CHAPTER 18

Africa and the World

ca. 1400–1800

The fifteenth-century voyages of Portuguese mariners eager to identify and exploit new trade opportunities ushered in an era of violence, exploitation, and slavery on the African continent. However, Africa's story during these four centuries was not simply one of involuntary participation in a European-dominated system of colonization and enslavement. For centuries, diverse African states had played an important role in global trade, and foreign and indigenous influences combined to produce powerful and enduring cultures. Neither was slavery new to African culture. However, the traditional African idea of slavery was transformed by the dehumanizing profit motive of European capitalism and plantation economies. Many coastal societies facilitated the massive transatlantic slave trade by capturing people from the African interior and delivering them to European slave ships. The documents in this chapter depict both continuity and transformation in African society during this period of European incursion.

DOCUMENT 18-1

NZINGA MBEMBA (ALFONSO I)
From Letters to the King of Portugal
1526

King of the powerful central West African state of Kongo, Nzinga Mbemba ruled from around 1506 to 1543. Like his father, he was baptized a Catholic by Portuguese explorers in 1491, taking the Christian name Alfonso I. As king, he embraced many aspects of Portuguese society, including both Catholicism and material culture, which became important symbols of

Basil Davidson, trans., *The African Coast* (London: Curtis Brown, Ltd., 1964), 54–57.

influence and power in his kingdom. In the 1520s, Alfonso noted with dismay the increasing Portuguese abuses of the thriving Kongolese slave markets and of his kingdom generally. The letters excerpted here represent his attempt to seek redress from his Portuguese counterpart.

Sir, Your Highness should know how our Kingdom is being lost in so many ways that it is convenient to provide for the necessary remedy, since this is caused by the excessive freedom given by your agents and officials to the men and merchants who are allowed to come to this Kingdom to set up shops with goods and many things which have been prohibited by us, and which they spread throughout our Kingdoms and Domains in such an abundance that many of our vassals, whom we had in obedience, do not comply because they have the things in greater abundance than we ourselves; and it was with these things that we had them content and subjected under our vassalage and jurisdiction, so it is doing a great harm not only to the service of God, but the security and peace of our Kingdoms and State as well.

And we cannot reckon how great the damage is, since the mentioned merchants are taking every day our natives, sons of the land and the sons of our noblemen and vassals and our relatives, because the thieves and men of bad conscience grab them wishing to have the things and wares of this Kingdom which they are ambitious of; they grab them and get them to be sold; and so great, Sir, is the corruption and licentiousness that our country is being completely depopulated, and Your Highness should not agree with this nor accept it as in your service. And to avoid it we need from those (your) Kingdoms no more than some priests and a few people to teach in schools, and no other goods except wine and flour for the holy sacrament. That is why we beg of Your Highness to help and assist us in this matter, commanding your factors that they should not send here either merchants or wares, because it is *our will that in these Kingdoms there should not be any trade of slaves nor outlet for them.* Concerning what is referred [to] above, again we beg of Your Highness to agree with it, since otherwise we cannot remedy such an obvious damage. Pray Our Lord in His mercy to have Your Highness under His guard and let you do forever the things of His service. I kiss your hands many times.

At our town of Kongo, written on the sixth day of July, [secretary] João Teixeira did it in 1526.
The King. Dom [Lord] Alfonso.

✳ ✳ ✳

Moreover, Sir, in our Kingdoms there is another great inconvenience which is of little service to God, and this is that many of our people, keenly desirous as they are of the wares and things of your Kingdoms, which are brought here by your people, and in order to satisfy their voracious appetite, seize many of our people, freed and exempt men, and very often it happens that they kidnap even noblemen and the sons of noblemen, and our relatives, and take them to be sold to the white men who are in our Kingdoms; and for this purpose they have concealed them; and others are brought during the night so that they might not be recognized.

And as soon as they are taken by the white men they are immediately ironed and branded with fire, and when they are carried to be embarked, if they are caught by our guards' men the whites allege that they have bought them but they cannot say from whom, so that it is our duty to do justice and to restore to the freemen their freedom, but it cannot be done if your subjects feel offended, as they claim to be.

And to avoid such a great evil we passed a law so that any white man living in our Kingdoms and wanting to purchase goods in any way should first inform three of our noblemen and officials of our court whom we rely upon in this matter, and these are Dom Pedro Manipanza and Dom Manuel Manissaba, our chief usher, and Gonçalo Pires our chief freighter, who should investigate if the mentioned goods are captives or free men, and if cleared by them there will be no further doubt nor embargo for them to be taken and embarked. But if the white men do not comply with it they will lose the aforementioned goods. And if we do them this favor and concession it is for the part Your Highness has in it, since we know that it is in your service too that these goods are taken from our Kingdom, otherwise we should not consent to this. . . .

* * *

Sir, Your Highness has been kind enough to write to us saying that we should ask in our letters for anything we need, and that we shall be provided with everything, and as the peace and the health of our Kingdom depend on us, and as there are among us old folks and people who have lived for many days, it happens that we have continuously many and different diseases which put us very often in such a weakness that we reach almost the last extreme; and the same happens to our children, relatives and natives owing to the lack in this country of physicians and surgeons who might know how to cure properly such diseases. And as we have got neither dispensaries nor drugs which might help us in this forlornness, many of those who had been already confirmed and instructed in the holy faith of Our Lord Jesus Christ perish and die; and the rest of the people in their majority cure themselves with herbs and breads and other ancient methods, so that they put all their faith in the mentioned herbs and cere- monies if they live, and believe that they are saved if they die; and this is not much in the service of God.

And to avoid such a great error and inconvenience, since it is from God in the first place and then from your Kingdoms and from Your High- ness that all the good and drugs and medicines have come to save us, we beg of you to be agreeable and kind enough to send us two physicians and two apothecaries and one surgeon, so that they may come with their drug- stores and all the necessary things to stay in our kingdoms, because we are in extreme need of them all and each of them. We shall do them all good and shall benefit them by all means, since they are sent by Your Highness, whom we thank for your work in their coming. We beg of Your Highness as a great favor to do this for us, because besides being good in itself it is in the service of God as we have said above.

READING AND DISCUSSION QUESTIONS

1. What complaints does Alfonso present to the Portuguese king, and what actions does he seek?

2. To justify his requests, Alfonso claims that the Portuguese are not act- ing "in the service of God." How might Alfonso's Christianity subject him to Portuguese control? How is it a useful tool for him?

3. Alfonso states that it is his will that the slave trade end in his country. Given the thriving slave markets that existed before contact with the Portuguese, what do you think about his decision to end the slave trade in Kongo? What seems to have motivated his choice?

DOCUMENT 18-2

LEO AFRICANUS
A Description of Timbuktu
1526

Leo Africanus (ca. 1465–1550) was one of thousands of Muslims expelled from the Iberian Peninsula after the "reconquest" of Spain by the Catholic monarchs Ferdinand and Isabella. Captured as a slave and given to Pope Leo X, Leo Africanus was baptized in 1519 and sent to Africa to observe and report back to the pope. The resulting work, published first in a larger collection by an Italian geographer, exemplified a new kind of travel writing that boasted careful research and meticulous, firsthand detail. In this excerpt, Leo Africanus relates his travels to the city of Timbuktu, which for centuries had been a center of international trade and Islamic higher learning.

The name of this kingdom is a modern one, after a city which was built by a king named Mansa Suleyman in the year 610 of the hegira[1] around twelve miles from a branch of the Niger River.

The houses of Timbuktu are huts made of clay-covered wattles [supports] with thatched roofs. In the center of the city is a temple built of stone and mortar, built by an architect named Granata, and in addition there is a large palace, constructed by the same architect, where the king lives. The shops of the artisans, the merchants, and especially weavers of cotton cloth are very numerous. Fabrics are also imported from Europe to Timbuktu, borne by Berber [North African] merchants.

The women of the city maintain the custom of veiling their faces, except for the slaves who sell all the foodstuffs. The inhabitants are very rich, especially the strangers who have settled in the country; so much so that the current king has given two of his daughters in marriage to two brothers, both businessmen, on account of their wealth. There are many

Paul Brians, et al., *Reading About the World*, vol. 2, 3d ed. (Harcourt Brace College Custom Books).

[1] **year 610 of the hegira**: Arabic for "migration," the hegira (hijra) was Muhammad's emigration to Medina in 622, the first year of the Islamic calendar. Therefore, Suleyman's city dates to the early thirteenth century.

wells containing sweet water in Timbuktu; and in addition, when the Niger is in flood canals deliver the water to the city. Grain and animals are abundant, so that the consumption of milk and butter is considerable. But salt is in very short supply because it is carried here from Tegaza, some 500 miles from Timbuktu. I happened to be in this city at a time when a load of salt sold for eighty ducats. The king has a rich treasure of coins and gold ingots. One of these ingots weighs 970 pounds.

The royal court is magnificent and very well organized. When the king goes from one city to another with the people of his court, he rides a camel and the horses are led by hand by servants. If fighting becomes necessary, the servants mount the camels and all the soldiers mount on horseback. When someone wishes to speak to the king, he must kneel before him and bow down; but this is only required of those who have never before spoken to the king, or of ambassadors. The king has about 3,000 horsemen and infinity of foot-soldiers armed with bows made of wild fennel which they use to shoot poisoned arrows. This king makes war only upon neighboring enemies and upon those who do not want to pay him tribute. When he has gained a victory, he has all of them — even the children — sold in the market at Timbuktu.

Only small, poor horses are born in this country. The merchants use them for their voyages and the courtiers to move about the city. But the good horses come from Barbary. They arrive in a caravan and, ten or twelve days later, they are led to the ruler, who takes as many as he likes and pays appropriately for them.

The king is a declared enemy of the Jews. He will not allow any to live in the city. If he hears it said that a Berber merchant frequents them or does business with them, he confiscates his goods. There are in Timbuktu numerous judges, teachers and priests, all properly appointed by the king. He greatly honors learning. Many hand-written books imported from Barbary are also sold. There is more profit made from this commerce than from all other merchandise.

Instead of coined money, pure gold nuggets are used; and for small purchases, cowrie shells which have been carried from Persia, and of which 400 equal a ducat. Six and two-thirds of their ducats equal one Roman gold ounce.

The people of Timbuktu are of a peaceful nature. They have a custom of almost continuously walking about the city in the evening (except for those that sell gold), between 10 PM and 1 AM, playing musical instruments and dancing. The citizens have at their service many slaves, both men and women.

The city is very much endangered by fire. At the time when I was there on my second voyage, half the city burned in the space of five hours. But the wind was violent and the inhabitants of the other half of the city began to move their belongings for fear that the other half would burn.

There are no gardens or orchards in the area surrounding Timbuktu.

READING AND DISCUSSION QUESTIONS

1. Describe the tone that Africanus uses. For whom do you imagine this work would be useful or interesting?

2. Leo Africanus notes that trade in books is worth more than any other form of commerce in the city. What does this suggest about life in Timbuktu?

DOCUMENT 18-3

JAMES BARBOT

A Voyage to New Calabar River

1699

James Barbot and his brother John were British subjects of French birth who took part in slaving expeditions in the late 1600s. James kept a journal of his 1699 voyage on a British ship — of which he was part owner — to the Rio Real, or New Calabar River. Prominent states along the river like Ibani and Kalabari (or Bonny and Calabar, as they were called by Europeans) profited from their coastal locations by trading between Europeans and inland societies. The tone of Barbot's journal reflects the practical, profit-minded nature of the negotiations between European and Ibani traders for various goods, including human beings.

Awnsham Churchill and John Churchill, eds., *Collections of Voyages and Travels,* 3d ed., 8 vols. (London: H. Lintor, 1744–1747), vol. 5:459. Modernized by A. J. Andrea.

June 30, 1699, being ashore, had a new conference which produced nothing. Then Pepprell, the king's brother, delivered a message from the king:

He was sorry we would not accept his proposals. It was not his fault, since he had a great esteem and regard for the whites, who had greatly enriched him through trade. His insistence on thirteen bars [of iron, Ibani currency] for male and ten for female slaves was due to the fact that the people of the country maintained a high price for slaves at their inland markets, seeing so many large ships coming to Bonny for them. However, to moderate matters and to encourage trade with us, he would be content with thirteen bars for males and nine bars and two brass rings for females, etc.

We offered thirteen bars for men and nine for women and proportionately for boys and girls, according to their ages. Following this we parted, without concluding anything further.

On July 1, the king sent for us to come ashore. We stayed there till four in the afternoon and concluded the trade on the terms offered them the day before. The king promised to come aboard the next day to regulate it and be paid his duties. . . .

The second [of July]. . . . At two o'clock we fetched the king from shore, attended by all his Caboceiros [chiefs and elders] and officers, in three large canoes. Entering the ship, he was saluted with seven guns. The king had on an old-fashioned scarlet coat, laced with gold and silver, very rusty, and a fine hat on his head, but bare-footed. All his attendants showed great respect to him and, since our arrival, none of the natives have dared to come aboard or sell the least thing, till the king adjusted trade matters.

We had again a long talk with the king and Pepprell, his brother, concerning the rates of our goods and his customs. This Pepprell was a sharp black and a mighty talking black, perpetually making objections against something or other and teasing us for this or that dassy [gift] or present, as well as for drinks, etc. Would that such a one as he were out of the way, to facilitate trade. . . .

Thus, with much patience, all our affairs were settled equitably, after the fashion of a people who are not very scrupulous when it comes to finding excuses or objections for not keeping to the word of any verbal contract. For they do not have the art of reading and writing, and we therefore are forced to stand to their agreement, which often is no longer than they think fit to hold it themselves. The king ordered the public crier to proclaim permission to trade with us, with the noise of his trumpets . . . , we paying sixteen brass rings to the fellow for his fee. The blacks objected against our wrought pewter and tankards, green beads, and other goods, which they would not accept. . . .

We gave the usual presents to the king. . . . To Captain Forty, the king's general, Captain Pepprell, Captain Boileau, alderman Bougsbyu, my lord Willyby, duke of Monmouth, drunken Henry, and some others [the king's chiefs and elders] two firelocks, eight hats, nine narrow Guinea stuffs [bolts of Indian cloth]. We adjusted with them the reduction of our merchandise into bars of iron, as the standard coin, namely: one bunch of beads, one bar; four strings of rings, ten rings each, one ditto; four copper bars, one ditto. . . . And so on pro rata for every sort of goods. . . .

The price of provisions and wood was also regulated. Sixty king's yams, one bar; one hundred and sixty slave's yams, one bar; for fifty thousand yams to be delivered to us. A butt [large cask] of water, two rings. For the length of wood, seven bars, which is dear, but they were to deliver it ready cut into our boat. For one goat, one bar. A cow, ten or eight bars, according to its size. A hog, two bars. A calf, eight bars. A jar of palm oil, one bar and a quarter.

We also paid the king's duty in goods; five hundred slaves, to be purchased at two copper rings a head.

READING AND DISCUSSION QUESTIONS

1. What are Barbot's opinions of the various Ibani figures with whom he has contact? How does he demonstrate those opinions?

2. Compare Barbot's description of the purchase of "provisions and wood" to the purchase of slaves.

3. Which party — European or African — seems to have the greater advantage in these negotiations, and why? How does that influence your perception of the transatlantic slave trade as a system?

DOCUMENT 18-4

OLAUDAH EQUIANO

From The Interesting Narrative of Olaudah Equiano

1789

One of the few enslaved Africans able to purchase their freedom, Olaudah Equiano (ca. 1745–1797) drew on his remarkable education and experiences to write an autobiographical account of kidnapping and slavery in Africa and the Americas. It was published with the help of British abolitionists, and he promoted his work in Britain with the equivalent of a modern book tour. Recently discovered evidence suggests that Equiano may have been born in South Carolina, and therefore would not have experienced life in Africa and the Middle Passage. However, his popular narrative is generally consistent with other accounts of the kidnapping and enslavement of Africans, and its power to inspire the abolitionist movement is unquestioned.

One day, when all our people were gone out to their works as usual, and only I and my dear sister were left to mind the house, two men and a woman got over our walls, and in a moment seized us both, and, without giving us time to cry out, or make resistance, they stopped our mouths, and ran off with us into the nearest wood. Here they tied our hands, and continued to carry us as far as they could, till night came on, when we reached a small house, where the robbers halted for refreshment, and spent the night. We were then unbound, but were unable to take any food; and, being quite overpowered by fatigue and grief, our only relief was some sleep, which allayed our misfortune for a short time. The next morning we left the house, and continued travelling all the day. For a long time we had kept [to] the woods, but at last we came to a road which I believed I knew. I now had some hopes of being delivered; for we had advanced but a little way before I discovered some people at a distance, on which I began to cry out for their assistance; but my cries had no other effect that to make them tie me faster and stop my mouth, and then they put me in a large sack. They also stopped my sister's mouth, and tied her hands; and in this

---

Olaudah Equiano, *The Interesting Narrative of Olaudah Equiano* (London, 1789).

manner we proceeded till we were out of sight of these people. When we went to rest the following night, they offered us some victuals, but we refused it; and the only comfort we had was in being in one another's arms all that night, and bathing each other with our tears. But alas! we were soon deprived of even the small comfort of weeping together.

The next day proved a day of greater sorrow that I had yet experienced; for my sister and I were then separated, while we lay clasped in each other's arms. It was in vain that we besought them not to part us; she was torn from me, and immediately carried away, while I was left in a state of distraction not to be described. I cried and grieved continually; and for several days did not eat anything but what they forced into my mouth. At length, after many days' travelling, during which I had often changed masters, I got into the hands of a chieftain, in a very pleasant country. This man had two wives and some children, and they all used me extremely well, and did all they could to comfort me; particularly the first wife, who was something like my mother. Although I was a great many days' journey from my father's house, yet these people spoke exactly the same language with us. . . .

From the time I left my own nation, I always found somebody that understood me till I came to the sea coast. The languages of different nations did not totally differ, nor were they so copious as those of the Europeans,[2] particularly the English. They were therefore easily learned; and, while I was journeying thus through Africa, I acquired two or three different tongues. In this manner I had been travelling for a considerable time, when, one evening, to my great surprise, whom should I see brought to the house where I was but my dear sister! As soon as she saw me, she gave a loud shriek, and ran into my arms — I was quite overpowered; neither of us could speak, but, for a considerable time, clung to each other in mutual embraces, unable to do anything but weep. Our meeting affected all who saw us; and, indeed, I must acknowledge, in honor of those sable destroyers of human rights, that I never met with any ill treatment, or saw any offered to their slaves, except tying them, when necessary, to keep them from running away.

When these people knew we were brother and sister, they indulged us to be together; and the man, to whom I suppose we belonged, lay with us, he in the middle, while she and I held one another by the hands across his breast all night; and thus for a while we forgot our misfortunes, in the joy of being together; but even this small comfort was soon to have an end; for

---

[2] **nor were they so copious . . . Europeans**: Equiano is saying that African languages had less extensive vocabularies than European languages.

scarcely had the fatal morning appeared when she was again torn from me forever! I was now more miserable, if possible, than before. The small relief which her presence gave me from pain, was gone, and the wretchedness of my situation was redoubled by my anxiety after her fate, and my apprehensions lest her sufferings should be greater than mine, when I could not be with her to alleviate them. . . .

I continued to travel, sometimes by land, sometimes by water, through different countries and various nations, till, at the end of six or seven months after I had been kidnapped, I arrived at the sea coast. . . .

The first object which saluted my eyes when I arrived on the coast, was the sea, and a slave ship, which was then riding at anchor, and waiting for its cargo. These filled me with astonishment, which was soon converted into terror, when I was carried on board. I was immediately handled, tossed up to see if I were sound, by some of the crew, and I was now persuaded that I had gotten into a world of bad spirits, and that they were going to kill me. Their complexions, too, differing so much from ours, their long hair, and the language they spoke (which was very different from any I had ever heard), united to confirm me in this belief. Indeed, such were the horrors of my views and fears at the moment, that, if ten thousand worlds had been my own, I would have freely parted with them all to have exchanged my condition with that of the meanest slave in my own country. When I looked round the ship too, and saw a large furnace of copper boiling, and a multitude of black people of every description chained together, every one of their countenances expressing dejection and sorrow. I no longer doubted of my fate, and, quite overpowered with horror and anguish, I fell motionless on the deck and fainted. When I recovered a little, I found some black people about me, who I believed were some of those who had brought me on board, and had been receiving their pay; they talked to me in order to cheer me, but all in vain. I asked them if we were not to be eaten by these white men with horrible looks, red faces, and long hair. They told me I was not, and one of the crew brought me a small portion of spirituous liquor in a wine glass; but being afraid of him, I would not take it out of his hand. One of the blacks therefore took it from him and gave it to me, and I took a little down my palate, which, instead of reviving me, as they thought it would, threw me into the greatest consternation at the strange feeling it produced, having never tasted any such liquor before. Soon after this, the blacks who brought me on board went off, and left me abandoned to despair. . . .

At last, when the ship we were in, had got in all her cargo, they made ready with many fearful noises, and we were all put under deck, so that we could not see how they managed the vessel. But this disappointment was the least of my sorrow. The stench of the hold while we were on the coast was so intolerably loathsome, that it was dangerous to remain there for any time, and some of us had been permitted to stay on the deck for the fresh air; but now that the whole ship's cargo was confined together, it became absolutely pestilential. The closeness of the place, and the heat of the climate, added to the number in the ship, which was so crowded that each had scarcely room to turn himself, almost suffocated us. This produced copious perspirations, so that the air soon became unfit for respiration, from a variety of loathsome smells, and brought on a sickness among the slaves, of which many died — thus falling victims to the improvident avarice, as I may call it, of their purchasers. This wretched situation was again aggravated by the galling of the chains, now became insupportable, and the filth of the necessary tubs [latrines], into which the children often fell, and were almost suffocated. The shrieks of the women, and the groans of the dying, rendered the whole a scene of horror almost inconceivable. Happily, perhaps, for myself, I was soon reduced so low here that it was thought necessary to keep me almost always on deck, and from my extreme youth I was not put in fetters. In this situation I expected every hour to share the fate of my companions, some of whom were almost daily brought upon deck at the point of death, which I began to hope would soon put an end to my miseries. Often did I think of the many inhabitants of the deep much more happy than myself. I envied them [for] the freedom they enjoyed, and as often wished I could change my condition for theirs. Every circumstance I met with, served only to render my state more painful, and heightened my apprehensions, and my opinion of the cruelty of the whites.

One day they had taken a number of fishes; and when they had killed and satisfied themselves with as many as they thought fit, to our astonishment who were on deck, rather than give any of them to us to eat, as we expected, they tossed the remaining fish into the sea again, although we begged and prayed for some as well we could, but in vain. . . .

One day, when we had a smooth sea and a moderate wind, two of my wearied countrymen who were chained together (I was near them at the time), preferring death to such a life of misery, somehow made through the nettings and jumped into the sea; immediately, another quite dejected fellow, who, on account of his illness, was suffered to be out of irons, also followed their example; and I believe many more would have soon done the same, if they had not been prevented by the ship's crew, who were instantly alarmed. . . .

At last we came in sight of the island of Barbadoes, at which the whites on board gave a great shout, and made many signs of joy to us. We did not know what to think of this; but as the vessel grew nearer, we plainly saw the harbor, and other ships of different kinds and sizes, and we soon anchored among them, off Bridgetown. Many merchants and planters now came on board, though it was in the evening. They put us in separate parcels, and examined us attentively. They also made us jump, and pointed to the land, signifying we were to go there. We thought by this, we should be eaten by these ugly men, as they appeared to us; and, when soon after we were all put down under deck again, there was much dread and trembling among us, and nothing but bitter cries to be heard all the night from these apprehensions, insomuch, that at last the white people got some old slaves from the land to pacify us. They told us we were not to be eaten, but to work, and were soon to go on land, where we would see many of our country people. This report eased us much. And sure enough, soon after we were landed, there came to us Africans of all languages.

We were immediately conducted to the merchant's yard, where we were all pent up together, like so many sheep in a fold, without regard to sex or age. As every object was new to me, everything I saw filled me with surprise. What struck me first, was, that the houses were built with bricks and stories, and every other respect different from those I had seen in Africa; but I was still more astonished on seeing people on horseback.[3] I did not know what this could mean; and, indeed, I thought these people were full of nothing but magical arts. While I was in this astonishment, one of my fellow prisoners spoke to a countryman of his, about the horses, who said they were the same kind they had in their country. I understood them, though they were from a distant part of Africa; and I thought it odd I had not seen any horses there; but afterwards, when I came to converse with different Africans, I found they had many horses amongst them, and much larger than those I then saw.

We were not many days in the merchant's custody, before we were sold in the usual manner, which is this: On a signal given (as the beat of a drum), the buyers rush at once into the yard where the slaves are confined, and make a choice of that parcel they like best. The noise and clamor with which this is attended, and the eagerness visible in the countenances of the buyers, serve not a little to increase the apprehension of terrified

---

[3] **people on horseback**: Equiano would have been unfamiliar with horses in West Africa, where they were susceptible to sleeping sickness, a lethal disease transmitted by the tsetse fly.

Africans, who may well be supposed to consider them as the ministers of that destruction to which they think themselves devoted. In this manner, without scruple, are relations and friends separated, most of them never to see each other again.

I remember, in the vessel in which I was brought over, in the men's apartment, there were several brothers, who, in the sale, were sold in different lots; and it was very moving on this occasion, to see and hear their cries at parting. O, ye nominal Christians! might not an African ask you — Learned you this from your God, who says unto you, Do unto all men as you would men should do unto you? Is it not enough that we are torn from our country and friends, to toil for your luxury and lust of gain? Must every tender feeling be likewise sacrificed to your avarice? Are the dearest friends and relations, now rendered more dear by their separation from their kindred, still to be parted from each other, and thus prevented from cheering the gloom of slavery, with the small comfort of being together, and mingling their sufferings and sorrows? Why are parents to lose their children, brothers their sisters, or husbands their wives? Surely, this is a new refinement in cruelty, which, while it has no advantage to atone for it, thus aggravates distress, and adds fresh horrors even to the wretchedness of slavery.

READING AND DISCUSSION QUESTIONS

1. How does Equiano contrast his experiences as a slave in Africa with his experiences aboard the slave ship?

2. To whom does Equiano appeal at the end of his narrative, and on what grounds?

3. At times, Equiano describes people as "white" or "black" — at others, he distinguishes between people of his own nation and other "blacks," and elsewhere he refers to "Africans." What is the significance of these different categorizations?

COMPARATIVE QUESTIONS

1. Compare the accounts of Olaudah Equiano and Leo Africanus, both of whom experienced slavery. How does the tone of each reflect their intended audience? With which of Equiano's arguments might Leo Africanus sympathize based on his description of slavery in Timbuktu?

2. Both James Barbot and Nzinga Mbemba/Alfonso I describe the difficulties of trading with people from another culture. How do those difficulties color their opinion of the other culture? How do they deal with, or propose to deal with, problems of trade?

3. Both Equiano and Mbemba/Alfonso I are Africans who use Christianity to make a point. How are the positions taken by each similar, and how are they different? Based on these examples, explain whether you think that the adoption of Christianity helped or harmed Africans.

4. Compare Barbot's travelogue to that of Africanus. For what purpose did each man write? What language reveals their assumptions or motives?

5. The issue of slavery looms large in any consideration of Africa from 1400 to 1800. What different kinds of slavery are depicted by Barbot, Equiano, and Mbemba/Alfonso I? What judgments — implicit or explicit — do these authors make about slavery?

CHAPTER 19

The Islamic World Powers

ca. 1400–1800

With the decline of the Mongol Empire in the late thirteenth and fourteenth centuries, power shifted to a number of Turkish territories. By the sixteenth century, three areas had developed into major Islamic empires: the Safavid in Persia, the Ottoman in Anatolia, and the Mughal in India. Their collective territories stretched from Eastern Europe and West Africa through present-day Bangladesh. As each state flourished, it made significant political, economic, intellectual, and artistic contributions. Islamic culture was enriched by the states' interactions with one another and with the increasingly mobile peoples of Christian Europe. However, the impressive extent of Islamic society and culture represented by the three states belies the sharp and often violent differences among them. The following documents reveal the splendor of and tension between the Ottoman, Safavid, and Mughal Empires, as well as their sense of the growing presence of Western European travelers.

DOCUMENT 19-1

SULTAN SELIM I
From a Letter to Shah Ismail of Persia
1514

Sultan Selim I (r. 1512–1520) presided over a massive territorial expansion of the Ottoman Empire, conquering much of the Middle East, including the holy cities of Mecca and Medina. After defeating the Mamluk Dynasty in Egypt in 1517, Selim assumed the title of caliph — a political and religious

---

John J. Saunders, ed., *The Muslim World on the Eve of Europe's Expansion* (Englewood Cliffs, N.J.: Prentice-Hall, 1966), 41–43.

successor to Muhammad — thereby declaring Sunni Ottoman leadership of the Muslim world. The excerpt that follows is from Selim's letter to Shah Ismail of Persia, the young founder of the Shi'ite Safavid Empire and a growing threat to Selim's power. The ensuing conflict in 1514 marked an important moment in Sunni-Shi'ite power struggles in the Islamic world.

The Supreme Being who is at once the sovereign arbiter of the destinies of men and the source of all light and knowledge, declares in the holy book [the Qur'an] that the true faith is that of the Muslims, and that whoever professes another religion, far from being hearkened to and saved, will on the contrary be cast out among the rejected on the great day of the Last Judgment; He says further, this God of truth, that His designs and decrees are unalterable, that all human acts are perforce reported to Him, and that he who abandons the good way will be condemned to hell-fire and eternal torments. Place yourself, O Prince, among the true believers, those who walk in the path of salvation, and who turn aside with care from vice and infidelity. . . .

I, sovereign chief of the Ottomans, master of the heroes of the age; . . . I, the exterminator of idolators, destroyer of the enemies of the true faith, the terror of the tyrants and pharaohs of the age; I, before whom proud and unjust kings have humbled themselves, and whose hand breaks the strongest scepters; I, the great Sultan-Khan, son of Sultan Bayezid-Khan, son of Sultan Muhammad-Khan, son of Sultan Murad-Khan, I address myself graciously to you, Emir Ismail, chief of the troops of Persia, comparable in tyranny to Sohak and Afrasiab [legendary Asian kings], and predestined to perish . . . in order to make known to you that the works emanating from the Almighty are not the fragile products of caprice or folly, but make up an infinity of mysteries impenetrable to the human mind. The Lord Himself says in his holy book: "We have not created the heavens and the earth in order to play a game" [Qur'an, 21:16]. Man, who is the noblest of the creatures and the summary of the marvels of God, is in consequence on earth the living image of the Creator. It is He who has set up Caliphs on earth, because, joining faculties of soul with perfection of body, man is the only being who can comprehend the attributes of the divinity and adore its sublime beauties; but he possesses this rare intelligence, he attains this divine knowledge only in our religion and by observing the precepts of the prince of prophets . . . the right arm of the God of Mercy [Muhammad]; it is then only by practicing the true religion that man will prosper in this world and merit eternal life in the other. As to you,

Emir Ismail, such a recompense will not be your lot; because you have denied the sanctity of the divine laws; because you have deserted the path of salvation and the sacred commandments; because you have impaired the purity of the dogmas of Islam; because you have dishonored, soiled, and destroyed the altars of the Lord, usurped the scepter of the East by unlawful and tyrannical means; because coming forth from the dust, you have raised yourself by odious devices to a place shining with splendor and magnificence; because you have opened to Muslims the gates of tyranny and oppression; because you have joined iniquity, perjury, and blasphemy to your sectarian impiety; because under the cloak of the hypocrite, you have sowed everywhere trouble and sedition; because you have raised the standard of irreligion and heresy; because yielding to the impulse of your evil passions, and giving yourself up without rein to the most infamous disorders, you have dared to throw off the control of Muslim laws and to permit lust and rape, the massacre of the most virtuous and respectable men, the destruction of pulpits and temples, the profanation of tombs, the ill-treatment of the ulama,[1] the doctors [teachers] and emirs [military commanders and princes] descended from the Prophet, the repudiation of the Quran, the cursing of the legitimate Caliphs.[2] Now as the first duty of a Muslim and above all of a pious prince is to obey the commandment, "O, you faithful who believe, be the executors of the decrees of God!" the ulama and our doctors have pronounced sentence of death against you, perjurer and blasphemer, and have imposed on every Muslim the sacred obligation to arm in defense of religion and destroy heresy and impiety in your person and that of all your partisans.

Animated by the spirit of this fatwa [religious decree], conforming to the Quran, the code of divine laws, and wishing on one side to strengthen Islam, on the other to liberate the lands and peoples who writhe under your yoke, we have resolved to lay aside our imperial robes in order to put on the shield and coat of mail [armor], to raise our ever victorious banner, to assemble our invincible armies, to take up the gauntlet of the avenger, to march with our soldiers, whose sword strikes mortal blows, and whose point will pierce the enemy even to the constellation of Sagittarius. In pursuit of this noble resolution, we have entered upon the campaign, and

---

[1] ulama: Religious teachers and interpreters of Muslim law.

[2] the legitimate Caliphs: Shi'ites broke with mainstream Islam over a dispute about the early caliphate. They believe that Muhammad's cousin and son-in-law Ali (the fourth caliph) should have been the first caliph. Shi'ites thus believe that the first three caliphs are illegitimate.

guided by the hand of the Almighty, we hope soon to strike down your tyrannous arm, blow away the clouds of glory and grandeur which trouble your head and cause your fatal blindness, release from your despotism your trembling subjects, smother you in the end in the very mass of flames which your infernal jinn [supernatural spirit] raises everywhere along your passage, accomplishing in this way on you the maxim which says: "He who sows discord can only reap evils and afflictions." However, anxious to conform to the spirit of the law of the Prophet, we come, before commencing war, to set out before you the words of the Quran, in place of the sword, and to exhort you to embrace the true faith; this is why we address this letter to you. . . .

We urge you to look into yourself, to renounce your errors, and to march towards the good with a firm and courageous step; we ask further that you give up possession of the territory violently seized from our state and to which you have only illegitimate pretensions, that you deliver it back into the hands of our lieutenants and officers; and if you value your safety and repose, this should be done without delay.

But if, to your misfortune, you persist in your past conduct, puffed up with the idea of your power and your foolish bravado, you wish to pursue the course of your iniquities, you will see in a few days your plains covered with our tents and inundated with our battalions. Then prodigies of valor will be done, and we shall see the decrees of the Almighty, Who is the God of Armies, and sovereign judge of the actions of men, accomplished. For the rest, victory to him who follows the path of salvation!

READING AND DISCUSSION QUESTIONS

1. What is Selim's principal complaint against Ismail? How does he state it?

2. Where in the letter does Selim use the rhetoric of religion against Ismail, and where does he accuse Ismail of political failings? How do the two arguments work together?

DOCUMENT 19-2

ANTONIO MONSERRATE

From The Commentary of Father Monserrate: On Mughal India

ca. 1580

In 1580, Portuguese Jesuit missionary Antonio Monserrate (1536–1600) arrived in Mughal India (present-day India). At the request of the sovereign Akbar, who had a keen interest in other religions, Monserrate had been sent from Portuguese Goa with illustrated Bibles and other religious materials. He was appointed as a tutor to Akbar's son Murad, and he remained with Akbar for some years, accompanying him on military ventures and engaging with the emperor on theological points. Monserrate's Commentary, *commissioned by his superior in the Jesuit order, which never reached his superiors and only resurfaced in the early 1900s in Calcutta, offers valuable insight into the European perception of Akbar and his realm.*

The wives of the Brachman — a famous class of nobly-born Hindus — are accustomed, in accordance with an ancient tradition of their religion, to burn themselves on the same pyres as their dead husbands. The King ordered the priests to be summoned to see an instance of this. They went in ignorance of what was to take place; but when they found out, they plainly indicated by their saddened faces how cruel and savage they felt that crime to be. Finally Rudolf [a Jesuit] publicly reprimanded the King for showing openly by his presence there that he approved of such a revolting crime, and for supporting it by his weighty judgment and explicit approbation, (for he was heard to say that such fortitude could only come from God). Such was Zelaldinus' [Akbar's] kindness and favor towards the priests that he showed no resentment; and a certain chief, a great favorite of his, a Brahman by birth, who held the office of Superintendent of sacred observances, could no longer persuade him to attend such spectacles. The wretched women are rendered quite insensible by means of certain drugs, in order that they may feel no pain. For this purpose opium is

The Commentary of Father Monserrate, S. J., on His Journey to the Court of Akbar (London: Oxford University Press, 1922), 61–63.

used, or a soporific herb named bang, or — more usually — the herb "duturo," which is known to the Indians, although entirely unfamiliar alike to modern Europeans and to the ancients. Sometimes they are half-drugged: and, before they lose their resolution, are hurried to the pyre with warnings, prayers, and promises of eternal fame. On arriving there they cast themselves into the flames. If they hesitate, the wretched creatures are driven on to the pyre: and if they try to leap off again, are held down with poles and hooks. The nobles who were present were highly incensed at the Fathers' interference. They did not dare to gainsay the King; but they grumbled loudly amongst themselves, saying, "Away with you, black-clothed Franks." The whole city was filled with praise and admiration when news was brought that the Franks had dared to rebuke the King regarding this affair.

On one occasion, the Fathers met a crowd of worthless profligates [male prostitutes], some of those who dress and adorn themselves like women. The priests were rightly disgusted at this, and took the first opportunity of privately complaining to the King (since he was so favorable to them) about this disgraceful matter. They declared with the greatest emphasis that they were astonished at his permitting such a class of men to live in his kingdom, let alone in his city, and almost under his eyes. They must be banished, as though they were a deadly plague, to his most distant territories; even better, let them be burnt up by devouring flames. They never would have believed that such men could be found in the court itself and in the royal city, where lived a king of such piety, integrity, and prudence. Therefore let him give orders that these libertines should never again be seen in Fattepurum, seeing that his remarkable prophet [Muhammad] had guaranteed that good men should never suffer for their good actions. The King laughed at this piece of sarcasm and retired, saying that he would attend to the matter.

READING AND DISCUSSION QUESTIONS

1. What two phenomena does Monserrate describe?

2. What is Monserrate's opinion of the two phenomena? What type of language does he use to make this clear?

3. How does Monserrate present Akbar's interactions with the priests?

4. From Monserrate's account, what is the status of Catholic priests in Akbar's court? What level of influence do they have?

DOCUMENT 19-3

ABUL FAZL

From Akbarnama

ca. 1580–1602

Abul Fazl (1551–1602) was a companion and advisor to Akbar, who is often noted as the greatest Mughal sovereign. Akbar was a successful military leader whose reputation for ethnic and religious tolerance helped foster valuable political and economic coalitions within his realm. Fazl's official history of Akbar, accompanied by rich illustrations, survives as a brilliant example of Mughal culture.

THE SIEGE OF SURAT

One of the occurrences of the siege[3] was that a large number of Christians came from the port of Goa[4] and its neighborhood to the foot of the sublime throne, and were rewarded by the bliss of an interview. Apparently they had come at the request of the besieged in order that the latter might make the fort over to them, and so convey themselves to the shore of safety. But when that crew saw the majesty of the imperial power, and had become cognizant of the largeness of the army, and of the extent of the siege-train they represented themselves as ambassadors and performed the kornish [act of worship]. They produced many of the rarities of their country, and the appreciative Khedive [Akbar] received each one of them with special favor and made inquiries about the wonders of Portugal and the manners and customs of Europe. It seemed as if he did this from a desire of knowledge, for his sacred heart is a storehouse of spiritual and physical sciences. But his . . . soul wished that these inquiries might be the means of civilizing this savage race [i.e., the Portuguese].

THE COMMODITIES OF GOA

One of the occurrences was the dispatch of Haji Habibu-llah Kashi to Goa. At the time when the country of Gujarat became included among

---

Henry Beveridge, trans., *The Akbar Nama of Abu-l-Fazl*, 3 vols. (New Delhi: Ess Ess Publications, 1902–1939), 1:37, 207, 322–323, 368–370, 410–411.

[3] **the siege:** Siege of the port of Surat in 1573, which gave Akbar access to the sea.
[4] **Goa:** A Portuguese stronghold in India since 1510.

the imperial dominions, and when many of the ports of the country came into possession, and the governors of the European ports became submissive,[5] many of the curiosities and rarities of the skilled craftsmen of that country became known to His Majesty. Accordingly the Haji,[6] who for his skill, right thinking and powers of observation was one of the good servants of the court, was appointed to take with him a large sum of money, and the choice articles of India to Goa, and to bring for His Majesty's delectation the wonderful things of that country. There were sent with him clever craftsmen, who to ability and skill added industry, in order that just as the wonderful productions of that country [Goa and Europe] were being brought away, so also might rare crafts be imported [into Akbar's dominions].

The Musicians of Goa

One of the occurrences was the arrival [at court] of Haji Habibu-llah. It has already been mentioned that he had been sent to the port of Goa with a large sum of money and skillful craftsmen in order that he might bring to his country the excellent arts and rarities of that place. On the 9th he came to do homage, attended by a large number of persons dressed up as Christians and playing European drums and clarions [trumpets]. He produced before His Majesty the choice articles of that territory. Craftsmen who had gone to acquire skill displayed the arts which they had learned and received praises in the critical place of testing. The musicians of that territory breathed fascination with the instruments of their country, especially with the organ. Ear and eye were delighted and so was the mind.

Thursday Night at the House of Worship

One night, the assembly in the Ibadatkhana[7] was increasing the light of truth. Padre Radif [a Jesuit missionary], one of the Nazarene [Christian] sages, who was singular for his understanding and ability, was making points in that feast of intelligence. Some of the untruthful bigots[8] came forward in a blundering way to answer him. Owing to the calmness of the august assembly, and the increasing light of justice, it became clear that

---

[5] **governors . . . became submissive**: In 1573, Akbar conquered the northwest coastal region of Gujarat.

[6] **the Haji**: Habibu-llah bore the title of haji because he had completed the hajj, or pilgrimage, to Mecca.

[7] **Ibadatkhana**: The house of worship where Akbar held weekly discussions on theological issues with teachers of various religions.

[8] **the untruthful bigots**: The Muslim religious teachers considered to be hypocrites by Abul Fazl, who pursued a policy of religious and cultural toleration.

each of these was weaving a circle of old acquisitions, and was not following the highway of proof, and that the explanation of the riddle of truth was
not present to their thoughts. The veil was nearly being stripped, once for
all, from their procedure. They were ashamed, and abandoned such discourse, and applied themselves to perverting the words of the Gospels. But
they could not silence their antagonist by such arguments. The Padre quietly and with an air of conviction said, "Alas, that such things should be
thought to be true! In fact, if this faction have such an opinion of our Book,
and regard the Furqan [the Qur'an] as the pure word of God, it is proper
that a heaped fire be lighted. We shall take the Gospel in our hands, and
the Ulama of that faith shall take their book, and then let us enter that
testing-place of truth. The escape of any one will be a sign of his truth-
fulness." The liverless and black-hearted fellows wavered, and in reply to
the challenge had recourse to bigotry and wrangling. This cowardice and
effrontery displeased Akbar's equitable soul, and the banquet of enlightenment was made resplendent by acute observations. Continually, in those
day-like nights, glorious subtleties and profound words dropped from his
pearl-filled mouth.

Among them was this: "Most persons, from intimacy with those who
adorn their outside but are inwardly bad, think that outward semblance,
and the letter of Islam, profit without internal conviction. Hence we by
fear and force compelled many believers in the Brahman [i.e., Hindu]
religion to adopt the faith of our ancestors. Now that the light of truth has
taken possession of our soul, it has become clear that in this distressful
place of contrarities [the world], where darkness of comprehension and
conceit are heaped up, fold upon fold, a single step cannot be taken without the torch of proof, and that creed is profitable which is adopted with
the approval of wisdom. To repeat the creed, to remove a piece of skin [i.e.,
to circumcise] and to place the end of one's bones on the ground [i.e., bow
the head in adoration] from dread of the Sultan [Akbar], is not seeking
after God.

European-Held Ports

One of the occurrences was the appointing of an army to capture the
European ports.[9] Inasmuch as conquest is the great rule of princes, and by
the observance of this glory-increasing practice, the distraction of plurality
[multiple rulers] places its foot in the peacefulness of unity, and the

---

[9] **European ports**: The ports of Diu and Bassein. This expedition was unsuccessful.

harassed world composes her countenance, the officers of the provinces of Gujarat and Malwa were appointed to this service under the leadership of Qutbu-d-din Khan on 18 Bahman, Divine month [February 1580]. The rulers of the Deccan were also informed that the troops had been sent in that direction in order to remove the Faringis [Europeans] who were a stumbling-block in the way of the pilgrims to the Hijaz.[10]

READING AND DISCUSSION QUESTIONS

1. How does Abul Fazl describe Akbar's interactions with Europeans?
2. Why do you think Fazl documented Akbar's encounters with Europeans?

DOCUMENT 19-4

NURUDDIN SALIM JAHANGIR
From the Memoirs of Jahangir
ca. 1580–1600

Akbar's third son, Prince Salim (1569–1628), succeeded his father as the Mughal sovereign in 1605 and took the name Jahangir, or "World Conqueror." During his reign, he continued many of his father's policies, including (limited) religious tolerance and wars of territorial expansion. Jahangir found himself locked in a familiar pattern of Mughal succession when his son Khurram rebelled in 1622, just as Jahangir rebelled against his own father. The passages here are taken from Jahangir's autobiography. In the

---

The *Tūzuk-i-Jahāngīrī* or *Memoirs of Jahāngīr*, eds. Alexander Rogers and Henry Beveridge (London: Royal Asiatic Society, 1909–1914), 2, 105.

[10] **pilgrims to the Hijaz**: Pilgrims to Mecca, which is located in the Hijaz, Arabia's west coast. Many Muslim pilgrims complained that when embarking at Portuguese ports they were forced to purchase letters of passage imprinted with images of Jesus and Mary. Orthodox Muslims consider such images blasphemous, and some Muslim ulama went so far as to argue that it was better to forego the pilgrimage than to submit to such sacrilege.

first section, he presents measures to promote justice and social welfare in the realm. In the second part, Jahangir describes a hunting trip with his favorite wife, Nur Jahan.

After my accession, the first order that I gave was for the fastening up of the Chain of Justice, so that if those engaged in the administration of justice should delay or practice hypocrisy in the matter of those seeking justice, the oppressed might come to this chain and shake it so that its noise might attract attention. Its fashion was this: I ordered them to make a chain of pure gold, 30 gaz in length and containing 60 bells. Its weight was 4 Indian maunds, equal to 42 'Irāqī maunds. One end of it they made fast to the battlements of the Shāh Burj of the fort at Agra and the other to a stone post fixed on the bank of the river. I also gave twelve orders to be observed as rules of conduct in all my dominions —

1. Forbidding the levy of cesses [taxes] under the names of tamghā and mīr baḥrī [river tolls], and other burdens which the jāgīrdārs[11] of every province and district had imposed for their own profit.
2. On roads where thefts and robberies took place, which roads might be at a little distance from habitations, the jāgīrdārs of the neighborhood should build sarā'īs [public rest-houses], mosques, and dig wells, which might stimulate population, and people might settle down in those sarā'īs. If these should be near a khāliṣa estate,[12] the administrator of that place should execute the work.
3. The bales of merchants should not be opened on the roads without informing them and obtaining their leave.
4. In my dominions if anyone, whether unbeliever or Musalman, should die, his property and effects should be left for his heirs, and no one should interfere with them. If he should have no heir, they should appoint inspectors and separate guardians to guard the property, so that its value might be expended in lawful expenditure, such as the building of mosques and sarā'īs, the repair of broken bridges, and the digging of tanks and wells.
5. They should not make wine or rice-spirit or any kind of intoxicating drug, or sell them; although I myself drink wine, and from the age of

---

[11] jāgīrdārs: Regional rulers whose income came primarily from taxes imposed within their districts.
[12] khāliṣa estate: Land controlled by the state.

18 years up till now, when I am 38, have persisted in it. When I first took a liking to drinking I sometimes took as much as twenty cups of double-distilled spirit; when by degrees it acquired a great influence over me I endeavored to lessen the quantity, and in the period of seven years I have brought myself from fifteen cups to five or six. My times for drinking were varied; sometimes when three or four sidereal hours of the day remained I would begin to drink, and sometimes at night and partly by day. This went on till I was 30 years old. After that I took to drinking always at night. Now I drink only to digest my food.

6. They should not take possession of any person's house.

7. I forbade the cutting off the nose or ears of any person, and I myself made a vow by the throne of God that I would not blemish anyone by this punishment.

8. I gave an order that the officials of the Crown lands and the jāgīrdārs should not forcibly take the ryots' [farmers'] lands and cultivate them on their own account.

9. A government collector or a jāgīrdār should not without permission intermarry with the people of the pargana [district] in which he might be.

10. They should found hospitals in the great cities, and appoint physicians for the healing of the sick; whatever the expenditure might be, should be given from the <u>kh</u>āliṣa establishment.

11. In accordance with the regulations of my revered father, I ordered that each year from the 18th of Rabī'u-l-awwal, which is my birthday, for a number of days corresponding to the years of my life, they should not slaughter animals [for food]. Two days in each week were also forbidden, one of them Thursday, the day of my accession, and the other Sunday, the day of my father's birth. He held this day in great esteem on this account, and because it was dedicated to the Sun, and also because it was the day on which the Creation began. Therefore it was one of the days on which there was no killing in his dominions.

12. I gave a general order that the offices and jāgīrs [land plots] of my father's servants should remain as they were. Later, the manṣabs [ranks or offices] were increased according to each one's circumstances by not less than 20 percent to 300 or 400 percent. The subsistence money of the aḥadīs was increased by 50 percent, and I raised the pay of all domestics by 20 percent. I increased the allowances of all the veiled ladies of my father's harem from 20 percent to 100 percent, according to their condition and relationship. By one stroke of the pen I confirmed the subsistence lands of the holders of aimas [charity lands]

within the dominions, who form the army of prayer, according to the deeds in their possession. I gave an order to Mīrān Ṣadr Jahān, who is one of the genuine Sayyids of India [descendants of Muhammad], and who for a long time held the high office of ṣadr [ecclesiastical officer] under my father, that he should every day produce before me deserving people [worthy of charity]. I released all criminals who had been confined and imprisoned for a long time in the forts and prisons. . . .

On the 25th the contingent of I'timādu-d-daulah passed before me in review on the plain under the jharoka.[13] There were 2,000 cavalry well horsed, most of whom were Moghuls, 500 foot armed with bows and guns, and fourteen elephants. The bakhshis reckoned them up and reported that this force was fully equipped and according to rule. On the 26th a tigress was killed. On Thursday, the 1st Urdībihisht, a diamond that Muqarrab Khān had sent by runners was laid before me; it weighed 23 surkh, and the jewellers valued it at 30,000 rupees. It was a diamond of the first water, and was much approved. I ordered them to make a ring of it. On the 3rd the mansab [military rank] of Yūsuf Khān was, at the request of Bābā Khurram, fixed at 1,000 with 1,500 horses, and in the same way the mansabs of several of the Amirs [nobles] and mansabdars [office holders] were increased at his suggestion.[14] On the 7th, as the huntsmen had marked down four tigers, when two watches and three gharis [a length of time] had passed I went out to hunt them with my ladies. When the tigers came in sight Nūr-Jahān Begam submitted that if I would order her she herself would kill the tigers with her gun. I said, "Let it be so." She shot two tigers with one shot each and knocked over the two others with four shots. In the twinkling of an eye she deprived of life the bodies of these four tigers. Until now such shooting was never seen, that from the top of an elephant and inside of a howdah [carriage atop an elephant] six shots should be made and not one miss, so that the four beasts found no opportunity to spring or move. As a reward for this good shooting I gave her a pair of bracelets of diamonds worth 100,000 rupees and scattered 1,000 ashrafis [over her].

---

[13] jharoka: Balcony used for architectural ornamentation and for spying.
[14] fixed at 1,000 . . . suggestion: System of military ranking that also determined compensation. High-ranking commanders were in one of three classes according to the proportion of horsemen in their unit.

READING AND DISCUSSION QUESTIONS

1. What is the purpose of Jahangir's Chain of Justice? What impression does it create of Jahangir?

2. Jahangir's twelve orders deal with a variety of issues. How would you categorize them? What order is most striking to you, and why?

3. What is the effect of Jahangir's frequent references to gold and jewels in both of these excerpts? What image does that create of him and his realm?

4. Jahangir describes both military forces and a hunting expedition with his wives. How would you compare the tone of this passage with his comments about justice and social order?

COMPARATIVE QUESTIONS

1. Compare and contrast how Selim, Fazl, and Monserrate present "other" cultures. What is the relative status of each culture? What kind of power does each culture command, and how is that power displayed?

2. Compare the way that Selim and Jahangir depict themselves as rulers. What do their depictions say about their individual motivations and values?

3. Fazl, Monserrate, and Jahangir attempted to describe events or places for future readers. How does the style of writing in each document communicate a certain idea or image of the subject to readers?

4. Compare Fazl's description of Akbar and his religious tolerance to Monserrate's description. How might each author's background influence his description?

CHAPTER 20

Continuity and Change in East Asia

ca. 1400–1800

From 1400 to 1800, East Asian countries experienced important changes at all levels of society. Despite the growing presence of Europeans in East Asia, both China and Japan remained relatively free from the influence of European commercial expansion. Chinese thinkers in the Ming and early Qing periods were primarily concerned with internal development and regional conflicts involving other Asian states. In Japan, the Tokugawa regime ended the chaotic Warring States Period and fostered domestic economic and cultural improvements. According to Chinese Confucian thought, merchants — who unlike scholars, farmers, and artisans, produced nothing for society — had relatively low social standing. In Tokugawa Japan, samurai replaced scholars at the top of a rigid social hierarchy borrowed from the same Confucian tradition. In the late 1700s, a sea change began. The Industrial Revolution spurred increased European (especially British) interest in the massive Chinese market. The growing wealth and power of merchant classes, as well as the extravagant urban culture that it supported, posed a challenge to Confucian social order in both countries.

DOCUMENT 20-1

ZHANG HAN

From "On Strange Tales" and "On Merchants"

ca. 1577

Zhang Han (1511–1593) was a Ming government official who wrote treatises on the four classes of the traditional Confucian social order: scholars, farmers, artisans, and merchants. His work on merchants is regarded as an important window on the economic life of Ming China, especially its discussion of the tensions between government control and economic freedom. Unlike many Confucian scholars in government, Zhang argued that a thriving merchant economy relatively free from government intervention would in turn benefit the state and society as a whole.

"On Strange Tales"

Ancestor Yian was of a humble family and made liquor as his profession, In the years of Chenghua (1465–1487) there was a flood. At that time my great-grandfather was living beside a river, and when the water flooded it entered the building. All the liquor he was making was completely spoiled. For several evenings he went out to look at his spoiled liquor and inundated jugs. One evening as he was returning home, someone suddenly called him from behind. My great-grandfather turned to greet him, and was handed something warm. Suddenly the person was not to be seen. When he got home he lit the lamp and shone it on what turned out to be a small ingot of silver. With this he gave up making liquor and bought a loom. He wove ramie and silk of several colors, and achieved a very high level of craftsmanship. Every time a roll of fabric came off the loom, people competed to buy it. He calculated his profit at 20 percent. After saving for twenty years he bought another loom. Later he increased his looms to over twenty. The merchants who dealt in textiles constantly thronged the house inside and out, and still he couldn't meet their orders. Hereafter, the family profession brought great wealth. The next four ancestors carried on the profession, each gaining wealth in the tens of thousands. The story of his receiving silver late that night is very strange, yet . . . it has been passed down. How is it that it should have started with a spirit's gift?

"On Merchants"

How important to people are wealth and profit! Human disposition is such that people pursue what is profitable to them, and with this profit in mind they will even face harm. They gallup [gallop] in pursuit of it day and night, never satisfied with what they have, though it wears down their spirits

Zhang Han, "On Strange Tales" and "Essays on Merchants"; Timothy Brooks, "The Merchant Network in 16th Century China," *Journal of the Economic and Social History of the Orient* XXIV (May 1981):186–208.

and exhausts them physically. Profit is what people covet. Since all covet it, they rush after it like torrents pouring into a valley: they come and go without end, never resting day or night, never reaching the point at which the raging floods within them subside such that they finally come to rest. . . . They use up all their energy chasing after the most negligible profits, and become forgetful of their diurnal [daily] exhaustion. How is this any different from thinking the hair's tip big and the mountain small? . . . It is as though they were being led on by the nose and pushed from behind.

Thus it has come to be that the children of merchants may take pleasure in their food and clothing. Their ornamented stallions are harnessed into teams, their carriages stretch on one after the other like bolts of cloth across the land or like ripples across a river; . . . Crafty, clever men latch on to their wealth and power, flattering them and scurrying about at their disposal. The young women . . . and the girls . . . play on string and reed instruments, perform on zithers, dangle long sleeves and trip about in pointed slippers, vying for beauty and currying favor.

The merchants boast that their knowledge and ability are sufficient to get them anything they want. They set their minds on monopolizing the operations of change in the natural world and scheme to exploit the natural transformations of man and animal. They shift with the times; when they offer their goods for sale, they control the prices. Tallying it all up, they do not let a hundredth part slip by. Yet they are unembarrassed by the pettiness of this knowledge and ability.

*   *   *

In ancient times the sage kings [mythical rulers] . . . valued agriculture and depreciated commerce. Hence the commercial taxes were double the agricultural taxes. From the time that Emperor Wu of the Han adopted Sang Hongyang's[1] policies, monopolizing all commodities in the empire, and selling them when they were dear and buying them when were cheap, merchants had no way to realize profits and the prices of goods remained stable. . . . He further decreed that merchants could not wear silk, ride in carriages, serve at court, or become officials. He increased their taxes and duties, and thereby disgraced them with misfortune. From this time on, those who pursued this profession saw their possessions exhausted because of this severity. . . .

---

[1] **Sang Hongyang:** High official who favored state intervention in the economy.

At the beginning of the Tang dynasty [618–907 C.E.] . . . legal structure became rather lax. The government forced down the prices on merchants' goods, which was purchasing in name but confiscation in fact.

The Song dynasty [960–1279 C.E.] forestalled the corrupt practices of the Tang. The Office of Miscellaneous Purchasing was established, engaging capital officials and eunuchs to run it jointly. . . . When the state storehouses were sufficiently provided for, they were ordered to discontinue purchasing. The rich and powerful merchants were all suspicious and uneasy, watching this but not daring to act, and so the whole point of trading was gone. . . .

Ming dynasty [1368–1644 C.E.] . . . has been more meticulous than previous dynasties. Transport is supervised by the Customs Houses under the jurisdiction of the Ministry of Revenue. Wood products are supervised by the Office of Produce Levies under the jurisdiction of the Ministry of Works. The salt taxation system has both Distribution Commissions and Distribution Superintendancies; as well, there are censors to review it. The administration of the tea tax is also handled in this way. The rest is controlled by the Ministry of Revenue. Thus the laws for exactions on merchants are precise and comprehensive.

* * *

In the capital [Beijing] the merchants' task is heavy. It is flat land, facing mountains. The area offers rich profits in millet, grain, donkeys, horses, fruits, and vegetables. As well, goods from all over the country collect in the markets of the larger cities and then are brought here on carts or carried on shoulders. What is displayed and bartered here goes beyond just the fruits of the land or the necessities of clothing. The larger objects clutter up rooms and the precious curios fill trunks, and all are costly in the extreme. Tibetan jade, Hainan pearls, Yunnanese gold, Annamese[2] feathers — all the treasures of the mountains and seas — are what the central kingdom lacks. So men from strange and distant lands do not shirk the dangers of expeditions, and converge here in wave after wave. . . .

South of the capital, Henan takes its place in the center of the empire, with Kaifeng as its capital. One can go north down the Wei and Zhang Rivers right to the edge of the national capital, or follow east along the Bian and Si Rivers to the Han and the Yangzi. Land communications

---

[2] **Hainan . . . Yunnanese . . . Annamese**: Hainan is an island in the South China Sea; Yunnan is a southern Chinese province; Annam is the eastern coastal region of Indochina.

extend in all directions, and merchants delight in gathering here. The region is rich in lacquer, fine hemp fiber, nettle hemp fiber, ramie [used in rope], cotton thread, cotton wadding, tin, wax, and leather. . . .

To the west of the Yellow River is the old territory of Yong, today called Shaanxi. Being closed in on all four sides by mountains and rivers, it was once called "the fort of heaven." . . . The region is abundant in donkeys, horses, cattle, sheep, felt, fur, meat, and bones. . . .

South of the Yangzi is Iguang. The profit in fish and grain here in the upper reaches extends throughout the empire. . . .

Further down the Yangzi is Nanjing, the place where the first Ming emperor founded his dynasty. . . . From all directions people come like spokes to a hub, from all places in the world they pour into this region. The eunuchs of the Office of the Emperor's Wardrobe value the clothes and shoes here. From the north and the south of the empire, merchants clamor to come. . . . To the east are Songjiang and Changshu, and in the middle is Suzhou. The wealth which the people derive through fish and rice is extreme, and the superb and ornate objects of the artisans are enough to dazzle the people's minds. Those who are set on wealthy extravagance rush in after them. . . .

Guangdong and Guangxi are between the mountains and the sea. . . . The capital of Guangdong is Guangzhou. . . . Various foreigners come and go along the seacoast between Leizhou and Qiongzhou: they are intent on trade and not on pillaging the border. . . .

Pearls, rhinoceros horn, drugs, tortoise shell, gold, and feathers mostly come by the foreigners' ships, and so merchants gather in Guangdong. . . .

✳ ✳ ✳

As for the border markets in the northwest and the maritime markets in the southeast, we should compare their profits and losses, and their advantages and disadvantages. . . . The markets on the border began by dealing in silks adulterated with ramie, but today they deal in brocades [a lustrous textile]. Horses are all that the tribal chieftains trade in return. I think that if China exchanged adulterated silk for broken horses, the profit is still on our side. They carry it off and no harm comes of it. Today however we sell our brocaded silk. Once they take the gold thread and go, they never return it. When the tribesmen get the silk worn in China for useless hacks, doesn't that go against common sense? . . .

In the southeast, the various foreigners gain profits from our Chinese goods, and China also gains profits from the foreigners' goods. Trading what we have for what we lack is China's intention in trade. . . . Why shrink from doing so? You might say, "The foreigners frequently invade;

the situation is such that we cannot do business with them." But you don't understand that the foreigners will not do without their profits from China, just as we cannot do without our profits from them. Prohibit this, keep them from contact, and how can you avoid their turning to piracy?[3] I maintain that once the maritime markets are opened, the aggressors will cease of their own accord. . . . What is paid out through the border markets is entirely the precious reserves of the state or the wealth of the rich. What is traded in the maritime market is entirely goods produced among the people, of no consequence to the finances of the state. The border markets operate at a loss and no gain results, whereas the maritime markets could operate at a profit and no harm would ensue. Why don't the government planners think of this?

* * *

As for taxes on China's merchants, even though they do contribute to the government's revenue, they are exacted through too many channels. This must be stopped. At every point where a merchant passes a customs house or a ford, the officials there either insist on unloading the carts or docking the boats and checking through the sacks and crates, or just overestimate the value and collect excessive payment. What has passed the customs house or ford has already been taxed, yet the markets then tax it again. One piece of merchandise should be subject to one taxing. There are the institutionalized surtax and the regular tax. The merchants cannot bear the interference caused by the further demands of constables and the exactions of sub-officials. How can merchants who have to pay double what they should not feel heavily afflicted?

READING AND DISCUSSION QUESTIONS

1. What language and stories does Zhang use to convey the social identity of merchants? Is this impression positive, negative, or mixed?

2. How does Zhang portray the role of commerce in connecting different parts of China?

3. How does Zhang treat the question of commercial contact with foreign countries?

---

[3] **turning to piracy:** Pirate raids on the southeast coast were a major problem in late Ming China. Most of the pirates were Japanese.

DOCUMENT 20-2

KAIBARA EKIKEN AND KAIBARA TŌKEN
Common Sense Teachings for Japanese Children and Greater Learning for Women
ca. 1700

Kaibara Ekiken (1630–1714) was a physician, educator, and author from the samurai class during the enforced peace of the Tokugawa period (1603–1867). His works combined neo-Confucian principles of self-reliance and humaneness with careful and practical attention to life in early modern Japan. His writings were printed and distributed widely thanks to the vibrant publishing world of urban Tokugawa Japan. The following selections (the latter probably coauthored with his wife, Tōken) show his concern with daily life and "common sense" and his interest in maintaining gender and social roles in the Confucian social order.

COMMON SENSE TEACHINGS FOR JAPANESE CHILDREN

In January when children reach the age of six, teach them numbers one through ten, and the names given to designate 100, 1,000, 10,000, and 100,000,000. Let them know the four directions, East, West, North, and South. Assess their native intelligence and differentiate between quick and slow learners. Teach them Japanese pronunciation from the age of six or seven, and let them learn how to write. . . . From this time on, teach them to respect their elders, and let them know the distinctions between the upper and lower classes and between the young and old. Let them learn to use the correct expressions.

When the children reach the age of seven, do not let the boys and girls sit together, nor must you allow them to dine together. . . .

For the eighth year. This is the age when the ancients began studying the book *Little Learning*.[4] Beginning at this time, teach the youngsters etiquette befitting their age, and caution them not to commit an act of

---

David J. Lu, *Japan: A Documentary History* (Armonk, N.Y.: M. E. Sharpe, 1997), 258–261.

[4] ***Little Learning***: An instruction book for young children that contained rules of behavior.

impoliteness. Among those which must be taught are: daily deportment, the manners set for appearing before one's senior and withdrawing from his presence, how to speak or respond to one's senior or guest, how to place a serving tray or replace it for one's senior, how to present a wine cup and pour rice wine and to serve side dishes to accompany it, and how to serve tea. Children must also learn how to behave while taking their meals.

Children must be taught by those who are close to them the virtues of filial piety and obedience. To serve the parents well is called filial piety, and to serve one's seniors well is called obedience. The one who lives close to the children and who is able to teach must instruct the children in the early years of their life that the first obligation of a human being is to revere the parents and serve them well. Then comes the next lesson which includes respect for one's seniors, listening to their commands and not holding them in contempt. One's seniors include elder brothers, elder sisters, uncles, aunts, and cousins who are older and worthy of respect. . . . As the children grow older, teach them to love their younger brothers and to be compassionate to the employees and servants. Teach them also the respect due the teachers and the behavior codes governing friends. The etiquette governing each movement toward important guests — such as standing, sitting, advancing forward, and retiring from their presence — and the language to be employed must be taught. Teach them how to pay respect to others according to the social positions held by them. Gradually the ways of filial piety and obedience, loyalty and trustworthiness, right deportment and decorum, and sense of shame must be inculcated in the children's minds and they must know how to implement them. Caution them not to desire the possessions of others, or to stoop below one's dignity in consuming excessive amounts of food and drink. . . .

Once reaching the age of eight, children must follow and never lead their elders when entering a gate, sitting, or eating and drinking. From this time on they must be taught how to become humble and yield to others. Do not permit the children to behave as they please. It is important to caution them against "doing their own things."

At the age of ten, let the children be placed under the guidance of a teacher, and tell them about the general meaning of the five constant virtues and let them understand the way of the five human relationships.[5] Let them read books by the Sage [Confucius] and the wise men of old and

---

[5] **five constant virtues . . . human relationships**: The *five virtues* are human heartedness, righteousness, propriety, wisdom, and good faith. The *five relationships* are ruler-subject, father-son, husband-wife, older brother-younger brother, and friend-friend.

cultivate the desire for learning. . . . When not engaged in reading, teach them the literary and military arts. . . .

Fifteen is the age when the ancients began the study of the *Great Learning*.[6] From this time on, concentrate on the learning of a sense of justice and duty. The students must also learn to cultivate their personalities and investigate the way of governing people. . . .

Those who are born in the high-ranking families have the heavy obligations of becoming leaders of the people, of having people entrusted to their care, and of governing them. Therefore, without fail, a teacher must be selected for them when they are still young. They must be taught how to read and be informed of the ways of old, of cultivating their personalities, and of the way of governing people. If they do not learn the way of governing people, they may injure the many people who are entrusted to their care by the Way of Heaven. That will be a serious disaster. . . .

GREATER LEARNING FOR WOMEN

Seeing that it is a girl's destiny, on reaching womanhood, to go to a new home, and live in submission to her father-in-law, it is even more incumbent upon her than it is on a boy to receive with all reverence her parents' instructions. Should her parents, through their tenderness, allow her to grow up self-willed, she will infallibly show herself capricious in her husband's house, and thus alienate his affection; while, if her father-in-law be a man of correct principles, the girl will find the yoke of these principles intolerable. She will hate and decry her father-in-law, and the end of those domestic dissensions will be her dismissal from her husband's house and the covering of herself with ignominy. Her parents, forgetting the faulty education they gave her, may indeed lay all the blame on the father-in-law. But they will be in error; for the whole disaster should rightly be attributed to the faulty education the girl received from her parents.

* * *

More precious in a woman is a virtuous heart than a face of beauty. The vicious woman's heart is ever excited; she glares wildly around her, she vents her anger on others, her words are harsh and her accent vulgar. When she speaks, it is to set herself above others, to upbraid others, to envy others, to be puffed up with individual pride, to jeer at others, to outdo others — all things at variance with the way in which a woman should

---

[6] *Great Learning*: A chapter in the *Record of Rituals*, one of the four works that came to be known within the Confucian classics as the Four Books.

walk. The only qualities that befit a woman are gentle obedience, chastity, mercy, and quietness.

From her earliest youth a girl should observe the line of demarcation separating women from men. The customs of antiquity did not allow men and women to sit in the same apartment, to keep their wearing apparel in the same place, to bathe in the same place, or to transmit to each other anything directly from hand to hand. A woman . . . must observe a certain distance in her relations even with her husband and with her brothers. In our days the women of lower classes, ignoring all rules of this nature, behave disorderly; they contaminate their reputations, bring down reproach upon the head of their parents and brothers, and spend their whole lives in an unprofitable manner. Is not this truly lamentable?

* * *

It is the chief duty of a girl living in the parental house to practice filial piety towards her father and mother. But after marriage her duty is to honor her father-in-law and mother-in-law, to honor them beyond her father and mother, to love and reverence them with all ardor, and to tend them with practice of every filial piety. . . . Even if your father-in-law and mother-in-law are inclined to hate and vilify you, do not be angry with them, and murmur not. If you carry piety towards them to its utmost limits, and minister to them in all sincerity, it cannot be but that they will end by becoming friendly to you.

* * *

The great lifelong duty of a woman is obedience. . . . When the husband issues his instructions, the wife must never disobey them. In a doubtful case, she should inquire of her husband and obediently follow his commands. . . .

Should her husband be roused at any time to anger, she must obey him with fear and trembling, and not set herself up against him in anger and forwardness. A woman should look upon her husband as if he were Heaven itself, and never weary of thinking how she may yield to her husband and thus escape celestial castigation.

Her treatment of her servant girls will require circumspection. Those low-born girls have had no proper education; they are stupid, obstinate, and vulgar in their speech. . . . Again, in her dealings with those lowly people, a woman will find many things to disapprove of. But if she be always reproving and scolding, and spend her time in hustle and anger, her household will be in a continual state of disturbance. When there is real wrongdoing, she should occasionally notice it, and point out the path of amendment, while lesser faults should be quietly endured without anger. . . .

READING AND DISCUSSION QUESTIONS

1. What values does Ekiken emphasize for children's education? How are they to be instilled?

2. How is concern for social hierarchy and propriety evident in Ekiken's work on children? On women?

3. Based on these readings, what potential do you see for women to have power in Tokugawa society?

4. What, if any, assumptions does Ekiken make about his likely audience? What gives you that impression?

DOCUMENT 20-3

MITSUI TAKAFUSA

From "Some Observations on Merchants"

ca. 1720–1730

Mitsui Takafusa (1684–1748) was a member of the Mitsui merchant family, whose success spawned financial and commercial institutions that played an important role in Japan's modern history. Mitsui's writings here, directed to fellow merchants, betray a careful negotiation between financial success and social deference at a time when the growing wealth of the merchant classes threatened the orthodox social order of Tokugawa Japan.

QUALITIES OF A SUCCESSFUL MERCHANT

There was a man of Edo rather ill-favored by nature. He had, nevertheless, a considerable fortune. Once when he met with other persons of the same status, they all asked: "What should we do to make money like yourself? Please pass on the formula." Thereupon he replied, "If only you are fond of money, you can do it any time." The people answered that there was no one who was not fond of money. "In that case," the man inquired, "if each of you now had as much money as he wanted, what would you do? I would

"Some Observations on Merchants: A Translation of Mitsui Takafusa's *Choni Koken Roku*," ed. and trans. E. S. Crawcour in *Transactions of the Asiatic Society of Japan*, 3d ser. (Tokyo, 1961), 8:39–41, 49, 56, 57, 77, 78, 82, 103, 121.

like to have your reflections on the subject." They each gave their views, that if they had so much money they would put so much aside and with the rest restore their unsightly houses or pay off their debts and so on. "Since this is how you all feel," the man said, "you cannot have money. You actually are planning to spend it before you even have it. I do not worry about the state of my house. Nor do I have clothes made. The only thing I am keen on is money." How truly right these golden words are. This little story should be weighed thoroughly.

* * *

When a deficiency appears in their financial positions, they should own up immediately to their poverty and declare their inability to pay. This should be the time to make plans to stay in business, but what they do is to think first of their reputations and borrow as much as they can to cover up their financial position. When at their wit's end, they are exposed and thus wind up like this [bankrupt]. . . . This is the meaning of the maxim that a bud may be nipped with the hand but if left will later have to be chopped with an axe.

* * *

Whatever business you get your start in, you must always continue to recognize the value of that business and put your heart and soul into it. Most people, however, when they have made a fortune, with large holdings of gold and silver, forget where it came from and think that the way to make a living is to engage in financing, which does not require many assistants. They leave their former business clerks and think they can live at ease through financing, but it is scarcely possible to make a living as easily as that. There are many examples in this world of people eventually going bankrupt by risking not only their own capital but even borrowed money. After all, though it may be a slower process, if you pay for all your personal expenses out of the profits of the trade in which you originally prospered, regard the money which you have as your stock in trade and work single-mindedly at your own business, it is only natural that as a divine reward your house will continue. . . .

MERCHANTS' MISSTEPS

This business of lending to daimyo [feudal lords] is like gambling. Instead of being cut in the first place while they are small, losses become a kind of bait. Using the argument that if further loans are made the original ones will be reactivated, the officials and financial agents of daimyo who raise loans decoy the lenders with specious talk. This is like setting fried bean curd for mice, as the saying has it, and finally they are caught in the trap.

They thus incur heavier losses than before. Such being the case, one should give up making loans of this sort. However, no gambler places a bet expecting from the beginning that he will lose. . . . If in lending to daimyo the dealings go according to contract, certainly there is no better business. It does not require a large staff. With one account book and one pair of scales, the thing is settled. This is really genuinely making money while you sleep. As the classical saying goes, however, "for every profit there is a loss." Such a fine business as this is liable to turn out very badly in the end. Consider well that you should never rely on lending to daimyo.

* * *

Samurai employ stratagems with victory as their sole aim. To do so is their military duty. Merchants may think that they can make profits to a reasonable extent and write off their losses. Samurai, however, are the highest of the four social classes, and their officials, who combine cleverness with cunning, see through your tricks and turn the tables on you. As soon as they have what they want out of the other party, they seize control and default. The bamboo spears of merchants, you might say, are pitted against the true swords of samurai, and you are no match for your adversary. . . . In books on military strategy, it is said that only he who knows the enemy as well as his own side can be called a great general. Any merchant who tries to trick samurai does not know his enemy.

* * *

Many in times both past and present have ruined their families through becoming involved in speculative ventures. In Edo, by so-called gold extraction,[7] or the smelting of gold from copper, people obtained some gold from bar copper and showed it to amateurs, whom they tricked into putting a lot of money into the idea. Eventually those "gold extractors" absconded with the money they had raised. They say that a little gold generally can be extracted by processing copper. If the cost of charcoal and laborers is taken into account, however, it hardly provides a living. I am told that in Holland they do smelt gold from copper. In Japan, though how to do this is known, it does not pay for the above reason, and so the copper is handed over as it is.

As regards gold mines, they say that small amounts of gold and silver exist everywhere but that the mining of them is not a commercial proposition because, as with the extraction of gold from copper, the yield is too small. Despite this, just because someone shows them something supposed

---

[7] **gold extraction:** Europeans introduced the process of extracting gold and silver from copper ore to Japan in the late sixteenth century.

to be ore from a mine and talks glibly, there are many people about who, being somewhat rash by nature, are ready to risk everything and, finally being talked into it, and by losing what little they had.

The Merchant's Place in Society

The Juemon I and Juemon II[8] possessed many fine household articles which they had bought. One of these was the "Misoya Katatsuki" tea container, which was bought from Kameya someone or other for a thousand gold pieces. They say the purchase money was loaded on a cart and dragged around in broad daylight to make the payment and take delivery.

Juemon II built a Zen temple at Narutaki, on the western side of Kyoto. He deposited with the temple an image of Hitomaro[9] and built for it a hall called Hitomaro Hall. The interior of this he lined with gold brocade. It is commonly known as the Gold Brocade Hall of Narutaki. Through his interest in Japanese poetry, he, though a merchant, mixed with distinguished Court nobles, forgot the real nature of his status and finally lost his large fortune. He was one who did not know his proper station.

* * *

Again, a merchant called Ishikawa Rokubei, of Edo, who started off in the brokerage business, had a wife who was extraordinarily extravagant and went to the limit in finery. Retribution finally caught up with them. Along the route of the valiant [the shogun's heir apparent], when this Rokubei's wife and her servants were all decked out, the valiant prince, thinking that she was the wife of a daimyo or of some family of high rank, graciously had his aides make inquiries and was told that she was the wife of that fellow [the merchant]. After he had returned to the palace, Rokubei and his wife were summoned to the office of the town magistrate. It was considered that their extravagance beyond their station and particularly their lack of respect for their superiors were outrageous. Their family property was forfeited, and, by the Shogun's mercy, they got off with banishment from Edo.

As they say, a curse always falls on the house where the hen does the crowing. If a wife is extravagant in defiance of her husband and runs the household just as she likes, it is the same as for a hen to crow the time. This must be the meaning of the golden words which say that such a house invariably perishes. . . .

---

[8] **Juemon I and Juemon II**: Juemon I is Itoya Juemon, a Kyoto-based rice trader; Juemon II was his son.

[9] **Hitomaro**: A famous poet of the late seventh and the early eighth centuries venerated as the god of poetry.

The Merchant's Calling

When great men are extravagant, they lose their territories, but lesser folk lose their livelihood. Even if one cannot add further profits to the money which one's forebear, acquiring merit through difficulties, accumulated by sweating away at money-making day and night, one at least should reflect on the debt of gratitude owing to one's forebear and take good care to keep his fortune intact. What can we say of one who does neither of these things and finally ruins his family through extravagance! Losses through miscalculation in trading, as well as losses in financial operations, may be due to insufficient concentration of one's proper calling. This is your livelihood, however, and as such cannot be shirked. Understand thoroughly that these things are only matters of prudence. . . . It is the law of nature that birds and beasts and in fact all things which dwell between heaven and earth — and above all, human beings — should seek their sustenance by working at their callings. This being so, such behavior on the part of people far from being in their dotage displays ignorance of the will of heaven.

READING AND DISCUSSION QUESTIONS

1. What qualities of a successful merchant does Mitsui enumerate? Are these qualities particular to Mitsui's situation or generally applicable to universal business dealings?

2. What indications does Mitsui provide of the delicate relationship between samurai and merchants? What is the implicit power relationship between samurai and merchants?

3. List at least three situations that Mitsui says can lead to an unwise merchant's ruin.

4. How does Mitsui support or contest the Confucian notion of the samurai's position over merchants?

EMPEROR QIANLONG

Edict on Trade with Great Britain

1793

The Qianlong emperor (r. 1736–1796) was responsible for an impressive flourishing of Chinese culture and power. In addition to sponsoring enormous compilations of scholarly and artistic works, Qianlong oversaw the conquest and integration of Muslim lands and peoples into the Chinese empire, which doubled China's territory. His early fascination with Western knowledge and technology seems absent from this 1793 missive to King George III of England, in which he stresses China's preeminent position among nations and its indifference to foreign trade.

You, O King, from afar have yearned after the blessings of our civilization, and in your eagerness to come into touch with our converting influence have sent an Embassy across the sea bearing a memorial [memorandum]. I have already taken note of your respectful spirit of submission, have treated your mission with extreme favor and loaded it with gifts, besides issuing a mandate to you, O King, and honoring you with the bestowal of valuable presents. Thus has my indulgence been manifested.

Yesterday your Ambassador petitioned my Ministers to memorialize me regarding your trade with China, but his proposal is not consistent with our dynastic usage and cannot be entertained. Hitherto, all European nations, including your own country's barbarian merchants, have carried on their trade with our Celestial Empire at Guangzhou. Such has been the procedure for many years, although our Celestial Empire possesses all things in prolific abundance and lacks no product within its own borders. There was therefore no need to import the manufactures of outside barbarians in exchange for our own produce. But as the tea, silk, and porcelain which the Celestial Empire produces are absolute necessities to European nations and to yourselves, we have permitted, as a signal mark of favor, that *hongs*[10] should be established at Guangzhou, so that your wants

---

Emperor Qianlong, "Edict on Trade with Great Britain," in J. O. P. Brand, *Annals and Memoirs of the Court of Peking* (Boston: Houghton Mifflin, 1914), 325–331.

[10] *hongs*: Chinese merchant guilds that were licensed to trade with Westerners.

might be supplied and your country thus participate in our beneficence. But your Ambassador has now put forward new requests which completely fail to recognize the Throne's principle to "treat strangers from afar with indulgence," and to exercise a pacifying control over barbarian tribes the world over. Moreover, our dynasty, ruling over the myriad races of the globe, extends the same benevolence towards all. Your England is not the only nation trading at Guangzhou. If other nations, following your bad example, wrongfully importune my ear with further impossible requests, how will it be possible for me to treat them with easy indulgence? Nevertheless, I do not forget the lonely remoteness of your island, cut off from the world by intervening wastes of sea, nor do I overlook your excusable ignorance of the usages of our Celestial Empire. I have consequently commanded my Ministers to enlighten your Ambassador on the subject, and have ordered the departure of the mission. But I have doubts that after your Envoy's return he may fail to acquaint you with my view in detail or that he may be lacking in lucidity, so that I shall now proceed . . . to issue my mandate on each question separately. In this way you will, I trust, comprehend my meaning. . . .

Your request for a small island near Zhoushan,[11] where your merchants may reside and goods be warehoused, arises from your desire to develop trade. As there are neither *hongs* nor interpreters in or near Zhoushan, where none of your ships has ever called, such an island would be utterly useless for your purposes. Every inch of the territory of our Empire is marked on the map and the strictest vigilance is exercised over it all: even tiny islets and far-lying sand-banks are clearly defined as part of the provinces to which they belong. Consider, moreover, that England is not the only barbarian land which wishes to establish . . . trade with our Empire: supposing that other nations were all to imitate your evil example and beseech me to present them each and all with a site for trading purposes, how could I possibly comply? This also is a flagrant infringement of the usage of my Empire and cannot possibly be entertained.

The next request, for a small site in the vicinity of Guangzhou city, where your barbarian merchants may lodge or, alternatively, that there be no longer any restrictions over their movements at Macao,[12] has arisen from the following causes. Hitherto, the barbarian merchants of Europe have had a definite locality assigned to them at Macao for residence and trade, and have been forbidden to encroach an inch beyond the limits assigned to that locality. . . . If these restrictions were withdrawn, friction

---

[11] **Zhoushan:** Group of islands in the East China Sea.
[12] **Macao:** An island colony west of Hong Kong where Europeans could trade.

would inevitably occur between the Chinese and your barbarian subjects, and the results would militate against the benevolent regard that I feel towards you. From every point of view, therefore, it is best that the regulations now in force should continue unchanged. . . .

Regarding your nation's worship of the Lord of Heaven, it is the same religion as that of other European nations. Ever since the beginning of history, sage Emperors and wise rulers have bestowed on China a moral system and inculcated a code [i.e., Confucianism], which from time immemorial has been religiously observed by the myriads of my subjects. There has been no hankering after heterodox doctrines. Even the European officials [missionaries] in my capital are forbidden to hold intercourse with Chinese subjects; they are restricted within the limits of their appointed residences, and may not go about propagating their religion. The distinction between Chinese and barbarian is most strict, and your Ambassador's request that barbarians shall be given full liberty to disseminate their religion is utterly unreasonable.

It may be, O King, that the above proposals have been wantonly made by your Ambassador on his own responsibility, or peradventure you yourself are ignorant of our dynastic regulations and had no intention of transgressing them when you expressed these wild ideas and hopes. . . . If, after the receipt of this explicit decree, you lightly give ear to the representations of your subordinates and allow your barbarian merchants to proceed to [port cities] Zhejiang and Tianjin, with the object of landing and trading there, the ordinances of my Celestial Empire are strict in the extreme, and the local officials, both civil and military, are bound reverently to obey the law of the land. Should your vessels touch the shore, your merchants will assuredly never be permitted to land or to reside there, but will be subject to instant expulsion. In that event your barbarian merchants will have had a long journey for nothing. Do not say that you were not warned in due time! Tremblingly obey and show no negligence! A special mandate!

READING AND DISCUSSION QUESTIONS

1. How does the emperor envision the relationship between Great Britain and China?

2. What reasons does the Qianlong emperor give for refusing British demands?

3. Based on your reading, was the Qianlong emperor's refusal in China's best interest? Why or why not?

COMPARATIVE QUESTIONS

1. Many of these documents imply that social hierarchy and custom are in some way tied to wealth and the influence of trade. Summarize the relationship between custom and trade as presented in each work.

2. While Zhang Han's work seems to advocate more freedom for the merchant class in Ming China, Mitsui Takafusa's observations of Tokugawa Japan merchants seem to push for limiting their status and power. How do you explain the difference in these works? From what perspective is each author writing?

3. Kaibara's work on the education of women and children is the only document to focus on anyone other than men in Chinese and Japanese societies. Compare Kaibara's suggestions for the "proper" roles of women and children with Mitsui's or Zhang's work on merchants. Which document suggests more freedom for a particular group?

CHAPTER 21

The Revolution in Politics

1775–1815

B eginning with the American Revolution in 1775, the intellectual projects of the Enlightenment in Europe intersected with the economic logic of overseas colonial empires to generate optimism and upheaval in the Atlantic world. Colonists in British North America, members of the third estate in France, and slaves in the French colony of Saint-Domingue (Haiti) all used Enlightenment values to justify rebellion. The bloody expression of notions of freedom, equality, and national integrity in the American, French, and Haitian Revolutions, along with the Napoleonic wars of conquest in Europe, challenged many aspects of traditional European society at home and in the colonies. However, the endurance of sexual, class-based, and ethnic discrimination and the recurrence of violence and war complicate the era's story of egalitarianism and democracy. The following documents set forth the central ideologies of these revolutionary movements and some important critiques.

DOCUMENT 21-1

From The Declaration of Independence of the United States of America

1776

The Declaration of Independence formally announced the American colonies' intent to separate from Great Britain. It was authored primarily by Thomas Jefferson (1743–1826), a Virginia delegate to the Continental Congress and an adherent to Enlightenment ideals of human rights and freedom. From Jefferson's first draft, begun June 12, the document was revised

---

U.S. National Archives and Records Administration, Washington, D.C.

repeatedly both by the drafting committee and by the full Congress until its final printing on July 4, 1776. The Declaration was quickly disseminated to the new states and printed in newspapers.

When, in the course of human events, it becomes necessary for one people to dissolve the political bands which have connected them with another, and to assume, among the powers of the earth, the separate and equal station to which the laws of nature and of nature's God entitle them, a decent respect to the opinions of mankind requires that they should declare the causes which impel them to the separation.

We hold these truths to be self-evident: That all men are created equal; that they are endowed by their Creator with certain unalienable rights; that among these are life, liberty, and the pursuit of happiness; that, to secure these rights, governments are instituted among men, deriving their just powers from the consent of the governed; that whenever any form of government becomes destructive of these ends, it is the right of the people to alter or to abolish it, and to institute a new government, laying its foundation on such principles, and organizing its powers in such form, as to them shall seem most likely to effect their safety and happiness. Prudence, indeed, will dictate that governments long established should not be changed for light and transient causes; and accordingly all experience hath shown that mankind are more disposed to suffer, while evils are sufferable, than to right themselves by abolishing the forms to which they are accustomed. But when a long train of abuses and usurpations, pursuing invariably the same object, evinces a design to reduce them under absolute despotism, it is their right, it is their duty, to throw off such government, and to provide new guards for their future security. Such has been the patient sufferance of these colonies; and such is now the necessity which constrains them to alter their former systems of government. The history of the present King of Great Britain is a history of repeated injuries and usurpations, all having in direct object the establishment of an absolute tyranny over these States. To prove this, let facts be submitted to a candid world. . . .

READING AND DISCUSSION QUESTIONS

1. Who is the intended audience for the Declaration?
2. Who is the "villain" here? To what are the colonists objecting?
3. How do Jefferson and the Congress justify their arguments?

DOCUMENT 21-2

The Declaration of the Rights of Man and Citizen

1789

On June 17, 1789, during a meeting of the Estates General, the traditional advisory body under the absolutist French monarchy, delegates of the third estate voted to form a new National Assembly of France. They were joined by clergy and noblemen from the first and second estates, one of whom, the Marquis de Lafayette (1757–1834), outlined the assembly's aims in the Declaration of the Rights of Man and Citizen. The assembly approved the document in August, after the Revolution had begun, and trumpeted it throughout Europe and the world. This declaration, like the Declaration of Independence of the United States, is an important codification of Enlightenment ideas.

The representatives of the French people, organized as a National Assembly, believing that the ignorance, neglect, or contempt of the rights of man are the sole cause of public calamities and of the corruption of governments, have determined to set forth in a solemn declaration the natural, inalienable, and sacred rights of man, in order that this declaration, being constantly before all the members of the social body, shall remind them continually of their rights and duties; in order that the acts of the legislative power, as well as those of the executive power, may be compared at any moment with the objects and purposes of all political institutions and may thus be more respected; and, lastly, in order that the grievances of the citizens, based hereafter upon simple and incontestable principles, shall tend to the maintenance of the constitution and redound to the happiness of all. Therefore the National Assembly recognizes and proclaims, in the presence and under the auspices of the Supreme Being, the following rights of man and of the citizen:

ARTICLE 1. Men are born and remain free and equal in rights. Social distinctions may be founded only upon the general good.

James Harvey Robinson, ed., *Readings in European History* (Boston: Ginn, 1904), 2:409–411.

2. The aim of all political association is the preservation of the natural and imprescriptible rights of man. These rights are liberty, property, security, and resistance to oppression.

3. The principle of all sovereignty resides essentially in the nation. No body nor individual may exercise any authority which does not proceed directly from the nation.

4. Liberty consists in the freedom to do everything which injures no one else; hence the exercise of the natural rights of each man has no limits except those which assure to the other members of the society the enjoyment of the same rights. These limits can only be determined by law.

5. Law can only prohibit such actions as are hurtful to society. Nothing may be prevented which is not forbidden by law, and no one may be forced to do anything not provided for by law.

6. Law is the expression of the general will. Every citizen has a right to participate personally, or through his representative, in its formation. It must be the same for all, whether it protects or punishes. All citizens, being equal in the eyes of the law, are equally eligible to all dignities and to all public positions and occupations, according to their abilities, and without distinction except that of their virtues and talents.

7. No person shall be accused, arrested, or imprisoned except in the cases and according to the forms prescribed by law. Any one soliciting, transmitting, executing, or causing to be executed, any arbitrary order, shall be punished. But any citizen summoned or arrested in virtue of the law shall submit without delay, as resistance constitutes an offense.

8. The law shall provide for such punishments only as are strictly and obviously necessary, and no one shall suffer punishment except it be legally inflicted in virtue of a law passed and promulgated before the commission of the offense.

9. As all persons are held innocent until they shall have been declared guilty, if arrest shall be deemed indispensable, all harshness not essential to the securing of the prisoner's person shall be severely repressed by law.

10. No one shall be disquieted on account of his opinions, including his religious views, provided their manifestation does not disturb the public order established by law.

11. The free communication of ideas and opinions is one of the most precious of the rights of man. Every citizen may, accordingly, speak, write, and print with freedom, but shall be responsible for such abuses of this freedom as shall be defined by law.

12. The security of the rights of man and of the citizen requires public military forces. These forces are, therefore, established for the good of all and not for the personal advantage of those to whom they shall be intrusted.

13. A common contribution is essential for the maintenance of the public forces and for the cost of administration. This should be equitably distributed among all the citizens in proportion to their means.

14. All the citizens have a right to decide, either personally or by their representatives, as to the necessity of the public contribution; to grant this freely; to know to what uses it is put; and to fix the proportion, the mode of assessment and of collection and the duration of the taxes.

15. Society has the right to require of every public agent an account of his administration.

16. A society in which the observance of the law is not assured, nor the separation of powers defined, has no constitution at all.

17. Since property is an inviolable and sacred right, no one shall be deprived thereof except where public necessity, legally determined, shall clearly demand it, and then only on condition that the owner shall have been previously and equitably indemnified.

READING AND DISCUSSION QUESTIONS

1. To what are the French citizens objecting in this document? What is the proposed solution, if any?

2. What is the role of law in this declaration? Who makes the laws, and whom do they protect?

3. Which of these rights seems most important to you? Which seems least applicable to your life? Why?

DOCUMENT 21-3

EDMUND BURKE

From Reflections on the Revolution in France

1791

Edmund Burke (1729-1797) was a British politician whose opposition to the French Revolution helped cement his status as an important voice in the founding of modern conservatism. As a member of Britain's House of

---

Edmund Burke, *The Works of the Right Honourable Edmund Burke*, vol. III (London: John C. Nimmo, 1887).

*Commons, he spoke out for tradition and nationalism, against imperialism,
and in support of the cause of American independence. This excerpt from
his* Reflections on the Revolution in France, *written as an open letter to
French society, reveals Burke's appreciation of tradition and his disapproval
of violence.*

Kings, in one sense, are undoubtedly the servants of the people, because
their power has no other rational end than that of the general advantage;
but it is not true that they are, in the ordinary sense, (by our Constitution,
at least,) anything like servants, — the essence of whose situation is to obey
the commands of some other, and to be removable at pleasure. But the king
of Great Britain obeys no other person; all other persons are individually,
and collectively too, under him, and owe to him a legal obedience. . . .

Ill would our ancestors at the Revolution have deserved their fame for
wisdom, if they had found no security for their freedom, but in rendering
their government feeble in its operations and precarious in its tenure, — if
they had been able to contrive no better remedy against arbitrary power
than civil confusion. Let these gentlemen state who that representative
public is to whom they will affirm the king, as a servant, to be responsible.
It will be then time enough for me to produce to them the positive statute
law which affirms that he is not.

The ceremony of cashiering kings, of which these gentlemen talk so
much at their ease, can rarely, if ever, be performed without force. It then
becomes a case of war, and not of constitution. . . . As it was not made for
common abuses, so it is not to be agitated by common minds. The speculative line of demarcation, where obedience ought to end and resistance
must begin, is faint, obscure, and not easily definable. It is not a single act
or a single event which determines it. Governments must be abused and
deranged indeed, before it can be thought of; and the prospect of the
future must be as bad as the experience of the past. When things are in that
lamentable condition, the nature of the disease is to indicate the remedy to
those whom Nature has qualified to administer in extremities this critical,
ambiguous, bitter potion to a distempered state. Times and occasions and
provocations will teach their own lessons. The wise will determine from
the gravity of the case; the irritable, from sensibility to oppression; the
high-minded, from disdain and indignation at abusive power in unworthy
hands; the brave and bold, from the love of honorable danger in a generous cause: but, with or without right, a revolution will be the very last
resource of the thinking and the good.

The third head of right asserted by the pulpit of the Old Jewry,[1] namely, the "right to form a government for ourselves," has, at least, as little countenance from anything done at the Revolution, either in precedent or principle, as the two first of their claims. The Revolution was made to preserve our ancient indisputable laws and liberties, and that ancient constitution of government which is our only security for law and liberty. . . . Such a claim is as ill-suited to our temper and wishes as it is unsupported by any appearance of authority. The very idea of the fabrication of a new government is enough to fill us with disgust and horror. We wished at the period of the Revolution, and do now wish, to derive all we possess as an inheritance from our forefathers. . . .

You will observe, that, from Magna Charta to the Declaration of Right, it has been the uniform policy of our Constitution to claim and assert our liberties as an entailed inheritance derived to us from our forefathers, and to be transmitted to our posterity, — as an estate specially belonging to the people of this kingdom, without any reference whatever to any other more general or prior right. By this means our Constitution preserves an unity in so great a diversity of its parts. We have an inheritable crown, an inheritable peerage, and a House of Commons and a people inheriting privileges, franchises, and liberties from a long line of ancestors. . . .

You had all these advantages in your ancient states; but you chose to act as if you had never been molded into civil society, and had everything to begin anew. You began ill, because you began by despising everything that belonged to you. You set up your trade without a capital. If the last generations of your country appeared without much luster in your eyes, you might have passed them by, and derived your claims from a more early race of ancestors. Under a pious predilection for those ancestors, your imaginations would have realized in them a standard of virtue and wisdom beyond the vulgar practice of the hour; and you would have risen with the example to whose imitation you aspired. Respecting your forefathers, you would have been taught to respect yourselves. You would not have chosen to consider the French as a people of yesterday, as a nation of low-born, servile wretches until the emancipating year of 1789. . . . Had you made it to be understood, that, in the delusion of this amiable error, you had gone further than your wise ancestors, — that you were resolved to resume your ancient privileges, whilst you preserved the spirit of your ancient and your recent loyalty and honor; or if, diffident of yourselves, and not clearly discerning the almost obliterated Constitution of your ancestors, you had

---

[1] **The Old Jewry**: An ancient meetinghouse in London that hosted a variety of speakers.

looked to your neighbors in this land, who had kept alive the ancient principles and models of the old common law of Europe, meliorated and adapted to its present state, — by following wise examples you would have given new examples of wisdom to the world. You would have rendered the cause of liberty venerable in the eyes of every worthy mind in every nation. You would have shamed despotism from the earth, by showing that freedom was not only reconcilable, but, as, when well disciplined, it is, auxiliary to law. You would have had an unoppressive, but a productive revenue. You would have had a flourishing commerce to feed it. You would have had a free Constitution, a potent monarchy, a disciplined army, a reformed and venerated clergy, — a mitigated, but spirited nobility, to lead your virtue, not to overlay it; you would have had a liberal order of commons, to emulate and to recruit that nobility; you would have had a protected, satisfied, laborious, and obedient people, taught to seek and to recognize the happiness that is to be found by virtue in all conditions, — in which consists the true moral equality of mankind, and not in that monstrous fiction which, by inspiring false ideas and vain expectations into men destined to travel in the obscure walk of laborious life, serves only to aggravate and embitter that real inequality which it never can remove, and which the order of civil life establishes as much for the benefit of those whom it must leave in an humble state as those whom it is able to exalt to a condition more splendid, but not more happy. You had a smooth and easy career of felicity and glory laid open to you, beyond anything recorded in the history of the world; but you have shown that difficulty is good for man.

Compute your gains; see what is got by those extravagant and presumptuous speculations which have taught your leaders to despise all their predecessors, and all their contemporaries, and even to despise themselves, until the moment in which they became truly despicable. By following those false lights, France has bought undisguised calamities at a higher price than any nation has purchased the most unequivocal blessings. France has bought poverty by crime. France has not sacrificed her virtue to her interest; but she has abandoned her interest, that she might prostitute her virtue. All other nations have begun the fabric of a new government, or the reformation of an old, by establishing originally, or by enforcing with greater exactness, some rites or other of religion. All other people have laid the foundations of civil freedom in severer manners, and a system of a more austere and masculine morality. France, when she let loose the reins of regal authority, doubled the license of a ferocious dissoluteness in manners, and of an insolent irreligion in opinions and practices, — and has extended through all ranks of life, as if she were communicating some privilege, or laying open some secluded benefit, all the unhappy corruptions that usually were the disease of wealth and power. This is one of the new principles of equality in France. . . .

After I had read over the list of the persons and descriptions elected into the Tiers État [France's third estate], nothing which they afterwards did could appear astonishing. Among them, indeed, I saw some of known rank, some of shining talents; but of any practical experience in the state not one man was to be found. The best were only men of theory. But whatever the distinguished few may have been, it is the substance and mass of the body which constitutes its character, and must finally determine its direction. In all bodies, those who will lead must also, in a considerable degree, follow. They must conform their propositions to the taste, talent, and disposition of those whom they wish to conduct: therefore, if an assembly is viciously or feebly composed in a very great part of it, nothing but such a supreme degree of virtue as very rarely appears in the world, and for that reason cannot enter into calculation, will prevent the men of talents disseminated through it from becoming only the expert instruments of absurd projects. If, what is the more likely event, instead of that unusual degree of virtue, they should be actuated by sinister ambition and a lust of meretricious glory, then the feeble part of the assembly, to whom at first they conform, becomes, in its turn, the dupe and instrument of their designs. In this political traffic, the leaders will be obliged to bow to the ignorance of their followers, and the followers to become subservient to the worst designs of their leaders. . . .

Judge, Sir, of my surprise, when I found that a very great proportion of the Assembly (a majority, I believe, of the members who attended) was composed of practitioners in the law. It was composed, not of distinguished magistrates, who had given pledges to their country of their science, prudence, and integrity, — not of leading advocates, the glory of the bar, — not of renowned professors in universities, — but for the far greater part, as it must in such a number, of the inferior, unlearned, mechanical, merely instrumental members of the profession. There were distinguished exceptions; but the general composition was of obscure provincial advocates, of stewards of petty local jurisdictions, country attorneys, notaries, and the whole train of the ministers of municipal litigation, the fomenters and conductors of the petty war of village vexation. From the moment I read the list, I saw distinctly, and very nearly as it has happened, all that was to follow.

The degree of estimation in which any profession is held becomes the standard of the estimation in which the professors hold themselves. Whatever the personal merits of many individual lawyers might have been, (and in many it was undoubtedly very considerable,) in that military kingdom no part of the profession had been much regarded, except the highest of all, who often united to their professional offices great family splendor, and were invested with great power and authority. These certainly were highly respected, and even with no small degree of awe. The next rank was not much esteemed; the mechanical part was in a very low degree of repute.

Whenever the supreme authority is vested in a body so composed, it must evidently produce the consequences of supreme authority placed in the hands of men not taught habitually to respect themselves, — who had no previous fortune in character at stake, — who could not be expected to bear with moderation or to conduct with discretion a power which they themselves, more than any others, must be surprised to find in their hands. Who could flatter himself that these men, suddenly, and as it were by enchantment, snatched from the humblest rank of subordination, would not be intoxicated with their unprepared greatness? . . . Was it to be expected that they would attend to the stability of property, whose existence had always depended upon whatever rendered property questionable, ambiguous, and insecure? Their objects would be enlarged with their elevation; but their disposition, and habits, and mode of accomplishing their designs must remain the same.

Well! but these men were to be tempered and restrained by other descriptions, of more sober minds and more enlarged understandings. Were they, then, to be awed by the supereminent authority and awful dignity of a handful of country clowns, who have seats in that assembly, some of whom are said not to be able to read and write, — and by not a greater number of traders, who, though somewhat more instructed, and more conspicuous in the order of society, had never known anything beyond their counting-house? No! both these descriptions were more formed to be overborne and swayed by the intrigues and artifices of lawyers than to become their counterpoise. With such a dangerous disproportion, the whole must needs be governed by them. . . .

READING AND DISCUSSION QUESTIONS

1. What is Burke's point of contrast between British and French society?
2. Based on this reading, does Burke seem categorically opposed to revolution? To social change?
3. Burke describes the "true moral equality of all mankind." What is that equality? How does it fit into his idea of social classes and occupations?

MARY WOLLSTONECRAFT

From A Vindication of the Rights of Woman

1792

In response to a 1791 report to the French National Assembly by diplomat Charles Talleyrand (1754–1838), British author Mary Wollstonecraft (1759–1797) argued for the importance of equal educational opportunities for women. Her Vindication of the Rights of Woman *is viewed as an important early contribution to feminist theory, but it is also provides insight on some of the controversy surrounding the French Revolution. Wollstonecraft's earlier publication,* A Vindication of the Rights of Man *(1790), argued against Edmund Burke's traditionalist critique of the French Revolution.* Rights of Woman *highlights how the French Revolution encouraged new debates and perspectives on gender relations in modern societies.*

But, if strength of body be, with some show of reason, the boast of men, why are women so infatuated as to be proud of a defect? Rousseau has furnished them with a plausible excuse, which could only have occurred to a man, whose imagination had been allowed to run wild, and refine on the impressions made by exquisite senses; — that they might, forsooth, have a pretext for yielding to a natural appetite without violating a romantic species of modesty, which gratifies the pride and libertinism of man.

Women, deluded by these sentiments, sometimes boast of their weakness, cunningly obtaining power by playing on the *weakness* of men; and they may well glory in their illicit sway, for, like Turkish bashaws [i.e., pashas, or Lords], they have more real power than their masters: but virtue is sacrificed to temporary gratifications, and the respectability of life to the triumph of an hour.

Women, as well as despots, have now, perhaps, more power than they would have if the world, divided and subdivided into kingdoms and families, were governed by laws deduced from the exercise of reason; but in obtaining it, to carry on the comparison, their character is degraded, and

---

Mary Wollstonecraft, *A Vindication of the Rights of Woman: With Strictures on Political and Moral Subjects* (London: T. Fisher Unwin, 1891), 74–84.

licentiousness spread through the whole aggregate of society. The many become pedestal to the few. I, therefore, will venture to assert, that till women are more rationally educated, the progress of human virtue and improvement in knowledge must receive continual checks. And if it be granted that woman was not created merely to gratify the appetite of man, or to be the upper servant, who provides his meals and takes care of his linen, it must follow, that the first care of those mothers, or fathers, who really attend to the education of females, should be, if not to strengthen the body, at least, not to destroy the constitution by mistaken notions of beauty and female excellence; nor should girls ever be allowed to imbibe the pernicious notion that a defect can, by any chemical process of reasoning, become an excellence. . . .

. . . But should it be proved that woman is naturally weaker than man, whence does it follow that it is natural for her to labor to become still weaker than nature intended her to be? Arguments of this cast are an insult to common sense, and savor of passion. The *divine right* of husbands, like the divine right of kings, may, it is to be hoped, in this enlightened age, be contested without danger, and, though conviction may not silence many boisterous disputants, yet, when any prevailing prejudice is attacked, the wife will consider, and leave the narrow-minded to rail with thoughtless vehemence at innovation.

The mother, who wishes to give true dignity of character to her daughter, must, regardless of the sneers of ignorance, proceed on a plan diametrically opposite to that which Rousseau has recommended with all the deluding charms of eloquence and philosophical sophistry: for his eloquence renders absurdities plausible, and his dogmatic conclusions puzzle, without convincing, those who have not ability to refute them.

Throughout the whole animal kingdom every young creature requires almost continual exercise, and the infancy of children, conformable to this intimation, should be passed in harmless gambols, that exercise the feet and hands, without requiring very minute direction from the head, or the constant attention of a nurse. In fact, the care necessary for self-preservation is the first natural exercise of the understanding, as little inventions to amuse the present moment unfold the imagination. But these wise designs of nature are counteracted by mistaken fondness or blind zeal. The child is not left a moment to its own direction, particularly a girl, and thus rendered dependent — dependence is called natural. . . .

Let not men then in the pride of power, use the same arguments that tyrannic kings and venal ministers have used, and fallaciously assert that woman ought to be subjected because she has always been so. But, when man, governed by reasonable laws, enjoys his natural freedom, let him despise woman, if she do not share it with him; and, till that glorious period arrives, in descanting on the folly of the sex, let him not overlook his own.

Women, it is true, obtaining power by unjust means, by practicing or fostering vice, evidently lose the rank which reason would assign them, and they become either abject slaves or capricious tyrants. They lose all simplicity, all dignity of mind, in acquiring power, and act as men are observed to act when they have been exalted by the same means.

It is time to effect a revolution in female manners — time to restore to them their lost dignity — and make them, as a part of the human species, labor by reforming themselves to reform the world. It is time to separate unchangeable morals from local manners. If men be demi-gods — why let us serve them! And if the dignity of the female soul be as disputable as that of animals — if their reason does not afford sufficient light to direct their conduct whilst unerring instinct is denied — they are surely of all creatures the most miserable! and, bent beneath the iron hand of destiny, must submit to be a *fair defect* in creation. But to justify the ways of [Divine] Providence respecting them, by pointing out some irrefragable reason for thus making such a large portion of mankind accountable and not accountable, would puzzle the subtlest casuist.[2]

READING AND DISCUSSION QUESTIONS

1. How does Wollstonecraft use the ideas of physical strength and exercise in her call for women's education?

2. How does Wollstonecraft connect the relationship between men and women to the relationship between ruler and ruled?

3. How does Wollstonecraft describe the ideal relationship between men and women? What is the level of equality in this relationship?

---

[2] **would puzzle the subtlest casuist:** A casuist attempts to solve moral problems. The author is suggesting that accepting that women are a weaker sex de facto is ludicrous, and that any person capable of reason should be able to deduce as much.

DOCUMENT 21-5

The Haitian Declaration of Independence

1804

The Haitian Revolution represents one of modern history's most thorough political and social transformations. Beginning in 1791, slaves of African descent on the sugar and coffee plantations in the French colony of Saint-Domingue staged a series of uprisings against white plantation owners, ultimately forcing France to abolish slavery in its colonies. After Napoleonic forces sought to regain control of the colony and imprisoned Saint-Domingue's charismatic leader, Toussaint L'Ouverture (1743–1803), his lieutenant Jean-Jacques Dessalines (1758–1806) took command and expelled the French in 1803. His declaration of independence in 1804 invoked Enlightenment values and rhetoric to address racial inequality.

THE COMMANDER IN CHIEF TO THE PEOPLE OF HAITI

Citizens:

It is not enough to have expelled the barbarians who have bloodied our land for two centuries; it is not enough to have restrained those ever-evolving factions that one after another mocked the specter of liberty that France dangled before you. We must, with one last act of national authority, forever ensure liberty's reign in the country of our birth; we must take any hope of re-enslaving us away from the inhumane government that for so long kept us in the most humiliating stagnation. In the end we must live independent or die.

Independence or death . . . let these sacred words unite us and be the signal of battle and of our reunion.

Citizens, my countrymen, on this solemn day I have brought together those courageous soldiers who, as liberty lay dying, spilled their blood to save it; these generals who have guided your efforts against tyranny have not yet done enough for your happiness; the French name still haunts our land.

Thomas Madiou, *Histoire d'Haïti* (Port-au-Prince, 1847–1848), 3:146–150. Excerpted in *Slave Revolution in the Caribbean, 1789–1804: A Brief History with Documents*, Laurent Dubois and John D. Garrigus, eds. (Boston: Bedford/St. Martin's, 2006), 188–191.

Everything revives the memories of the cruelties of this barbarous people: our laws, our habits, our towns, everything still carries the stamp of the French. Indeed! There are still French in our island, and you believe yourself free and independent of that republic, which, it is true, has fought all the nations, but which has never defeated those who wanted to be free.

What! Victims of our [own] credulity and indulgence for fourteen years; defeated not by French armies, but by the pathetic eloquence of their agents' proclamations; when will we tire of breathing the air that they breathe? What do we have in common with this nation of executioners? The difference between its cruelty and our patient moderation, its color and ours, the great seas that separate us, our avenging climate, all tell us plainly that they are not our brothers, that they never will be, and that if they find refuge among us, they will plot again to trouble and divide us.

Native citizens, men, women, girls, and children, let your gaze extend on all parts of this island: look there for your spouses, your husbands, your brothers, your sisters. Indeed! Look there for your children, your suckling infants, what have they become? . . . I shudder to say it . . . the prey of these vultures.

Instead of these dear victims, your alarmed gaze will see only their assassins, these tigers still dripping with their blood, whose terrible presence indicts your lack of feeling and your guilty slowness in avenging them. What are you waiting for before appeasing their spirits? Remember that you had wanted your remains to rest next to those of your fathers after you defeated tyranny; will you descend into their tombs without having avenged them? No! Their bones would reject yours.

And you, precious men, intrepid generals, who, without concern for your own pain, have revived liberty by shedding all your blood, know that you have done nothing if you do not give the nations a terrible, but just example of the vengeance that must be wrought by a people proud to have recovered its liberty and jealous to maintain it. Let us frighten all those who would dare try to take it from us again; let us begin with the French. Let them tremble when they approach our coast, if not from the memory of those cruelties they perpetrated here, then from the terrible resolution that we will have made to put to death anyone born French whose profane foot soils the land of liberty.

We have dared to be free, let us be thus by ourselves and for ourselves. Let us imitate the grown child: his own weight breaks the boundary that has become an obstacle to him. What people fought for us? What people wanted to gather the fruits of our labor? And what dishonorable absurdity to conquer in order to be enslaved. Enslaved? . . . Let us leave this description for the French; they have conquered but are no longer free.

Let us walk down another path; let us imitate those people who, extending their concern into the future and dreading to leave an example of cowardice for posterity, preferred to be exterminated rather than lose their place as one of the world's free peoples.

Let us ensure, however, that a missionary spirit does not destroy our work; let us allow our neighbors to breathe in peace; may they live quietly under the laws that they have made for themselves, and let us not, as revolutionary firebrands, declare ourselves the lawgivers of the Caribbean, nor let our glory consist in troubling the peace of the neighboring islands. Unlike that which we inhabit, theirs has not been drenched in the innocent blood of its inhabitants; they have no vengeance to claim from the authority that protects them.

Fortunate to have never known the ideals that have destroyed us, they can only have good wishes for our prosperity.

Peace to our neighbors; but let this be our cry: "Anathema to the French name! Eternal hatred of France!"

Natives of Haiti! My happy fate was to be one day the sentinel who would watch over the idol to which you sacrifice; I have watched, sometimes fighting alone, and if I have been so fortunate as to return to your hands the sacred trust you confided to me, know that it is now your task to preserve it. In fighting for your liberty, I was working for my own happiness. Before consolidating it with laws that will guarantee your free individuality, your leaders, who I have assembled here, and I, owe you the final proof of our devotion.

Generals and you, leaders, collected here close to me for the good of our land, the day has come, the day which must make our glory, our independence, eternal.

If there could exist among us a lukewarm heart, let him distance himself and tremble to take the oath which must unite us. Let us vow to ourselves, to posterity, to the entire universe, to forever renounce France, and to die rather than live under its domination; to fight until our last breath for the independence of our country.

And you, a people so long without good fortune, witness to the oath we take, remember that I counted on your constancy and courage when I threw myself into the career of liberty to fight the despotism and tyranny you had struggled against for fourteen years. Remember that I sacrificed everything to rally to your defense; family, children, fortune, and now I am rich only with your liberty; my name has become a horror to all those who want slavery. Despots and tyrants curse the day that I was born. If ever you refused or grumbled while receiving those laws that the spirit guarding your fate dictates to me for your own good, you would deserve the fate of an ungrateful people. But I reject that awful idea; you will sustain the liberty that you cherish and support the leader who commands you. Therefore, vow before me to live free and independent and to prefer death to anything that will try to place you back in chains. Swear, finally, to pursue forever the traitors and enemies of your independence.

Done at the headquarters of Gonaïves, the first day of January 1804, the first year of independence.

READING AND DISCUSSION QUESTIONS

1. How does the Haitian Declaration of Independence inspire nationalist feelings in its audience?

2. How does the document justify the Haitian Revolution?

3. Describe the tone of the Declaration. Who is speaking, and to whom?

COMPARATIVE QUESTIONS

1. Compare and contrast the three declarations. How does each declaration describe past problems and how does each present a vision of a new world? What values do all three embrace, and where do the documents diverge?

2. Edmund Burke argues strongly against the radical nature of the French Revolution. How might the author of the Haitian Declaration of Independence and Mary Wollstonecraft answer Burke's charge that legitimate social change must not break with tradition?

3. Based on his assessment of the French Revolution, how do you think Burke would respond to the use of violence in the Haitian Revolution?

CHAPTER 22

The Industrial Revolution in Europe

ca. 1780–1860

The Industrial Revolution, though less visibly dramatic than the bloody political and social revolutions taking place in Europe and the Americas, did more to transform human societies around the world than any single development since the beginning of agriculture. Changes in agriculture, manufacturing, and domestic and foreign trade — first in Britain, and then in Europe and beyond — resulted in unprecedented economic growth. At the same time, shifts in social relations revealed obvious and disturbing inequalities between prosperous business owners and their often-abused workers. In the following documents, British politicians, workers, and intellectuals address some of the social effects of rapid industrialization. Whether seeking protection for women and children in the workplace, demanding universal male suffrage, or analyzing the challenges of a rapidly increasing population, these texts show ways in which people tried to understand and navigate their changing social and economic worlds.

DOCUMENT 22-1

THOMAS ROBERT MALTHUS
From An Essay on the Principle of Population
1798

Anglican priest and scholar Thomas Robert Malthus (1766–1834) revised and republished his influential 1798 work on population numerous times to respond to critics and changing circumstances. His views on the relationships

Thomas Robert Malthus, "An Essay on the Principle of Population," in Walter Arnstein, ed., *The Past Speaks*, 2d ed. (Lexington, Mass.: D.C. Heath, 1993), 2:144–146.

between population, resources, and human happiness met with considerable
opposition, especially from thinkers such as William Godwin (1756–1836),
husband of the author Mary Wollstonecraft and author of a book that Mal-
thus attacked directly. Malthus's attempts to fold natural and social sciences
together, though frequently misunderstood or misappropriated, continue to
inform debates over social policy and natural resources.

I have read some of the speculations on the perfectibility of man and of
society with great pleasure. I have been warmed and delighted with the
enchanting picture which they hold forth. I ardently wish for such happy
improvements. But I see great, and, to my understanding, unconquerable
difficulties in the way to them. These difficulties it is my present purpose
to state; declaring, at the same time, that so far from exulting in them, as a
cause of triumphing over the friends of innovation, nothing would give me
greater pleasure than to see them completely removed. . . .

I think I may fairly make two postulata.

First, That food is necessary to the existence of man.

Secondly, That the passion between the sexes is necessary, and will
remain nearly in its present state. . . .

Assuming, then, my postulata as granted, I say, that the power of
population is indefinitely greater than the power in the earth to produce
subsistence for man.

Population, when unchecked, increases in a geometrical ratio. Subsistence only increases in an arithmetical ratio. A slight acquaintance with numbers will show the immensity of the first power in comparison of the second.

By that law of our nature which makes food necessary to the life of
man, the effects of these two unequal powers must be kept equal.

This implies a strong and constantly operating check on population
from the difficulty of subsistence. This difficulty must fall some where; and
must necessarily be severely felt by a large portion of mankind. . . .

The ultimate check to population appears then to be a want of food
arising necessarily from the different ratios according to which population
and food increase. But this ultimate check is never the immediate check,
except in cases of actual famine.

The immediate check may be stated to consist in all those customs,
and all those diseases which seem to be generated by a scarcity of the
means of subsistence; and all those causes, independent of this scarcity,
whether of a moral or physical nature, which tend prematurely to weaken
and destroy the human frame.

In every country some of these checks are, with more or less force, in constant operation; yet, notwithstanding their general prevalence, there are few states in which there is not a constant effort in the population to increase beyond the means of subsistence. This constant effort as constantly tends to subject the lower classes of society to distress, and to prevent any great permanent melioration of their condition.

These effects, in the present state of society, seem to be produced in the following manner. We will suppose the means of subsistence in any country just equal to the easy support of its inhabitants. The constant effort toward population, which is found to act even in the most vicious societies, increases the number of people before the means of subsistence are increased. The food, therefore, which before supported eleven millions, must now be divided among eleven millions and a half. The poor consequently must live much worse, and many of them be reduced to severe distress. The number of laborers also being above the proportion of work in the market, the price of labor must tend to fall, while the price of provisions would at the same time tend to rise. The laborer therefore must do more work to earn the same as he did before. During this season of distress, the discouragements to marriage and the difficulty of rearing a family are so great, that the progress of population is retarded. In the meantime, the cheapness of labor, the plenty of laborers, and the necessity of an increased industry among them, encourage cultivators to employ more labor upon their land, to turn up fresh soil, and to manure and improve more completely what is already in tillage, till ultimately the means of subsistence may become in the same proportion to the population as at the period from which we set out. The situation of the laborer being then again tolerably comfortable, the restraints to population are in some degree loosened; and, after a short period, the same retrograde and progressive movements, with respect to happiness, are repeated. . . .

READING AND DISCUSSION QUESTIONS

1. According to Malthus, what features are constant in modern populations?

2. In Malthus's view, who bears the brunt of the cycle of reproduction and food production? What seems to be Malthus's attitude toward these people?

3. What do you imagine might be solutions to the cycle that Malthus describes?

DOCUMENT 22-2

SADLER COMMITTEE AND
ASHLEY COMMISSION

Testimonies Before Parliamentary Committees on Working Conditions in England

1832, 1842

The Industrial Revolution depended on men, women, and children working under harsh and often deadly conditions. Troubled by the social changes wrought by Britain's rapid industrialization, politician Michael Sadler (1780–1835) formed the Committee on the Labour of Children in the Mills and Factories of the United Kingdom. The committee's 1832 report shocked the public and mobilized support for labor reform. In 1840, another labor reform advocate, Lord Ashley (1801–1885), established the Children's Employment Commission. Its 1842 report shed light on the practice of child labor in coal mines. Both of these reports prompted legislation and raised public awareness of the human cost of the Industrial Revolution.

TESTIMONY BEFORE THE SADLER COMMITTEE, 1832[1]

Elizabeth Bentley, Called in; and Examined

What age are you? — Twenty-three. . . .

What time did you begin to work at a factory? — When I was six years old. . . .

What kind of mill is it? — Flax-mill. . . .

What was your business in that mill? — I was a little doffer.[2]

What were your hours of labor in that mill? — From 5 in the morning till 9 at night, when they were thronged [busy].

John Bowditch, ed. *Voices of the Industrial Revolution* (Ann Arbor: University of Michigan Press, 1961), 82–90.

[1] **Testimony . . . 1832**: Michael Sadler first proposed a ten-hour workday in 1831; his bill was rejected by Parliament but prompted the formation of this investigative committee.

[2] **doffer**: A young child whose job was to clean the machinery.

For how long a time together have you worked that excessive length of time? — For about half a year.

What were your usual hours of labor when you were not so thronged? — From 6 in the morning till 7 at night.

What time was allowed for your meals? — Forty minutes at noon.

Had you any time to get your breakfast or drinking? — No, we got it as we could.

And when your work was bad, you had hardly any time to eat it at all? — No; we were obliged to leave it or take it home, and when we did not take it, the overlooker took it, and gave it to his pigs.

Do you consider doffing a laborious employment? — Yes.

Explain what it is you had to do. — When the frames are full, they have to stop the frames, and take the flyers off, and take the full bobbins off, and carry them to the roller; and then put empty ones on, and set the frames on again.

Does that keep you constantly on your feet? — Yes, there are so many frames and they run so quick.

Your labor is very excessive? — Yes; you have not time for anything.

Suppose you flagged a little, or were too late, what would they do? — Strap us.

Are they in the habit of strapping those who are last in doffing? — Yes.

Constantly? — Yes.

Girls as well as boys? — Yes.

Have you ever been strapped? — Yes.

Severely? — Yes.

Could you eat your food well in that factory? — No, indeed, I had not much to eat, and the little I had I could not eat it, my appetite was so poor, and being covered with dust; and it was no use to take it home, I could not eat it, and the overlooker took it, and gave it to the pigs. . . .

Did you live far from the mill? — Yes, two miles.

Had you a clock? — No, we had not.

Supposing you had not been in time enough in the morning at the mills, what would have been the consequence? — We should have been quartered.

What do you mean by that? — If we were a quarter of an hour too late, they would take off half an hour; we only got a penny an hour, and they would take a halfpenny more. . . .

Were you generally there in time? — Yes, my mother has been up at 4 o'clock in the morning, and at 2 o'clock in the morning; the colliers used to go to their work about 3 or 4 o'clock, and when she heard them stirring she has got up out of her warm bed, and gone out and asked them the time, and I have sometimes been at Hunslet Car at 2 o'clock in the morning, when it was streaming down with rain, and we have had to stay till the mill was opened. . . .

Testimony Before the Ashley Committee on the Conditions in Mines, 1842[3]

Edward Potter

I am a coal viewer, and the manager of the South Hetton colliery. We have about 400 bound people (contract laborers), and in addition our bank people (foremen), men and boys about 700. In the pits 427 men and boys; of these, 290 men. . . .

Of the children in the pits we have none under eight, and only three so young. We are constantly beset by parents coming making application to take children under the age, and they are very anxious and very dissatisfied if we do not take the children; and there have been cases in times of brisk trade, when the parents have threatened to leave the colliery, and go elsewhere if we did not comply. At every successive binding, which takes place yearly, constant attempts are made to get the boys engaged to work to which they are not competent from their years. In point of fact, we would rather not have boys until nine years of age complete. If younger than that, they are apt to fall asleep and get hurt; some get killed. It is no interest to the company to take any boys under nine. . . .

Hannah Richardson

I've one child that works in the pit; he's going on ten. He is down from 6 to 8. . . . he's not much tired with the work, it's only the confinement that tires him. He likes it pretty well, for he'd rather be in the pit than to go to school. There is not much difference in his health since he went into the pit. He was at school before, and can read pretty well, but can't write. He is used pretty well; I never hear him complain. I've another son in the pit, 17 years old. . . . He went into the pit at eight years old. It's not hurt his health nor his appetite, for he's a good size. It would hurt us if children were prevented from working till 11 or 12 years old, because we've not jobs enough to live now as it is. . . .

---

[3] **Testimony . . . 1842**: This testimony led to the Mines Act of 1842, which prohibited boys under the age of ten and women from working in the mines.

Mr. George Armitage

I am now a teacher at Hoyland school; I was a collier at Silkstone until I was 22 years old and worked in the pit above 10 years. . . . I hardly know how to reprobate the practice sufficiently of girls working in pits; nothing can be worse. I have no doubt that debauchery is carried on, for which there is every opportunity; for the girls go constantly, when hurrying, to the men, who work often alone in the bank-faces apart from every one. I think it scarcely possible for girls to remain modest who are in pits, regularly mixing with such company and hearing and such language as they do — it is next to impossible. I dare venture to say that many of the wives who come from pits know nothing of sewing or any household duty, such as women ought to know — they lose all disposition to learn such things; they are rendered unfit for learning them also by being overworked and not being trained to the habit of it. I have worked in pits for above 10 years, where girls were constantly employed, and I can safely say it is an abominable system; indecent language is quite common. I think, if girls were trained properly, as girls ought to be, that there would be no more difficulty in finding suitable employment for them than in other places. Many a collier spends in drink what he has shut up a young child the whole week to earn in a dark cold corner as a trapper. The education of the children is universally bad. They are generally ignorant of common facts in Christian history and principles, and, indeed, in almost everything else. Little can be learned merely on Sundays, and they are too tired as well as indisposed to go to night schools. . . .

The Rev. Robert Willan, Curate of St. Mary's, Barnsley

I have been resident here as chief minister for 22 years. I think the morals of the working classes here are in an appalling state. . . . The ill manners and conduct of the weavers are daily presented to view in the streets, but the colliers work under ground and are less seen, and we have less means of knowing. . . . The master-sin among the youths is that of gambling; the boys may be seen playing at pitch-and-toss on the Sabbath and on week-days; they are seen doing this in all directions. The next besetting sin is promiscuous sexual intercourse; this may be much induced by the manner in which they sleep — men, women, and children often sleeping in one bed-room. I have known a family of father and mother and 12 children, some of them up-grown, sleeping on a kind of sacking and straw bed, reaching from one side of the room to the other, along the floor; they were an English family. Sexual intercourse begins very young. This and gambling pave the way; then drinking ensues, and this is the vortex which draws in every other sin.

Thomas Wilson, Esq., Owner of Three Collieries

I object on general principles to government interference in the conduct of any trade, and I am satisfied that in the mines it would be productive of the greatest injury and injustice. The art of mining is not so perfectly understood as to admit of the way in which a colliery shall be conducted being dictated by any person, however experienced, with such certainty as would warrant an interference with the management of private business. I should also most decidedly object to placing collieries under the present provisions of the Factory Act[4] with respect to the education of children employed therein. First, because, if it is contended that coal-owners, as employers of children, are bound to attend to their education, this obligation extends equally to all other employers, and therefore it is unjust to single out one class only; secondly, because, if the legislature asserts a right to interfere to secure education, it is bound to make that interference general; and thirdly, because the mining population is in this neighborhood so intermixed with other classes, and is in such small bodies in any one place, that it would be impossible to provide separate schools for them.

READING AND DISCUSSION QUESTIONS

1. How do these testimonies present the realities of child labor? Give specific examples.

2. Both reports make particular note of the gender of workers. What is the effect of calling attention to female labor? How would you describe the attitudes toward gender differences conveyed in these reports?

3. Summarize the arguments presented in the Ashley Commission report for and against the regulation of female and child labor in mines. How is the issue of education used in each argument?

---

[4]**Factory Act**: The Factory Act of 1833 restricted the workday to eight hours for children between the ages of nine and fourteen and twelve hours for those between fourteen and eighteen.

DOCUMENT 22-3

Chartism: The People's Petition

1838

In 1837, a group of twelve men — six members of Parliament and six members of the British working class — composed and circulated a list of demands for electoral reforms including universal male suffrage. These demands were later incorporated into the People's Charter, from which the Chartist movement took its name. In 1838, the petition excerpted below was submitted to Parliament. Despite garnering more than a million signatures, the proposal met with little support from the rest of Parliament and among the middle classes and it failed to pass on several occasions. Nevertheless, the Chartist movement was an important early milestone in the struggle for individual rights during the Industrial Revolution.

Unto the Honorable the Commons of the United Kingdom of Great Britain and Ireland in Parliament assembled, the Petition of the undersigned, their suffering countrymen.

HUMBLY SHEWETH,

That we, your petitioners, dwell in a land whose merchants are noted for enterprise, whose manufacturers are very skilful, and whose workmen are proverbial for their industry.

The land itself is goodly, the soil rich, and the temperature wholesome; it is abundantly furnished with the materials of commerce and trade; it has numerous and convenient harbors; in facility of internal communication it exceeds all others.

For three-and-twenty years we have enjoyed a profound peace.

Yet, with all these elements of national prosperity, and with every disposition and capacity to take advantage of them, we find ourselves overwhelmed with public and private suffering.

We are bowed down under a load of taxes; which, notwithstanding, fall greatly short of the wants of our rulers; our traders are trembling on the

William Lovett, *The Life and Struggles of William Lovett* (New York: Knopf, 1920), 478–482.

verge of bankruptcy; our workmen are starving; capital brings no profit, and labor no remuneration; the home of the artificer is desolate, and the warehouse of the pawnbroker is full; the workhouse is crowded, and the manufactory is deserted.

We have looked on every side, we have searched diligently in order to find out the causes of a distress so sore and so long continued.

We can discover none in nature, or in Providence.

Heaven has dealt graciously by the people; but the foolishness of our rulers has made the goodness of God of none effect.

The energies of a mighty kingdom have been wasted in building up the power of selfish and ignorant men, and its resources squandered for their aggrandizement.

The good of a party has been advanced to the sacrifice of the good of the nation; the few have governed for the interest of the few, while the interest of the many has been neglected, or insolently and tyrannously trampled upon.

It was the fond expectation of the people that a remedy for the greater part, if not for the whole, of their grievances, would be found in the Reform Act of 1832.

They were taught to regard that Act as a wise means to a worthy end; as the machinery of an improved legislation, when the will of the masses would be at length potential.

They have been bitterly and basely deceived.

The fruit which looked so fair to the eye has turned to dust and ashes when gathered.

The Reform Act has effected a transfer of power from one domineering faction to another, and left the people as helpless as before.

Our slavery has been exchanged for an apprenticeship to liberty, which has aggravated the painful feeling of our social degradation, by adding to it the sickening of still deferred hope.

We come before your Honorable House to tell you, with all humility, that this state of things must not be permitted to continue; that it cannot long continue without very seriously endangering the stability of the throne and the peace of the kingdom; and that if by God's help and all lawful and constitutional appliances, an end can be put to it, we are fully resolved that it shall speedily come to an end.

We tell your Honorable House that the capital of the master must no longer be deprived of its due reward; that the laws which make food dear, and those which by making money scarce, make labor cheap, must be abolished; that taxation must be made to fall on property, not on industry;

that the good of the many, as it is the only legitimate end, so must it be the sole study of the Government.

As a preliminary essential to these and other requisite changes; as means by which alone the interests of the people can be effectually vindicated and secured, we demand that those interests be confided to the keeping of the people.

When the State calls for defenders, when it calls for money, no consideration of poverty or ignorance can be pleaded in refusal or delay of the call.

Required as we are, universally, to support and obey the laws, nature and reason entitle us to demand, that in the making of the laws, the universal voice shall be implicitly listened to.

We perform the duties of freemen; we must have the privileges of freemen.

WE DEMAND UNIVERSAL SUFFRAGE.

The suffrage to be exempt from the corruption of the wealthy, and the violence of the powerful, must be secret.

The assertion of our right necessarily involves the power of its uncontrolled exercise.

WE DEMAND THE BALLOT.

The connection between the representatives and the people, to be beneficial must be intimate.

The legislative and constituent powers, for correction and for instruction, ought to be brought into frequent contact.

Errors, which are comparatively light when susceptible of a speedy popular remedy, may produce the most disastrous effects when permitted to grow inveterate through years of compulsory endurance.

To public safety as well as public confidence, frequent elections are essential.

WE DEMAND ANNUAL PARLIAMENTS.

With power to choose, and freedom in choosing, the range of our choice must be unrestricted.

We are compelled, by the existing laws, to take for our representatives, men who are incapable of appreciating our difficulties, or who have little sympathy with them; merchants who have retired from trade, and no longer feel its harassings; proprietors of land who are alike ignorant of its evils and their cure; lawyers, by whom the honors of the senate are sought after only as means of obtaining notice in the courts.

The labors of a representative, who is sedulous in the discharge of his duty, are numerous and burdensome.

It is neither just, nor reasonable, nor safe, that they should continue to be gratuitously rendered.

We demand that in the future election of members of your Honorable House, the approbation of the constituency shall be the sole qualification; and that to every representative so chosen shall be assigned, out of the public taxes, a fair and adequate remuneration for the time which he is called upon to devote to the public service.

Finally, we would most earnestly impress on your Honorable House, that this petition has not been dictated by any idle love of change; that it springs out of no inconsiderate attachment to fanciful theories; but that it is the result of much and long deliberation, and of convictions, which the events of each succeeding year tend more and more to strengthen.

The management of this mighty kingdom has hitherto been a subject for contending factions to try their selfish experiments upon.

We have felt the consequences in our sorrowful experience — short glimmerings of uncertain enjoyment swallowed up by long and dark seasons of suffering.

If the self-government of the people should not remove their distresses, it will at least remove their repinings.

Universal suffrage will, and it alone can, bring true and lasting peace to the nation; we firmly believe that it will also bring prosperity.

May it therefore please your Honorable House to take this our petition into your most serious consideration; and to use your utmost endeavors, by all constitutional means, to have a law passed, granting to every male of lawful age, sane mind, and unconvicted of crime, the right of voting for members of Parliament; and directing all future elections of members of Parliament to be in the way of secret ballot; and ordaining that the duration of Parliaments so chosen shall in no case exceed one year; and abolishing all property qualifications in the members; and providing for their due remuneration while in attendance on their Parliamentary duties.

READING AND DISCUSSION QUESTIONS

1. What complaints does the People's Petition enumerate?

2. Do the authors of this document seem more concerned with the economic or political outcome of their demands? Support your conclusion with evidence from the document.

3. Explain which of the six specific demands would be relevant to your own life, and which would not.

COMPARATIVE QUESTIONS

1. Compare the societal problems outlined in each document. Which seems the most pressing problem; why? The least pressing? What solutions do they offer?

2. Both the testimonies to the parliamentary committees and the People's Petition reflect attempts by the British government to correct social ills. What seems to be the relationship between the British government and British businesses during the Industrial Revolution?

3. What moral issues do these documents raise? What practical issues? In what issues do morality and practicality intersect?

CHAPTER 23

The Triumph of Nationalism in Europe

1815–1914

Following the defeat of Napoleon and his imperial aspirations, a period of ideological development promised to transform the economic and political foundations of Europe. Born in part out of calls for national mobilization in Revolutionary France, nationalism gained strength as cultural groups began to seek their own political identity as "nation-states." This movement led to uprisings and revolutions, but also strengthened states by standardizing culture and language; mobilizing the populace in concerted economic, military, and civic projects; and creating a sense of internal solidarity. The documents in this chapter reflect the development and communication of national identity and the tensions within such movements, as well as a new ideology that challenged nationalism in favor of a unified working class solidarity.

DOCUMENT 23-1

KARL MARX AND FRIEDRICH ENGELS
From The Communist Manifesto

1848

Published in 1848, the Manifesto of the Communist Party *was commissioned by the Communist League, an early socialist organization that advocated for workers' rights and societal reforms. Party members Karl Marx (1818–1883) and Friedrich Engels (1820–1895) set forth the group's analysis*

Karl Marx and Friedrich Engels, "The Communist Manifesto," in Arthur P. Mendel, *The Essential Works of Marxism* (New York: Bantam, 1961), 13–17, 19, 23, 40–44.

of social conditions under capitalism, their historical basis, and the roles of the bourgeoisie (middle-class property holders) and proletariat (urban workers) in social change. Written in German, the document was translated into English in 1850 but received little attention. In later years, however, Marx's writings spurred great debate in England and around the world.

A specter is haunting Europe — the specter of communism. All the powers of old Europe have entered into a holy alliance to exorcise this specter: Pope and Czar, Metternich and Guizot,[1] French Radicals and German police-spies. . . .

Communism is already acknowledged by all European powers to be itself a power.

It is high time that Communists should openly, in the face of the whole world, publish their views, their aims, their tendencies, and meet this nursery tale of the specter of communism with a Manifesto of the party itself. . . .

The history of all hitherto existing society is the history of class struggles. . . .

Modern industry has established the world market, for which the discovery of America paved the way. This market has given an immense development to commerce, to navigation, to communication by land. This development has, in its turn, reacted on the extension of industry; and in proportion as industry, commerce, navigation, railways extended, in the same proportion the bourgeoisie developed, increased its capital, and pushed into the background every class handed down from the Middle Ages. . . .

The bourgeoisie, historically, has played a most revolutionary part.

The bourgeoisie, wherever it has got the upper hand, has put an end to all feudal, patriarchal, idyllic relations. It has pitilessly torn asunder the motley feudal ties that bound man to his "natural superiors," and has left remaining no other nexus between man and man than naked self-interest, than callous "cash payment." It has drowned the most heavenly ecstasies of religious fervor, of chivalrous enthusiasm, of philistine sentimentalism, in the icy water of egotistical calculation. It has resolved personal worth into exchange value, and in place of the numberless indefeasible chartered

---

[1] **Metternich and Guizot**: Prince Klemens von Metternich (1773–1859) was foreign minister and chancellor of the Austrian Empire (1809–1848); François Guizot (1787–1874) was a French politician who served as prime minister from 1847 to 1848.

freedoms, has set up that single, unconscionable freedom — Free Trade. In a word, for exploitation, veiled by religious and political illusions, it has substituted naked, shameless, direct, brutal exploitation.

The bourgeoisie has stripped of its halo every occupation hitherto honored and looked up to with reverent awe. It has converted the physician, the lawyer, the priest, the poet, and the man of science into its paid wage-laborers.

The bourgeoisie has torn away from the family its sentimental veil and has reduced the family relation to a mere money relation. . . .

The bourgeoisie has subjected the country to the rule of the towns. It has created enormous cities, greatly increased the urban population as compared with the rural, and thus rescued a considerable part of the population from the idiocy of rural life. . . .

The bourgeoisie, during its rule of scarcely one hundred years, has created more massive and more colossal productive forces than have all preceding generations together. . . .

But not only has the bourgeoisie forged the weapons that bring death to itself; it has also called into existence the men who are to wield those weapons — the modern working class — the proletariat.

In proportion as the bourgeoisie, i.e., capital, develops, in the same proportion the proletariat, the modern working class, develops — a class of laborers, who live only so long as they find work, and who find work only so long as their labor increases capital. These laborers, who must sell themselves piecemeal, are a commodity, like every other article of commerce, and are consequently exposed to all the vicissitudes of competition, to all the fluctuations of the market. . . .

Of all the classes that stand face to face with the bourgeoisie today, the proletariat alone is a really revolutionary class. The other classes decay and finally disappear in the face of modern industry; the proletariat is its special and essential product. . . .

The socialist and communist systems properly so called, those of Saint-Simon, Fourier, Owen[2] and others, spring into existence in the early undeveloped period, described above, of the struggle between proletariat and bourgeoisie. . . .

Such fantastic pictures of future society, painted at a time when the proletariat is still in a very undeveloped state and has but a fantastic

---

[2] **Saint-Simon, Fourier, Owen**: French utopian socialists Henri de Saint-Simon (1760–1825) and Charles Fourier (1772–1837) and Welsh utopian socialist Robert Owen (1771–1858) believed that capitalists and workers could overcome their antagonism and work cooperatively for the common good.

conception of its own position, correspond with the first instinctive yearnings of that class for a general reconstruction of society.

But these socialist and communist publications contain also a critical element. They attack every principle of existing society. . . .

The Communists fight for the attainment of the immediate aims, for the enforcement of the momentary interests of the working class; but in the movement of the present, they also represent and take care of the future of that movement. . . .

The Communists turn their attention chiefly to Germany, because that country is on the eve of a bourgeois revolution that is bound to be carried out under more advanced conditions of European civilization, and with a much more developed proletariat, than that of England was in the seventeenth, and of France in the eighteenth century, and because the bourgeois revolution in Germany will be but the prelude to an immediately following proletarian revolution.

In short, the Communists everywhere support every revolutionary movement against the existing social and political order of things.

In all these movements they bring to the fore, as the leading question in each, the property question, no matter what its degree of development at the time.

Finally, they labor everywhere for the union and agreement of the democratic parties of all countries.

The Communists disdain to conceal their views and aims. They openly declare that their ends can be attained only by the forcible overthrow of all existing social conditions. Let the ruling classes tremble at a Communistic revolution. The proletarians have nothing to lose but their chains. They have a world to win.

WORKING MEN OF ALL COUNTRIES, UNITE!

READING AND DISCUSSION QUESTIONS

1. Evaluate the actions of the bourgeoisie described by Marx and Engels. Which actions seem positive and which seem negative? What do Engels and Marx mean when they say that the bourgeoisie has "played a most revolutionary part" in history?

2. According to Marx and Engels, what is the purpose of their manifesto? How successful is it in achieving that purpose?

DOCUMENT 23-2

HEINRICH VON TREITSCHKE

From History of Germany in the Nineteenth Century *and* Historical and Political Writings

1879, 1896

Prussian historian and politician Heinrich von Treitschke (1834–1896) was an important voice in the establishment of German national consciousness. Active as both a writer and a member of the German Reichstag, or parliament, Treitschke called for the unification of German states and the aggressive pursuit of colonial territories. His History of Germany in the Nineteenth Century *reflects the importance of historical narrative in nationalist movements. It also conveys the themes of the importance of an all-encompassing state, the value of war, and the superiority of the German national character. Treitschke's writings, including those excerpted below, fueled nationalistic pride among the German people.*

ON THE GERMAN CHARACTER

Depth of thought, idealism, cosmopolitan views; a transcendent philosophy which boldly oversteps (or freely looks over) the separating barriers of finite existence, familiarity with every human thought and feeling, the desire to traverse the world-wide realm of ideas in common with the foremost intellects of all nations and all times. All that has at all times been held to be characteristic of the Germans and has always been praised as the essence of German character and breeding.

The simple loyalty of the Germans contrasts remarkably with the lack of chivalry in the English character. This seems to be due to the fact that in England physical culture is sought, not in the exercise of noble arms, but in sports like boxing, swimming, and rowing, sports which undoubtedly have their value, but which obviously tend to encourage a brutal and purely athletic point of view, and the single and superficial ambition of getting a first prize.

Heinrich von Treitschke, *History of Germany in the Nineteenth Century* and *Historical and Political Writings*, in Louis Snyder, ed., *Documents of German History* (Piscataway, NJ: Rutgers University Press, 1958), 259–262.

On the State

The state is a moral community, which is called upon to educate the human race by positive achievement. Its ultimate object is that a nation should develop in it, a nation distinguished by a real national character. To achieve this state is the highest moral duty for nation and individual alike. All private quarrels must be forgotten when the state is in danger.

At the moment when the state cries out that its very life is at stake, social selfishness must cease and party hatred be hushed. The individual must forget his egoism, and feel that he is a member of the whole body.

The most important possession of a state, its be-all and end-all, is power. He who is not man enough to look this truth in the face should not meddle in politics. The state is not physical power as an end in itself, it is power to protect and promote the higher interests. Power must justify itself by being applied for the greatest good of mankind. It is the highest moral duty of the state to increase its power. . . .

Only the truly great and powerful states ought to exist. Small states are unable to protect their subjects against external enemies; moreover, they are incapable of producing genuine patriotism or national pride and are sometimes incapable of Kultur [culture] in great dimensions. Weimar produced a Goethe and a Schiller[3]; still these poets would have been greater had they been citizens of a German national state.

On Monarchy

The will of the state is, in a monarchy, the expression of the will of one man who wears the crown by virtue of the historic right of a certain family; with him the final authority rests. Nothing in a monarchy can be done contrary to the will of the monarch. In a democracy, plurality, the will of the people, expresses the will of the state. A monarchy excels any other form of government, including the democratic, in achieving unity and power in a nation. It is for this reason that monarchy seems so natural, and that it makes such an appeal to the popular understanding. We Germans had an experience of this in the first years of our new empire.[4] How wonderfully the idea of a united Fatherland was embodied for us in the person of the venerable Emperor! How much it meant to us that we could feel once more: "That man is Germany; there is no doubting it!"

---

[3] **a Goethe and a Schiller**: Johann Wolfgang von Goethe (1749–1832) and Johann von Schiller (1759–1805) were poets and dramatists who lived in Weimar.

[4] **our new empire**: When Germany became a unified state in 1871, the king of Prussia, William I, became emperor of Germany.

On War

The idea of perpetual peace is an illusion supported only by those of weak character. It has always been the weary, spiritless, and exhausted ages which have played with the dream of perpetual peace. A thousand touching portraits testify to the sacred power of the love which a righteous war awakes in noble nations. It is altogether impossible that peace be maintained in a world bristling with arms, and even God will see to it that war always recurs as a drastic medicine for the human race. Among great states the greatest political sin and the most contemptible is feebleness. . . .

War is elevating because the individual disappears before the great conception of the state. The devotion of the members of a community to each other is nowhere so splendidly conspicuous as in war.

Modern wars are not waged for the sake of goods and resources. What is at stake is the sublime moral good of national honor, which has something in the nature of unconditional sanctity, and compels the individual to sacrifice himself for it. . . .

The grandeur of war lies in the utter annihilation of puny man in the great conception of the State, and it brings out the full magnificence of the sacrifice of fellow-countrymen for one another. In war the chaff is winnowed from the wheat. Those who have lived through 1870 cannot fail to understand Niebuhr's[5] description of his feelings in 1813, when he speaks of how no one who has entered into the joy of being bound by a common tie to all his compatriots, gentle and simple alike, can ever forget how he was uplifted by the love, the friendliness, and the strength of that mutual sentiment.

It is war which fosters the political idealism which the materialist rejects. What a disaster for civilization it would be if mankind blotted its heroes from memory. The heroes of a nation are the figures which rejoice and inspire the spirit of its youth, and the writers whose words ring like trumpet blasts become the idols of our boyhood and our early manhood. He who feels no answering thrill is unworthy to bear arms for his country. To appeal from this judgment to Christianity would be sheer perversity, for does not the Bible distinctly say that the ruler shall rule by the sword, and again that greater love hath no man than to lay down his life for his friend? To Aryan[6] races, who are before all things courageous, the foolish

---

[5]**Niebuhr**: Prussian civil servant and historian Barthold Georg Niebuhr (1776–1831) lectured for a time at the University of Berlin and is best known for his three-volume history of Rome.

[6]**Aryan**: The Aryans migrated from Central Asia to Europe and India in the distant past. In the racial mythology of Hitler and the Nazis (see Documents 29-3 and 30-2), the Aryans provided Europe's original racial stock.

preaching of everlasting peace has always been in vain. They have always been man enough to maintain with the sword what they have attained through the spirit. . . .

On the English

The hypocritical Englishman, with the Bible in one hand and a pipe of opium[7] in the other, possesses no redeeming qualities. The nation was an ancient robber-knight, in full armor, lance in hand, on every one of the world's trade routes.

The English possess a commercial spirit, a love of money which has killed every sentiment of honor and every distinction of right and wrong. English cowardice and sensuality are hidden behind unctuous, theological fine talk which is to us free-thinking German heretics among all the sins of English nature the most repugnant. In England all notions of honor and class prejudices vanish before the power of money, whereas the German nobility has remained poor but chivalrous. That last indispensable bulwark against the brutalization of society — the duel — has gone out of fashion in England and soon disappeared, to be supplanted by the riding whip.[8] This was a triumph of vulgarity. The newspapers, in their accounts of aristocratic weddings, record in exact detail how much each wedding guest has contributed in the form of presents or in cash; even the youth of the nation have turned their sports into a business, and contend for valuable prizes, whereas the German students wrought havoc on their countenances [i.e., been scarred in duels] for the sake of a real or imaginary honor.

On Jews

The Jews at one time played a necessary role in German history, because of their ability in the management of money. But now that the Aryans have become accustomed to the idiosyncrasies of finance, the Jews are no longer necessary. The international Jew, hidden in the mask of different nationalities, is a disintegrating influence; he can be of no further use to the world. It is necessary to speak openly about the Jews, undisturbed by the fact that the Jewish press befouls what is purely historical truth.

---

[7] **the Bible in one hand . . . opium**: Treitschke views the British as hypocritical — professed Christians who sell opium to the Chinese.
[8] **last indispensable bulwark . . . whip**: Aristocratic males frequently settled disputes concerning their honor by dueling. To Treitschke, dueling was more honorable than other pursuits, such as riding and hunting.

READING AND DISCUSSION QUESTIONS

1. How does Treitschke describe the German character? How does he characterize the English and the Jews to make his points? How might these descriptions appeal to a German reader?

2. What is Treitschke's argument about the state and the monarch? How does he view the individual German citizen?

3. What does Treitschke say about war and peace? What reasons does he give for waging war? Do you agree or disagree with his explanation; why?

DOCUMENT 23-3

LEO PINSKER

From Auto-Emancipation: *The Case for a Jewish Homeland*

1882

Physician and activist Leo (or Leon) Pinsker (1821–1891) was initially an advocate of Jewish assimilation into European society. Later, disenchanted by violent Russian anti-Semitism, he became a leader of the group Lovers of Zion (Hovevei Zion), which pushed for a homeland for Jewish people where a transformation of Jewish social, economic, and cultural life could take place. His pamphlet Auto-Emancipation, *written in 1882, offered both philosophical support and practical proposals for the establishment of such a homeland and the Zionist movement. It added significantly to the growing international attention to Jewish nationalism.*

> "If I am not for myself, who will be for me?
> And if not now, when?"
>
> — Hillel[9]

Leon Pinsker, *Auto-Emancipation: An Appeal to His People, By a Russian Jew*, trans. Dr. D. S. Blondheim, Federation of American Zionists, 1916 (Masada: Youth Zionist Organization of America, 1939).

[9] **Hillel**: A Jewish scholar and leader active in the first century B.C.E., and one of the fathers of Jewish law.

That hoary problem, subsumed under the Jewish question, today, as ever in the past, provokes discussion. Like the squaring of the circle it remains unsolved, but unlike it, continues to be the ever-burning question of the day. That is because the problem is not one of mere theoretical interest: it renews and revives in every-day life and presses ever more urgently for solution.

This is the kernel of the problem, as we see it: the Jews comprise a distinctive element among the nations under which they dwell, and as such can neither assimilate nor be readily digested by any nation.

Hence the solution lies in finding a means of so readjusting this exclusive element to the family of nations, that the basis of the Jewish question it will be permanently removed. . . .

A fear of the Jewish ghost has passed down the generations and the centuries. First a breeder of prejudice, later in conjunction with other forces we are about to discuss, it culminated in Judeophobia.

Judeophobia, together with other symbols, superstitions, and idiosyncrasies, has acquired legitimacy among all the peoples of the earth with whom the Jews had intercourse. Judeophobia is a variety of demonopathy[10] with the distinction that it is not peculiar to particular races but is common to the whole of mankind, and that this ghost is not disembodied like other ghosts but partakes of flesh and blood, must endure pain inflicted by the fearful mob that imagines itself endangered.

Judeophobia is a psychic aberration. As a psychic aberration it is hereditary, and as a disease transmitted for two thousand years it is incurable. . . .

The Jews are aliens who can have no representatives, because they have no country. Because they have none, because their home has no boundaries within which they can be entrenched, their misery too is boundless. The general law does not apply to the Jews as true aliens, but there are everywhere laws for the Jews, and if the general law is to apply to them, a special and explicit by-law is required to confirm it. Like the Negroes, like women, and unlike all free peoples, they must be emancipated. If, unlike the Negroes, they belong to an advanced race, and if, unlike women, they can produce not only women of distinction, but also distinguished men, even men of greatness, then it is very much the worse for them.

---

[10] **demonopathy**: A mental disorder in which the victim believes that he or she is possessed by a demon. Pinsker is comparing Judeophobia to mental illness, not to the belief in possession.

Since the Jew is nowhere at home, nowhere regarded as a native, he remains an alien everywhere. That he himself and his ancestors as well are born in the country does not alter this fact in the least.

In the great majority of cases, he is treated as a stepchild, as a Cinderella; in the most favorable cases he is regarded as an adopted child whose rights may be questioned; never is he considered a legitimate child of the fatherland.

The German proud of his Teutonism [distinctly German character], the Slav, the Celt, not one of them admits that the Semitic Jew is his equal by birth; and even if he be ready, as a man of culture, to admit him to all civil rights, he will never quite forget that his fellow-citizen is a Jew. The legal emancipation of the Jews is the culminating achievement of our century. But legal emancipation is not social emancipation, and with the proclamation of the former the Jews are still far from being emancipated from their exceptional social position. . . .

This degrading dependence of the ever alien Jew upon the non-Jew is reinforced by another factor, which makes amalgamation of the Jews with the original inhabitants of a land absolutely impossible. In the great struggle for existence, civilized peoples readily submit to laws which help to transform their struggle into a peaceful competition, a noble emulation. In this respect a distinction is usually made between the native and the foreigner, the first, of course, always receiving the preference. Now, if this distinction is drawn even against the foreigner of equal birth, how harshly is it applied to the ever alien Jew! The beggar who dares to cast longing eyes upon a country not his own is in the position of a young virgin's suitor, guarded against him by jealous relatives! And if he nevertheless prosper and succeed in plucking a flower here and there from its soil, woe to the ill-fated man! He must expect the fate of the Jews of Spain and Russia.

The Jews, moreover, do not suffer only when they meet with notable success. Wherever they are congregated in large numbers, they must, by their very preponderance, hold an advantage in competition with the non-Jewish population. Thus, in the western provinces [of Russia] we see the Jews squeezed together, leading a wretched existence in dreadful poverty, while charges of Jewish exploitation are continually pressed.

To sum up then, to the living the Jew is a corpse, to the native a foreigner, to the homesteader a vagrant, to the proprietary a beggar, to the poor an exploiter and a millionaire, to the patriot a man without a country, for all a hated rival. . . .

If we already knew where to direct our steps, were we compelled to emigrate again, we could surely make a vast step forward. We must set vigorously to work to complete the great task of self-liberation. We must use all the resources which human intellect and human experience have devised, instead of leaving our national regeneration to blind chance. The territory to be acquired must be fertile, well-situated, and sufficiently extensive to allow the settlement of several millions. The land, as national property, must be inalienable. Its selection is, of course, of the first and highest importance, and must not be left to off-hand decision or to certain preconceived sympathies of individuals, as has alas, happened lately. This land must be uniform and continuous in extent, for it lies in the very nature of our problem that we must possess as a counterpoise to our disposition one single refuge, since a number of refuges would again be equivalent to our old dispersion. Therefore, the selection of a permanent, national land, meeting all requirements, must be made with every precaution and confided to one single body, through a committee of experts selected from our directorate. Only such a supreme tribunal will be able, after thorough and comprehensive investigation, to give an opinion and decide upon which of the two continents and upon which territory in them our final choice should fall. Only then, and not before, should the directorate, together with an associated body of capitalists, as founders of a stock company later to be organized, acquire a tract of land sufficient for the settlement, in the course of time, of several million Jews. This tract might form a small territory in North America, or a sovereign Pashalik [jurisdiction of a Pasha] in Asiatic Turkey recognized by the [Ottoman] Porte and the other Powers as neutral. It would certainly be an important duty of the directorate to secure the assent of the Porte, and probably of the other European cabinets to this plan. Under the supervision of the directorate, the land purchased would have to be divided by surveyors into small parcels, which could be assigned according to the local conditions to agricultural, building, or manufacturing purposes. Every parcel laid off thus (for agricultural, house and garden, town-hall, factory, etc.) would form a lot which would be transferred to the purchaser in accordance with his wishes.

After a complete survey and the publication of detailed maps and a comprehensive description of the land, a part of the lots would be sold to Jews for an adequate payment at a price, exactly fixed in proportion to the original purchase price, perhaps a little above it. Part of the proceeds of the sale, together with the profits, would belong to the stock company, and part would flow into a fund to be administered by the directorate, for the maintenance of destitute immigrants. For the establishment of this fund the directorate could also open a national subscription. It is definitely to be expected that our brethren everywhere would hail with joy such an appeal for subscriptions and that the most liberal donations would be made for so sacred a purpose.

Each title-deed delivered to the purchaser, with his name entered and signed by the directorate and the company, must bear the exact number of the lot upon the general map so that each purchaser would know exactly the location of the piece of ground — field, or building lot — which he purchases as his individual property.

Assuredly, many a Jew, who is still bound to his old home by an unenviable occupation, would gladly grasp the opportunity to throw out an anchor to windward by such a deed and to escape those sad experiences so numerous in the immediate past.

That part of the territory which would be assigned to the directorate for free distribution, against the national subscription mentioned and the expected profits, would be given to destitute but able-bodied immigrants, recommended by local committees.

Since the donations to the national subscription would not come in at once, but say in annual contributions, the colonization, also, would be carried out gradually and in a fixed order.

If the experts find in favor of Palestine or Syria, this decision would not be based on the assumption that the country could be transformed in time by labor and industry into a quite productive one. In this event the price of land would rise in proportion. But should they prefer North America, however, we must hasten. If one considers that in the last thirty-eight years the population of the United States of America has risen from seventeen millions to fifty millions, and that the increase in population for the next forty years will probably continue in the same proportion, it is evident that immediate action is necessary, if we do not desire to eliminate for all time the possibility of establishing in the New World a secure refuge for our unhappy brethren.

Every one who has the slightest judgment can see at first glance that the purchase of lands in America would, because of the swift rise of that country, not be a risky, but a lucrative enterprise.

Whether this act of national self-help on our part might turn out profitably or otherwise, however, is of little consequence as compared with the great significance which such an undertaking would have for the future of our unsettled people; for our future will remain insecure and precarious unless a radical change in our position is made. This change cannot be brought about by the civil emancipation of the Jews in this or that state, but only by the auto-emancipation of the Jewish people as a nation, the foundation of a colonial community belonging to the Jews, which is some day to become our inalienable home, our country.

There will certainly be plenty of counter-arguments. We will be charged with reckoning without our host. What land will grant us permission to settle a nation within its borders? At first glance, our building would appear from this standpoint to be a house of cards to divert children and wits. We think, however, that only thoughtless childhood could be diverted by the sight of shipwrecked voyagers who desire to build a little boat in order to leave inhospitable shores. We even go as far as to say that we expect, strangely enough, that those inhospitable people will aid us in our departure. Our "friends" will see us leave with the same pleasure with which we turn our back upon them.

Of course, the establishment of a Jewish refuge cannot come about without the support of the governments. In order to obtain the latter and to insure the perpetual existence of a refuge, the molders of our national regeneration must proceed with caution and perseverance. What we seek is at bottom neither new nor dangerous to anyone. Instead of the many refuges which we have always been accustomed to seek, we would fain have one single refuge, the existence of which, however, would have to be politically assured.

Let "Now or never" be our watchword. Woe to our descendants, woe to the memory of our Jewish contemporaries, if we let this moment pass by!

The Jews are not a living nation: they are everywhere aliens; therefore they are despised.

The civil and political emancipation of the Jews is not sufficient to raise them in the estimation of the peoples.

The proper, the only solution, is in the creation of a Jewish nationality, of a people living upon its own soil, the auto-emancipation of the Jews; their return to the ranks of the nations by the acquisition of a Jewish homeland.

We must not persuade ourselves that humanity and enlightenment alone can cure the malady of our people.

The lack of national self-respect and self-confidence of political initiative and of unity, are the enemies of our national renaissance.

That we may not be compelled to wander from one exile to another, we must have an extensive, productive land of refuge, a center which is our own. The present moment is the most favorable for this plan.

The international Jewish question must have a national solution. Of course, our national regeneration can only proceed slowly. We must take the first step. Our descendants must follow us at a measured and not over-precipitant speed.

The national regeneration of the Jews must be initiated by a congress of Jewish notables. No sacrifice should be too great for this enterprise which will assure our people's future, everywhere endangered.

The financial execution of the undertaking does not present insur-mountable difficulties.

Help yourselves, and God will help you!

READING AND DISCUSSION QUESTIONS

1. What does Pinsker present as the essential problem faced by Jews?

2. According to Pinsker, what is the effect of not having a Jewish home-land? How does he describe the Jewish nation?

3. Pinsker gives a detailed set of recommendations for the establishment of a Jewish homeland. What are they? Where does he want to locate this homeland, and what reasons does he give for this location?

DOCUMENT 23-4

THEODOR HERZL

From The Jews' State

1896

No one is more prominently associated with the Zionist movement than journalist, playwright, and activist Theodor Herzl (1860–1904). Born in Pest (now part of Budapest, Hungary), Herzl's activism was inspired by the anti-Semitism of the Dreyfus affair. He believed that a separate Jewish state was necessary for the survival of the Jewish people, and his commitment to

Theodor Herzl, "The Jews' State," in Henk Overberg, ed. and trans., *The Jews' State* (Amsterdam: Jason Aronson, Inc., 1977), 123, 129, 130, 134, 135, 139, 140, 144–146, 148, 149, 196.

Zionism brought him into contact with various world leaders and govern-ment figures. He became president of the Zionist Organization, founded the weekly newspaper Die Welt, *and authored the political tract* The Jews' State *and the novel* The Old-New Land *(1902), both of which articulated his vision for Zionism.*

Preamble and Introduction

The concept with which I am dealing in this paper is very old. It is the establishment of the Jews' State.

The world resounds with clamor against Jews, and that arouses this concept out of its sleep. . . .

I consider the issue of the Jews neither in social nor religious terms, even though these things do come into it. It is a national issue, and if we are to find a solution, we must make it a political question for the whole world, to be tackled in counsel with all civilized peoples.

We are a people, one people.

We have tried everywhere in all honesty to assimilate into the com-munities around us, while preserving the faith of our fathers. We are not allowed to. We are faithful and often even over-enthusiastic patriots — in vain. We make the same sacrifices in life and limb as our countrymen — in vain. We do our utmost to further the reputation of our home countries in the fields of arts and science — in vain. We toil to increase the wealth of our lands with our commerce and trade — in vain. In our home countries, where we have been living for centuries, we are decried as foreign, often by those whose forebears were not even living there when our forebears were already being persecuted. . . . Therefore we are good patriots every-where in vain, just like the Huguenots,[11] who were forced to go elsewhere. If they only left us in peace. . . .

But I believe they will not leave us in peace.

For deep down within the feelings of peoples there are old prejudices anchored against us. If you want evidence, you only need to listen where the people express themselves simply and truthfully: folktales and proverbs are antisemitic. . . .

The collective personality of the Jews as a people, however, cannot, will not, and must not perish. It cannot perish, because external enemies hold it together. It will not perish; it has demonstrated that during two

---

[11] **Huguenots:** Protestants in predominantly Catholic France whose grant of religious toleration was revoked by Louis XIV in 1685. Many Huguenots left France and settled in England, the Netherlands, and Prussia.

millennia under enormous suffering. It must not perish; that is what I seek to demonstrate in this publication after many other Jews who never gave up hope. Whole branches of Jewry may well die away and fall off; the tree lives. . . .

No one person has sufficient strength or wealth to transplant a whole people from one domicile to another. Only an idea is powerful enough to do that. The idea of the state has such power. For the whole night of their history Jews have not stopped dreaming the royal dream. "Next year in Jerusalem" is our ancient watchword. The question now is to demonstrate that the dream can be turned into an idea as bright as day. . . .

THE ISSUE OF THE JEWS

Day by day, attacks on Jews increase in the parliaments, at meetings, in the press, on the pulpit, in the street; when they travel, they are denied entry into hotels or places of amusement. The character of these persecutions varies, depending on country or social circle. In Russia they plunder Jewish villages, in Rumania they beat a few people to death, in Germany Jews are on the receiving end of a good thrashing now and again, in Austria public life is terrorized by antisemites, in Algeria there are preachers roaming the countryside extolling hatred, in Paris high society closes ranks and shuts itself off against Jews. The variety is endless. However, this is not an attempt to provide a melancholy list of all Jewish hardships. We will not worry about details, however painful.

It is not my intention to create an atmosphere sympathetic to us. All that would be useless, in vain, and unworthy of us. For me it is sufficient to ask the Jews: is it not a fact that in countries where we live in significant numbers, the position of Jewish lawyers, doctors, technicians, teachers, and all types of public servants is becoming increasingly unbearable? Is it not a fact that our whole Jewish middle class is under serious threat? Is it not a fact that all the passions of the lower classes are being marshaled against our wealthy people? Is it not a fact that the poor among us suffer much more than the rest of the proletariat? . . .

The fact is that it amounts to the same thing everywhere, and it can be summarized in the classic slogan of the Berliners: Away with the Jews!

I will now express the issue of the Jews in its most concise form: if we must be away, then where to?

Or can we still stay put? And for how long?

Let us first tackle the question of staying put. Can we hope for better times, can we be patient, put our faith in God and wait until the rulers and peoples of the world get into a more benign mood towards us? I say we cannot expect a turnaround in the general trend. Why not? Kings and emperors cannot protect us, even if they wished to treat us equally. They would only inflame hatred against the Jews if they showed the Jews too much sympathy. And this "too much sympathy" would at any rate still amount to less than what is normally due to every normal citizen or social group.

The peoples with whom Jews live are all anti-semites, without exception, discreetly or brazenly. . . .

EFFECTS OF ANTI-SEMITISM

The pressure exerted upon us does not make us any better. We are no different from other human beings. It is quite true that we do not love our enemies. . . . Pressure naturally evokes in us hostility against our oppressors; and then our hostility in turn increases the pressure. It is impossible to break the vicious circle.

"Nevertheless," so the gentle daydreamers will say, "nevertheless, it is possible by working patiently to draw out what is good in people."

Do I really still have to demonstrate that this is just sentimental twaddle? If you wanted to improve your situation by relying on the good will of people, you would certainly be writing a utopian romance.

I have already mentioned our "assimilation." I do not say for a moment that I want it. Our national character is historically too famous and, despite all humiliation, too proud to wish for its demise. But perhaps we could merge without a trace into the peoples around us if we were left in peace for a couple of generations. They will not leave us in peace. After short spells of tolerance the hostility against us awakens anew. There seems to be something in our prosperity that irritates people, because the world has been accustomed to seeing us as the most despised among the poor. At the same time they do not notice, whether from ignorance or narrow-mindedness, that our prosperity weakens us as Jews and dissipates our character. Only pressure keeps us close to the old tribe, only the hatred that surrounds us turns us into strangers. . . .

We are a people — the enemy turns us into one against our wishes — that has been the same throughout history. In oppression we stand together, and then we suddenly discover our power. Yes, we have the power to create a state, even a state that would stand as a model for all. We possess all the necessary human and material means.

THE PLAN

In its basic form the whole plan is infinitely simple: it just has to be if it is to be understood by everyone.

We should be given sovereignty over a piece of the earth's surface sufficient for the legitimate needs of our people. We will look after everything else. . . .

As I have already said, the departure of the Jews should not be seen as a sudden phenomenon. It will occur gradually and will take decades. First the poorest Jews will go and make the land arable. In accordance with a previously developed concept they will build the streets, bridges, and railways, they will construct the telegraph system, they will regulate the rivers and build homes for themselves. Their work will lead to business, business will bring markets, markets will entice new immigrants to come. Everyone will come of their own free will, and bear their own costs and risks. . . . Jews will not take long to realize that a new and lasting target has been opened up for their spirit of enterprise, for which hitherto they have been hated and despised. . . .

If the Great Powers are prepared to grant the Jews as a people sovereignty over a neutral land, then the Society will enter into negotiations about the land which is to be selected. Two regions will be considered: Palestine and Argentina. . . .

In terms of natural resources Argentina is one of the wealthiest countries in the world, enormous in size, sparsely populated, and with a moderate climate. It would be in the interest of the Argentinian republic to cede us a piece of territory. Unfortunately, the present infiltration of Jews has created ill feeling there; we would have to explain to Argentina the fundamental difference of the new Jewish migration.

Palestine is our unforgettable historical home. This very name would already be an enormously powerful rallying cry for our people. If His Majesty the Sultan were to give us Palestine,[12] we could undertake the responsibility of putting the finances of Turkey completely in order. To Europe we would represent a part of the barrier against Asia; we would serve as the outpost of civilization against barbarism. As a neutral state we would remain allied to all of Europe, which in turn would have to guarantee our existence. An internationally acceptable arrangement would be found to guarantee the extra-territorial status of the holy places of Christendom. We would form the guard of honor around the holy places, and guarantee the execution of this duty with our very existence. This guard of honor would be the great symbol of the solution of the issue of the Jews after eighteen centuries of agony.

---

[12] **Palestine**: A province of the Ottoman Empire at this time.

THE TRANSPLANT

Up to now we have simply indicated how the emigration is to be effected without economic upheaval. However, such an emigration is also associated with strong, deep, personal disorientation. There are old customs, and memories which tie us people to specific places. We have cradles, we have graves, and we know the place of graves in the hearts of Jews. The cradles we will take with us — in them slumbers our smiling and rosy future. Our dear graves will have to be left behind — I believe this separation will weigh heavily on our possessive people. But it must be.

Economic distress, political oppression, and social hatred already separate us from our home towns and from our graves. Jews already leave one country for the next at every moment; a strong movement even leads overseas to the United States, where we are not welcome either. Where will we ever be welcome, so long as we do not have a country to call our own?

We, however, want to give the Jews a home country. Not by tearing them forcibly out of their present land. No, by lifting them carefully with all their roots and transplanting them into a better soil. Just as we want to create new conditions in the economic and political sphere, we will respect the sanctity of old ways in the cultural sphere. . . .

THEOCRACY

Will we end up having a theocracy? No! Faith will hold us together, science makes us free. We will not even allow the theocratic inclinations of our spiritual leaders to raise their ugly heads. We will know how to keep them in their temples, just as we will know how to keep our professional army in the barracks. Army and clerics will be highly honored, as much as is right and proper in the light of their beautiful functions. They have no say in the state which treats them with deference, for they will only conjure up external and internal difficulties.

Everybody is as free and unfettered in practicing his belief or unbelief as he is in his nationality. And should it come to pass that persons of other faiths or nationalities live among us, then we will accord them honorable protection and equality before the law. Tolerance we have learnt in Europe, and I am not even being sarcastic when I say this. Only in a few isolated instances can you equate modern antisemitism with the old religious intolerance. It is in most cases a movement among the civilized peoples, with which they want to ward off a ghost from their own past.

READING AND DISCUSSION QUESTIONS

1. How does Herzl describe the condition of Jews around the world? What examples does he cite?

2. Herzl presents his plan in some detail. Where does he propose to locate the Jewish homeland, and why there? How will Jews be convinced to leave their homes and relocate to the new Jewish state?

3. Herzl argues that the new state would not be a theocracy, but a tolerant environment. Why do you think he felt it necessary to make this point? To what extent is his proposal specifically pertinent to the Jewish people, and to what extent could it apply to any people suffering from prejudice and discrimination?

COMPARATIVE QUESTIONS

1. Which of the documents in this chapter seems most directly concerned with nationalism? Use evidence from the documents to support your assertion.

2. How do Treitschke and Herzl define nationalism? Based on their definitions, would you consider *The Communist Manifesto* to be a nationalistic document? Why or why not?

3. What differences within the Zionist movement can you discern from reading the documents by Pinsker and Herzl? Compare their arguments regarding unity.

4. Compare the ways that Marx and Engels and Treitschke address diversity of opinion.

CHAPTER 24

Africa, Southwest Asia, and Western Imperialism

1800–1914

T he rise of industrial economies in Europe drove European nations to expand their empires in Africa and Asia. In search of markets, resources, and occasionally adventure, Europeans gained control of an increasingly large part of the globe by way of commerce and colonization. At the same time, states like the Ottoman Empire mixed Western European notions of civilization with their own cultures to develop alternative versions of a "modern society." The documents in this chapter present different perspectives on the global processes of modernization and Westernization: one from an African who fought and then submitted to British colonial rule, and two from the Ottoman Empire's government as it sought to draw on modern Western ideas to reform and strengthen its state. All three documents offer insight on how non-Western peoples adapted and endured as nationalism, progress, and empire changed their worlds.

DOCUMENT 24-1

SULTAN ABDUL MEJID

Imperial Rescript

1856

Building on the work of previous rulers to enact military and administrative reforms, many of which were inspired by modern Western institutions, Sultan Abdul Mejid or Abdulmecid (r. 1839–1861) instituted a period of

E. A. Van Dyck, *Report upon the Capitulations of the Ottoman Empire since the Year 1150*, pt. 1 (Washington, D.C : U.S. Government Printing Office, 1881, 1882), 106–108.

"reorganization," or Tanzimat, *in the aging Ottoman Empire. Various non-Turkish groups had been pulling away from Ottoman rule since the early 1800s, and large-scale violence against non-Muslim subjects was not uncommon. In this Imperial Rescript, or official proclamation, the sultan affirms his policy of "Ottomanism," or equal treatment of all citizens without regard to race, language, or religion. Ottomanism may be seen as a doomed and even hypocritical attempt to reassert central authority; however, the rescript represented real reform in Ottoman society.*

Let it be done as herein set forth. . . . It being now my desire to renew and enlarge still more the new Institutions ordained with the view of establishing a state of things conformable with the dignity of my Empire and — . . . by the kind and friendly assistance of the Great Powers, my noble Allies.[1] . . . The guarantees promised on our part by the Hatti-Humaïoun of Gülhané,[2] and in conformity with the Tanzimat, . . . are today confirmed and consolidated, and efficacious measures shall be taken in order that they may have their full and entire effect.

All the privileges and spiritual immunities granted by my ancestors from time immemorial, and at subsequent dates, to all Christian communities or other non-Muslim persuasions established in my empire, under my protection, shall be confirmed and maintained.

Every Christian or other non-Muslim community shall be bound within a fixed period, and with the concurrence of a commission composed . . . of members of its own body, to proceed with my high approbation and under the inspection of my Sublime Porte,[3] to examine into its actual immunities and privileges, and to discuss and submit to my Sublime Porte the reforms required by the progress of civilization and of the age. The powers conceded to the Christian Patriarchs and Bishops[4] by the Sultan Mehmed II[5] and his successors, shall be made to harmonize with

---

[1] **the Great Powers, my noble allies**: During the Crimean War (1853–1856) the Ottoman Empire fought with Great Britain and France against Russia.

[2] **The guarantees . . . Gülhané**: The Noble Rescript of 1839, also written by Sultan Abdul Mejid, guaranteed personal security, a fair tax system, controlled military conscriptions, and full rights to citizens regardless of faith.

[3] **Sublime Porte**: A building that housed the grand vizier and other high officials of the Ottoman state.

[4] **Christian Patriarchs and Bishops**: Ruling officials of the Greek and Armenian churches in the Ottoman Empire.

[5] **Sultan Mehmed II**: Ottoman ruler from 1451 to 1481.

the new position which my generous and beneficent intentions ensure to these communities. . . . The ecclesiastical dues, of whatever sort of nature they be, shall be abolished and replaced by fixed revenues of the Patriarchs and heads of communities. . . . In the towns, small boroughs, and villages, where the whole population is of the same religion, no obstacle shall be offered to the repair, according to their original plan, of buildings set apart for religious worship, for schools, for hospitals, and for cemeteries. . . .

Every distinction or designation tending to make any class whatever of the subjects of my Empire inferior to another class, on account of their religion, language, or race, shall be forever effaced from Administrative Protocol. The laws shall be put in force against the use of any injurious or offensive term, either among private individuals or on the part of the authorities. . . .

As all forms of religion are and shall be freely professed in my dominions, no subject of my Empire shall be hindered in the exercise of the religion that he professes. . . . No one shall be compelled to change their religion . . . and . . . all the subjects of my Empire, without distinction of nationality, shall be admissible to public employments. . . . All the subjects of my Empire, without distinction, shall be received into the civil and military schools of the government. . . . Moreover, every community is authorized to establish public schools of science, art, and industry. . . .

All commercial, correctional, and criminal suits between Muslims and Christian or other non-Muslim subjects, or between Christian or other non-Muslims of different sects, shall be referred to Mixed Tribunals. The proceedings of these Tribunals shall be public; the parties shall be confronted, and shall produce their witnesses, whose testimony shall be received, without distinction, upon an oath taken according to the religious law of each sect. . . .

Penal, correctional, and commercial laws, and rules of procedure for the Mixed Tribunals, shall be drawn up as soon as possible, and formed into a code. . . . Proceedings shall be taken, for the reform of the penitentiary system. . . .

The organization of the police . . . shall be revised in such a manner as to give to all the peaceable subjects of my Empire the strongest guarantees for the safety both of their persons and property. . . . Christian subjects, and those of other non-Muslim sects, . . . shall, as well as Muslims, be subject to the obligations of the Law of Recruitment [for military service]. The principle of obtaining substitutes, or of purchasing exemption, shall be admitted.

Proceedings shall be taken for a reform in the constitution of the Provincial and Communal Councils, in order to ensure fairness in the choice of the deputies of the Muslim, Christian, and other communities, and freedom of voting in the Councils. . . .

As the laws regulating the purchase, sale, and disposal of real property are common to all the subjects of my Empire, it shall be lawful for foreigners to possess landed property in my dominions. . . .

The taxes are to be levied under the same denomination from all the subjects of my Empire, without distinction of class or of religion. The most prompt and energetic means for remedying the abuses in collecting the taxes, and especially the tithes, shall be considered. The system of direct collection shall gradually, and as soon as possible, be substituted for the plan of farming,[6] in all the branches of the revenues of the state.

A special law having been already passed, which declares that the budget of the revenue and the expenditure of the state shall be drawn up and made known every year, the said law shall be most scrupulously observed. . . .

The heads of each community and a delegate, designated by my Sublime Porte, shall be summoned to take part in the deliberations of the Supreme Council of Justice on all occasions which might interest the generality of the subjects of my Empire. . . .

Steps shall be taken for the formation of banks and other similar institutions, so as to effect a reform in the monetary and financial system, as well as to create funds to be employed in augmenting the sources of the material wealth of my Empire.

Everything that can impede commerce or agriculture shall be abolished. To accomplish these objects means shall be sought to profit by science, the art, and the funds of Europe, and thus gradually to execute them.

READING AND DISCUSSION QUESTIONS

1. What specific measures does the sultan take to ensure religious and ethnic equality? What do these measures imply about life in the Ottoman Empire before the rescript was issued?

---

[6] **farming**: Tax farming, in which the government contracted with private financiers who collected taxes for a profit.

2. The sultan is careful to extend military service to people of all religious and ethnic backgrounds. How does this right compare to rights regarding public employment, education, taxation, and real estate?

3. The rescript mentions communities of Christian and non-Muslim people and villages or small areas where all people share a common religion. What does this imply about the integration of different religious groups in Ottoman society?

4. In explaining the purpose of his rescript, the sultan refers to the "dignity" of his empire and mentions the Ottoman Empire's relationship with European "Great Powers." How do you think the ideas of religious equality, social reform, and international relations and the dignity of the empire work together?

DOCUMENT 24-2

An Ottoman Government Decree on the "Modern" Citizen

1870

In June 1870, this official document was presented to Farhan Pasha, an Istanbul-educated sheikh of the Shammar tribe in what is now Iraq. The document drew on Western notions of "civilization" in order to push the local Bedouin population, a formerly nomadic people, into settled agricultural life. It demonstrates that the Ottoman Empire was challenged by divisions within its Muslim populations as well as those between Muslim and non-Muslim groups. With the rise of ethnic nationalisms in the late 1800s, the rift between Arab and Turkish populations in the Ottoman Empire would widen and further weaken the empire.

To the model of proverbs and peers, His Excellency Firhan Pasha Zayd 'Alwa. It is known that if one compares the tribes and people who live in

Ottoman Government Decree Issued to the Amir of Shamr, His Excellency Firhan Pasha, June 19, 1870, trans. Akram Khater. Ottoman Archives of Directorate General of State Archives at the Prime Ministry (Tapu Tahrir: Mosul, 1869–1872).

the lifestyle of Bedouins [nomadic tribes] with those urbane people who live in the cities and villages, one will note the complexity in the customs of city-folk. In contrast, it will be noted that in comparison to the original creation of man and his internal self, the way of life of Bedouins is simple. In fact, the primitive and original state of man is most likely the same as that of the Bedouin. However, God has graced human beings with a characteristic that is absent from any other [species]. According to this characteristic, man cannot remain in his original state of creation but should prepare all that is needed for his food, drink, and clothing, and after this he must gather knowledge and develop commerce and other human necessities. He seeks to obtain other necessities as well, and every time he reaches a stage of acquisition, then he sees the need to advance and progress beyond what he had in the past. . . . Thus, it is apparent that even if the first state of man is to be a Bedouin, urbanity is a characteristic that cannot be separated from him. For the human being has become civilized . . . and the virtues of humanity cannot be attained except through the path of urbanization and civilization. Those who surpass their brethren and control all elements of this world, completely or partially, are those who live in the cities and who are civilized.

After proving that this is the case, we would like to explain and specify the reasons those people demand to remain in this state [of being Bedouins]. They remain in this state of deprivation of the virtues of humanity and the characteristics of civilization for several reasons. The first is that these people are ignorant of the state of the world and the nations. Because of their ignorance we have found our fathers desiring to stay unchanged in the state to which they were born. Secondly, the basis of the wealth of the tribes and clans is animals — in particular camels — and since it is difficult to manage and raise animals and camels in the cities — where they cannot find pasture — the people remain in their original state of being. . . . The third reason is that the mentioned peoples are like wild animals who enjoy what they have gotten used to in terms of stealing and raiding the property of others of their own people and killing them. This has become a reason for their wildness and their insistence on staying in the state of Bedouinism. It should be obvious that the first reason — which is ignorance and illiteracy — is an ugly and unacceptable characteristic in all the creatures of this world. And the second reason is the subordination [to tradition] characteristic of animals, and it is contrary to the image according to which man was created, for God has created the human being to be the most honorable of all creatures, and He made all breathing creatures subservient to him. He who is a Bedouin has become accustomed to the opposite of this natural order, so that although he used to be over other creatures, he has become subservient.

The truth is that this fallen state is an insult to humanity, and accordingly if we investigate the immense harm these tribes cause to each other, we will find that it has no equivalence in magnitude. For the human being has been commanded to protect those of his kind and treat them well, and is not commanded to do the opposite. In fact, all the religions command this [good treatment of others], and in particular the Mohammedan Shari'a [body of Islamic religious law]. After proving that this is contrary to what has been commanded and is prohibited in all religions and in the Mohammedan Shari'a, then anyone with intelligence will see that harming people and robbing them of their money and their cattle is contrary to humanity and Islam. He who dares to commit that which we have mentioned must be punished. In addition, we see that this implies that since living as a Bedouin . . . leads to these harmful results, then no one should stay in that state of being, especially since we have arrived at a time and epoch . . . where to stay in this fallen and immoral state of existence appears as an ugly habit in the eyes of the world. For these explained reasons, these people cannot stay even for a short period in this state, and these tribes and clans should be settled and gain good human characteristics. It is imperative upon the Sublime Government to facilitate the emergence of these moral characteristics. This is particularly the case since those tribes and clans that have been settled during the past two years have faced difficulties and material needs, and they have remained in their original state because they are deprived of access to agriculture and commerce. Thus, and in order to feed their children, they have dared to attack the fields belonging to the inhabitants of the cities and towns. And in that case the government will have to reimburse the farmers for their losses and to dispatch imperial troops to punish the perpetrators, all of which costs money. Thus, and before matters reach this state, we would advise to give the lands that extend from Tikrit [village in Iraq] to the borders of Mosul [main city in northern Iraq] and that are located east of the Tigris River to the Shamr clan. Furthermore, we recommend that these lands be designated as a Mutassarifiya [provincial government within the Ottoman Empire] and be named as Sandjak [province] of Shamr, and that they [the clan of Shamr] be settled in these lands until they dig the necessary canals to the Tigris and reclaim the lands and plant them like other people. Once it is apparent that they are settled, then this place should be designated as a Mutassarifiya, like the Mutassarifiya of al-Muntafak, and this Mutassarifiya should be placed under your authority, O, Pasha! . . . Because those [people] are used to being Bedouins, and because it will be difficult to sever those ties all at once, then we should grant some of them with animals a permit to pasture their animals on some of the lands, provided that they return to their places of residence. In order to encourage development of these lands, we should exempt those who reclaim the lands and dig the ditches and canals from all but the Miri tax. . . . Once this Sandjak is formed according to what has preceded, and a Mutassarifiya is subsequently established, then troops should be sent to keep the peace, and the Mutassarif should be assigned a deputy and a tax collector and all that he requires in terms of government officials. . . .

This official Ottoman decree has been issued by the ministry of the Vilayet of Baghdad, and let it be known to all.

READING AND DISCUSSION QUESTIONS

1. What is the motivation for this decree? What specific situation does the Ottoman government feel must be remedied?

2. The decree distinguishes between Bedouins and non-Bedouins. What are the assumptions behind these different definitions? Do you agree with them?

3. How does the document use religion to make its argument? How does it use the idea of "civilization"? How do the two ideas work together, or separately, to define both the Bedouin and those who have attained the "virtues of humanity"?

DOCUMENT 24-3

NDANSI KUMALO
On the British Incursion in Zimbabwe
1932

Ndansi Kumalo was a member of the Ndebele people who lived in what is now Zimbabwe, where the Ndebele had settled after years of struggle with

Margery Perham, ed., *Ten Africans* (London: Faber & Faber, 1936).

Zulu and Dutch forces. The Ndebele sovereign Lobengula negotiated with the new wave of British colonizers intent on access to the region's mineral resources, but tensions mounted and conflict broke out in the 1890s. Kumalo, a witness to the British incursion, was hired to play the role of Lobengula in a 1932 British film about the life of colonizer Cecil Rhodes (1853–1902). While filming in England, Kumalo met the African scholar Margery Perham, who recorded the following firsthand account of British colonization.

We were terribly upset and very angry at the coming of the white men, for Lobengula . . . was under her . . . [the Queen's] protection and it was quite unjustified that white men should come with force into our country.[7] . . . Lobengula had no war in his heart: he had always protected the white men and been good to them. If he had meant war, would he have sent our regiments far away to the north at this moment? As far as I know the trouble began in this way. Gandani, a chief who was sent out, reported that some of the Mashona[8] had taken the king's cattle; some regiments were detailed to follow and recover them. They followed the Mashona to Ziminto's people. Gandani had strict instructions not to molest the white people established in certain parts and to confine himself to the people who had taken the cattle. The commander was given a letter which he had to produce to the Europeans and tell them what the object of the party was. But the members of the party were restless and went without reporting to the white people and killed a lot of Mashonas. The pioneers were very angry and said, "You have trespassed into our part." They went with the letter, but only after they had killed some people, and the white men said, "You have done wrong, you should have brought the letter first and then we should have given you permission to follow the cattle." The commander received orders from the white people to get out, and up to a certain point which he could not possibly reach in the time allowed. A force followed them up and they defended themselves. When the pioneers turned out there was a fight at Shangani and at Bembezi. . . .

---

[7] **under her . . . our country:** In an 1888 agreement Lobengula made with Cecil Rhodes, the British government guaranteed there would be no incursion of English settlers on Ndebele land, and that Lobengula's authority would continue. Unhappy with Lobengula's concessions, many Ndebele warriors began to press for war against the Europeans.

[8] **the Mashona:** A people who raised livestock and were ruled by the Ndebele.

The next news was that the white people had entered Bulawayo; the King's kraal [stockade] had been burnt down and the King had fled. Of the cattle very few were recovered; most fell into the hands of the white people. Only a very small portion were found and brought to Shangani where the King was, and we went there to give him any assistance we could. . . . Three of our leaders mounted their horses and followed up the King and he wanted to know where his cattle were; they said they had fallen into the hands of the whites, only a few were left. He said, "Go back and bring them along." But they did not go back again; the white forces had occupied Bulawayo and they went into the Matoppos [hills]. Then the white people came to where we were living and sent word round that all chiefs and warriors should go into Bulawayo and discuss peace, for the King had gone and they wanted to make peace. . . . The white people said, "Now that your King has deserted you, we occupy your country. Do you submit to us?" What could we do? "If you are sincere, come back and bring in all your arms, guns, and spears." We did so. . . .

So we surrendered to the white people and were told to go back to our homes and live our usual lives and attend to our crops. But the white men sent native police who did abominable things; they were cruel and assaulted a lot of our people and helped themselves to our cattle and goats. These policemen were not our own people; anybody was made a police-man. We were treated like slaves. They came and were overbearing and we were ordered to carry their clothes and bundles. They interfered with our wives and our daughters and molested them. In fact, the treatment we received was intolerable. We thought it best to fight and die rather than bear it. How the rebellion started I do not know; there was no organization, it was like a fire that suddenly flames up. We had been flogged by native police and then they rubbed salt water in the wounds. There was much bitterness because so many of our cattle were branded and taken away from us; we had no property, nothing we could call our own. We said, "It is no good living under such conditions; death would be better — let us fight." Our King gone, we had submitted to the white people and they ill-treated us until we became desperate and tried to make an end of it all. We knew that we had very little chance because their weapons were so much superior to ours. But we meant to fight to the last, feeling that even if we could not beat them we might at least kill a few of them and so have some sort of revenge.

I fought in the rebellion. We used to look out for valleys where the white men were likely to approach. We took cover behind rocks and trees and tried to ambush them. We were forced by the nature of our weapons not to expose ourselves. I had a gun, a breech-loader [rear-loading gun]. They — the white men — fought us with big guns and Maxims [early machine guns] and rifles.

I remember a fight in the Matoppos when we charged the white men. There were some hundreds of us; the white men also were as many. We charged them at close quarters: we thought we had a good chance to kill them but the Maxims were too much for us. We drove them off at the first charge, but they returned and formed up again. We made a second charge, but they were too strong for us. I cannot say how many white people were killed, but we think it was quite a lot. . . . Many of our people were killed in this fight: I saw four of my cousins shot. One was shot in the jaw and the whole of his face was blown away — like this — and he died. One was hit between the eyes; another here, in the shoulder; another had part of his ear shot off. We made many charges but each time we were beaten off, until at last the white men packed up and retreated. But for the Maxims, it would have been different. . . .

So peace was made. Many of our people had been killed, and now we began to die of starvation; and then came the rinderpest [an infectious cow disease] and the cattle that were still left to us perished. We could not help thinking that all these dreadful things were brought by the white people. We struggled, and the Government helped us with grain; and by degrees we managed to get crops and pulled through. Our cattle were practically wiped out, but a few were left and from them we slowly bred up our herds again. We were offered work in the mines and farms to earn money and so were able to buy back some cattle. At first, of course, we were not used to going out to work, but advice was given that the chief should advise the young people to go out to work, and gradually they went. At first we received a good price for our cattle and sheep and goats. Then the tax came. It was 10s.[9] a year. Soon the Government said, "That is too little, you must contribute more; you must pay £1." We did so. Then those who took more than one wife were taxed; 10s. for each additional wife. The tax is heavy, but that is not all. We are also taxed for our dogs; 5s. for a dog. Then we were told we were living on private land; the owners wanted rent in addition to the Government tax; some 10s. some £1, some £2 a year. . . .

Would I like to have the old days back? Well, the white men have brought some good things. For a start, they brought us European implements — plows; we can buy European clothes, which are an advance. The

---

[9] **10s.**: Ten shillings.

Government has arranged for education and through that, when our children grow up, they may rise in status. We want them to be educated and civilized and make better citizens. Even in our own time there were troubles, there was much fighting and many innocent people were killed. It is infinitely better to have peace instead of war, and our treatment generally by the officials is better than it was at first. But, under the white people, we still have our troubles. Economic conditions are telling on us very severely. We are on land where the rainfall is scanty, and things will not grow well. In our own time we could pick our own country, but now all the best land has been taken by the white people. We get hardly any price for our cattle; we find it hard to meet our money obligations. If we have crops to spare we get very little for them; we find it difficult to make ends meet and wages are very low. When I view the position, I see that our rainfall has diminished, we have suffered drought and have poor crops and we do not see any hope of improvement, but all the same our taxes do not diminish. We see no prosperous days ahead of us. There is one thing we think an injustice. When we have plenty of grain the prices are very low, but the moment we are short of grain and we have to buy from Europeans at once the price is high. If when we have hard times and find it difficult to meet our obligations some of these burdens were taken off us it would gladden our hearts. As it is, if we do raise anything, it is never our own: all, or most of it, goes back in taxation. We can never save any money. If we could, we could help ourselves: we could build ourselves better houses; we could buy modern means of traveling about, a cart, or donkeys or mules.

As to my own life, I have had twelve wives altogether, five died and seven are alive. I have twenty-six children alive, five have died. Of my sons five are married and are all at work farming; three young children go to school. I hope the younger children will all go to school. I think it is a good thing to go to school.

There are five schools in our district. Quite a number of people are Christians, but I am too old to change my ways. In our religion we believe that when anybody dies the spirit remains and we often make offerings to the spirits to keep them good-tempered. But now the making of offerings is dying out rapidly, for every member of the family should be present, but the children are Christians and refuse to come, so the spirit-worship is dying out. A good many of our children go to the mines in the Union, for the wages are better there. Unfortunately a large number do not come back at all. And some send money to their people — others do not. Some men have even deserted their families, their wives, and children. If they cannot go by train they walk long distances.

READING AND DISCUSSION QUESTIONS

1. What reasons does Kumalo give for rebelling against British colonial forces? What caused the initial violence, and what was the outcome?

2. If the Ndebele leader Gandani had delivered the letter to the British and not acted in haste, do you think the British pioneers would have responded as violently as they did? What gives you that impression?

3. What is Kumalo's opinion of British colonial influence in Africa? Cite examples to support your answer.

COMPARATIVE QUESTIONS

1. All of the documents in this chapter are written from a non-Western perspective and address modernization of older cultures. What are some of the changes that modernization brings? How are the authors' attitudes toward these changes similar, and how do they differ?

2. Compare the 1856 Ottoman rescript on equality to the 1870 Ottoman decree describing Bedouin backwardness. Are the two compatible? If not, how can you explain the transformation in Ottoman policy?

3. Compare Kumalo's views on civilization to those expressed or implied in each of the Ottoman documents. What do these views suggest about the authors' understanding of other cultures?

CHAPTER 25

Asia in the Era of Imperialism

1800–1914

Though not colonized as directly or thoroughly as Africa, Asia was heavily influenced by the imperial aspirations of Western industrial societies. British colonial rule directly reshaped the Indian economy and Indian culture, forcibly incorporating many Indians into the British-dominated world economy. In East Asia, treaties gave multiple Western powers — and Japan — economic, political, and military control over key areas of China. Spared the full brunt of Western attention, Japan incorporated Western ideas as it pushed to become an industrial power in its own right. But in every case, Asian nations wrestled with the presence of Western ideas and Westerners as well as their own domestic transformations. The documents in this chapter reflect the broad range of strategies that Asians used to appropriate and/or contest what they understood to be a new framework of international power.

DOCUMENT 25-1

LIN ZEXU

From a Letter to Queen Victoria

1839

Lin Zexu (1785–1850) was a Confucian scholar-bureaucrat of the highest rank, who was tapped by the Daoguang emperor in 1838 to stop the influx of opium illegally imported by Great Britain and other foreign powers. In 1839, he arrived in Guangzhou and, after increasingly hostile negotiations, seized and destroyed more than two million pounds of raw opium from

Lin Zexu, "Letter to Queen Victoria, 1839," in Dun J. Li, ed. *China in Transition, 1517–1911* (New York: Van Nostrand Reinhold, 1969), 64–67.

British warehouses. This action, viewed as heroic by Chinese and Britons alike, ignited the First Opium War (1839–1842). Lin wrote to Queen Victoria, pleading with her to stop the British opium trade. Although his letter was never sent to the queen, it was published in Guangdong and later in Britain, where it aroused both outrage and sympathy.

His Majesty the Emperor comforts and cherishes foreigners as well as Chinese: he loves all the people in the world without discrimination. Whenever profit is found, he wishes to share it with all men; whenever harm appears, he likewise will eliminate it on behalf of all of mankind. His heart is in fact the heart of the whole universe.

Generally speaking, the succeeding rulers of your honorable country have been respectful and obedient. Time and again they have sent petitions to China, saying: "We are grateful to His Majesty the Emperor for the impartial and favorable treatment he has granted to the citizens of my country who have come to China to trade," etc. I am pleased to learn that you, as the ruler of your honorable country, are thoroughly familiar with the principle of righteousness and are grateful for the favor that His Majesty the Emperor has bestowed upon your subjects. Because of this fact, the Celestial Empire, following its traditional policy of treating foreigners with kindness, has been doubly considerate towards the people from England. You have traded in China for almost 200 years, and as a result, your country has become wealthy and prosperous.

As this trade has lasted for a long time, there are bound to be unscrupulous as well as honest traders. Among the unscrupulous are those who bring opium to China to harm the Chinese; they succeed so well that this poison has spread far and wide in all the provinces. You, I hope, will certainly agree that people who pursue material gains to the great detriment of the welfare of others can be neither tolerated by Heaven nor endured by men. . . .

Your country is more than 60,000 *li*[1] from China. The purpose of your ships in coming to China is to realize a large profit. Since this profit is realized in China and is in fact taken away from the Chinese people, how can foreigners return injury for the benefit they have received by sending this poison to harm their benefactors? They may not intend to harm others on purpose, but the fact remains that they are so obsessed with material gain that they have no concern whatever for the harm they can cause to others.

---

[1] *li*: Approximately one-third of a mile.

Have they no conscience? I have heard that you strictly prohibit opium in your own country, indicating unmistakably that you know how harmful opium is.[2] You do not wish opium to harm your own country, but you choose to bring that harm to other countries such as China. Why?

The products that originate from China are all useful items. They are good for food and other purposes and are easy to sell. Has China produced one item that is harmful to foreign countries? For instance, tea and rhubarb[3] are so important to foreigners' livelihood that they have to consume them every day. Were China to concern herself only with her own advantage without showing any regard for other people's welfare, how could foreigners continue to live? Foreign products like woolen cloth and beiges [undyed wool fabric] rely on Chinese raw materials such as silk for their manufacturing. Had China sought only her own advantage, where would the foreigners' profit come from? The products that foreign countries need and have to import from China are too numerous to enumerate: from food products such as molasses, ginger, and cassia [similar to cinnamon] to useful necessities such as silk and porcelain. The imported goods from foreign countries, on the other hand, are merely playthings which can be easily dispensed with without causing any ill effect. Since we do not need these things really, what harm would come if we should decide to stop foreign trade altogether? The reason why we unhesitantly allow foreigners to ship out such Chinese products as tea and silk is that we feel that wherever there is an advantage, it should be shared by all the people in the world. . . .

I have heard that you are a kind, compassionate monarch. I am sure that you will not do to others what you yourself do not desire. I have also heard that you have instructed every British ship that sails for Guangzhou not to bring any prohibited goods to China. It seems that your policy is as enlightened as it is proper. The fact that British ships have continued to bring opium to China results perhaps from the impossibility of making a thorough inspection of all of them owing to their large numbers. I am sending you this letter to reiterate the seriousness with which we enforce the law of the Celestial Empire and to make sure that merchants from your honorable country will not attempt to violate it again.

I have heard that the areas under your direct jurisdiction such as London, Scotland, and Ireland do not produce opium; it is produced instead

---

[2] **I have heard . . . opium is**: Lin was mistaken; the use of opium was not prohibited in England at the time he wrote his letter.

[3] **rhubarb**: Rhubarb roots were used in medicines.

in your Indian possessions such as Bengal, Madras, Bombay, Patna, and Malwa. In these possessions the English people not only plant opium poppies that stretch from one mountain to another but also open factories to manufacture this terrible drug. As months accumulate and years pass by, the poison they have produced increases in its wicked intensity, and its repugnant odor reaches as high as the sky. Heaven is furious with anger, and all the gods are moaning with pain! It is hereby suggested that you destroy and plow under all of these opium plants and grow food crops instead, while issuing an order to punish severely anyone who dares to plant opium poppies again. If you adopt this policy of love so as to produce good and exterminate evil, Heaven will protect you, and gods will bring you good fortune. Moreover, you will enjoy a long life and be rewarded with a multitude of children and grandchildren! In short, by taking this one measure, you can bring great happiness to others as well as yourself. Why do you not do it? . . .

For every government, past or present, one of its primary functions is to educate all the people living within its jurisdiction, foreigners as well as its own citizens, about the law and to punish them if they choose to violate it. Since a foreigner who goes to England to trade has to obey the English law, how can an Englishman not obey the Chinese law when he is physically within China? The present law calls for the imposition of the death sentence on any Chinese who has peddled or smoked opium. Since a Chinese could not peddle or smoke opium if foreigners had not brought it to China, it is clear that the true culprits of a Chinese's death as a result of an opium conviction are the opium traders from foreign countries. Being the cause of other people's death, why should they themselves be spared from capital punishment? A murderer of one person is subject to the death sentence; just imagine how many people opium has killed! This is the rationale behind the new law which says that any foreigner who brings opium to China will be sentenced to death by hanging or beheading. Our purpose is to eliminate this poison once and for all and to the benefit of all mankind.

Our Celestial Empire towers over all other countries in virtue and possesses a power great and awesome enough to carry out its wishes. But we will not prosecute a person without warning him in advance; that is why we have made our law explicit and clear. If the merchants of your honorable country wish to enjoy trade with us on a permanent basis, they must fearfully observe our law by cutting off, once and for all, the supply of opium. Under no circumstance should they test our intention to enforce the law by deliberately violating it. You, as the ruler of your honorable country, should do your part to uncover the hidden and unmask the wicked. It is hoped that you will continue to enjoy your country and become more and more respectful and obeisant. How wonderful it is that we can all enjoy the blessing of peace!

READING AND DISCUSSION QUESTIONS

1. Describe the tone of Lin's letter. What language or phrases establish Lin's understanding of the relationship between China and Great Britain?

2. According to Lin, what should motivate Queen Victoria's to halt the opium trade? How will she be rewarded?

3. What does Lin say about trade between China and the world? In his opinion, whom does this trade benefit? How do you imagine a British trader would respond to Lin's assertions?

DOCUMENT 25-2

Two Proclamations of the Boxer Rebellion

1898, 1900

Following the Guangxu emperor's optimistic but unsuccessful attempt to modernize China during the 100 Days' Reform period of 1898, a local martial arts organization in Shandong village, the Society of Righteous and Harmonious Boxers, emerged as a violently antimodern, anti-Western, and anti-Christian force. Encouraged by the Qing government and eschewing modern military techniques, the Boxers killed thousands of foreign and Chinese Christians and in 1900 laid siege to the area in Beijing where foreign officials were quartered. A multinational force, including both Western and Japanese troops, ended the siege within two months, and the resulting Boxer Protocol of 1901 forced the Qing government to pay war reparations. The proclamations here outline the Boxers' beliefs and their exhortations to Chinese citizens.

The Society of Righteous and Harmonious Boxers, "The Gods Assist the Boxers" in the Peking and Tientsin *Times*, May 5, 1900. "Attention" in Ssu-ya Teng and John K. Fairbank, *China's Response to the West* (Cambridge: Harvard University Press, 1954), 190.

The Gods assist the Boxers,
The Patriotic Harmonious corps,
It is because the "Foreign Devils" disturb the "Middle Kingdom"
    [China].
Urging the people to join their religion,
To turn their backs on Heaven,
Venerate not the Gods and forget the ancestors.
Men violate the human obligations,
Women commit adultery,
"Foreign Devils" are not produced by mankind,
If you do not believe,
Look at them carefully.
The eyes of all the "Foreign Devils" are bluish,
No rain falls,
The earth is getting dry,
This is because the churches stop Heaven,
The Gods are angry;
The Genii [minor spirits] are vexed;
Both come down from the mountain to deliver the doctrine.
This is no hearsay,
The practices of boxing[4] will not be in vain;
Reciting incantations and pronouncing magic words,
Burn up yellow written prayers,
Light incense sticks
To invite the Gods and Genii of all the grottoes.
The Gods come out from grottoes,
The Genii come down from mountains,
Support the human bodies to practice the boxing.
When all the military accomplishments or tactics
Are fully learned,
It will not be difficult to exterminate the "Foreign Devils" then.
Push aside the railway tracks,
Pull out the telegraph poles,
Immediately after this destroy the steamers.
The great France

---

[4] **practices of boxing**: Society members trained in Chinese martial arts techniques, which included intense physical and mental discipline and meditation techniques. Essentially, they believed that their physical prowess enabled them to deflect bullets.

Will grow cold and downhearted.
The English and Russians will certainly disperse.
Let the various "Foreign Devils" all be killed.
May the whole Elegant Empire of the Great Qing Dynasty[5] be ever
    prosperous!

Attention: all people in markets and villages of all provinces in China —
now, owing to the fact that Catholics and Protestants have vilified our gods
and sages, have deceived our emperors and ministers above, and oppressed
the Chinese people below, both our gods and our people are angry at
them, yet we have to keep silent. This forces us to practice the Yike[6] magic
boxing so as to protect our country, expel the foreign bandits and kill
Christian converts, in order to save our people from miserable suffering.
After this notice is issued to instruct you villagers, no matter which village
you are living in, if there are Christian converts, you ought to get rid of
them quickly. The churches which belong to them should be unreserv-
edly burned down. Everyone who intends to spare someone, or to disobey
our order by concealing Christian converts, will be punished according to
the regulation when we come to his place, and he will be burned to death
to prevent his impeding our program. We especially do not want to punish
anyone by death without warning him first. We cannot bear to see you suffer innocently. Don't disobey this special notice!

READING AND DISCUSSION QUESTIONS

1. What are the Boxers' complaints?

2. How do the Boxers characterize the distinction between the West and
   China?

3. How do you imagine Chinese citizens might have responded to the
   Boxers' proclamations?

---

[5] **Great Qing Dynasty**: Chinese imperial family between 1644 and 1912. The Qing
encouraged the Boxer uprising.
[6] **Yike**: The type of martial arts practiced by the Boxers.

DOCUMENT 25-3

ABDOOL REHMAN

Memorandum to Lord Selborne

1905

British colonization of India had a significant adverse impact on domestic Indian manufacturing, and many South Asians emigrated — often in slave-like indentured servitude — to other British colonies and beyond. A large number settled in the British territories that would later comprise South Africa, where discrimination against nonwhites was a near-constant feature of colonial society. In this memo, the secretary of the local Indian Associa-tion, Abdool Rehman, issues a formal protest to the British official Lord Sel-borne regarding the treatment of Indian merchants.

Did we not know that what has been called the Anti-Asiatic Vigilance Society is to make representations to Your Excellency with reference to the British Indians, so far as regards Potchefstroom [city in South Africa], we would not have given any trouble whatsoever to Your Excellency, espe-cially as we are aware that Your Excellency is to meet very shortly a depu-tation of the British Indian Association at Johannesburg.[7]

Mr. Loveday it was who stated that Potchefstroom was being inundated with indentured Indians from Natal. To this we beg to give an empathic contradiction. Some of us know the Natal laws, and we know that [it] is next to impossible for an indentured Indian to escape. In any case not a single instance has been brought forward to prove the statement above referred to.

Another statement was made by the mayor of Johannesburg when he was here. He is reported to have said that, whereas there were nineteen licenses issued to Asiatics before the war,[8] now there were ninety-six

---

Abdool Rehman, "Memorandum to Lord Selborne, High Commissioner of Trans-vaal, October 1905," in *Collected Works of Mahatma Gandhi*, V:96–98.

[7] **a deputation . . . Johannesburg**: A member of the Anti-Asiatic Vigilance Society.
[8] **the war**: The South African War (1899–1902), also known as the Anglo-Boer War, ended in victory for the British over South Africans of Dutch descent who had sought independence from British rule.

traders' licenses and thirty-seven hawkers' [street vendors'] licenses. This statement, so far as traders are concerned, is not true. We supplied before the war a list of British Indian traders in the town of Potchefstroom to the British Agent, and there were twenty-two British Indian stores in the town of Potchefstroom, as distinguished from the district. We have a true copy of the list that was sent to the British Agent, and we are today in a position, not only to give the names, but to locate each of the store-keepers. Seeing that Mr. Goch[9] mentions ninety-six traders' licenses in connection with the nineteen before the war, we take it that he refers to ninety-six traders' licenses for the town of Potchefstroom. If so, this is grossly untrue. There are only twenty-four British Indian stores in this town at the present day. We state this with a full sense of responsibility and knowledge, and we challenge our detractors to prove the contrary.

A third statement that has been made against us in Potchefstroom is with reference to the so-called insanitary condition of our dwellings and shops. These, indeed, speak for themselves, but when the charge was made, we took the opportunity of showing our places to the district surgeon of Potchefstroom, and the following is the report that [he] gave:

In going through the various premises, I am pleased to say I was greatly impressed with the general condition of each place I visited, both internally as well as externally. Taking all things into consideration, the backyards are all perfectly clean and sanitary. I saw no accumulation of rubbish, this I understand being carried away daily by the contractor. The bucket system is enforced as in other parts of the town, which is also attended to by the Sanitary Department, and I can find no fault from what I saw. There appears to me to be no overcrowding as regards sleeping accommodation. At the back of each business premise, in addition, I noticed a kind of mess room capable of seating about five to eight persons, and each has its own kitchen; these are also well kept.

We mention these things to show under what disadvantages, we have to labor, and what misrepresentations are made against us. We have no hesitation in saying that the whole of the anti-Asiatic agitation is due to trade jealousy. Nothing can be further from our wish than to enter into an unfair competition with the white store-keepers.

Much has been said against our mode of life. We are proud to think that we are sober and simple in our habits, and if thereby we have an advantage over the rival white traders, we hardly think that it should be brought up against us in order to traduce and degrade us. It is totally

---

[9] **Mr. Goch**: George H. Goch, the mayor of Johannesburg (1904–1905).

forgotten, in this connection, by those who denounce us, that the white traders have other advantages which we cannot dream of having, namely their European connection, their knowledge of the English language, and their better organizing powers. Moreover, we are able to carry on our trade only because of the goodwill of the poor whites, and our ability to please the poorest class of customers; also, we have the support of wholesale European houses.

It has been said that our competition resulted in many European shops being closed. We deny this. In the first instance, some of the shops that have been closed were not shops with which we could possibly enter into competition, for instance hairdressers and others. Some general goods stores have undoubtedly closed, but to connect their closing with Asiatic competition would be [as] unfair as to connect the closing of several Asiatic shops with European competition in this town. There is trade depression all over South Africa, and it has only resulted in getting rid of overtrading that was indulged in soon after the war, based, as it was, on high expectations which have never been fulfilled.

May we also, in this connection, state that much of the agitation against us is kept up not by bona-fide British subjects but by aliens who can have very little indeed to complain of against us. The policy adopted to drive us out of the township is a policy of irritation and insults which, though petty in themselves, are galling enough to be very much felt by us.

Without the slightest occasion, we are now served at special counters in the Post Office. We are debarred from having a breath of fresh air in a park which is called a "public" park, and which is kept up from rates which we are called upon to pay in common with other citizens. We mention these instances to draw Your Excellency's attention to the awkward position in which we are placed without any fault of ours. No opportunity is missed of degrading us and humiliating us. We do not wish to burden Your Excellency with such other instances. We have a right, we submit, to expect the British Government to protect us from such humiliation, and insure for us that freedom to which, as loyal British subjects, we are entitled wherever the Union Jack flies.

We beg to thank Your Excellency for giving us a patient hearing, and in conclusion hope that, as a result of Your Excellency's visit to this township, there will be an amelioration in our condition.

READING AND DISCUSSION QUESTIONS

1. What claims do the Anti-Asiatic Vigilance Society and other whites make against the Indian populations of Natal and Transvaal?

2. How does Rehman answer these claims, and what does he say motivates them?

3. What complaints does Rehman make regarding the quality of life for Indians in South Africa?

DOCUMENT 25-4

SUN YAT-SEN

On the Three People's Principles and the Future of the Chinese People

1906

Trained as a Western physician in Hong Kong, Sun Yat-Sen (1866–1925) studied and traveled extensively and became an important revolutionary during the final years of the Qing Dynasty (1644–1912). While in exile after a failed coup, he formed the Tongmenghui revolutionary organization and won support among Chinese expatriates through his "Three Principles of the People," presented in this excerpt of a 1906 speech in Tokyo. Although the 1911 revolution occurred in his absence, he was selected as provisional president of the new Republic of China, a post he occupied for less than three months. However, his legacy as founder of the Guomindang (Nationalist Party) and position as an iconic figure of Chinese modernity remain strong.

Let us pause to consider for a moment: Where is the nation? Where is the political power? Actually, we are already a people without a nation! The population of the globe is only one billion, several hundred million; we Han,[10] being 400 million, comprise one-fourth of that population.

Prescriptions for Saving China: Selected Writings of Sun Yat-sen, eds. Julie Lee Wei, Ramon H. Myers, and Donald G. Gillin (Palo Alto, CA: Hoover Institution Press, 1994).

[10] **Han**: The Chinese people.

Our nation is the most populous, most ancient, and most civilized in the world, yet today we are a lost nation. Isn't that enormously bizarre? The African nation of the Transvaal has a population of only 200,000, yet when Britain tried to destroy it, the fighting lasted three years.[11] The Philippines have a population of only several million, but when America tried to subdue it, hostilities persisted for several years.[12] Is it possible that the Han will gladly be a lost nation?

We Han are now swiftly being caught up in a tidal wave of nationalist revolution, yet the Manchus continue to discriminate against the Han. They boast that their forefathers conquered the Han because of their superior unity and military strength and that they intend to retain these qualities so as to dominate the Han forever. . . . Certainly, once we Han unite, our power will be thousands of times greater than theirs, and the success of the nationalist revolution will be assured.

As for the Principle of Democracy, it is the foundation of the political revolution. . . . For several thousand years China has been a monarchical autocracy, a type of political system intolerable to those living in freedom and equality. A nationalist revolution is not itself sufficient to get rid of such a system. Think for a moment: When the founder of the Ming dynasty expelled the Mongols and restored Chinese rule, the nationalist revolution triumphed, but his political system was only too similar to those of the Han, Tang, and Song dynasties.[13] Consequently, after another three hundred years, foreigners again began to invade China. This is the result of the inadequacy of the political system, so that a political revolution is an absolute necessity. . . . The aim of the political revolution is to create a constitutional, democratic political system. . . .

*   *   *

Now, let me begin by discussing the origins of the Principle of the People's Livelihood, a principle that began to flourish only in the latter part of the nineteenth century. . . . As civilization advanced, people relied less on physical labor and more on natural forces, since electricity and steam

---

[11] **The African nation . . . three years**: A reference to the South African War, or Anglo-Boer War (1899–1902).

[12] **The Philippines . . . several years**: Between 1899 and 1901, Filipinos fought against the United States after the United States took over the Philippines from Spain at the end of the Spanish-American War.

[13] **When the founder . . . dynasties**: The Ming Dynasty ruled from 1368 to 1644 C.E.; the Han (202 B.C.E.–220 C.E.), Tang (618–906 C.E.), and Song (960–1279 C.E.) were earlier Chinese dynasties.

could accomplish things a thousand times faster than human physical strength. For example, in antiquity a single man tilling the land could harvest at best enough grain to feed a few people, notwithstanding his toil and trouble. Now, however, as a result of the development of scientific agriculture, one man can grow more than enough to feed a thousand people because he can use machinery instead of his limbs, with a consequent increase in efficiency. . . .

In view of this, everyone in Europe and America should be living in a state of plenty and happiness undreamed of in antiquity. If we look around, however, we see that conditions in those countries are precisely the opposite. Statistically, Britain's wealth has increased more than several thousandfold over the previous generation, yet poverty of the people has also increased several thousandfold over the previous generation. Moreover, the rich are extremely few, and the poor extremely numerous. This is because the power of human labor is no match for the power of capital. In antiquity, agriculture and industry depended completely on human labor; but now, with the development of natural forces that human labor cannot match, agriculture and industry have fallen completely into the hands of capitalists. The greater the amount of capital, the more abundant the resources that can be utilized. Unable to compete, the poor have naturally been reduced to destitution. . . .

Indeed, this constitutes a lesson for China. . . . Civilization yields both good and bad fruits, and we should embrace the good and reject the bad. In the countries of Europe and America, the rich monopolize the good fruits of civilization, while the poor suffer from its evil fruits. . . . Our current revolution will create a nation that not only belongs to the citizenry but is socially responsible. Certainly, there will be nothing comparable to it in Europe or America.

Why have Europe and America failed to solve their social problems? Because they have not solved their land problem. Generally speaking, wherever civilization is advanced, the price of land increases with each passing day. . . . In China capitalists have not yet emerged, so that for several thousand years there has been no increase in land prices. . . . After the revolution, however, conditions in China will be different. For example, land prices in Hong Kong and Shanghai are currently as much as several hundred times higher than those in the interior. This increment is the result of the advance of civilization and the development of communications. It is inevitable that, as the entire nation advances, land prices everywhere will rise accordingly. . . . Fifty years ago, land along the banks of the Huangpu River in Shanghai was worth up to a million dollars a *mou*

[1.5 acres]. This is evidence of the clearest sort, from which we can see that in the future the rich will get richer every day, and the poor poorer. . . . Consequently, we must come up with a solution now. . . .

With respect to a solution, although the socialists have different opinions, the procedure I most favor is land valuation. For example, if a landlord has land worth 1,000 dollars, its price can be set at 1,000 or even 2,000 dollars. Perhaps in the future, after communications have been developed, the value of his land will rise to 10,000 dollars; the owner should receive 2,000, which entails a profit and no loss, and the 8,000 increment will go to the state. Such an arrangement will greatly benefit both the state and the people's livelihood. Naturally, it will also eliminate the shortcomings that have permitted a few rich people to monopolize wealth. This is the simplest, most convenient, and most feasible method. . . .

Once we adopt this method, the more civilization advances, the greater the wealth of the nation, and then we can be sure our financial problems will not become difficult to handle. After the excessive taxes of the present have been abolished, the price of consumer goods will gradually fall and the people will become increasingly prosperous. We will forever abolish the vicious taxation policies that have prevailed for several thousand years. . . . After China's social revolution is accomplished, private individuals will never again have to pay taxes. The collection of land revenues alone will make China the richest nation on earth. . . .

Obviously, . . . it is necessary to give considerable attention to what the constitution of the Republic of China should be. . . . The British constitution embodies the so-called separation of powers into executive, legislative, and judicial, all mutually independent. . . . The Frenchman[14] later embraced the British system and melded it with his own ideals to create his own school of thought. The American constitution was based on Montesquieu's theories but went further in clearly demarcating the separation of powers. . . . As to the future constitution of the Republic of China, I propose that we introduce a new principle, that of the "five separate powers."

Under this system, there will be two other powers in addition to the three powers just discussed. One is the examination power. . . . American officials are either elected or appointed. . . .

With respect to elections, those endowed with eloquence ingratiated themselves with the public and won elections, while those who had

---

[14] **The Frenchman**: Montesquieu (1689–1755); a French political philosopher who argued that individual freedom is safest when the three powers of government — the judicial, executive, and legislative — are kept separate in a state.

learning and ideals but lacked eloquence were ignored. Consequently, members of America's House of Representatives have often been foolish and ignorant people who have made its history quite ridiculous. As for appointees, they all come and go with the president. The Democratic and Republican parties have consistently taken turns holding power, and whenever a president is replaced, cabinet members and other officials, comprising no fewer than 60,000–70,000 people, including the postmaster general, are also replaced. As a result, the corruption and laxity of American politics are unparalleled among the nations of the world. . . . Therefore, the future constitution of the Republic of China must provide for an independent branch expressly responsible for civil service examinations. Furthermore, all officials, however high their rank, must undergo examinations in order to determine their qualifications. Whether elected or appointed, officials must pass those examinations before assuming office. This procedure will eliminate such evils as blind obedience, electoral abuses, and favoritism. . . .

The other power is the supervisory power, responsible for monitoring matters involving impeachment. For reasons that should be evident to all, such a branch is indispensable to any nation. The future constitution of the Republic of China must provide for an independent branch. Since ancient times, China had a supervisory organization, the Censorate,[15] to monitor the traditional social order. Inasmuch as it was merely a servant of the monarchy, however, it was ineffectual. . . .

With this added to the four powers already discussed, there will be five separate powers. That constitution will form the basis of the sound government of a nation that belongs to its own race, to its own citizens, and to its own society. This will be the greatest good fortune for our 400 million Han people. I presume that you gentlemen are willing to undertake and complete this task. It is my greatest hope.

READING AND DISCUSSION QUESTIONS

1. Sun presents his first principle only indirectly in the first three paragraphs of this speech. Describe what you think that principle is, based on your reading of the speech.

---

[15] **the Censorate**: A unique feature of Chinese government during the Ming and Qing eras; also called the Board of Censors, which was responsible for reviewing the conduct of officials and reporting any offences to the emperor.

2.   Sun mentions the Han and Manchu. Why do you think he uses eth-
     nic groups to describe the situation in China?

3.   What are Sun's second and third principles? What distinction does he
     make between the third principle and socialism?

4.   How does Sun invoke Western countries to strengthen the argument
     for his three principles?

DOCUMENT 25-5

THE BLACK DRAGON SOCIETY

Anniversary Statement

1930

*The Black Dragon Society, or Amur River Society, was founded in 1901 by
the ultranationalist adventurer Uchida Ryōhei (1873–1937), who strongly
opposed Russian influence in Siberia and promoted Japan's international
expansion through a Japanese-directed form of pan-Asianism. Uchida traveled
to Russia and Korea in order to foment rebellion, and the society continued
to mobilize for Japanese power in Asia until it was disbanded during the
Allied occupation of Japan in 1946. The society's 1930 history of the Japanese colonization and annexation of Korea, excerpted below, interprets and
defends Japanese imperialism and spells out its international and domestic
platforms.*

From the first, we members of the Amur [Black Dragon] Society have
worked in accordance with the imperial mission for overseas expansion to
solve our overpopulation; at the same time, we have sought to give support
and encouragement to the peoples of East Asia. Thus we have sought the
spread of humanity and righteousness throughout the world by having the
imperial purpose extend to neighboring nations.

Earlier, in order to achieve these principles, we organized the Heavenly Blessing Heroes in Korea in 1894 and helped the Tong Hak rebellion

The Black Dragon Society, "Anniversary Statement," in Wm. Theodore de Bary and
Donald Keene, eds., *Sources of Japanese Tradition*, vol. 2 (New York: Columbia
University Press, 1964) 256–258.

there in order to speed the settlement of the dispute between Japan and China.[16] In 1899 we helped Aguinaldo in his struggle for independence for the Philippines.[17] In 1900 we worked with other comrades in helping Sun Yat-sen start the fires of revolution in South China. In 1901 we organized this Society and became exponents of the punishment of Russia, and thereafter we devoted ourselves to the annexation of Korea while continuing to support the revolutionary movement of China. . . .

During this period we have seen the fulfillment of our national power in the decisive victories in the two major wars against China and Russia,[18] in the annexation of Korea, the acquisition of Formosa [Taiwan] and Sakhalin,[19] and the expulsion of Germany from the Shandong peninsula.[20] Japan's status among the empires of the world has risen until today she ranks as one of the three great powers, and from this eminence she can support other Asiatic nations. . . .

However, in viewing recent international affairs it would seem that the foundation established by the great Meiji emperor is undergoing rapid deterioration. The disposition of the gains of the war with Germany was left to foreign powers, and the government, disregarding the needs of national defense, submitted to unfair demands to limit our naval power.[21] Moreover, the failure of our China policy[22] made the Chinese more and more contemptuous of us, so much so that they have been brought to

---

[16] **helped the Tong Hak rebellion . . . China**: The Tonghak was a late-nineteenth-century Korean religious movement that drew on Daoist, Buddhist, Confucian, and Catholic traditions. Members rebelled in 1894 against the China-oriented government of Korea, which sparked Japanese and Chinese intervention and led to the Sino-Japanese War of 1894–1895, which ultimately led to Korean independence.

[17] **helped Aguinaldo . . . Philippines**: Emilio Aguinaldo (1869–1964) led an insurrection against Spain in 1898 and established the Philippine Republic in January 1899.

[18] **the decisive victories . . . Russia**: Victories over China in the Sino-Japanese War (1894–1895) and Russia in the Russo-Japanese War (1904–1905).

[19] **the acquisition of . . . Sakhalin**: Japan was granted control over former German areas of influence in China's Shandong province after World War I.

[20] **the expulsion . . . peninsula**: Japan received Taiwan (Formosa) after the Sino-Japanese War.

[21] **the government . . . our naval power**: The Washington Conference of 1921 estimated Japan's naval strength to be 60 percent of that of the United States and Great Britain.

[22] **the failure of our China policy**: The Twenty-One Demands would have established extensive Japanese influence over the Chinese government. China successfully resisted these demands.

demand the surrender of our essential defense lines in Manchuria and Mongolia. Furthermore, in countries like the United States and Australia our immigrants have been deprived of rights which were acquired only after long years of struggle, and we now face a highhanded anti-Japanese expulsion movement which knows no bounds.[23] Men of purpose and of humanity who are at all concerned for their country cannot fail to be upset by the situation.

When we turn our attention to domestic affairs, we feel more than deep concern. There is a great slackening of discipline and order. Men's hearts are becoming corrupt. Look about you! Are not the various government measures and establishments a conglomeration of all sorts of evils and abuses? The laws are confusing, and evil grows apace. The people are overwhelmed by heavy taxes, the confusion in the business world complicates the livelihood of the people, the growth of dangerous thought threatens social order, and our national polity, which has endured for three thousand years, is in danger. This is a critical time for our national destiny; was there ever a more crucial day? What else can we call this time if it is not termed decisive?

And yet, in spite of this our government, instead of pursuing a far-sighted policy, casts about for temporary measures. The opposition party simply struggles for political power without any notion of saving our country from this crisis. And even the press, which should devote itself to its duty of guiding and leading society, is the same. For the most part it swims with the current, bows to vulgar opinions, and is chiefly engrossed in money making. Alas! Our empire moves ever closer to rocks which lie before us. . . .

Therefore we of the Amur Society have determined to widen the scope of our activity. Hereafter, besides our interest in foreign affairs, we will give unselfish criticism of internal politics and of social problems, and we will seek to guide public opinion into proper channels. . . . We . . . are resolved to reform the moral corruption of the people, restore social discipline, and ease the insecurity of the people's livelihood by relieving the crises in the financial world, restore national confidence, and increase the national strength, in order to carry out the imperial mission to awaken the countries of Asia. In order to clarify these principles, we here set forth our platform to all our fellow patriots.

---

[23] **we now face . . . no bounds**: Australia and the United States severely restricted Japanese and Chinese immigration in the 1920s.

PLATFORM

1. Developing the great plan of the founders of the country, we will widen the great Way [Dao] of Eastern culture, work out a harmony of Eastern and Western cultures, and take the lead among Asian peoples.
2. We will bring to an end many evils, such as formalistic legalism; it restricts the freedom of the people, hampers common sense solutions, prevents efficiency in public and private affairs, and destroys the true meaning of constitutional government. Thereby we will show forth again the essence of the imperial principles.
3. We shall rebuild the present administrative systems. We will develop overseas expansion through the activation of our diplomacy, further the prosperity of the people by reforms in internal government, and solve problems of labor and management by the establishment of new social policies. Thereby we will strengthen the foundations of the empire.
4. We shall carry out the spirit of the Imperial Rescript[24] to Soldiers and Sailors and stimulate a martial spirit by working toward the goal of a nation in arms. Thereby we look toward the perfection of national defense.
5. We plan a fundamental reform of the present educational system, which is copied from those of Europe and America; we shall set up a basic study of a national education originating in our national polity. Thereby we anticipate the further development and heightening of the wisdom and virtue of the Yamato race.[25]

READING AND DISCUSSION QUESTIONS

1. What is the overall goal of the Black Dragon Society?
2. How does the society's statement deal with the topic of international relations — both within Asia and with non-Asian countries?
3. The society mentions the deprivation of Japanese immigrant rights in the United States and Australia. How is this relevant to the society's mission?

---

[24] **Imperial Rescript**: An 1882 decree by the emperor that gave the emperor command of the armed forces, thus strengthening the military's independence from civilian control.
[25] **Yamato race**: According to tradition, Japan's imperial line can be traced back to a descendant of the Sun Goddess on the Yamato plain.

4. This document represents a shift in focus to domestic affairs. What are the society's complaints about Japanese society, and how does it propose to rectify them?

COMPARATIVE QUESTIONS

1. How do some of the documents in this chapter convey a willingness to engage with Western ideas, and how do some insist on rejecting them? Which tactic seems to be more successful? Why?

2. Compare the attitudes of the Black Dragon Society and the Boxers toward the West and their approaches to both international and domestic affairs.

3. Compare the letters of Lin Zexu and Abdool Rehman, who both protest the treatment of their people at the hands of the British. How much does each author seem to know of Western culture, and how is that knowledge — or lack of knowledge — important to their argument?

4. Which of these documents are directed toward a Western audience, and which are directed toward an indigenous audience? Are any directed to both? What is the effect of this choice by the author(s)?

CHAPTER 26

Nation Building in the Western Hemisphere and Australia

Duning the nineteenth century, rebellions and revolutions overturned long-established patterns of European colonial rule throughout the Western Hemisphere and in Australia. As newly independent countries focused on nation building and economic development, they struggled to establish systems of government and new trade patterns, and to address issues of land management, urbanization, and regional and racial differences. Their struggles produced markedly different results: the United States, Canada, and Australia created stable democratic societies, whereas Latin American countries grappled with ongoing political and economic instability. The United States transformed into an industrial power rivaling Europe, while Canada and Australia remained largely agricultural economies. In every instance, however, national leaders — typically descendants of European settlers or settlers themselves — experienced status anxiety, which often manifested in discriminatory policies that ensured their higher standing and power over native populations.

DOCUMENT 26-1

A Spanish Colonist Protests the Marriage of His Daughter

1784–1785

Concerned about preserving racial and ethnic and class standing among Spanish colonists in the Americas, in 1776 the Spanish Crown passed

Christian Büschges, "Don Manuel Valdivieso y Carrión Protests the Marriage of His Daughter to Don Teodoro Jaramillo, a Person of Lower Social Standing (Quito, 1784–85)," in Richard Boyer and Geoffrey Spurling, eds., *Colonial Lives: Documents in Latin American History, 1550–1850* (London: Oxford University Press, 2000), 224–235.

marriage legislation governing all its colonies. Its Royal Pragmatic (Real Pragmática) gave fathers (or other relatives) the right to prevent marriages between their children and members of a lower social class. The dozens of lawsuits contesting these regulations reveal shifting notions of social status and hierarchy. In the case recounted below, Manuel Valdivieso y Carrión of Loja seeks to block the marriage of his daughter Baltasara — which he had previously approved — to Don Teodoro Jaramillo.

18.1 COURT SUMMARY OF A QUESTIONNAIRE, WITH RECORDED TESTIMONIES, PRESENTED BY DON MANUEL VALDIVIESO

[Asked] if they know or have heard publicly that it is well known and well recognized that don Manuel Valdivieso and his ancestors have been of distinguished nobility and have obtained in Loja and other provinces the most honorable offices, they all confirm [that this is true].

[Asked] if they know that doña María Aguilera, don Manuel Valdivieso's wife, and her ancestors have enjoyed an equivalent reputation, without any reduction of the noble privileges. All of them confirm.

[Asked] if they know publicly that don Juan Teodoro is of low birth, very inferior in origin and *calidad* [social standing] to don Manuel Valdivieso and his wife. Don José Vivanco says that he has not heard anything about it, either publicly or privately, that he is ignorant of the *calidad* of the parents of don Teodoro, that he has seen [Teodoro's] mother wearing lady's clothing, dressed as a *beata*,[1] and that he has heard in public that Jaramillo was inferior in descent to don Manuel Valdivieso and his wife. Don Maríano Piedra [says] that he considered don Juan Teodoro a plebeian man [commoner] and of low birth, but that he regarded him as neither mean nor ignoble, and he knows Jaramillo's origin is very much inferior to that of don Manuel and his wife. Don Agustin Vasquez [says] that he has heard that he is not of noble birth, [but] that he also has heard that he is the grandchild of a distinguished gentleman. Don Bernardo Aguirre [says] that he knows that the [honorific] "don" was not given to Teodoro at first, but not because he was ignoble or mean; and he has considered him [Teodoro] a white man, and he has heard he descends from the Jaramillo family, which is reputed to be noble. No one can doubt that the family] of Valdivieso and his wife is of the most illustrious kind. Don Mateo Vasquez [says] he has considered Jaramillo neither ignoble, mean, nor plebeian, [and] that he has known him as a Spanish man, but it is certain that he is

---

[1] *beata*: Vivanco compares Teodoro's mother to a pious woman who dressed and in some ways lived like a nun but did not officially become one.

not equal to don Manuel and his wife. Don Francisco Moreno [says] that he has not considered don Juan Teodoro a mean and ignoble man, and he does not know anything about his lineage; he has judged him to be a man not of the highest distinction but also not contemptible since he has seen him held in esteem and high regard. He also knows that he [Teodoro] is not an equal of don Manuel and his wife, and that during this lawsuit he has heard [things] in favor and in disfavor of the *calidad* of Jaramillo. Don José Murillo [says] that he has considered don Teodoro a white man and of inferior *calidad* to that of don Manuel. Doña Micaela Castillo [says] that she does not know if don Teodoro is a mean or ignoble man and that she has regarded him as a white and decent man.

[Asked] if they know that Jaramillo was a silversmith by profession, like his uncle Esteban Oreha. Don Maríano Piedra [says] that he has seen him in the silversmith's shop in the company of Esteban Ureña, but he is not sure if he was practicing this craft [though] he has heard this in public on the occasion of this lawsuit. Don Agustin Vasquez does not know if he was or was not [a silversmith]; he says that [Jaramillo] has led caravans of mules owned by Miguel Carrión, getting paid a salary for his work. Don Mateo Vasquez [says] that he saw [Jaramillo] as a child learning the silversmith's trade in the company of his uncle Ureña, and after a short time he left it [the craft]; [don Mateo Vasquez says] that Jaramillo ran the *fábrica* [business operations] of the house of don Miguel Carrión at the rank of steward, I and he led the mules of don Miguel and his son, earning a salary. All the witnesses agree that Jaramillo served in the business and led Carrión's mule caravans. . . .

[Asked] if they know or have heard etc.[2] Don Bernardo Valdivieso [says], concerning the paternal ancestors, he knows and has heard that the sons of don Juan Jaramillo and Margarita González [Teodoro Jaramillo's paternal grandparents] were regarded as plebeians, as were the maternal [ancestors] of Teodoro, and they did not hold any honorable offices. Don Bernardo Valdivieso says] that Francisco Jaramillo is the great-uncle of don Juan Teodoro, and that the descendants of don Francisco have served, because of their family branch or line, in the top occupations. Piedra [says] that he does not know [if] the ancestors of Jaramillo had obtained honorable occupations or manual ones, but that since his grandfather they have been reputed to be plebeians. Aguirre [says] that he does not know anything regarding [Jaramillo's] maternal [ancestors], but that the Jaramillos have served in honorable occupations. Don Mateo Vasquez [says] that he

---

[2] **Asked if they know . . . etc.**: The rest of this question is missing from the original document.

[has] heard that don Teodoro is related to and descends from Jaramillos, noble persons. . . .

[Asked] if they have heard or known that don Juan Jaramillo etc. Don Francisco Riofrío [says] that on this same occasion he has heard in various conversations that don Juan Jaramillo married Margarita González, reputed to be the daughter of an Indian woman from Saraguro. Don Mateo Vasquez [says] that he has only heard that don Juan Jaramillo married badly and unequally for his noble station. The other [witnesses] do not know.

[Asked] if they know that Juan Jaramillo and González etc. Vivanco [says] that he only knows that the mother of Jaramillo had a son called José, and as a widow she married Bartolo Galvez, a humble man who due to his poverty works as a *truquero*.[3] Don Maríano Piedra [says] that he did not know if María Regalado [Teodoro Jaramillo's mother] was a plebeian, but that he has regarded her as such. . . .

Don Mateo Vasquez adds that María Regalado was a white woman, and that he never saw her in the clothing of a plebeian. . . .

[Asked] if they know that José Aguirre etc. Don Bernardo Valdivieso testifies that Francisca, sister of Teodoro, is the wife of Maríano Riofrío, bastard son of an Indian woman. Piedra [says] that Riofrío is the son of an Indian woman. Don Agustin Vasquez [states] that it is said in public that Riofrío is the son of a gentleman of distinguished nobility; although [Vasquez] has heard talk that [Riofrío] is a *mestizo*, he does not know anything about his mother. . . .

[Asked] if they know that Josefa Córdova, Juan Teodoro Jaramillo's former wife etc. . . . . Moreno testifies that he regards Josefa not as a plebeian, although she is of humble birth, and that her father had married an Indian woman. . . .

[Asked] if José de Herique[4] is a child born out of wedlock etc. Don Bernardo Valdivieso publicly clears him of the accusation that he [José de Herique] was the son of an Indian woman. [Don Bernardo says] that at first Herique carried out the profession of a smith and that he is an intimate friend of don Teodoro. . . . Aguirre clears him according to what he has heard regarding the *calidad* of Herique, and adds that as an honorable man of good behavior and virtue he [Herique] has taken some measures to end the hostilities and disturbances occasioned by the proposed matrimony, and that, although many years ago he had worked as a smith, he now maintains himself as a trader (*mercader*), respected by everyone.

---

[3] *truquero*: Gaming table operator.
[4] **José de Herique**: Teodoro's good friend.

18.2 PETITION SUBMITTED TO THE COURT BY RAMON JARAMILLO, ATTORNEY FOR DON MANUEL VALDIVIESO

I, Ramon Jaramillo, attorney, in the name of don Manuel Valdivieso y Carrión, citizen of the city of Loja, in virtue of the power he has invested in me to act in the lawsuit against Juan Teodoro Jaramillo, concerning the marriage that he requests to doña Baltasara Valdivieso, daughter of my client, thinking himself noble, and with the rest inferred, I say that in the name of justice [and] in order to serve the superior judgment of Your Highness, [you should] declare, with a just and clear judgment, that the named Jaramillo is plebeian and of humble birth and cannot and shall not enter into marriage with doña Baltasara. If she anticipates this decision with irregular and wrongful actions, in contradiction to her known nobility and *hidalguía*, she should suffer precisely the penalties prescribed [i.e., disinheritance] in the latest publicly announced Royal Pragmatic [*Real Pragmatica*], that all in these realms are ordered to follow, guard, fulfill, and execute. The court should condescend to resolve and judge the case, both because the law is clearly on my client's side and because, despite the cunning lobbying, with which Teodoro has tried, with no other merit than his moneyed wealth, to aspire to a much higher station than that [appropriate to] his low birth, he does not cease to be the son of Juan Jaramillo, who was himself born of another don Juan Jaramillo and Margarita González, Valdivieso, o Montesdoca, who, not knowing with certitude the identity of her father, must be classified as an Indian like her mother. Nor does Teodoro cease being the son of María de Ureña, known as the Maco Regala, wife of the *truquero* Bartolome Galvez, both low people, who as such occupied the servile and mechanical stations appropriate to their birth. Because of his low birth, Jaramillo worked in the profession of silversmith under the shadow of his uncle Esteban Ureña, who instructed him publicly as an apprentice, until he went on to serve as steward in the house *fábrica* of don Miguel Carrión, and then as muleteer, or driver of his mules, a profession he carried out for many years in the company of don Pedro Javier Valdivieso, without neglecting all the activities with which he made his fortune. He then bought the Catamayo hacienda, which has increased his means and made him conceited, so that, forgetting his humble beginnings, he claims not only to equal but even to exceed the distinguished *calidad* of my client. And his whole family, conspiring with their witnesses, who are of the same extraction as his, showing disrespect for the constant echo of the truth and the sacred religion of the oath, have insisted on ennobling their mean descent, not only through the [honorific] don, with which they prodigiously honor themselves, but also through nobility itself, which they ascribe to their ancestors, who, due to their contemptible *calidad*, never held any honorable position of the kind held by subjects of distinction. And as [they have always carried out the] low, manual trades, they have not passed beyond being silversmiths and servants. Jaramillo himself, with all his fortune, hardly exudes the dignity of a steward of the city, this being a position that the illustrious citizens of the most distinguished nobility have never obtained. . . .

That a corrupt or indulgent patron might give the title of don, which these days plebeian men often enjoy, does not mean that they therefore can constitute themselves as nobles without the requisites that laws and rights prescribe. . . .

The unfortunate witnesses had wished to distinguish the family of the Ureñas, Regalados and Lopez, who have earned nothing more than the honor of being either silversmiths or servants. Even if they might not have been of mixed origin, but had been Spaniards, they would not pass beyond the rank of montañeses, who are commonly known as *mestizos* [of European-Indian descent] of a slightly better class than the children of an Indian woman and a Spaniard. . . .

That is why the inequality which exists between Jaramillo and doña Baltasara is irrefutable, he descending from subjects of obscure birth and the lowest plebs, and she from the most distinguished, who, corresponding to their eminent nobility, have occupied the most honorable offices of the republic, as is consistent and publicly known.

18.3 Defense Submitted to the Court by Tomás Garcia y Sierra, Attorney for Don Juan Teodoro Jaramillo

I, Tomás Garcia y Sierra, in the name of don Juan Teodoro Jaramillo, citizen of the city of Loja, in virtue of the power he has invested in me to act in the lawsuit against don Manuel Valdivieso y Carrión . . . state that:

I will examine the foundations on which the complaint is based, and, as one cannot deny that don Manuel and his daughter doña Baltasara are accepted as noble and esteemed as such without dispute, it only remains to see if the lineage of my client has the claimed social distance to consider that matrimony is seriously offensive to the honor of the family of don Manuel, [considering] the [appropriate] degree [of relationship] laid out in the Royal Pragmatic of 1776. And in fact, the evidence given by both parties does not justify the [accusation of] low origin and extremely ignoble extraction which has been made against my client; on the contrary, the purity of his blood and his *hidalguía* are demonstrated, all of which refutes the insults and invectives he has been exposed to. . . . All his uncles and cousins, legitimate descendants of don Juan Jaramillo, have been regarded as persons of known nobility and distinguished *calidad*, for which reason they had obtained the best offices of that community (*republica*) and were married to women of the same class, as is entirely confirmed in detail by the certificate presented by don Manuel Jaramillo, second cousin of my client and, at the moment, *alcalde ordinario* of the city of Loja. This document should be kept in mind because it accurately enumerates the offices, honors, and marriages from the first don Juan Jaramillo, who was born in Alcala de Henares. . . .

The copious number of witnesses that my client presented before the corregidor [original arbiter of the case] confirmed unanimously that [Jaramillo's] ancestors, dona Margarita included, were not of the race of *negros*, Indians, and *mulattos*.

The nobility of his mother [is] impossible to deny, as it is confirmed by an extensive number of witnesses who affirm that they had known dona María, that she was the daughter of don Pedro Regalado de Ureña and dona Clara Lopez de la farina, and that he [Pedro] was the son of the captain Antonio de Ureña and dona Isabel de Solorzano, and that doña Clara was the legitimate daughter of don Marcos Lopez de la Parilla and doña Elena Roman, all of them noble persons, free (*limpia*: literally, "clean") of people [descendants] from other castes.

The Royal Pragmatic does not require a mathematical equality between prospective husbands and wives when it obliges the parents, relatives, or guardians to give their assent. And it only requires assent when matrimony does not seriously offend the honor of the family, declaring just cause for dissent in the case of a serious offense. And no one doubts that not every inequality is seriously offensive, since to be so it is necessary that the social difference be too striking and excessive. . . .

All of this evidence [about the standing of Juan Teodoro] is enhanced by the extensive proof that my client has offered concerning his good habits and behavior. Although the opposing attorney characterizes this justification as useless and superfluous to this lawsuit, my client thought to present it as more relevant to the honor of his person, since he has well understood, by what the arbitristas teach, that the political nobility that consists in good habits is better than the legal and civil one derived from blood, that moral virtue exceeds natural virtue, and that the nobility of heroic actions exceeds the nobility of blood. It is the same as when a philosopher, asked what nobility consists of, answers that in the case of the beasts it refers to the good constitution of the body, in the case of men to their good and laudable actions. One may infer, then, that, far from being superfluous to the lawsuit, this evidence is most suitable to prove that my client has this double nobility that makes him worthy of the esteem that has been granted to his person in private and public acts in this neighborhood (*vecindario*). Also, it [has not] been proven otherwise that the office and profession [of steward of the city], to which he had been appointed in the year 1781, is appropriate only to plebeian men as, on the contrary, it has clearly been carried out by nobles. . . .

When asked if the nobility loses its privileges through the practice of ignoble and mechanical professions, A.A. [the *arbitristas*] resolve that it is not denigrated if the nobility derives from blood and not from privilege, and that is the general opinion. . . .

The earlier consent [of Manuel Valdivieso] was directed toward removing, through the remedy of matrimony, the public infamy that doña Baltasara must have suffered because of the illicit contact she had with my client for over two years without her parents having said a word in opposition in all this time. . . .

It would not be reasonable to thwart this marriage of doña Baltasara, because, under these circumstances, no one would want her to be his wife, nor would it be possible for her to find another husband who, knowing about her former relationship (*amistad*), would extend to her the appropriate respect. It is also not tolerable that my client be scorned when he aspires to grace through [the sacrament of] matrimony, having been valued during the illicit relationship, letting it be known through such irregular means that his notion of nobility prevails over [the obligations of] religion. One should conclude from this argument, and from the sufficient proof I have presented to demonstrate the hidalguía of my client, that the petition of don Manuel Valdivieso should be declared unfounded and unjust. . . .

READING AND DISCUSSION QUESTIONS

1. How does lineage factor into the discussion of Jaramillo's worthiness to marry Valdivieso's daughter?

2. Witnesses and attorneys all discuss the issues of honor and nobility in making their cases. Based on their testimony, how are these terms defined?

3. What evidence is offered to establish the supposed inequality of Jaramillo to Valdivieso's family?

4.   What consequences might blocking this marriage have on Baltasara, the intended bride, and what does this reveal about gender roles in Spanish colonies?

DOCUMENT 26-2

Cherokee Nation versus the State of Georgia

1831

The economic development of the United States in the nineteenth century rested, in part, on expanding the nation's landholdings westward onto Indian lands, even if that meant violating earlier treaties. In 1828, Georgia passed several laws to remove the Cherokee from their homeland. Cherokee chief John Ross fought back, appealing first to Congress and, after passage of the federal Cherokee Removal Act, by filing suit in 1830 on behalf of his tribe. In 1931, Supreme Court Justice John Marshall wrote the following opinion dismissing the case, thereby denying self-governance to the Cherokee. Seven years later, President Martin Van Buren enforced his predecessor Andrew Jackson's decision to resettle the Cherokee from Georgia to Oklahoma in a forced march that became known as the Trail of Tears.

Mr. Chief Justice MARSHALL delivered the opinion of the Court:

This bill is brought by the Cherokee Nation, praying an injunction to restrain the state of Georgia from the execution of certain laws of that state, which as is alleged, go directly to annihilate the Cherokees as a political society, and to seize, for the use of Georgia, the lands of the nation which have been assured to them by the United States in solemn treaties repeatedly made and still in force.

If courts were permitted to indulge their sympathies, a case better calculated to excite them can scarcely be imagined. A people once numerous, powerful, and truly independent, found by our ancestors in the quiet and uncontrolled possession of an ample domain, gradually sinking beneath our superior policy, our arts, and our arms, have yielded their lands by successive treaties, each of which contains a solemn guarantee of the

Cherokee Nation v. Georgia, 30 U.S. 1 (1831).

residue, until they retain no more of their formerly extensive territory than is deemed necessary to their comfortable subsistence. To preserve this remnant the present application is made.

Before we can look into the merits of the case, a preliminary inquiry presents itself. Has this Court jurisdiction of the cause?

The 3rd Article of the Constitution describes the extent of the judicial power. The 2nd Section closes an enumeration of the cases to which it is extended, with controversies between a state or the citizens thereof, and foreign states, citizens, or subjects. A subsequent clause of the same section gives the Supreme Court original jurisdiction in all cases in which a state shall be a party. The party defendant may then unquestionably be sued in this Court. May the plaintiff sue in it? Is the Cherokee Nation a foreign state in the sense in which that term is used in the Constitution?

The counsel for the plaintiffs have maintained the affirmative of this proposition with great earnestness and ability. So much of the argument as was intended to prove the character of the Cherokees as a state, as a distinct political society separated from others, capable of managing its own affairs and governing itself, has, in the opinion of a majority of the judges, been completely successful. They have been uniformly treated as a state from the settlement of our country. The numerous treaties made with them by the United States recognize them as a people capable of maintaining the relations of peace and war, of being responsible in their political character for any violation of their engagements, or for any aggression committed on the citizens of the United States by any individual of their community. Laws have been enacted in the spirit of these treaties. The acts of our government plainly recognize the Cherokee Nation as a state, and the courts are bound by those acts.

A question of much more difficulty remains. Do the Cherokees constitute a foreign state in the sense of the Constitution?

The counsel have shown conclusively that they are not a state of the Union, and have insisted that individually they are aliens, not owing allegiance to the United States. An aggregate of aliens composing a state must, they say, be a foreign state. Each individual being foreign, the whole must be foreign.

This argument is imposing, but we must examine it more closely before we yield to it. The condition of the Indians in relation to the United States is perhaps unlike that of any other two people in existence. In the general, nations not owing a common allegiance are foreign to each other. The term foreign nation is, with strict propriety, applicable by either to the other. But the relation of the Indians to the United States is marked by peculiar and cardinal distinctions which exist nowhere else.

The Indian Territory is admitted to compose part of the United States. In all our maps, geographical treatises, histories, and laws, it is so considered. In all our intercourse with foreign nations, in our commercial regulations, in any attempt at intercourse between Indians and foreign nations, they are considered as within the jurisdictional limits of the United States, subject to many of those restraints which are imposed upon our own citizens. They acknowledge themselves in their treaties to be under the protection of the United States; they admit that the United States shall have the sole and exclusive right of regulating the trade with them and managing all their affairs as they think proper; and the Cherokees in particular were allowed by the Treaty of Hopewell,[5] which preceded the Constitution, to send a deputy of their choice, whenever they think fit, to Congress. Treaties were made with some tribes by the state of New York under a then unsettled construction of the Confederation, by which they ceded all their lands to that state, taking back a limited grant to themselves in which they admit their dependence.

Though the Indians are acknowledged to have an unquestionable and, heretofore, unquestioned right to the lands they occupy until that right shall be extinguished by a voluntary cession to our government, yet it may well be doubted whether those tribes which reside within the acknowledged boundaries of the United States can, with strict accuracy, be denominated foreign nations. They may more correctly, perhaps, be denominated domestic dependent nations. They occupy a territory to which we assert a title independent of their will, which must take effect in point of possession when their right of possession ceases. Meanwhile, they are in a state of pupilage. Their relation to the United States resembles that of a ward to his guardian.

They look to our government for protection; rely upon its kindness and its power; appeal to it for relief to their wants; and address the President as their great father. They and their country are considered by foreign nations, as well as by ourselves, as being so completely under the sovereignty and dominion of the United States that any attempt to acquire their lands or to form a political connection with them would be considered by all as an invasion of our territory and an act of hostility.

These considerations go far to support the opinion that the framers of our Constitution had not the Indian tribes in view when they opened the courts of the Union to controversies between a state or the citizens thereof and foreign states.

---

[5] **Treaty of Hopewell**: Signed on November 28, 1785, this treaty between the United States and Cherokee Indians defined the westernmost boundary for white settlement.

In considering this subject, the habits and usages of the Indians in their intercourse with their white neighbors ought not to be entirely disregarded. At the time the Constitution was framed, the idea of appealing to an American court of justice for an assertion of right or a redress of wrong had perhaps never entered the mind of an Indian or of his tribe. Their appeal was to the tomahawk, or to the government. This was well understood by the statesmen who framed the Constitution of the United States, and might furnish some reason for omitting to enumerate them among the parties who might sue in the courts of the Union. Be this as it may, the peculiar relations between the United States and the Indians occupying our territory are such that we should feel much difficulty in considering them as designated by the term foreign state were there no other part of the Constitution which might shed light on the meaning of these words. But we think that in construing them, considerable aid is furnished by that clause in the 8th Section of the 3rd Article, which empowers Congress to regulate commerce with foreign nations, and among the several states, and with the Indian tribes.

In this clause they are as clearly contradistinguished by a name appropriate to themselves from foreign nations as from the several states composing the Union. They are designated by a distinct appellation; and as this appellation can be applied to neither of the others, neither can the appellation distinguishing either of the others be in fair construction applied to them. The objects to which the power of regulating commerce might be directed are divided into three distinct classes: foreign nations, the several states, and Indian tribes. When forming this article, the Convention considered them as entirely distinct. We cannot assume that the distinction was lost in framing a subsequent article, unless there be something in its language to authorize the assumption.

Foreign nations is a general term, the application of which to Indian tribes, when used in the American Constitution, is at best extremely questionable. In one article in which a power is given to be exercised in regard to foreign nations generally, and to the Indian tribes particularly, they are mentioned as separate in terms clearly contradistinguishing them from each other. We perceive plainly that the Constitution in this article does not comprehend Indian tribes in the general term foreign nations; not, we presume, because a tribe may not be a nation but because it is not foreign to the United States. When, afterward, the term foreign state is introduced, we cannot impute to the Convention the intention to desert its former meaning and to comprehend Indian tribes within it, unless the context force that construction on us. We find nothing in the context and nothing in the subject of the article which leads to it.

The Court has bestowed its best attention on this question and, after mature deliberation, the majority is of opinion that an Indian tribe or nation within the United States is not a foreign state in the sense of the Constitution, and cannot maintain an action in the courts of the United States.

A serious additional objection exists to the jurisdiction of the Court. Is the matter of the bill the proper subject for judicial inquiry and decision? It seeks to restrain a state from the forcible exercise of legislative power over a neighboring people, asserting their independence; their right to which the state denies. On several of the matters alleged in the bill, for example on the laws making it criminal to exercise the usual powers of self-government in their own country by the Cherokee Nation, this Court cannot interpose, at least in the form in which those matters are presented.

That part of the bill which respects the land occupied by the Indians, and prays the aid of the Court to protect their possession, may be more doubtful. The mere question of right might perhaps be decided by this Court in a proper case with proper parties. But the Court is asked to do more than decide on the title. The bill requires us to control the legislature of Georgia, and to restrain the exertion of its physical force. The propriety of such an interposition by the Court may be well questioned. It savors too much of the exercise of political power to be within the proper province of the Judicial Department. But the opinion on the point respecting parties makes it unnecessary to decide this question.

If it be true that the Cherokee Nation have rights, this is not the tribunal in which those rights are to be asserted. If it be true that wrongs have been inflicted and that still greater are to be apprehended, this is not the tribunal which can redress the past or prevent the future.

The motion for an injunction is denied.

READING AND DISCUSSION QUESTIONS

1. How does Justice Marshall define "foreign nation"?
2. What are the unique qualities of the U.S. relationship with Indians according to Marshall?
3. Why does Marshall use the phrase "domestic dependent nations" in relation to Native Americans?
4. Why does Marshall say that the Court is not the place to address the rights of the Cherokee in this matter?

| DOCUMENT 26-3 |

ALEXIS DE TOCQUEVILLE
From Democracy in America
1840

French thinker Alexis de Tocqueville (1805–1859) spent much of the early 1800s touring the United States and writing about the uniqueness of the American democratic experiment. His incisive observations revealed the strengths and inherent weaknesses of a political and economic system based on the notion of equality. One area in which democracy seemed to contradict itself was military service and the quest for peace. Tocqueville's comments on this topic were published a decade after the wars for independence in Latin and South America left parts of those regions under military rule and other areas plagued by violence and the need to recruit armies by force.

BOOK III
CHAPTER XXII
WHY DEMOCRATIC NATIONS NATURALLY DESIRE PEACE, AND DEMOCRATIC ARMIES, WAR

The same interests, the same fears, the same passions that deter democratic nations from revolutions deter them also from war; the spirit of military glory and the spirit of revolution are weakened at the same time and by the same causes. The ever increasing numbers of men of property who are lovers of peace, the growth of personal wealth which war so rapidly consumes, the mildness of manners, the gentleness of heart, those tendencies to pity which are produced by the equality of conditions, that coolness of understanding which renders men comparatively insensible to the violent and poetical excitement of arms, all these causes concur to quench the military spirit. I think it may be admitted as a general and constant rule that among civilized nations the warlike passions will become more rare and less intense in proportion as social conditions are more equal.

War is nevertheless an occurrence to which all nations are subject, democratic nations as well as others. Whatever taste they may have for peace,

---

Alexis de Tocqueville, *Democracy in America*, 3d ed., ed. Francis Bowen, trans. Henry Reeve (Cambridge: Sever & Francis, 1863), II:326–332.

they must hold themselves in readiness to repel aggression, or, in other words, they must have an army. Fortune, which has conferred so many peculiar benefits upon the inhabitants of the United States, has placed them in the midst of a wilderness, where they have, so to speak, no neighbors; a few thousand soldiers are sufficient for their wants. But this is peculiar to America, not to democracy.

The equality of conditions and the manners as well as the institutions resulting from it do not exempt a democratic people from the necessity of standing armies, and their armies always exercise a powerful influence over their fate. It is therefore of singular importance to inquire what are the natural propensities of the men of whom these armies are composed.

Amongst aristocratic nations, especially among those in which birth is the only source of rank, the same inequality exists in the army as in the nation; the officer is noble, the soldier is a serf; the one is naturally called upon to command, the other to obey. In aristocratic armies the private soldier's ambition is therefore circumscribed within very narrow limits. Nor has the ambition of the officer an unlimited range. An aristocratic body not only forms a part of the scale of ranks in the nation, but contains a scale of ranks within itself; the members of whom it is composed are placed one above another in a particular and unvarying manner. Thus one man is born to the command of a regiment, another to that of a company. When once they have reached the utmost object of their hopes, they stop of their own accord and remain contented with their lot.

There is, besides, a strong cause that in aristocracies weakens the officer's desire of promotion. Among aristocratic nations an officer, independently of his rank in the army, also occupies an elevated rank in society; the former is almost always, in his eyes, only an appendage to the latter. A nobleman who embraces the profession of arms follows it less from motives of ambition than from a sense of the duties imposed on him by his birth. He enters the army in order to find an honorable employment for the idle years of his youth and to be able to bring back to his home and his peers some honorable recollections of military life; but his principal object is not to obtain by that profession either property, distinction, or power, for he possesses these advantages in his own right and enjoys them without leaving his home.

In democratic armies all the soldiers may become officers, which makes the desire of promotion general and immeasurably extends the bounds of military ambition. The officer, on his part, sees nothing that naturally and necessarily stops him at one grade more than at another; and each grade has immense importance in his eyes because his rank in society almost always depends on his rank in the army. Amongst democratic nations it often happens that an officer has no property but his pay and no distinction but that of military honors; consequently, as often as his duties change, his fortune changes and he becomes, as it were, a new man. What was only an appendage to his position in aristocratic armies has thus become the main point, the basis of his whole condition.

Under the old French monarchy officers were always called by their titles of nobility; they are now always called by the title of their military rank. This little change in the forms of language suffices to show that a great revolution has taken place in the constitution of society and in that of the army.

In democratic armies the desire of advancement is almost universal: it is ardent, tenacious, perpetual; it is strengthened by all other desires and extinguished only with life itself. But it is easy to see that, of all armies in the world, those in which advancement must be slowest in time of peace are the armies of democratic countries. As the number of commissions is naturally limited while the number of competitors is almost unlimited, and as the strict law of equality is over all alike, none can make rapid progress; many can make no progress at all. Thus the desire of advancement is greater and the opportunities of advancement fewer there than elsewhere. All the ambitious spirits of a democratic army are consequently ardently desirous of war, because war makes vacancies and warrants the violation of that law of seniority which is the sole privilege natural to democracy.

We thus arrive at this singular consequence, that, of all armies, those most ardently desirous of war are democratic armies, and of all nations, those most fond of peace are democratic nations; and what makes these facts still more extraordinary is that these contrary effects are produced at the same time by the principle of equality.

All the members of the community, being alike, constantly harbor the wish and discover the possibility of changing their condition and improving their welfare; this makes them fond of peace, which is favorable to industry and allows every man to pursue his own little undertakings to their completion. On the other hand, this same equality makes soldiers dream of fields of battle, by increasing the value of military honors in the eyes of those who follow the profession of arms and by rendering those honors accessible to all. In either case the restlessness of the heart is the same, the taste for enjoyment is insatiable, the ambition of success as great; the means of gratifying it alone are different.

These opposite tendencies of the nation and the army expose democratic communities to great dangers. When a military spirit forsakes a people, the profession of arms immediately ceases to be held in honor and military men fall to the lowest rank of the public servants; they are little esteemed and no longer understood. The reverse of what takes place in aristocratic ages then occurs; the men who enter the army are no longer those of the highest, but of the lowest class. Military ambition is indulged only when no other is possible. Hence arises a circle of cause and consequence from which it is difficult to escape: the best part of the nation shuns the military profession because that profession is not honored, and the profession is not honored because the best part of the nation has ceased to follow it.

It is then no matter of surprise that democratic armies are often restless, ill-tempered, and dissatisfied with their lot, although their physical condition is commonly far better and their discipline less strict than in other countries. The soldier feels that he occupies an inferior position, and his wounded pride either stimulates his taste for hostilities that would render his services necessary or gives him a desire for revolution, during which he may hope to win by force of arms the political influence and personal importance now denied him.

The composition of democratic armies makes this last-mentioned danger much to be feared. In democratic communities almost every man has some property to preserve; but democratic armies are generally led by men without property, most of whom have little to lose in civil broils. The bulk of the nation is naturally much more afraid of revolutions than in the ages of aristocracy, but the leaders of the army much less so.

Moreover, as amongst democratic nations (to repeat what I have just remarked) the wealthiest, best-educated, and ablest men seldom adopt the military profession, the army, taken collectively, eventually forms a small nation by itself, where the mind is less enlarged and habits are more rude than in the nation at large. Now, this small uncivilized nation has arms in its possession and alone knows how to use them; for, indeed, the pacific temper of the community increases the danger to which a democratic people is exposed from the military and turbulent spirit of the army. Nothing is so dangerous as an army in the midst of an unwarlike nation; the excessive love of the whole community for quiet continually puts the constitution at the mercy of the soldiery.

It may therefore be asserted, generally speaking, that if democratic nations are naturally prone to peace from their interests and their propensities, they are constantly drawn to war and revolutions by their armies. Military revolutions, which are scarcely ever to be apprehended in aristocracies, are always to be dreaded among democratic nations. These perils must be reckoned among the most formidable that beset their future fate, and the attention of statesmen should be sedulously applied to find a remedy for the evil.

When a nation perceives that it is inwardly affected by the restless ambition of its army, the first thought which occurs is to give this inconvenient ambition an object by going to war. I do not wish to speak ill of war: war almost always enlarges the mind of a people and raises their character. In some cases it is the only check to the excessive growth of certain propensities that naturally spring out of the equality of conditions, and it must be considered as a necessary corrective to certain inveterate diseases to which democratic communities are liable.

War has great advantages, but we must not flatter ourselves that it can diminish the danger I have just pointed out. That peril is only suspended by it, to return more fiercely when the war is over; for armies are much more impatient of peace after having tasted military exploits. War could be a remedy only for a people who were always a thirst for military glory.

I foresee that all the military rulers who may rise up in great democratic nations will find it easier to conquer with their armies than to make their armies live at peace after conquest. There are two things that a democratic people will always find very difficult, to begin a war and to end it.

Again, if war has some peculiar advantages for democratic nations, on the other hand it exposes them to certain dangers which aristocracies have no cause to dread to an equal extent. I shall point out only two of these.

Although war gratifies the army, it embarrasses and often exasperates that countless multitude of men whose minor passions every day require peace in order to be satisfied. Thus there is some risk of its causing, under another form, the very disturbance it is intended to prevent.

No protracted war can fail to endanger the freedom of a democratic country. Not indeed that after every victory it is to be apprehended that the victorious generals will possess themselves by force of the supreme power, after the manner of Sulla and Caesar;[6] the danger is of another kind. War does not always give over democratic communities to military government, but it must invariably and immeasurably increase the powers of civil government; it must almost compulsorily concentrate the direction of all men and the management of all things in the hands of the administration. If it does not lead to despotism by sudden violence, it prepares men for it more gently by their habits. All those who seek to destroy the liberties of a democratic nation ought to know that war is the surest and the shortest means to accomplish it. This is the first axiom of the science.

---

[6] **Sulla and Caesar**: Sulla refers to Lucius Cornelius Sulla, a dictator who claimed power in Rome from 82 to 79 B.C.E.; Caesar is Julius Caesar, dictator of Rome from 45 to 44 B.C.E., when he was murdered by political leaders who feared his growing sense of self-importance.

One remedy, which appears to be obvious when the ambition of soldiers and officers becomes the subject of alarm, is to augment the number of commissions to be distributed by increasing the army. This affords temporary relief, but it plunges the country into deeper difficulties at some future period. To increase the army may produce a lasting effect in an aristocratic community, because military ambition is there confined to one class of men, and the ambition of each individual stops, as it were, at a certain limit, so that it may be possible to satisfy all who feel its influence. But nothing is gained by increasing the army among a democratic people, because the number of aspirants always rises in exactly the same ratio as the army itself. Those whose claims have been satisfied by the creation of new commissions are instantly succeeded by a fresh multitude beyond all power of satisfaction; and even those who were but now satisfied soon begin to crave more advancement, for the same excitement prevails in the ranks of the army as in the civil classes of democratic society, and what men want is, not to reach a certain grade, but to have constant promotion. Though these wants may not be very vast, they are perpetually recurring. Thus a democratic nation, by augmenting its army, allays only for a time the ambition of the military profession, which soon becomes even more formidable because the number of those who feel it is increased.

I am of the opinion that a restless and turbulent spirit is an evil inherent in the very constitution of democratic armies and beyond hope of cure. The legislators of democracies must not expect to devise any military organization capable by its influence of calming and restraining the military profession; their efforts would exhaust their powers before the object could be attained.

The remedy for the vices of the army is not to be found in the army itself, but in the country. Democratic nations are naturally afraid of disturbance and of despotism; the object is to turn these natural instincts into intelligent, deliberate, and lasting tastes. When men have at last learned to make a peaceful and profitable use of freedom and have felt its blessings, when they have conceived a manly love of order and have freely submitted themselves to discipline, these same men, if they follow the profession of arms, bring into it, unconsciously and almost against their will, these same habits and manners. The general spirit of the nation, being infused into the spirit peculiar to the army, tempers the opinions and desires engendered by military life, or represses them by the mighty force of public opinion. Teach the citizens to be educated, orderly, firm, and free and the soldiers will be disciplined and obedient.

Any law that, in repressing the turbulent spirit of the army, should tend to diminish the spirit of freedom in the nation and to overshadow the notion of law and right would defeat its object; it would do much more to favor than to defeat the establishment of military tyranny. After all, and in spite of all precautions, a large army in the midst of a democratic people will always be a source of great danger. The most effectual means of diminishing that danger would be to reduce the army, but this is a remedy that all nations are not able to apply.

READING AND DISCUSSION QUESTIONS

1. How is military rank determined in aristocratic nations? How is it determined in democratic countries?

2. According to Tocqueville, the principle of equality inspires different motivations among the soldiers and citizens of a democracy. What are these motivations, and why might they be a source of conflict?

3. Tocqueville says that laws won't keep armies from seeking to wage war. What does he see as the key to a lasting peace?

DOCUMENT 26-4

JOSÉ CARLOS MARÍATEGUI

From Seven Interpretive Essays on Peruvian
Reality: *On the Indian and Land*

1928

By the 1900s, several centuries of land grabbing by European settlers had left South American Indians in dire poverty. In Peru, a rising demand for agricultural products fueled new laws that enabled rich landowners to snatch up larger shares of Indian land, forcing many Indians to work as low-paid laborers and farmhands. A new cadre of intellectuals — many of them Marxists — began to explore the Indians' plight with genuine concern. Some, such as Peruvian journalist José Carlos Maríategui (1894–1930),

---

José Carlos Maríategui, "The Problem of the Indian," *Seven Interpretive Essays on Peruvian Reality*, trans. Marjory Urquidi (Austin, TX: University of Texas Press, 1971), 22–25, 31–33, 58–61.

countered prevailing ideas about the "inferiority" of Indians and argued that economic policies — especially those concerning land — were largely responsible for the vast gulf between rich whites and impoverished Indians.

[THE PROBLEM OF THE INDIAN]

Any treatment of the problem of the Indian . . . that fails or refuses to recognize it as a socio-economic problem is but a sterile, theoretical exercise destined to be completely discredited. . . . The socialist[7] critic exposes and defines the problem because he looks for its causes in the country's economy and not in its administrative, legal, or ecclesiastic machinery, its racial dualism or pluralism, or its cultural or moral conditions. The problem of the Indian is rooted in the land tenure system of our economy. Any attempt to solve it with administrative . . . measures, through education or by a road building program, is superficial and secondary as long as the feudalism of the *gamonales* [great landowners] continues to exist.

Gamonalismo[8] necessarily invalidates any law or regulation for the protection of the Indian. The hacienda owner, the *latifundista*[9] is a feudal lord. The written law is powerless against his authority, which is supported by custom and habit. Unpaid labor is illegal, yet unpaid and even forced labor survive in the latifundium. The judge, the subprefect, the commissary, the teacher, the tax collector, all are in bondage to the landed estate. The law cannot prevail against the *gamonales*. Any official who insisted on applying it would be abandoned and sacrificed by the central government. . . .

The oldest and most obvious mistake is, unquestionably, that of reducing the protection of the Indian to an ordinary administrative matter. From the days of Spanish colonial legislation, wise and detailed ordinances, worked out after conscientious study, have been quite useless. The republic, since independence [in 1824], has been prodigal in its decrees, laws, and provisions intended to protect the Indian against exaction and abuse. The *gamonal* of today, . . . however, has little to fear from administrative theory; he knows that its practice is altogether different.

---

[7] **socialist**: One who embraces the political and economic theory that government should own the means of production and manage and distribute resources.

[8] ***Gamonalismo***: Social and political domination of rural Peru by wealthy landowners; sometimes translated as "feudalism."

[9] **latifundista**: Owner of a *latifundio*, a large landed estate worked by farm laborers in a state of partial serfdom.

The individualistic character of the republic's legislation has favored the absorption of Indian property by the latifundium system. . . . The appropriation of most communal and individual Indian property is an accomplished fact. . . .

The assumption that the Indian problem is ethnic is sustained by the most outmoded repertory of imperialist ideas. The concept of inferior races was useful to the white man's West for purposes of expansion and conquest. To expect that the Indian will be emancipated through a steady crossing of the aboriginal race with white immigrants is an anti-sociological naiveté that could only occur to the primitive mentality of an importer of merino sheep. The people of Asia, who are in no way superior to the Indians, have not needed any transfusion of European blood in order to assimilate the most dynamic and creative aspects of Western culture. The degeneration of the Peruvian Indian is a cheap invention of sophists [distracters] who serve feudal interests. . . .

The tendency to consider the Indian problem as a moral one embodies a liberal, humanitarian, enlightened nineteenth-century attitude. . . . The anti-slavery conferences and societies in Europe that have denounced more or less futilely the crimes of the colonizing nations are born of this tendency, which always has trusted too much in its appeals to the conscience of civilization. . . .

Humanitarian teachings have not halted or hampered European imperialism, nor have they reformed its methods. The struggle against imperialism now relies only on the solidarity and strength of the liberation movement of the colonial masses. . . .

On a moral and intellectual plane, the church took a more energetic or at least a more authoritative stand centuries ago. This crusade, however, achieved only very wise laws and provisions. The lot of the Indian remained substantially the same. . . . To wipe out abuses, it would have been necessary to abolish land appropriation and forced labor, in brief, to change the entire colonial regime. Without the toil of the American Indian, the coffers of the Spanish treasury would have been emptied.

But today a religious solution is unquestionably the most outdated and antihistoric of all. . . . If the church could not accomplish its task in a medieval era, when its spiritual and intellectual capacity could be measured by friars like Las Casas,[10] how can it succeed with the elements in

---

[10] **Las Casas**: Bartolomé de Las Casas (1474–1566) was a Spanish friar who denounced the exploitation of Amerindians by the Spanish (see Document 15-1).

commands today? . . . The belief that the Indian problem is one of education does not seem to be supported by even a strictly and independently pedagogical criterion. . . . School and teacher are doomed to be debased under the pressure of the feudal regime, which cannot be reconciled with the most elementary concept of progress and evolution. When this truth becomes partially understood, the saving formula is thought to be discovered in boarding schools for Indians. But the glaring inadequacy of this formula is self-evident in view of the tiny percentage of the indigenous school population that can be boarded in these schools.

The pedagogical solution, advocated by many in good faith, has been discarded officially. . . .

The new approach locates the problem of the Indian in the land tenure system.

[THE PROBLEM OF LAND]

Those of us who approach and define the Indian problem from a Socialist point of view must start out by declaring the complete obsolescence of the humanitarian and philanthropic points of view. . . . We shall try to establish the basically economic character of the problem. First, we protest against the instinctive attempt of the criollo or mestizo[11] to reduce it to an exclusively administrative, pedagogical, ethnic, or moral problem in order to avoid at all cost recognizing its economic aspect. . . . We are not satisfied to assert the Indian's right to education, culture, progress, love, and heaven. We begin by categorically asserting his right to land. . . .

The agrarian problem is first and foremost the problem of eliminating feudalism in Peru, which should have been done by the democratic-bourgeois regime that followed the War of Independence.[12] But in its one hundred years as a republic, Peru has not had a genuine bourgeois class, a true capitalist class. The old feudal class — camouflaged or disguised as a republican bourgeoisie — has kept its position. . . . During a century of Republican rule, great agricultural property actually has grown stronger and expanded, despite the theoretical liberalism of our constitution and the practical necessities of the development of our capitalist economy. There are two expressions of feudalism that survive: the latifundium and

---

[11] **criollo or mestizo**: A criollo is a Peruvian of European descent; a mestizo is a person of European-Indian descent.

[12] **War of Independence**: Battles between Peru and the Spanish crown from 1809 to 1821 that resulted in Peru's liberation from Spanish rule.

servitude. Inseparable and of the same substance, their analysis leads us to the conclusion that the servitude oppressing the indigenous race cannot be abolished unless the latifundium is abolished. . . .

Everyone knows that the liberal solution for this problem, in conformity with individualist ideology, would be to break up the latifundio in order to create small landed properties. . . .

In conformity with my ideological position, I think that in Peru the hour for trying the liberal method, the individualist formula, has already passed. Leaving doctrinal reasons aside, I regard as fundamental an indisputable and concrete factor that gives a peculiar stamp to our agrarian problem: the survival of the Indian community and of elements of practical socialism in Indian life and agriculture.

In Peru, communal property does not represent a primitive economy that has gradually been replaced by a progressive economy founded on individual property. No; the "communities" have been despoiled of their land for the benefit of the feudal or semi-feudal latifundium, which is constitutionally incapable of technical progress.

The latifundium compares unfavorably with the "community" as an enterprise for agricultural production. . . . Large property seems to be justified by the interests of production, which are identified, at least in theory, with the interests of society. But this is not the case of the latifundium and, therefore, it does not meet an economic need. Except for sugarcane plantations — which produce *aguardiente* [liquor] to intoxicate and stupefy the Indian peasant — the latifundium of the sierra generally grows the same crops as the "community," and it produces no more. . . .

The "community," on the one hand, is a system of production that keeps alive in the Indian the moral incentives that stimulate him to do his best work. . . .

By dissolving or abandoning the "community," the system of the feudal latifundium has attacked not only an economic institution but also, and more important, a social institution, one that defends the indigenous tradition [and] maintains the function of the rural family. . . .

READING AND DISCUSSION QUESTIONS

1. What are some of the arguments that Europeans used to defend the latifundium system?

2. Why did laws that were designed to protect Indians ultimately prove useless?

3. What evidence does Maríategui offer as proof that a religious solution to the Indians' woes would fail?

4. What solutions does Maríategui see in community land ownership? What makes it superior to feudalism?

DOCUMENT 26-5

From Aborigines Protection Act

1909–1943

Beginning in 1869, Australian officials adopted new laws that reflected the uneasy coexistence of the island's native Aborigine and settler populations. The Aborigines Protection Act, which was amended several times through 1943, on the surface attempted to protect the native nomadic peoples. In reality, it sought to regulate their lives in numerous ways, including outlining where they could work and live. The most controversial aspect of the law was its application to Aborigine children, who could legally be taken from their parents — sometimes forcibly and permanently — at the discretion of the state.

ACT NO. 25, 1909.

An Act to provide for the protection and care of aborigines; to repeal the Supply of Liquors to Aborigines Prevention Act; to amend the Vagrancy Act, 1902, and the Police Offences (Amendment) Act, 1908; and for purposes consequent thereon or incidental thereto. [Assented to, 20th December, 1909.]

Be it enacted by the King's Most Excellent Majesty, by and with the advice and consent of the Legislative Council and Legislative Assembly of New South Wales in Parliament assembled, and by the authority of the same, as follows: —

1. This Act may be cited as the "Aborigines Protection Act, 1909," and shall come into force on a date to be fixed by proclamation of the Governor in the Gazette.

Public Acts of New South Wales, 1824–1957, eds. R. J. McKay, O. M. L. Davies, and S. G. O. Martin (Sydney, Australia: Law Book Co. of Australia PTY LTD., 1958).

2. The Acts specified in the Schedule hereto are, to the extent indicated, repealed.

3. In this Act, unless the context or subject matter otherwise indicates or requires: —

"Aborigine" means any full-blooded or half-caste aboriginal who is a native of Australia and who is temporarily or permanently resident in New South Wales.

"Adopted boarder" means a child who, if under the maximum age up to which he is compelled by law to attend school, is allowed by authority of the board to remain with a foster parent without payment of an allowance or, if over the maximum age up to which he is compelled by law to attend school, is allowed by authority of the board to remain with the foster parent on terms and conditions which do not require that the whole or any part of any wages earned by the child be paid to the board on behalf of such child,

"Board" means the Aborigines Welfare Board, constituted under this Act. . . .

"Reserve" means area of land heretofore or hereafter reserved from sale or lease under any Act dealing with Crown lands, or given by or acquired from any private person, for the use of aborigines. . . .

"Ward" means a child who has been admitted to the control of the board or committed to a home constituted and established under section eleven of this Act. . . .

7. (1) It shall be the duty of the board —

    (a) to, with the consent of the Minister, apportion, distribute, and apply as may seem most fitting, any moneys voted by Parliament, and any other funds in its possession or control, for the relief or benefit of aborigines or for the purpose of assisting aborigines in obtaining employment and of maintaining or assisting to maintain them whilst so employed, or otherwise for the purpose of assisting aborigines to become assimilated into the general life of the community;

    (b) To distribute blankets, clothing, and relief to aborigines at the discretion of the board;

    (c) To provide for the custody and maintenance of the children of aborigines;

    (d) To manage and regulate the use of reserves;

    (e) To exercise a general supervision and care over all aborigines and over all matters affecting the interests and welfare of aborigines, and to protect them against injustice, imposition, and fraud;

(f) to arrange for the inspection at regular intervals of each station and training school under the control of the board, by the Superintendent of Aborigines Welfare and one or more of the other members of the board, or by one or more of such other members. . . .

(2) The board may on the application of the parent or guardian of any child admit such child to the control of the board.

8. (1) All reserves shall be vested in the board, and it shall not be lawful for any person other than an aborigine, or an officer under the board, or a person acting under the board's direction, or under the authority of the regulations, or a member of the police force, to enter or remain upon or be within the limits of a reserve upon which aborigines are residing, for any purpose whatsoever:

Provided that the board may, by permit in the prescribed form, authorize, subject to such terms and conditions as it may think fit, any person apparently having an admixture of aboriginal blood to enter or remain upon or be within the limits of any such reserve.

(2) The board may remove from a reserve any aborigine or other person who is guilty of any misconduct, or who, in the opinion of the board, should be earning a living away from such reserve.

(3) Any building erected on a reserve shall be vested in and become the property of the board, also all cattle, horses, pigs, sheep, machinery, and property thereon purchased or acquired for the benefit of aborigines.

8A. (1) Where an aborigine or a person apparently having an admixture of aboriginal blood is, in the opinion of the board, living in insanitary or undesirable conditions, or should in the opinion of the board be placed under control, a stipendiary or police magistrate may, on the application of the board, order such aborigine or person to remove to a reserve or place controlled by the board, or, if such aborigine or person is but temporarily resident in this State, to return to the State whence he came within a time specified in the order.

(2) Any such order may on a like application be cancelled or varied by the same or another stipendiary or police magistrate.

(3) Until such an order is cancelled every aborigine or other person named therein in that behalf shall be and remain under the control of the board while he is in this State.

(4) The manner of making application under this section and the procedure to be adopted thereon and in connection therewith shall be as prescribed by regulations made under this Act.

8B. Whosoever, without lawful authority or excuse the proof whereof shall lie on him, removes an aborigine or causes, assists, entices, or persuades an aborigine to remove from a reserve shall be guilty of an offense against this Act. . . .

11. The board may constitute and establish under this Act homes for the reception, maintenance, education, and training of wards and may assign a name or names to such homes.

11A. (1) The board may, by indenture, bind or cause to be bound any ward as an apprentice or may, where apprenticeship conditions are not applicable or desirable, place any ward in other suitable employment.

(2) The indentures of apprenticeship and agreements shall be in the forms prescribed and shall contain provisions to the satisfaction of the board for the maintenance, training, care, and religious instruction of any ward concerned and for the due payment of any wages payable thereunder. Such indentures and agreements shall be exempt from the provisions of the Stamp Duties Act, 1920–1939.

(3) All wages earned by any ward except such part thereof as the employer is required to pay to the ward personally as pocket money, shall be paid by the employer to the board on behalf of such ward and shall be applied as prescribed.

(4) The wages due by any employer or person on account of any ward may be sued for and recovered in the name of the board, or any officer authorized by the board in that behalf, in any court of competent jurisdiction, for the benefit of such ward.

11B. (1) Where a ward is not regarded by the board as ready for placement in employment or for apprenticeship, such ward may be placed in a home for the purpose of being maintained, educated, and trained.

(2) Where the board is satisfied that any ward is not likely to succeed in his employment or as an apprentice, the board may, with the approval of the employer or guardian of such ward, cancel any indenture of apprenticeship or agreement, and may place such

ward in a home for the purpose of being maintained, educated, and trained.

11c. Upon complaint made by the board or any officer authorized by the board in that behalf, that any person with whom any ward has been placed in employment or apprenticed is not observing or performing the conditions of any indenture of apprenticeship or agreement or is unfit to have the further care of such ward any magistrate or justice may call upon such person to answer such complaint, and on proof thereof a children's court established under the Child Welfare Act, 1939, may order such agreement to be terminated and may direct that the ward be sent to a home constituted and established under section eleven of this Act pending arrangements for further employment or apprenticeship.

11D. (1) The board shall be the authority to —

(a) admit a child to its control;

(b) provide for the accommodation and maintenance of any child admitted to its control until he is apprenticed, placed in employment, boarded-out, or placed as an adopted boarder;

(c) pay foster parents such rates as may be prescribed;

(d) direct the removal or transfer of any ward (other than a ward who has been committed to an institution for a specified term);

(e) apprentice, place in employment, board-out, or place as an adopted boarder any ward (other than a ward who has been committed to an institution for a specified term);

(f) approve of persons applying for the custody of wards and of the homes of such persons;

(g) arrange the terms and conditions of the custody of any ward;

(h) direct the restoration of any ward (other than a ward who has been committed to an institution for a specified term) to the care of his parent or of any other person;

(i) direct the absolute discharge of any ward (other than a ward who has been committed to an institution for a specified term) from supervision and control.

(2) (a) The board may, under and in accordance with subsection one of this section, board out any child to the person for the time being in charge of any charitable depot, home, or hostel and may make to the person in charge of such charitable depot, home, or hostel, payments in respect of such child

at the rates prescribed for payments under paragraph (c) of that subsection.

(b) Where payments are, in accordance with paragraph (a) of this subsection, made to the person for the time being in charge of any charitable depot, home, or hostel an officer appointed for the purpose may, at any time inspect such charitable depot, home, or hostel and make such examinations into the state and management thereof and the conditions and treatment of the children and young persons (being inmates thereof) in respect of whom the payments are so made, as he thinks requisite, and the person for the time being in charge of the charitable depot, home, or hostel shall afford all reasonable facilities for such inspection and examination.

(c) In this subsection "charitable depot, home, or hostel" means a depot, home, or hostel established or maintained by a charitable organization and used wholly or in part for purposes analogous to the purposes referred to in subsection one of section twenty-one of the Child Welfare Act.

(3) The board may, upon such terms and conditions as may be prescribed or as it may, in any special case, approve, place a ward as an adopted boarder in the care of a foster parent.

When such ward is over the maximum age up to which he is compelled by law to attend school and is to be employed by the foster parent, but the foster parent is unable to pay the prescribed rate of wages the consent of the board and of the ward shall be obtained before he is so placed in the care of a foster parent.

(4) Payment to a foster parent for any ward shall not extend beyond the time when the ward shall have attained the maximum age up to which he is compelled by law to attend school unless —

(a) the ward is an invalid or is otherwise incapacitated; or

(b) the case possesses unusual features which call for special consideration,

and the board authorizes such payment.

(5) On attaining the maximum age up to which he is compelled by law to attend school a ward shall, except in the circumstances referred to in subsections three and four of this section, or except in such other circumstances as may be prescribed, be apprenticed or placed in employment. . . .

13B. In any case where an aborigine is living with, or employed by, any other person, and the board has reason to believe that such aborigine is not receiving fair and proper treatment, and is not being paid a reasonable wage, or the board is of opinion that his moral or physical well-being is likely to be impaired by continuance in such employment, or that he is being influenced to continue in such employment, the board shall have the power to terminate same and remove the aborigine concerned to such reserve, home, or other place as it may direct. For the purposes of this section any officer of the board, or member of the police force, shall have access to such aborigine at all reasonable times for the purpose of making such inspection and inquiries as he may deem necessary.

13c. In any case where it appears to the board to be in the best interests of the aborigine concerned and/or of his wife and/or children the board may direct employers or any employer to pay the wages of the aborigine to the Superintendent of Aborigines Welfare or some other officer named by him, and any employer who fails to observe such directions shall be deemed to have not paid such wages. The wages so collected shall be expended solely on behalf of the aborigine to whom they were due and/or of his wife and/or children, and an account kept of such expenditure. . . .

14a. The board may authorize the medical examination of any aborigine or person having apparently an admixture of aboriginal blood and may have such aborigine or person so examined, removed to and kept in a public hospital or other institution for appropriate curative treatment, or may require such aborigine or person to undergo such treatment as and where provided.

　　Any such examination shall be performed only by a medical practitioner authorized in that behalf either generally or in a particular case by the Chief Medical Officer of the Government. . . .

16.　(1) Where an aborigine under sixteen years of age has been admitted to the control of the board and is a ward, or where any order has been made by a children's court established under the Child Welfare Act, 1939, committing an aborigine under sixteen years of age —

　　(a) to the care of any person; or

　　(b) to the control of the board; or

　　(c) to a home constituted and established under section eleven of this Act,

　　the near relatives shall be liable to pay for or to contribute towards his maintenance.

READING AND DISCUSSION QUESTIONS

1. What duties does the board established by this act have in "protecting" the Aborigines?

2. Under what circumstances can a child be removed from the reserve (reservation) by government representatives? What powers does this act give the government regarding the treatment of such wards?

3. Who pays for the care of Aborigine children who become wards of the state?

4. What notions of race and caste does this legislation reveal?

COMPARATIVE QUESTIONS

1. What are the advantages of socialism and of democracy in addressing inequality, according to Maríategui and Tocqueville?

2. How did governments in Australia, Peru, and the United States understand their relationship with native populations?

3. What systems are employed in the regions discussed here to maintain racial boundaries and racial and ethnic superiority? Why is that important?

CHAPTER 27

The Great Break:
War and Revolution

W orld War I (1914–1918) changed the global balance of economic, military, and political power. Though the conflict started as a dispute between two small Eastern European nations over a political assassination, a web of national alliances and long-suppressed hostilities over lost territory helped escalate it into four years of war that involved most major countries. The "Great War" led to a rise in Asian nationalism, the decline of Great Britain, France, and Germany as world powers, and the ascent of the United States as a global force. People everywhere seized opportunities created by the war as an opportunity for change. Russia was transformed by a social revolution at home and Zionists across Europe sought support for a national homeland in Palestine.

DOCUMENT 27-1

HENRY S. CLAPHAM
From Mud and Khaki: Memoirs of an Incomplete Soldier

1915

Many British soldiers kept diaries of their World War I experiences, providing vivid chronicles of the horrendous conditions and difficulties of trench warfare. Henry S. Clapham served in the northern Belgium city of Ypres and participated in the second of three major battles there, during which Germany introduced the use of chlorine gas fired from cylinders or artillery shells. Later, gas masks and respirators would protect soldiers from poison gas, but

H. S. Clapham, *Mud and Khaki: Memoirs of an Incomplete Soldier* (London: Hutchinson & Co., 1930), 141–153.

early on, thousands of soldiers "drowned" to death when the gas triggered the production of excess fluid in their lungs.

JUNE 19, 1915

We started again at dusk and passed down the railway cutting, but, instead of turning off into the fields, we went on as far as the Menin Road, at what is known as "Hell Fire Corner." A few hundred yards down the road we found a resting place for the night in some shallow "jumping off" trenches, a few yards back from the front line. It was very dark, and the trench was small, and sitting in a huddle I got a cramp and felt miserable.

The Huns[1] started by putting over big crumps [shells] all around us. They seemed to aim for the relics of a building a hundred yards in the rear, and there the bricks were flying. . . . Then at 2:50 A.M. our own guns started and kept up a heavy bombardment of the trenches in front until 4:15, by which time it was quite light. . . .

At 4:15 a whistle blew. The men in the front line went over the top, and we scrambled out and took their places in the front trench. In front of us was a small field . . . split diagonally by an old footpath. On the other side of the field was a belt of trees in which lay the Hun trench.

In a few moments flags went up there, to show that it had been captured and that the troops were going on. Another whistle, and we ourselves scrambled over the parapet [mound protecting the front of the trench] and sprinted across the field. Personally I was so overweighted that I could only amble. . . . I took the diagonal path, as the line of least resistance, and most of my section did the same.

When I dropped into the Hun trench I found it a great place, only three feet wide, and at least eight deep, and beautifully made of white sandbags, back and front. At that spot there was no sign of any damage by our shells, but a number of dead Huns lay in the bottom. There was a sniper's post just where I fell in, a comfortable little square hole, fitted with seats and shelves, bottles of beer, tinned meats, and a fine helmet hanging on a hook.

Our first duty was to change the [barbed] wire, so . . . I slipped off my pack, and, clambering out again, started to move the wire from what was now the rear, to the new front of the trench. It was rotten stuff, most of it loose coils. . . . What there was movable of it, we got across without much difficulty, and we had just finished when we were ordered to move down the trench, as our diagonal advance had brought us too far to the right.

---

[1] **Huns:** A derogatory term for German soldiers in World War I.

We moved down along the belt of woodland, which was only a few yards broad, to a spot where one of our companies was already hard at work digging a communication trench[2] back to our old front line. Here there was really no trench at all. One or more of our own big shells had burst in the middle, filling it up for a distance of ten yards and practically destroying both parapet and parados [mound protecting the rear of the trench]. Some of us started building up the parapet with sandbags, and I saw the twins merrily at work hauling out dead Huns at least twice their own size.

There was a hedge along the back of the trench, so I scrambled through a hole in it, piled my pack, rifle, and other things, including the helmet, on the farther side, and started again on the wire. Hereabouts it was much better stuff, and it took us some time to get it across and pegged down. We had just got the last knife-rest across, when I saw a man who was placing sandbags on the parapet from the farther side swivel round, throw his legs into the trench, and collapse in a heap in the bottom. Several others were already lying there, and for the first time I realized that a regular hail of machinegun bullets was sweeping over the trench. . . .

We all started work at a feverish pace, digging out the trench and building up some sort of shelter in front. One chap, a very nice kid, was bowled over almost at once with a bullet in the groin, and lay in the trench, kicking and screaming while we worked. . . .

The attacking battalions had carried several more trenches and we were told that two at least had been held, but our own orders were to consolidate and hold on to the trench we were in at all costs. . . .

I had just filled a sandbag and placed it on the top of the parapet when I happened to glance down, and saw a slight movement in the earth between my feet. I stooped and scraped away the soil with my fingers and found what seemed like palpitating flesh. It proved to be a man's cheek, and a few minutes' work uncovered his head. I poured a little water down his throat, and two or three of us dug out the rest of him. He was undamaged except for his feet and ankles, which were a mass of pulp, and he recovered consciousness as we worked. The first thing he said was in English: "What Corps are you?" He was a big man, and told us he was forty-five and had only been a soldier for a fortnight.

We dragged him out and laid him under the hedge. There was nothing else we could do for him. He had another drink later, but he must have

___

[2]**communication trench**: Shallow trench built from the front line to a safer area in the rear. These trenches were used to supply front-line troops with food and ammunition.

died in the course of the day. I am afraid we forgot all about him, but nothing could have lived there until evening.

The Captain was the next to go. He insisted on standing on the parados, directing operations, and got a bullet in the lungs. He could walk, and two men were detailed to take him down to the dressing-station. One came back, to be killed later in the day, but the other stopped a bullet *en route*, and followed the Captain.

When we had got our big Hun out, he left a big hole in the ground, and we found a dead arm and hand projecting from the bottom. We dug about, but did not seem to be able to find the body, and when I seized the sleeve and pulled, the arm came out of the ground by itself. We had to dig deeper for our own sake, but there was nothing else left, except messy earth, which seemed to have been driven into the side of the trench. The man helping me turned sick, for it wasn't pretty work. . . .

About 5:30 A.M. the Huns started shelling, and the new communication trench soon became a death-trap. A constant stream of wounded who had come down another trench from the north, passed along the rear. The Huns made a target of the two traverses (unluckily including our own), from which the communication trench opened, and numbers of the wounded were caught just behind us. The trench itself was soon choked with bodies. . . .

The shelling got worse as the day wore on and several more of our men went down. They plastered us with crumps, shrapnel, and whizz-bangs [all different shell projectiles]. One of the latter took off a sandbag from the top of the parapet and landed it on my head. It nearly broke my neck and I felt ill for some time after. . . .

The worst of it was the inaction. Every minute several shells fell within a few yards and covered us with dust, and the smell of the explosives poisoned my mouth. All I could do was to crouch against the parapet and pant for breath, expecting every moment to be my last. And this went on for hours. I began to long for the shell which would put an end to everything, but in time my nerves became almost numbed, and I lay like a log until roused.

I think it must have been midday when something happened. An alarm was given and we manned the parapet, to see some scores of men retreating at a run from the trench in front. They ran right over us, men of half a dozen battalions, and many dropped on the way. As they passed, something was said of gas, but it appeared that nearly all the officers in the two front trenches had been killed or wounded, someone had raised an alarm of gas, and the men had panicked and run.

A lot of the runaways insisted on gathering by the hedge just behind us, in spite of our warnings not to do so, and I saw at least twenty hit by shrapnel within a few yards of us.

The Brigade-Major arrived, cursing, and called upon some of our own men to advance and reoccupy the trench in front. He led them himself, and they made a very fine dash across. I do not think more than twenty fell, and they reoccupied the trench and, I believe, the third also, before the Huns realized that they were empty. . . .

Soon the runaways began to return. They had been turned back, in some cases, at the point of the revolver, but when their first panic had been overcome, they came back quite willingly, although they must have lost heavily in the process. They crowded into our trench, and there was hardly room to move a limb.

It was scorchingly hot and no one could eat, although I tried to do so. All day long we were constantly covered with debris from the shell bursts. Great pieces fell all about us, and, packed like herrings, we crowded in the bottom of the trench. Hardly anything could be done for the wounded. If their wounds were slight, they generally risked a dash to the rear. Every now and then we stood to in expectation of a counterattack, but none developed.

About 6:00 P.M. the worst moment of the day came. The Huns started to bombard us with a shell which was quite new to us. It sounded like a gigantic fire-cracker, with two distinct explosions. These shells came over just above the parapet, in a flood, much more quickly than we could count them. After a quarter of an hour of this sort of thing, there was a sudden crash in the trench and ten feet of the parapet, just beyond me, was blown away and everyone around blinded by the dust. With my first glance I saw what looked like half a dozen bodies, mingled with sandbags, and then I smelt gas and realized that these were gas-shells. I had my respirator on in a hurry and most of our own men were as quick. The others were slower and suffered for it. One man was sick all over the sandbags and another was coughing his heart up. We pulled four men out of the debris un-harmed. One man was unconscious, and died of gas later. Another was hopelessly smashed up and must have got it full in the chest.

We all thought that this was the end and almost hoped for it, but luck-ily the gas-shells stopped, and after a quarter of an hour we could take off our respirators. I started in at once to build up the parapet again, for we had been laid open to the world in front, but the gas lingered about the hole for hours, and I had to give up delving in the bottom for a time. As it was it made me feel very sick.

A counter-attack actually commenced as soon as the bombardment ceased, and we had to stand to again. . . . As we leaned over the parapet, I saw the body of a Hun lying twenty yards out in front. It commenced to writhe and finally half-sat up. I suppose the gas had caught him. The man standing next me — a corporal in a county battalion — raised his rifle, and before I could stop him, sent a bullet into the body. It was a rotten thing to see, but I suppose it was really a merciful end for the poor chap, better than his own gas, at any rate.

The men in the front trenches had got it as badly as we had, and if the counter-attack was pressed, it did not seem humanly possible, in the condition we were in, to offer a successful defense. . . . Fortunately, our own guns started and apparently caught the Huns massing. The counter-attack accordingly crumpled up.

In the midst of it all, someone realized that the big gap in the parapet could not be manned, and four of us, including myself, were ordered to lie down behind what was left of the parados and cover the gap with our rifles. It was uncomfortable work, as . . . the place was a jumble of dead bodies. We could not stand up to clear them away, and in order to get a place at all, I had to lie across the body of a gigantic Hun. . . .

We managed to get some sort of parapet erected in the end. It was more or less bullet-proof, at any rate. At dusk some scores of men came back from the front line, wounded or gassed. They had to cross the open at a run or a shamble, but I did not see any hit. Then the Brigade-Major appeared, and cheered us by promising a relief that night. It still rained shells, although not so hard as before dusk, and we did not feel capable of standing much more of it.

READING AND DISCUSSION QUESTIONS

1. What discoveries does Clapham make while digging trenches?

2. Clapham describes a new kind of shelling. What was it and how did it affect the troops?

3. How does Clapham describe the fate of the German found after the poison gas stopped? In what ways, if any, do his descriptions of the German and British soldiers differ? What does this tell you about the nature of trench warfare?

4. What conditions does Clapham describe when he and others are charged with manning the parapet?

DOCUMENT 27-2

VLADIMIR ILYICH LENIN

On War and Revolution

1917

The Great War was the spark that ignited what came to be known as the Russian Revolution (ca. 1905–1917), an uprising by peasants and workers against the government. With its resources strained, casualties mounting, and a crisis in leadership, Russia was ripe for the socialist revolution that had been percolating for years under authoritarian leadership. Just months before the peasant uprisings that led the Bolsheviks to power in November 1917, leading revolutionary thinker Vladimir Lenin (1870–1924) outlined in a public address what he and other socialists considered to be the real causes of World War I — which differed from the participating capitalist nations' claims — and what it would take to end the war and prevent future conflicts.

WAR AND REVOLUTION

A Lecture Delivered May 14 (27), 1917

It seems to me that the most important thing that is usually overlooked in the question of the war, a key issue to which insufficient attention is paid and over which there is so much dispute useless, hopeless, idle dispute, I should say is the question of the class character of the war: what caused that war, what classes are waging it, and what historical and historico-economic conditions gave rise to it. As far as I have been able to follow the way the question of the war is dealt with at public and Party meetings, I have come to the conclusion that the reason why there is so much misunderstanding on the subject is because, all too often, when dealing with the question of the war, we speak in entirely different languages.

From the point of view of Marxism, that is, of modern scientific socialism, the main issue in any discussion by socialists on how to assess the war and what attitude to adopt towards it is this: what is the war being waged for, and what classes staged and directed it. We Marxists do not belong to

Lenin: Collected Works, trans. Isaacs Bernard (Moscow: Progress Publishers, 1964), 24:398–421.

that category of people who are unqualified opponents of all war. We say: our aim is to achieve a socialist system of society, which, by eliminating the division of mankind into classes, by eliminating all exploitation of man by man and nation by nation, will inevitably eliminate the very possibility of war. But in the war to win that socialist system of society we are bound to encounter conditions under which the class struggle within each given nation may come up against a war between the different nations, a war conditioned by this very class struggle. Therefore, we cannot rule out the possibility of revolutionary wars, i.e., wars arising from the class struggle, wars waged by revolutionary classes, wars which are of direct and immediate revolutionary significance. Still less can we rule this out when we remember that though the history of European revolutions during the last century, in the course of 125–135 years, say, gave us wars which were mostly reactionary, it also gave us revolutionary wars, such as the war of the French revolutionary masses against a united monarchist, backward, feudal, and semi-feudal Europe. No deception of the masses is more widespread today in Western Europe, and latterly here in Russia, too, than that which is practiced by citing the example of revolutionary wars. There are wars and wars. We must be clear as to what historical conditions have given rise to the war, what classes are waging it, and for what ends. Unless we grasp this, all our talk about the war will necessarily be utterly futile, engendering more heat than light. That is why I take the liberty, seeing that you have chosen war and revolution as the subject of today's talk, to deal with this aspect of the matter at greater length. . . .

War is a continuation of policy by other means. All wars are inseparable from the political systems that engender them. The policy which a given state, a given class within that state, pursued for a long time before the war is inevitably continued by that same class during the war, the form of action alone being changed.

War is a continuation of policy by other means. When the French revolutionary townspeople and revolutionary peasants overthrew the monarchy at the close of the eighteenth century by revolutionary means and established a democratic republic when they made short work of their monarch, and short work of their landowners, too, in a revolutionary fashion that policy of the revolutionary class was bound to shake all the rest of autocratic, tsarist, imperial, and semi-feudal Europe to its foundations. And the inevitable continuation of this policy of the victorious revolutionary class in France was the wars in which all the monarchist nations of Europe, forming their famous coalition, lined up against revolutionary France in a counter-revolutionary war. Just as within the country the revolutionary people of France had then, for the first time, displayed revolutionary energy on a scale it had never shown for centuries, so in the war at the close of the eighteenth century it revealed a similar gigantic revolutionary creativeness when it remodelled its whole system of strategy, broke with all the old rules and traditions of warfare, replaced the old troops with a new revolutionary people's army, and created new methods of warfare. This example, to my mind, is noteworthy in that it clearly demonstrates to us things which the bourgeois journalists are now always forgetting when they pander to the philistine prejudices and ignorance of the backward masses who do not understand this intimate economic and historical connection between every kind of war and the preceding policy of every country, every class that ruled before the war and achieved its ends by so-called "peaceful" means. So-called, because the brute force required to ensure "peaceful" rule in the colonies, for example, can hardly be called peaceful.

Peace reigned in Europe, but this was because domination over hundreds of millions of people in the colonies by the European nations was sustained only through constant, incessant, interminable wars, which we Europeans do not regard as wars at all, since all too often they resembled, not wars, but brutal massacres, the wholesale slaughter of unarmed peoples. The thing is that if we want to know what the present war is about we must first of all make a general survey of the policies of the European powers as a whole. . . . We must take the whole policy of the entire system of European states in their economic and political interrelations if we are to understand how the present war steadily and inevitably grew out of this system. . . .

What we have at present is primarily two leagues, two groups of capitalist powers. We have before us all the world's greatest capitalist powers Britain, France, America, and Germany who for decades have doggedly pursued a policy of incessant economic rivalry aimed at achieving world supremacy, subjugating the small nations, and making threefold and tenfold profits on banking capital, which has caught the whole world in the net of its influence. That is what Britain's and Germany's policies really amount to. . . . This fact can never be emphasized strongly enough, because if we forget this we shall never understand what this war is about, and we shall then be easy game for any bourgeois publicist who tries to foist lying phrases on us.

The real policies of the two groups of capitalist giants Britain and Germany, who, with their respective allies, have taken the field against each other policies which they were pursuing for decades before the war, should be studied and grasped in their entirety. If we did not do this we should not only be neglecting an essential requirement of scientific socialism and of all social science in general, but we should be unable to understand anything whatever about the present war. . . .

These policies show us just one thing continuous economic rivalry between the world's two greatest giants, capitalist economies. On the one hand we have Britain, a country which owns the greater part of the globe, a country which ranks first in wealth, which has created this wealth not so much by the labor of its workers as by the exploitation of innumerable colonies, by the vast power of its banks which have developed at the head of all the others into an insignificantly small group of some four or five super-banks handling billions of rubles, and handling them in such a way that it can be said without exaggeration that there is not a patch of land in the world today on which this capital has not laid its heavy hand, not a patch of land which British capital has not enmeshed by a thousand threads. This capital grew to such dimensions by the turn of the century that its activities extended far beyond the borders of individual states and formed a group of giant banks possessed of fabulous wealth. Having begotten this tiny group of banks, it has caught the whole world in the net of its billions. . . .

On the other hand, opposed to this, mainly Anglo-French group, we have another group of capitalists, an even more rapacious, even more predatory one, a group who came to the capitalist banqueting table when all the seats were occupied, but who introduced into the struggle new methods for developing capitalist production, improved techniques, and superior organization, which turned the old capitalism, the capitalism of the free-competition age, into the capitalism of giant trusts, syndicates, and cartels. This group introduced the beginnings of state-controlled capitalist production, combining the colossal power of capitalism with the colossal power of the state into a single mechanism and bringing tens of millions of people within the single organization of state capitalism. Here is economic history . . . it leads you to the conclusion that the present war, too, is the outcome of the policies of the classes who have come to grips in it, of the two supreme giants, who, long before the war, had caught the whole world, all countries, in the net of financial exploitation and economically divided the globe up among themselves. They were bound to clash, because a redivision of this supremacy, from the point of view of capitalism, had become inevitable.

The old division was based on the fact that Britain, in the course of several centuries, had ruined her former competitors. A former competitor was Holland, which had dominated the whole world. Another was France, which had fought for supremacy for nearly a hundred years. After a series of protracted wars Britain was able, by virtue of her economic power, her merchant capital, to establish her unchallenged sway over the world. In 1871 a new predator appeared, a new capitalist power arose, which developed at an incomparably faster pace than Britain. . . . This rapid development of capitalism in Germany was the development of a young strong predator, who appeared in the concert of European powers and said: "You ruined Holland, you defeated France, you have helped yourself to half the world now be good enough to let us have our fair share." What does "a fair share" mean? How is it to be determined in the capitalist world, in the world of banks? There power is determined by the number of banks, there power is determined in the way described by a mouthpiece of the American multimillionaires, which declared with typically American frankness and typically American cynicism: "The war in Europe is being waged for world domination. To dominate the world two things are needed: dollars and banks. We have the dollars, we shall make the banks and we shall dominate the world." This statement was made by a leading newspaper of the American multimillionaires. I must say, there is a thousand times more truth in this cynical statement of a blustering American multimillionaire than in thousands of articles by bourgeois liars who try to make out that this war is being waged for national interests, on national issues, and utter similar glaringly patent lies which dismiss history completely. . . .

When we argue about annexations . . . we always forget that these, generally, are what the war is being waged for; it is for the carve-up of conquered territories, or, to put it more popularly, for the division of the plundered spoils by the two robber gangs. We maintain that no newspaper, either of the chauvinists in general, who simply say that the fatherland must be defended, or of the social-chauvinists, has ever given a definition of annexation that would fit both Germany and Russia, that would be applicable to any side. It cannot do this for the simple reason that this war is the continuation of a policy of annexations, that is, a policy of conquest, of capitalist robbery on the part of both groups involved in the war. . . .

The present war is a continuation of the policy of conquest, of the shooting down of whole nationalities, of unbelievable atrocities committed by the Germans and the British in Africa, and by the British and the Russians in Persia, which of them committed most it is difficult to say. It was for this reason that the German capitalists looked upon them as their enemies. Ah, they said, you are strong because you are rich? But we are stronger, therefore we have the same "sacred" right to plunder. That is what the real history of British and German finance capital in the course of several decades preceding the war amounts to. . . . Forgetting the history of finance capital, the history of how this war had been brewing over the issue of redivision, they present the matter like this: two nations were living at peace, then one attacked the other, and the other fought back. All science, all banks are forgotten, and the peoples are told to take up arms, and so are the peasants, who know nothing about politics. All they have to do is to fight back! . . . In this way such a view of annexations could be justified. They can't tell the truth about annexations because the whole history of Russia, Britain, and Germany has been one of continuous, ruthless, and sanguinary war over annexations. Ruthless wars were waged in Persia and Africa by the Liberals, who flogged political offenders in India for daring to put forward demands which were being fought for here in Russia. The French colonial troops oppressed peoples too. There you have the prehistory, the real history of unprecedented plunder! Such is the policy of these classes, of which the present war is a continuation. . . . In every resolution, of which dozens are passed, and published . . . you will find the answer, poorly expressed: We don't want a war for supremacy over other nations, we are fighting for our freedom. That is what all the workers and peasants say, that is [their] . . . understanding of the war. They imply by this that if the war were in the interests of the working people against the exploiters they would be for such a war. So would we, and there is not a revolutionary party that could be against it. Where they go wrong, these movers of numerous resolutions, is when they believe that the war is being waged by them. We soldiers, we workers, we peasants are fighting for our freedom. . . . You're wrong, you are fighting because you are obeying your capitalist government; it's the governments, not the peoples, who are carrying on this war. . . . [The worker] doesn't understand that the war is being waged by the government, and that he is just a tool in the hands of that government. He can call himself a revolutionary people and write eloquent resolutions. [T]o Russians this means a lot, because this has come into their lives only recently. There has recently appeared a "revolutionary" declaration by the Provisional Government.[3] This doesn't mean anything. Other nations, more experienced than we are in the capitalist art of hoodwinking the masses by penning "revolutionary" manifestos, have long since broken all the world's records in this respect. . . . No, this war is an inevitable outgrowth of supercapitalism, especially banking capital, which resulted in some four banks in Berlin and five or six in London

---

[3] **Provisional Government**: Government that ruled Russia for eight months in 1917 following the March revolution.

dominating the whole world, appropriating the world's funds, reinforcing their financial policy by armed force, and finally clashing in a savage armed conflict because they had come to the end of their free tether in the matter of conquests. One or the other side had to relinquish its colonies. Such questions are not settled voluntarily in this world of capitalists. This issue could only be settled by war. . . .

The Russian revolution has not altered the war, but it has created organizations which exist in no other country and were seldom found in revolutions in the West. . . . In this we have the germ of hope that it may overcome the war. Besides the government of "near-socialist" ministers, the government of imperialist war, the government of offensive, a government tied up with Anglo-French capital besides this government and independent of it we have all over Russia a network of Soviets of Workers', Soldiers', and Peasants' Deputies. Here is a revolution which has not said its last word yet. Here is a revolution which Western Europe, under similar conditions, has not known. Here are organizations of those classes which really have no need for annexations, which have not put millions in the banks, and which are probably not interested in whether the Russian Colonel Lyakhov and the British Liberal ambassador divided Persia properly or not. Here is the pledge of this revolution being carried further, i.e., that the classes which have no interest in annexations, and despite the fact that they put too much trust in the capitalist government, despite the appalling muddle and appalling deception contained in the very concept "revolutionary defensism," despite the fact that they support the war loan, support the government of imperialist war despite all this have succeeded in creating organizations in which the mass of the oppressed classes are represented. These are the Soviets of Workers', Soldiers', and Peasants' Deputies, which, in very many local areas in Russia, have gone much further than the Petrograd Soviet in their revolutionary work. It is only natural, because in Petrograd we have the central authority of the capitalists. . . .

And when Skobelev[4] in his speech yesterday said: "We'll take all the profits, we'll take 100 percent," he was just letting himself go with ministerial *élan*. . . . We never suggested taking 100 percent of profits. Nevertheless, it is a valuable promise. If you take the resolution of our Party you will see that we propose there, only in a more closely reasoned form, exactly what I have been proposing. Control must be established over the

---

[4]**Skobelev**: Matvey Skobelev; a Russian politician who served on the Petrograd Soviet during the Provisional Government and as minister of labor after May 5, 1917.

banks, followed by a fair tax on incomes. And nothing more! Skobelev suggests taking a hundred kopeks in the ruble. We proposed and propose nothing of the sort. . . . Minister Skobelev may have the best of intentions. . . . Good intentions pave the road to hell. All the government offices are full of papers signed by our ministers, but nothing has changed as a result of it. If you want to introduce control, start it! . . . One day is enough to have a law on such control issued. The employees' council at every bank, the workers' council at every factory, and all the parties receive the right of control. But you can't do that, we shall be told. This is a commercial secret, this is sacred private property. Well, just as you like, make your choice. If you want to safeguard all those ledgers and accounts, all the transactions of the trusts, then don't chatter about control, about the country going to ruin.

In the two months following the revolution the industrialists have robbed the whole of Russia. Capitalists have made staggering profits; every financial report tells you that. And when the workers, two months after the revolution, had the "audacity" to say they wanted to live like human beings, the whole capitalist press throughout the country set up a howl. Every number of *Rech* is a wild howl about the workers wanting to rob the country, but all we promise is merely control over the capitalists. . . . Control can only be exercised by the people. You must arrange control by bank employees' councils, engineers' councils, and workers' councils, and start that control right away, tomorrow. Every official should be made responsible, on pain of criminal persecution, for any wrong information he may give in any of these institutions. It is a matter of life and death to the country. We want to know how much grain there is, how much raw material, how many work hands there are and where they are to be placed.

This brings me to the last question[,] that of how to end the war. The ridiculous view is ascribed to us that we are out for a separate peace. The German robber capitalists are making peace overtures, saying: "We'll give you a piece of Turkey and Armenia if you give us ore-bearing lands." . . . What nonsense it is to allege that we are for ending the war by a separate peace! . . . The war which the capitalists of all countries are waging cannot be ended without a workers' revolution against these capitalists. So long as control remains a mere phrase instead of deed, so long as the government of the capitalists has not been replaced by a government of the revolutionary proletariat, the government is doomed merely to reiterate: We are heading for disaster, disaster, disaster. Socialists are now being jailed in "free" Britain for saying what I am saying. In Germany Liebknecht has been imprisoned for saying what I am saying, and in Austria Friedrich

Adler[5] is in jail for saying the same thing with the help of a revolver (he may have been executed by now). The sympathy of the mass of workers in all countries is with these socialists and not with those who have sided with their capitalists. The workers' revolution is mounting throughout the world. . . . In other countries it is a more difficult matter, of course. They have no half-wits there like Nicholas and Rasputin.[6] There the best men of their class are at the head of the government. They lack conditions there for a revolution against autocracy. They have there a government of the capitalist class. The most talented representatives of that class have been governing there for a long time. That is why the revolution there, though it has not come yet, is bound to come. . . . The peasants refuse to give up their grain for money and demand implements, boots, and clothes. There is a great measure of profound truth in this decision. Indeed, the country has reached a stage of ruin when it now faces the same situation, although to a less intensive degree, that other countries have long been facing, a situation in which money has lost its value. The rule of capitalism is being so strongly undermined by the whole course of events that the peasants, for instance, refuse to accept money. They say: "What do we want money for?" And they are right. . . .

The peasant expresses what everybody sees that the power of money has been undermined. The only way out is for the Soviets to agree to give implements, boots, and clothes in exchange for grain. This is what we are coming to, this is the answer that life dictates. Without this, tens of millions of people will go hungry, without clothes and boots. Tens of millions of people are facing disaster and death; safeguarding the interests of the capitalists is the last thing that should bother us. The only way out is for all power to be transferred to the Soviets, which represent the majority of the population. Possibly mistakes may be made in the process. . . . We do not want a "seizure" of power, because the entire experience of past revolutions teaches us that the only stable power is the one that has the backing of the majority of the population.

---

[5] **Liebknecht . . . Adler**: Both men were members of the Communist Party. Adler (1879–1960) assassinated the minister-president of Austria, Count Karl von Stürgkh, in 1916 to protest Austria-Hungary's war policy.
[6] **Nicholas and Rasputin**: Tsar Nicholas II (r. 1894–1917) was seen as a weak leader, whose tragic decision in 1915 to lead the army at the Russia front enabled Tsarina Alexandra and her advisor Rasputin to take control, as the country spiraled toward revolution.

How can the war be ended? . . . We say: The war which the capitalist governments have started can only be ended by a workers' revolution. Those interested in the socialist movement should read the Basle Manifesto of 1912[7] adopted unanimously by all the socialist parties of the world, a manifesto that was published in our newspaper *Pravda*, a manifesto that can be published now in none of the belligerent countries, neither in "free" Britain nor in republican France, because it said the truth about war before the war. It said that there would be war between Britain and Germany as a result of capitalist competition. . . . It told us what the war would be fought for, and said that the war would lead to a proletarian revolution. Therefore, we tell those socialists who signed this Manifesto and then went over to the side of their capitalist governments that they have betrayed socialism. There has been a split among the socialists all over the world. Some are in ministerial cabinets, others in prison. All over the world some socialists are preaching a war build-up, while others, like Eugene Debs, the American Bebel,[8] who enjoys immense popularity among the American workers, say: "I'd rather be shot than give a cent towards the war. I'm willing to fight only the proletariat's war against the capitalists all over the world." That is how the socialists have split throughout the world. . . . We preach proletarian revolution the only true cause, for which scores of people have gone to the scaffold, and hundreds and thousands have been thrown into prison. These imprisoned socialists are a minority, but the working class is for them, the whole course of economic development is for them. All this tells us that there is no other way out. The only way to end this war is by a workers' revolution in several countries. In the meantime we should make preparations for that revolution, we should assist it. . . . The revolution is beginning to change the war on Russia's part. The capitalists are still continuing the war, and we say: Until there is a workers' revolution in several countries the war cannot be stopped, because the people who want that war are still in power. . . .

The soldiers at the front cannot tear the front away from the rest of the state and settle things their own way. The soldiers at the front are a part

---

[7] **Basle Manifesto of 1912**: Socialist manifesto assailing the imperialist nations of the world, which included text by Lenin advocating that if capitalist (i.e., Western) nations warred with each other, socialists should seize the moment to help speed capitalism's downfall.

[8] **Eugene Debs, the American Bebel**: Eugene Debs was a labor activist and leader of the Socialist Party in the United States; August Bebel helped found the German Social-Democratic Party.

of the country. So long as the country is at war the front will suffer along with the rest. Nothing can be done about it. The war has been brought about by the ruling classes and only a revolution of the working class can end it.

READING AND DISCUSSION QUESTIONS

1. What is the socialist system of society and how does Lenin believe it will make war obsolete?

2. What policies of the dominant world nations does Lenin see as the cause of World War I?

3. How do capitalist governments "trick" workers into supporting war, according to Lenin?

4. What does Lenin say must happen to bring about an end to the Great War?

DOCUMENT 27-3

THE ZIONIST ORGANIZATION

Memorandum to the Peace Conference in Versailles: On the Establishment of a Jewish State in Palestine

February 3, 1919

Zionists who had long sought to establish a Jewish state in the Middle East saw the Paris Peace Conference as an opportunity to gain support for their quest. Already backed by Great Britain, Zionist leaders recognized that the Allied powers would be addressing the redistribution of colonies around the globe and the future of the Middle East. Members of the Zionist Organization — an umbrella organization that merged Zionist groups in Europe and elsewhere — and their Arab counterparts were concerned about what this might mean for them, and Jewish leaders drafted a memo that made their case to the Allies for the creation of a Jewish state in Palestine.

David Hunter Miller, *My Diary at the Conference of Paris* (New York: Appeal Printing Company, 1924), 5:15–29.

The Zionist Organization respectfully submits the following draft resolutions for the consideration of the Peace Conference:

1. The High Contracting Parties recognize the historic title of the Jewish
   people to Palestine and the right of the Jews to reconstitute in Palestine their National Home.
2. The boundaries of Palestine shall be as declared in the Schedule
   annexed hereto.
3. The sovereign possession of Palestine shall be vested in the League of
   Nations and the Government entrusted to Great Britain as mandatary
   of [mandated by] the League.
4. (Provision to be inserted relating to the application in Palestine of
   such of the general conditions attached to mandates as are suitable to
   the case.)
5. The mandate shall be subject also to the following special conditions:
   I. Palestine shall be placed under such political, administrative, and
      economic conditions as will secure the establishment there of the
      Jewish National Home and ultimately render possible the crea-
      tion of an autonomous Commonwealth, it being clearly under-
      stood that nothing shall be done which may prejudice the civil
      and religious rights of existing non-Jewish communities in Pales-
      tine or the rights and political status enjoyed by Jews in any other
      country.
   II. To this end the Mandatary Power shall *inter alia* ["among other
       things"]
       a. Promote Jewish immigration and close settlement on the land,
           the established rights of the present non-Jewish population
           being equitably safeguarded.
       b. Accept the co-operation in such measures of a Council rep-
           resentative of the Jews of Palestine and of the world that may
           be established for the development of the Jewish National
           Home in Palestine and entrust the organization of Jewish
           education to such Council.
       c. On being satisfied that the constitution of such Council pre-
           cludes the making of private profit, offer to the Council in pri-
           ority any concession for public works or for the development
           of natural resources which may be found desirable to grant.
   III. The Mandatary Power shall encourage the widest measure of self-
        government for localities practicable in the conditions of the
        country.

IV. There shall be for ever the fullest freedom of religious worship for all creeds in Palestine. There shall be no discrimination among the inhabitants with regard to citizenship and civil rights, on the grounds of religion or of race.

V. (Provision to be inserted relating to the control of the Holy Places.)

THE BOUNDARIES OF PALESTINE SCHEDULE

The boundaries of Palestine shall follow the general lines set out below:

Starting on the North at a point on the Mediterranean Sea in the vicinity of Sidon and following the watersheds of the foothills of the Lebanon as far as Jisr El Karaon, thence to El Bire, following the dividing line between the two basins of the Wadi El Korn and the Wadi Et Teim thence in a southerly direction following the dividing line between the Eastern and Western slopes of the Hermon, to the vicinity West of Beit Jenn, thence Eastward following the northern watersheds of the Nahr Mughaniye close to and west of the Hedjaz Railway.

In the East a line close to and West of the Hedjaz Railway terminating in the Gulf of Akaba.

In the South a frontier to be agreed upon with the Egyptian Government. In the West the Mediterranean Sea.

The details of the delimitations, or any necessary adjustments of detail, shall be settled by a Special Commission on which there shall be Jewish representation.

STATEMENT

The Historic Title

The claims of the Jews with regard to Palestine rest upon the following main considerations:

1. The land is the historic home of the Jews; there they achieved their greatest development, from that center, through their agency, there emanated spiritual and moral influences of supreme value to mankind. By violence they were driven from Palestine, and through the ages they have never ceased to cherish the longing and the hope of a return.

2. In some parts of the world, and particularly in Eastern Europe, the conditions of life of millions of Jews are deplorable. Forming often a congested population, denied the opportunities which would make a healthy development possible, the need of fresh outlets is urgent, both

for their own sake and in the interest of the population of other races, among whom they dwell. Palestine would offer one such outlet. To the Jewish masses it is the country above all others in which they would most wish to cast their lot. By the methods of economic development to which we shall refer later, Palestine can be made now as it was in ancient times, the home of a prosperous population many times as numerous as that which now inhabits it.

3. But Palestine is not large enough to contain more than a proportion of the Jews of the world. The greater part of the fourteen millions or more scattered through all countries must remain in their present localities, and it will doubtless be one of the cares of the Peace Conference to ensure for them, wherever they have been oppressed, as for all peoples, equal rights and humane conditions. A Jewish National Home in Palestine will, however, be of high value to them also. Its influence will permeate the Jewries of the world: it will inspire these millions, hitherto often despairing, with a new hope; it will hold out before their eyes a higher standard; it will help to make them even more useful citizens in the lands in which they dwell.

4. Such a Palestine would be of value also to the world at large, whose real wealth consists in the healthy diversities of its civilizations.

5. Lastly the land itself needs redemption. Much of it is left desolate. Its present condition is a standing reproach. Two things are necessary for that redemption — a stable and enlightened Government, and an addition to the present population which shall be energetic, intelligent, devoted to the country, and backed by the large financial resources that are indispensable for development. Such a population the Jews alone can supply.

Inspired by these ideas, Jewish activities particularly during the last thirty years have been directed to Palestine within the measure that the Turkish administrative system allowed. Some millions of pounds sterling have been spent in the country particularly in the foundation of Jewish agricultural settlements. Those settlements have been for the most part highly successful.

With enterprise and skill the Jews have adopted modern scientific methods and have shown themselves to be capable agriculturalists. Hebrew has been revived as a living language, it is the medium of instruction in the schools and the tongue is in daily use among the rising generation. The foundations of a Jewish University have been laid at Jerusalem and considerable funds have been contributed for the creation of its building and for its endowment. Since the British occupation, the Zionist Organization has expended in Palestine approximately £50,000 a month upon relief, education, and sanitation. To promote the future development of the country great sums will be needed for drainage, irrigation, roads, railways, harbors, and public works of all kinds, as well as for land settlement and house building. Assuming a political settlement under which the establishment of a Jewish National Home in Palestine is assured the Jews of the world will make every effort to provide the vast sums of money that will be needed. . . .

[Here follow a recital of the Balfour Declaration[9] and of its endorsement by the French foreign minister and reference to support of Zionism and the Balfour Declaration by other allied governments.]

GREAT BRITAIN AS MANDATARY OF THE LEAGUE OF NATIONS

We ask that Great Britain shall act as Mandatary of the League of Nations for Palestine. The selection of Great Britain as Mandatary is urged on the ground that this is the wish of the Jews of the world and the League of Nations in selecting a Mandatary will follow as far as possible, the popular wish of the people concerned.

The preference on the part of the Jews for a British Trusteeship is unquestionably the result of the peculiar relationship of England to the Jewish Palestinian problem. The return of the Jews to Zion has not only been a remarkable feature in English literature, but in the domain of statecraft it has played its part, beginning with the readmission of the Jews under Cromwell.[10] It manifested itself particularly in the 19th century in the instructions given to British Consular representatives in the Orient after the Damascus Incident;[11] in the various Jewish Palestinian projects suggested by English non-Jews prior to 1881; in the letters of endorsement and support given by members of the Royal Family and Officers of the

---

[9] **Balfour Declaration**: The 1917 endorsement of a Jewish homeland in Palestine by the British government.

[10] **readmission of the Jews . . . Cromwell**: In 1290, under King Edward I, Jews were cast out of England. In 1656, during his rule as Lord Protector of the Commonwealth of England, Scotland, and Ireland (1653–1658), Oliver Cromwell allowed them to return, in part due to his religious tolerance, and in part to stimulate the British economy.

[11] **Damascus Incident**: In 1840, the Jews of Damascus were unjustly accused of ritual murder and imprisoned. England spearheaded a successful effort to rescue them.

Government to Lawrence Oliphant and finally, in the three consecutive acts which definitely associated Great Britain with Zionism in the minds of the Jews viz. — the El Arish offer in 1901; the East African offer in 1903, and lastly the British Declaration in favor of a Jewish National Home in Palestine in 1917.[12] Moreover, the Jews who have gained political experience in many lands under a great variety of governmental systems, wholeheartedly appreciate the advanced and liberal policies adopted by Great Britain in her modern colonial administration. . . .

[Here follows an account of the selection of Great Britain as mandatary power by the American Jewish Congress and a conference of Palestine Jews at Jaffa.]

BOUNDARIES

The boundaries above outlined are what we consider essential for the necessary economic foundation of the country. Palestine must have its natural outlets to the seas and the control of its rivers and their headwaters. The boundaries are sketched with the general economic needs and historic traditions of the country in mind, factors which necessarily must also be considered by the Special Commission in fixing the definite boundary lines. This Commission will bear in mind that it is highly desirable, in the interests of economical administration that the geographical area of Palestine should be as large as possible so that it may eventually contain a large and thriving population which could more easily bear the burdens of modern civilized government than a small country with a necessary limitation of inhabitants.

The economic life of Palestine, like that of every other semi-arid country depends on the available water supply. It is, therefore, of vital importance not only to secure all water resources already feeding the country, but also to be able to conserve and control them at their sources.

The Hermon[13] is Palestine's real "Father of Waters" and cannot be severed from it without striking at the very root of its economic life. The Hermon not only needs reforestation but also other works before it can again adequately serve as the water reservoir of the country. It must therefore be wholly under the control of those who will most willingly as well as most

---

[12] **various Jewish Palestinian projects . . . 1917**: Events in which England lent its support to the establishment of a Jewish homeland.
[13] **The Hermon**: Mountain range in Palestine with a vast waterfall at its base.

adequately restore it to its maximum utility. Some international arrangement must be made whereby the riparian rights of the people dwelling south of the Litani River may be fully protected. Properly cared for these head waters can be made to serve in the development of the Lebanon as well as of Palestine.

The fertile plains east of the Jordan, since the earliest Biblical times, have been linked economically and politically with the land west of the Jordan. The country which is now very sparsely populated, in Roman times supported a great population. It could now serve admirably for colonization on a large scale. A just regard for the economic needs of Palestine and Arabia demands that free access to the Hedjaz Railway throughout its length be accorded both Governments.

An intensive development of the agriculture and other opportunities of Transjordania make it imperative that Palestine shall have access to the Red Sea and an opportunity of developing good harbors on the Gulf of Akaba. Akaba, it will be recalled, was the terminus of an important trade route of Palestine from the days of Solomon onwards. The ports developed in the Gulf of Akaba should be free ports through which the commerce of the Hinterland may pass on the same principle which guides us in suggesting that free access be given to the Hedjaz Railway.

Proposals to the Mandatary Power

In connection with the Government to be set up by the Mandatary of the League of Nations until such time as the people of Palestine shall be prepared to undertake the establishment of representative and responsible Government proposals will be made in due course to the Mandatary Power to the following effect:

1. In any instrument establishing the constitution of Palestine the Declarations of the Peace Conference shall be recited as forming an integral part of that constitution.

2. The Jewish people shall be entitled to fair representation in the executive and legislative bodies and in the selection of public and civil servants. In giving such representation the Mandatary Power shall consult the Jewish Council hereinafter mentioned.

    Neither law nor custom shall preclude the appointment of a citizen of Palestine as chief of the executive.

3. That in encouraging the self government of localities the Mandatary Power shall secure the maintenance by local communities of proper standards of administration in matters of education, communal, or

regional activities. In granting or enlarging local autonomy regard shall be had to the readiness and ability of the community to attain such standards. Local autonomous communities shall be empowered and encouraged to combine and cooperate for common purposes.

4. Education without distinction of race shall be assisted from public funds.

5. Hebrew shall be one of the official languages of Palestine and shall be employed in all documents, decrees, and announcements and on all stamps, coins, and notes issued by the Government.

6. The Jewish Sabbath and Holy Days shall be recognized as legal days of rest.

7. All inhabitants continuing to reside in Palestine who on the _____ day of _____, 19_____, have their domicile in Palestine, except those who elect in writing within six months from such date to retain their foreign citizenship, shall become citizens of Palestine, and they and all persons in Palestine or naturalized under the laws of Palestine after the _____ day of _____, 19_____, shall be citizens thereof and entitled to the protection of the Mandatary Power on behalf of the Government of Palestine.

LAND COMMISSION

Recognizing that the general progress of Palestine must begin with the reform of the conditions governing land tenure and settlement, the Mandatary Power shall appoint a Commission (upon which the Jewish Council shall have representation) with power:

a. To make survey of the land and to schedule all lands that may be made available for close settlement, intensive cultivation, and public use.

b. To propose measures for determining and registering titles of ownership of land.

c. To propose measures for supervising transactions in land with a view of preventing land speculation.

d. To propose measures for the close settlement, intensive cultivation, and public use of land, where necessary by compulsory purchase at a fair pre-war price and further by making available all waste lands unoccupied and inadequately cultivated lands or lands without legal owners, and state lands.

e. To propose measures for the taxation and the tenure of land and in general any progressive measures in harmony with the policy of making the land available for close settlement and intensive cultivation.

f.   To propose measures whereby the Jewish Council may take over all lands available for close settlement and intensive cultivation.

g.   In all such measures the established rights of the present population shall be equitably safeguarded.

The Jewish Council for Palestine

1.   A Jewish Council for Palestine shall be elected by a Jewish Congress representative of the Jews of Palestine and of the entire world, which shall be convoked in Jerusalem on or before the First day of January, 1920, or as soon thereafter as possible, by the Provisional Jewish Council hereinafter mentioned.

The Jewish Congress shall determine its functions as well as the constitution and functions of the Jewish Council in conformity with the purpose and spirit of the Declarations of the Peace Conference and of the powers conferred by the Mandatary Power upon the Jewish Council.

2.   The Jewish Council shall be recognized as a legal entity and shall have power:

a.   To co-operate and consult with and to assist the Government of Palestine in any and all matters affecting the Jewish people in Palestine and in all such cases to be and to act as the representative of the Jewish people.

b.   To participate in the development and administration of immigration, close land settlement, credit facilities, public works, services, and enterprises, and every other form of activity conducive to the development of the country. The organization of Jewish education to be entrusted to such Council.

c.   To acquire and hold Real Estate.

d.   To acquire and exercise concessions for public works and the development of natural resources.

e.   With the consent of the Jewish inhabitants concerned or their accredited representatives, to assess such inhabitants for the purpose of stimulating and maintaining education, communal, charitable, and other public institutions (including the Jewish Council) and other activities primarily concerned with the welfare of the Jewish people in Palestine.

f.   With the approval of the Mandatary Power and upon such terms and conditions as the Mandatary Power may prescribe, to administer the immigration laws of Palestine in so far as they affect Jewish immigration.

g. With the approval of the Mandatary Power, to issue bonds, debentures, or other obligations, the proceeds of any or all of which to be expended by the Jewish Council for the benefit of the Jewish people or for the development of Palestine.

h. The Jewish Council shall hold all of its property and income in trust for the benefit of the Jewish people.

3. A provisional Jewish Council of representatives of the Zionist Organization, of the Jewish population in Palestine, and of such other approved Jewish organizations as are willing to co-operate in the development of a Jewish Palestine shall be formed forthwith by the Zionist Organization. Such Provisional Jewish Council shall exercise all of the powers and perform all of the duties of the Jewish Council until such time as the Jewish Council shall be formally constituted by the Jewish Congress.

4. Finally when in the opinion of the Mandatary Power, the inhabitants of Palestine shall be able to undertake the establishment of Representative and Responsible Government, such steps shall be taken as will permit the establishment of such government through the exercise of a democratic franchise, without regard to race or faith; and the inhabitants of Palestine under such government, shall continue to enjoy equal civil and political rights as citizens irrespective of race or faith. . . .

READING AND DISCUSSION QUESTIONS

1. How does the Zionist Organization justify its claims to a portion of Palestinian land as the Jewish National Home?

2. How do the authors of this memorandum seek to address the fears of Palestinians and others that the creation of such a Jewish homeland might inspire?

3. According to the Zionists, what is the symbolic importance of a national homeland for Jews everywhere?

4. Why do the Zionists want Great Britain to oversee this operation as the "Mandatary Power"?

DOCUMENT 27-4

GERMAN DELEGATION TO THE
PARIS PEACE CONFERENCE
On the Conditions of Peace
October 1919

The Treaty of Versailles, signed at the 1919 Paris Peace Conference, for-mally brought World War I to an end and set the conditions for peace. Orchestrated by the Allied powers — the United States, Great Britain, and France — the treaty blamed the war on Germany and ordered it to pay $33 billion in reparations, cede all of its colonies, dismantle its air force, and greatly reduce other military operations. It also established the League of Nations as an international peacekeeping organization. Russia did not attend the conference, and Germany — the nation most impacted by the treaty — was not permitted to contribute to the negotiations. Fearing inva-sion, Germany ultimately signed the treaty despite continued protests.

Although President Wilson, in his speech of October 20th, 1916, has acknowledged that "no single fact caused the war, but that in the last analysis the whole European system is in a deeper sense responsible for the war, with its combination of alliances and understandings, a complicated texture of intrigues and espionage that unfailingly caught the whole family of nations in its meshes," . . . Germany is to acknowledge that Germany and her allies are responsible for all damages which the enemy Govern-ments or their subjects have incurred by her and her allies' aggression. . . . Apart from the consideration that there is no incontestable legal founda-tion for the obligation for reparation imposed upon Germany, the amount of such compensation[14] is to be determined by a commission nominated solely by Germany's enemies, Germany taking no part. . . . The commis-sion is plainly to have power to administer Germany like the estate of a bankrupt.

"Comments of the German Delegation to the Paris Peace Conference on the Condi-tions of Peace, Oct., 1919," in *International Conciliation*, October 1919 (no. 143).

[14] **amount of such compensation**: A reparations commission appointed by the Peace Conference determined the final sum to be $33 billion in 1921.

As there are innate rights of man, so there are innate rights of nations. The inalienable fundamental right of every state is the right of self-preservation and self-determination. With this fundamental right the demand here made upon Germany is incompatible. Germany must promise to pay an indemnity, the amount of which at present is not even stated. The German rivers are to be placed under the control of an international body upon which Germany's delegates are always to be but the smallest minority. Canals and railroads are to be built on German territory at the discretion of foreign authorities.

These few instances show that that is not the just peace we were promised, not the peace "the very principle of which," according to a word of President Wilson, "is equality and the common participation in a common benefit. . . ."

In such a peace the solidarity of human interests, which was to find its expression in a League of Nations, would have been respected. How often Germany has been given the promise that this League of Nations would unite the belligerents, conquerors as well as conquered, in a permanent system of common rights! . . .

But in contradiction to them, the Covenant of the League of Nations has been framed without the cooperation of Germany. Nay, still more. Germany does not even stand on the list of those States that have been invited to join the League of Nations. . . . What the treaty of peace proposes to establish, is rather a continuance of the present hostile coalition which does not deserve the name of "League of Nations." . . . The old political system based on force and with its tricks and rivalries will thus continue to thrive!

Again and again the enemies of Germany have assured the whole world that they did not aim at the destruction of Germany. . . .

In contradiction to this, the peace document shows that Germany's position as a world power is to be utterly destroyed. The Germans abroad are deprived of the possibility of keeping up their old relations in foreign countries and of regaining for Germany a share in world commerce, while their property, which has up to the present been confiscated and liquidated, is being used for reparation instead of being restored to them. . . .

In this war, a new fundamental law has arisen which the statesmen of all belligerent peoples have again and again acknowledged to be their aim: the right of self-determination. To make it possible for all nations to put this privilege into practice was intended to be one achievement of the war. . . .

Neither the treatment described above of the inhabitants of the Saar region[15] as accessories to the [coal] pits nor the public form of consulting the population in the districts of Eupen, Malmédy, and Prussian Moresnet[16] — which, moreover, shall not take place before they have been put under Belgian sovereignty — comply in the least with such a solemn recognition of the right of self-determination.

The same is also true with regard to Alsace-Lorraine. If Germany has pledged herself "to right the wrong of 1871," this does not mean any renunciation of the right of self-determination of the inhabitants of Alsace-Lorraine. A cession of the country without consulting the population would be a new wrong, if for no other reason, because it would be inconsistent with a recognized principle of peace.

On the other hand, it is incompatible with the idea of national self-determination for two and one-half million Germans to be torn away from their native land against their own will. By the proposed demarcation of the boundary, unmistakably German territories are disposed of in favor of their Polish neighbors. Thus, from the Central Silesian districts of Guhrau and Militsch certain portions are to be wrenched away, in which, beside 44,900 Germans, reside at the utmost 3,700 Poles. . . .

This disrespect of the right of self-determination is shown most grossly in the fact that Danzig[17] is to be separated from the German Empire and made a free state. Neither historical rights nor the present ethnographical conditions of ownership of the Polish people can have any weight as compared with the German past and the German character of that city. . . . Likewise the cession of the commercial town of Memel, which is to be exacted from Germany, is in no way consistent with the right of self-determination. The same may be said with reference to the fact that millions of Germans in German-Austria are to be denied the union with Germany which they desire and that, further, millions of Germans dwelling along our frontiers are to be forced to remain part of the newly created Czecho-Slovakian State.

---

[15] **inhabitants of the Saar region**: After fifteen years, Saar inhabitants would vote in a plebiscite to decide if they would stay under the administration of a League of Nations commission or become part of France or Germany. In 1935 they voted to join Germany.

[16] **Prussian Moresnet**: Moresnet was annexed outright by Belgium. In Eupen and Malmédy, those who objected to the transferring the areas to Belgium could sign their names in a public registry. Both areas became Belgian.

[17] **Danzig**: Danzig was administered by the League of Nations.

Even as regards that part of the national territory that is to be left to Germany, the promised right of self-determination is not observed. A Commission for the execution of the indemnity shall be the highest instance for the whole State. Our enemies claim to have fought for the great aim of the democratization of Germany. To be sure, the outcome of the war has delivered us from our former authorities, but instead of them we shall have in exchange a foreign, dictatorial power whose aim can and must be only to exploit the working power of the German people for the benefit of the creditor states.[18] . . .

The fact that this is an age in which economic relations are on a world scale, requires the political organization of the civilized world. The German Government agrees with the Governments of the Allied and Associated Powers in the conviction that the horrible devastation caused by this war requires the establishment of a new world order, an order which shall insure the "effective authority of the principles of international law," and "just and honorable relations between the nations." . . .

There is no evidence of these principles in the peace document which has been laid before us. Expiring world theories, emanating from imperialistic and capitalistic tendencies, celebrate in it their last horrible triumph. As opposed to these views, which have brought unspeakable disaster upon the world, we appeal to the innate sense of right of men and nations, under whose token the English State developed, the Dutch People freed itself, the North American nation established its independence, France shook off absolutism. The bearers of such hallowed traditions cannot deny this right to the German people, that now for the first time has acquired in its internal polities the possibility of living in harmony with its free will based on law.

READING AND DISCUSSION QUESTIONS

1. What does the German delegation say is the real cause of the war?
2. What does the delegation mean when it invokes the "innate rights of nations"?

---

[18] **Commission for the execution . . . states:** After the Germans fell behind in their payments in 1923, the French-controlled reparations commission sent French, Belgian, and Italian technicians into Germany's Ruhr region to collect coal to make up for the delinquent payments.

3. How does the peace proposed by the treaty differ from that which Germany expected and says it was promised, particularly by Wilson?

4. According to the Germans, in what ways does the treaty violate the right of self-determination?

COMPARATIVE QUESTIONS

1. How did World War I facilitate the causes of both the Zionists and the Russian revolutionaries?

2. Based on Clapham's account of trench warfare, Lenin's speech, and the argument set forth by the German delegation to the Paris Peace Conference, what impact did the war have on soldiers and civilians in affected nations?

3. What postwar world visions do the writers of these documents offer? What might each author deem a "successful" outcome?

4. According to Lenin and the German delegation, why was the fate of colonies and the nations that controlled them such a critical component of the war and the peace that followed?

CHAPTER 28

Nationalism in Asia

1914–1939

Though World War I may have initially seemed like a strictly European conflict, the Great War would ultimately inspire popular
nationalist movements throughout Asia and evolve into a worldwide conflict. Asian nationalists sought to resist imperialism and free the region
from outside (Western) control, promising supporters that the resulting
freedom and prosperity would make any short-term sacrifices bearable. In
India, nationalists embraced nonviolence. Arab nationalists and Zionists
seeking a Jewish homeland in Palestine sought and received support from
leading Western powers including Great Britain. Some nationalist movements, particularly those in Turkey and the Middle East — empowered by
an "us versus them" mentality — would become quite brutal.

DOCUMENT 28-1

On the Education of Girls and the
Advancement of Iranian Society

1907, 1909

*In the wake of World War I, during which both Russia and Great Britain lost
their holds on Persia (renamed Iran in 1935), Persian nationalists heightened
their efforts to convert their undeveloped country into a unified, modern nation. Persia's leader, Reza Shah, faced a difficult task given the nation's vast
desert and mountain terrain, its disparate ethnic groups, and its large poor
and illiterate rural population. Some members of the middle class viewed the*

"Girls' Education Is the Basis of Civilization and Moral Refinement," *True Dawn*
(February 1907). "Girls' Schooling," *Watan*, 1, no. 1 (1909).

education of women and girls as the key to Iran's modernization and pre-
sented their arguments in Iranian magazines like those excerpted below.

"Girls' Education Is the Basis of Civilization and Moral Refinement"

The best path to civilization is the education, training of girls. The first necessity of moral refinement for girls is to be educated, trained, and cultured. Every nation that wants to become civilized has to begin educating and training girls from an early age. Each nation, according to their own religious laws and practices, should provide it [education] for them with any means possible.

Indeed, these girls will become mothers themselves, and their children will socialize with one another and their habits and disposition will spread among each other. But if they have all been educated in a good manner and with moral refinement, then there can be established in that nation a higher civilization. In this manner, the nation will develop and complete its march of progress by becoming civilized.

On the other hand, if the girls (children) are trained and raised by an uneducated mother, then the bad moods, habits, and disposition will have a bad affect on the children. Along with the growth and mental maturity, an indecent manner will be formed and become a habit; and it will also spread among the children. Therefore, barbarism will develop among the people and they will never become a civilized nation. One savant says: "Every behavior that comes to view, or any word that is said, whether good or bad, will have affect on the child either directly or indirectly. And if that word or behavior was proper, it will have a positive influence, and if it was improper, indeed it could have a negative result on the child. Truly, the child's mind and soul absorbs any word and behavior, good or bad, faster than the elders."

Every character and manner, good or bad, when experienced by a child will develop inside him and will be there. When Confucius, a Chinese savant, saw the moral refinement that resulted from educating girls, he understood that it is the greatest and most desired outcome from their education. He took advantage of this idea and instituted it as a law in the Chinese nation. Thus, each girl that is educated and trained in decent manner and has not committed a sin will receive a specific amount of money from government.

One day Napoleon arrived in one of the schools in France, and told the teachers: "I have provided the best necessities for education in France.

I have made any resources available for learning by any means, so why is public instruction not improving, and why are the children not learning or advancing in their knowledge?" The teachers replied: "The home school teachers in France are not educated. The reason for retrogression and the lack of children's learning is because of the uneducated and untrained mothers."

Therefore, our nation [Iran] which has taken off the tattered garment of barbarism and savagery, and has put on the sash of honor and civilization, should not neglect the importance of girls' education and culture.

"GIRLS' SCHOOLING"

It is essential to build a school for boys, but schools are more important for girls because boys do not go to school before the age of eight. Rather, [boys] are raised and learn their behavior from their mothers. Thus, if the mother gains her education through schools, her children will learn good behavior and virtue from her. In contrast, if the mother has not been to school, her child is compelled to ill-natured behavior, like her.

So it is obvious that good education for a mother has a direct effect on her child. In the past, any woman who had a good education left a good name in history. In addition, a girl who was well-educated was also well-respected by her father, husband, and relatives, and at any time in history, she was well-received by the public. Nor has Islam ever banned educational advancement in the family of the Prophet, or subsequent royal families. It has never been reported that Islam has said that a girl could not obtain education or should remain ignorant. According to Islam, women are equal to men with regard to human rights. For inheritance, Islam has given the son twice [the inheritance] as that of a daughter. The reason is simple, because the man has to provide food and shelter for the woman it would have been unjustified if both had equal inheritance. It is irrational to criticize Islamic principles for not giving man and woman equal inheritance. If you heard that man and woman have to be equal, it is not in the matter of inheritance, but rather in education, human qualities, and equality in thoughts and opinions. The first woman believers, Khadija, and Fatima Zahra,[1] praise be to them, because of their good qualities, chastity, and worship of God, were superior to all women throughout the world.

Ghatr Al-Tazy, the mother of Al-Muqtadir bi-Allah of the Abbasids [a medieval Islamic ruling dynasty], presided over civil trials and entertained

---

[1] **Khadija, and Fatima Zahra**: Khadija was the wife of the Prophet Muhammad; Fatima Zahra was their daughter.

foreign ambassadors. She earned the confidence of the Abbasids' Caliph. Zubayda, the wife of Haroun Al-Rashid, had an abundant knowledge in literature, and one of her public works is "Zubayda's Fountain" [built] on the Road to Mecca. Moreover, she financed the renovation of the city of Alexandria.

Buran, the daughter of Hassan ibn Sahl, and the secretary of Mamoun Al-Rashid's wife, was popular for her wisdom, politeness, and generosity. She built several hospitals at her own expense in Baghdad. Her Highness, Sakina Khatoon, the daughter of Husayn, son of Ali [the cousin of the Prophet], praise upon him, was outstanding in literature and the Arabic language. In royal families, during old times and new, there were always several women who became rulers. If they were not distinguished in wisdom and knowledge, they would not have reached those ranks.

His excellency, the editor of the newspaper, *Fareedeh ol 'Alam Al-Islami Fasli-Moshamma*, has written on this matter, which I do not want to repeat. But its conclusion and observations about this matter [are] that the Iranians, in every city, according to its population, should build schools for women. By doing so they would serve humanity. And there are indications that several individuals are taking steps to fulfill this. God willing, when this promise is fulfilled I will present it.

Prosperity for Iranians.

READING AND DISCUSSION QUESTIONS

1. How do the authors link motherhood with the nation's ability to modernize?

2. What historical examples do they use to make their case? Why might they use these specific examples?

3. How do the authors address religious concerns about educating females?

DOCUMENT 28-2

MARY L. GRAFFAM

*An Account of Turkish Violence
against Armenians*

1915

As young Turkish revolutionaries rose to power in Turkey after 1908, they sought to enforce a narrowly defined national identity that erased the country's multiculturalism and instead focused on Turkish language, culture, and race. Their efforts to consolidate what was left of the Ottoman Empire led to genocide against the Armenians. During World War I, while the international community was distracted by the war, the Turks massacred thousands of Armenians and deported others. Mary Graffam, a missionary from Massachusetts, was among the hundreds of U.S. and European workers and diplomats in Turkey who recorded the killings, starvation, and brutal deportations. These eyewitness accounts were later printed in newspapers around the world.

When we were ready to leave Sivas,[2] the Government gave forty-five ox-carts for the Protestant townspeople and eighty horses, but none at all for our pupils and teachers; so we bought ten ox-carts, two horse arabas [wagons], and five or six donkeys, and started out. In the company were all our teachers in the college, about twenty boys from the college and about thirty of the girls'-school. It was as a special favor to the Sivas people, who had not done anything revolutionary, that the Vali [provincial governor] allowed the men who were not yet in prison to go with their families.

The first night we were so tired that we just ate a piece of bread and slept on the ground wherever we could find a place to spread a yorgan [blanket]. It was after dark when we stopped, anyway. We were so near Sivas that the gendarmes [Armed Ottoman police] protected us, and no special harm was done; but the second night we began to see what was

---

Mary L. Graffam, reprinted from the *Missionary Herald* (Boston), December 1915.

[2] **Sivas**: City in North Central Turkey, where Mary Graffam was the principal of a girls' school.

before us. The gendarmes would go ahead and have long conversations with the villagers, and then stand back and let them rob and trouble the people until we all began to scream, and then they would come and drive them away. Yorgans and rugs, and all such things, disappeared by the dozen, and donkeys were sure to be lost. Many had brought cows; but from the first day those were carried off, one by one, until not a single one remained.

We got accustomed to being robbed, but the third day a new fear took possession of us, and that was that the men were to be separated from us at Kangal. . . . Our teacher from Mandjaluk was there, with his mother and sisters. They had left the village with the rest of the women and children, and when they saw that the men were being taken off to be killed the teacher fled to another village, four hours away, where he was found by the police and brought safely with his family to Kangal, because the tchaoush [officer] who had taken them from Mandjaluk wanted his sister. I found them confined in one room. I went to the Kaimakam [district official] and got an order for them all to come with us.

At Kangal some Armenians had become Mohammedans, and had not left the village, but the others were all gone. . . . They said that a valley near there was full of corpses. At Kangal we also began to see exiles from Tokat. The sight was one to strike horror to any heart; they were a company of old women, who had been robbed of absolutely everything. At Tokat the Government had first imprisoned the men, and from the prison had taken them on the road. . . . After the men had gone, they arrested the old women and the older brides, perhaps about thirty or thirty-five years old. There were very few young women or children. All the younger women and children were left in Tokat. . . .

When we looked at them we could not imagine that even the sprinkling of men that were with us would be allowed to remain. We did not long remain in doubt; the next day we . . . had come to Hassan Tehelebi . . . and it was with terror in our hearts that we passed through that village about noon. But we encamped and ate our supper in peace, and even began to think that perhaps it was not so, when the Mudir [official in charge] came round with gendarmes and began to collect the men. . . .

The night passed, and only one man came back to tell the story of how every man was compelled to give up all his money, and all were taken to prison. The next morning they collected the men who had escaped the night before and extorted forty-five liras from our company, on the promise that they would give us gendarmes to protect us. One "company" is supposed to be from 1,000 to 3,000 persons. Ours was perhaps 2,000, and the greatest number of gendarmes would be five or six. In addition to these they sewed a red rag on the arm of a Kurdish villager and gave him a gun, and he had the right to rob and bully us all he pleased.[3]

Broken-hearted, the women continued their journey. . . .

As soon as the men left us, the Turkish drivers began to rob the women, saying: "You are all going to be thrown into the Tokma Su [river], so you might as well give your things to us, and then we will stay by you and try to protect you." Every Turkish woman that we met said the same thing. The worst were the gendarmes, who really did more or less bad things. One of our schoolgirls was carried off by the Kurds twice, but her companions made so much fuss that she was brought back. . . .

As we approached the bridge over the Tokma Su, it was certainly a fearful sight. As far as the eye could see over the plain was this slow-moving line of ox-carts. For hours there was not a drop of water on the road, and the sun poured down its very hottest. As we went on we began to see the dead from yesterday's company, and the weak began to fall by the way. The Kurds working in the fields made attacks continually, and we were half-distracted. I piled as many as I could on our wagons, and our pupils, both boys and girls, worked like heroes. One girl took a baby from its dead mother and carried it until evening. Another carried a dying woman until she died. We bought water from the Kurds, not minding the beating that the boys were sure to get with it. I counted forty-nine deaths, but there must have been many more. One naked body of a woman was covered with bruises. I saw the Kurds robbing the bodies of those not yet entirely dead. . . .

The hills on each side were white with Kurds, who were throwing stones on the Armenians, who were slowly wending their way to the bridge. I ran ahead and stood on the bridge in the midst of a crowd of Kurds, until I was used up [exhausted]. I did not see anyone thrown into the water, but they said, and I believe it, that a certain Elmas, who has done handwork for me for years, was thrown over the bridge by a Kurd. Our Badvelli's wife was riding on a horse with a baby in her arms, and a Kurd took hold of her to throw her over, when another Kurd said: "She has a baby in her arms," and they let her go. . . .

The police for the first time began to interfere with me here, and it was evident that something was decided about me. The next morning after we arrived at this bridge, they wanted me to go to Malatia; but I insisted

---

[3] sewed a red rag . . . he pleased: The "red rag" was an arm band that gave the Kurds special status.

that I had permission to stay with the Armenians. During the day, however, they said that [I had been ordered] to come to Malatia, and that the others were going to Kiakhta. Soon after we heard that they were going to Ourfa, there to build villages and cities, &c.

In Malatia I went at once to the commandant, a captain who they say has made a fortune out of these exiles. I told him how I had gone to Erzeroum last winter, and how we pitied these women and children and wished to help them, and finally he sent me to the Mutessarif [district official]. The latter is a Kurd, apparently anxious to do the right thing; but he has been sick most of the time since he came, and the "beys" [Kurdish chiefs] here have had things more or less their own way, and certainly horrors have been committed. . . .

My friends here are very glad to have me with them, for they have a very difficult problem on their hands and are nearly crazy with the horrors they have been through here. The Mutessarif and other officials here and at Sivas have read me orders from Constantinople again and again to the effect that the lives of these exiles are to be protected, and from their actions I should judge that they must have received such orders; but they certainly have murdered a great many in every city. Here there were great trenches dug by the soldiers for drilling purposes. Now these trenches are all filled up, and our friends saw carts going back from the city by night. A man I know told me that when he was out to inspect some work he was having done, he saw a dead body which had evidently been pulled out of one of these trenches, probably by dogs. . . . The Beledia Reis [village chief] here says that every male over ten years old is being murdered, that not one is to live, and no woman over fifteen. The truth seems to be somewhere between these two extremes. . . .

READING AND DISCUSSION QUESTIONS

1. What happened to the men after Graffam's group left Tokat?
2. How were the women treated on this exile from Turkey?
3. Where were the Armenian exiles sent (and for what purpose) after Graffam was separated from them?
4. What do you suppose was the intended use of the trenches?

DOCUMENT 28-3

ARTHUR JAMES BALFOUR

Debating the Balfour Declaration:
The British Government Supports a
Jewish Homeland in Palestine

1917

The decision to support a Jewish homeland in Palestine posed a diplomatic dilemma for Great Britain. Though British Foreign Secretary Lord Balfour (1916–1919) would ultimately be authorized to endorse a Jewish homeland, the behind-the-scenes discussions excerpted below illustrate the War Department's concern about the consequences of such support. On the one hand, England hoped its actions might enlist American Zionists to push the U.S. Congress to back Britain in the war and would help Britain retain control of the Suez Canal; on the other, it risked its alliance with Arab leaders, who saw a separate Jewish state as contradictory to its government by majority rule.

THE BALFOUR DECLARATION, 1917

Foreign Office
November 2nd, 1917
Dear Lord Rothschild [a French Zionist],

I have much pleasure in conveying to you, on behalf of His Majesty's Government, the following declaration of sympathy with Jewish Zionist aspirations which has been submitted to, and approved by, the Cabinet.

"His Majesty's Government view with favor the establishment in Palestine of a national home for the Jewish people, and will use their best endeavors to facilitate the achievement of this object, it being clearly understood that nothing shall be done which may prejudice the civil and religious rights of existing non-Jewish communities in Palestine, or the rights and political status enjoyed by Jews in any other country."

"The Balfour Declaration," *Times* (London), November 9, 1917, p. 1.

I should be grateful if you would bring this declaration to the knowledge of the Zionist Federation.[4]

Yours sincerely,

Arthur James Balfour

1. Cambon Letter to Sokolow,[5] June 4, 1917

You were good enough to present the project to which you are devoting your efforts, which has for its object the development of Jewish colonization in Palestine. You consider that, circumstances permitting, and the independence of the Holy Places being safeguarded on the other hand, it would be a deed of justice and of reparation to assist, by the protection of the Allied Powers, in the renaissance of the Jewish nationality in that Land from which the people of *Israel* were exiled so many centuries ago.

The French Government, which entered this present war to defend a people wrongfully attacked, and which continues the struggle to assure the victory of right over might, can but feel sympathy for your cause, the triumph of which is bound up with that of the Allies.

I am happy to give you herewith such assurance.

2. Official Zionist Formula, 18 July 1917

H. M. Government, after considering the aims of the Zionist Organization,[6] accepts the principle of recognizing Palestine as the National Home of the Jewish people and the right of the Jewish people to build up its National life in Palestine under a protection to be established at the conclusion of Peace, following upon the successful issue of the war.

H. M. Government regards as essential for the realization of this principle the grant of internal autonomy to the Jewish nationality in Palestine, freedom of immigration for Jews, and the establishment of a Jewish National Colonizing Corporation for the re-settlement and economic development of the country.

The conditions and forms of the internal autonomy and a charter for the Jewish National Colonizing Corporation should, in the view of H. M.

---

[4]**Zionist Federation**: The British Federation of Zionists, an organization that lobbied the British government to support a Jewish homeland in Palestine.

[5]**Cambon . . . Sokolow**: Jules Cambon, secretary-general of the French Foreign Ministry and Nahum Sokolow, head of the Zionist Organization based in London.

[6]**Zionist Organization**: An umbrella organization that merged Zionist groups in Europe and elsewhere to establish a Jewish state in Palestine.

Government, be elaborated in detail and determined with the representatives of the Zionist Organization.

3. Minutes of War Cabinet Meeting No. 227, Minute No. 2, 3 September 1917

The War Cabinet had under consideration correspondence which had passed between the Secretary of State for Foreign Affairs and Lord Rothschild[7] on the question of the policy to be adopted towards the Zionist movement. In addition to the draft declaration of policy included in the above correspondence, they had before them an alternative draft prepared by Lord Milner. They had also before them a Memorandum by Mr. Montagu entitled "The Anti-Semitism of the present Government."

It was suggested that a question raising such important issues as to the future of Palestine ought, in the first instance, to be discussed with our Allies, and more particularly with the United States.

On the question of submitting Lord Milner's draft for the consideration of the United States Government, Mr. Montagu urged that the use of the phrase "the home of the Jewish people" would vitally prejudice the position of every Jew elsewhere and expand the argument contained in his Memorandum. Against this it was urged that the existence of a Jewish State or autonomous community in Palestine would strengthen rather than weaken the situation of Jews in countries where they were not yet in possession of equal rights, and that in countries like England, where they possessed such rights and were identified with the nation of which they were citizens, their position would be unaffected by the existence of a national Jewish community elsewhere. The view was expressed that, while a small influential section of English Jews were opposed to the idea, large numbers were sympathetic to it, but in the interests of Jews who wished to go from countries where they were less favorably situated, rather than from any idea of wishing to go to Palestine themselves.

With reference to a suggestion that the matter might be postponed, the Acting Secretary of State for Foreign Affairs pointed out that this was a question on which the Foreign Office had been very strongly pressed for a long time past. There was a very strong and enthusiastic organization, more particularly in the United States, who were zealous in this matter,

---

[7] **Lord Rothschild**: Walter Lord Rothschild was a former member of Parliament (1899–1910) and an ardent English Zionist who was influential in shaping the Balfour Declaration.

and his belief was that it would be of most substantial assistance to the Allies to have the earnestness and enthusiasm of these people enlisted on our side. To do nothing was to risk a direct breach with them, and it was necessary to face this situation.

The War Cabinet decided that —

The views of [U.S.] President Wilson should be obtained before any declaration was made, and requested the Acting Secretary of State for Foreign Affairs to inform the Government of the United States that His Majesty's Government were being pressed to make a declaration in sympathy with the Zionist movement, and to ascertain their views as to the advisability of such a declaration being made.

4. MINUTES OF WAR CABINET MEETING NO. 245, MINUTE NO. 18, 4 OCTOBER 1917

With reference to War Cabinet 227, Minute 2, the Secretary of State for Foreign Affairs stated that the German Government were making great efforts to capture the sympathy of the Zionist Movement. This Movement, though opposed by a number of wealthy Jews in this country, had behind it the support of a majority of Jews, at all events in Russia and America, and possibly in other countries. He saw nothing inconsistent between the establishment of a Jewish national focus in Palestine and the complete assimilation and absorption of Jews into the nationality of other countries. Just as English emigrants to the United States became, either in the first or subsequent generations, American nationals, so, in future, should a Jewish citizenship be established in Palestine, would Jews become either Englishmen, Americans, Germans, or Palestinians. What was at the back of the Zionist Movement was the intense national consciousness held by certain members of the Jewish race. They regarded themselves as one of the great historic races of the world, whose original home was Palestine, and these Jews had a passionate longing to regain once more this ancient national home. Other Jews had become absorbed into the nations among whom they and their forefathers had dwelt for many generations. Mr. Balfour then read a very sympathetic declaration by the French Government which had been conveyed to the Zionists, and he stated that he knew that President Wilson was extremely favorable to the Movement.

Attention was drawn to the contradictory telegrams received from Colonel House and Justice Brandeis.

The Secretary was instructed to take the necessary action.

The War Cabinet further decided that the opinions received upon this draft declaration should be collated and submitted to them for decision.

5. MINUTES OF WAR CABINET MEETING No. 259, MINUTE No. 12, 25 OCTOBER 1917

With reference to War Cabinet 245, Minute 18, the Secretary mentioned that he was being pressed by the Foreign Office to bring forward the question of Zionism, an early settlement of which was regarded as of great importance.

Lord Curzon stated that he had a Memorandum on the subject in course of preparation.

The question was adjourned until Monday, 29th October, or some other day early next week.

6. MINUTES OF WAR CABINET MEETING No. 261, MINUTE No. 12, 31 OCTOBER 1917

With reference to War Cabinet 245, Minute 18, the War Cabinet had before them a note by the Secretary, and also a memorandum by Lord Curzon on the subject of the Zionist movement.

The Secretary of State for Foreign Affairs stated that he gathered that everyone was now agreed that, from a purely diplomatic and political point of view, it was desirable that some declaration favorable to the aspirations of the Jewish nationalists should now be made. The vast majority of Jews in Russia and America, as, indeed, all over the world, now appeared to be favorable to Zionism. If we could make a declaration favorable to such an ideal, we should be able to carry on extremely useful propaganda both in Russia and America. He gathered that the main arguments still put forward against Zionism were twofold: —

(a.) That Palestine was inadequate to form a home for either the Jewish or any other people.
(b.) The difficulty felt with regard to the future position of Jews in Western countries.

With regard to the first, he understood that there were considerable differences of opinion among experts regarding the possibility of the settlement of any large population in Palestine, but he was informed that, if Palestine were scientifically developed, a very much larger population could be sustained than had existed during the period of Turkish misrule. As to the meaning of the words "national home," to which the Zionists attach so much importance, he understood it to mean some form of British, American, or other protectorate, under which full facilities would be given to the Jews to work out their own salvation and to build up, by means of education, agriculture, and industry, a real center of national culture and focus of national life. It did not necessarily involve the early establishment of an independent Jewish State, which was a matter for gradual development in accordance with the ordinary laws of political evolution.

With regard to the second point, he felt that, so far from Zionism hindering the process of assimilation in Western countries, the truer parallel was to be found in the position of an Englishman who leaves his country to establish a permanent home in the United States. In the latter case there was no difficulty in the Englishman or his children becoming full nationals of the United States, whereas, in the present position of Jewry, the assimilation was often felt to be incomplete, and any danger of a double allegiance or non-national outlook would be eliminated.

Lord Curzon[8] stated that he admitted the force of the diplomatic arguments in favor of expressing sympathy, and agreed that the bulk of the Jews held Zionist rather than anti-Zionist opinions. He added that he did not agree with the attitude taken up by Mr. Montagu. On the other hand, he could not share the optimistic views held regarding the future of Palestine. These views were not merely the result of his own personal experiences of travel in that country, but of careful investigations from persons who had lived for many years in the country. He feared that by the suggested declaration we should be raising false expectations which could never be realized. He attached great importance to the necessity of retaining the Christian and Moslem Holy Places in Jerusalem and Bethlehem, and, if this were to be effectively done, he did not see how the Jewish people could have a political capital in Palestine. However, he recognized that some expression of sympathy with Jewish aspirations would be a valuable adjunct to our propaganda, though he thought that we should be guarded in the language used in giving expression to such sympathy. . . .

READING AND DISCUSSION QUESTIONS

1. What do the various leaders envision will be the impact of creating a Jewish state on Jews living in other countries?

---

[8] **Lord Curzon**: George Nathaniel Curzon served in the British War Cabinet as Lord President of the Council (1916–1919).

2. What reasons do they give for the urgency to act on this matter and show support for Zionism?

3. What are their concerns about establishing a Jewish settlement within Palestine?

4. Why might some historians see the Balfour Declaration as the cause of later Palestinian-Jewish conflicts? Based on these excerpts, what could support that claim?

DOCUMENT 28-4

SAROJINI NAIDU

From "The Agony and Shame of the Punjab": An Indian Nationalist Condemns the British Empire

1920

Great Britain may have worried that World War I would intensify Indian efforts to break with British rule, but instead Indians rallied around Britain's war effort, offering soldiers, food, and other much-needed resources. After the war, however, Indian nationalism grew immensely, due in large part to Indians' disillusionment with the colonial powers. Feminist and nationalist leader Sarojini Naidu (1879–1949) expressed her country's outrage at British hypocrisy and betrayal of its democratic ideals, and used evidence of that betrayal to justify Indian independence and self-rule.

I speak to you today as standing arraigned because of the blood-guiltiness of those who have committed murder in my country. I need not go into the details. But I am going to speak to you as a woman about the wrongs committed against my sisters. Englishmen, you who pride yourselves upon your chivalry, you who hold more precious than your imperial treasures

Sarojini Naidu, Speech, "The Agony and Shame of the Punjab," in Padmini Sengupta, *Sarojini Naidu: A Biography* (London: Asia Publishing House, 1966), 161–162.

the honor and chastity of your women, will you sit still and leave un-avenged the dishonor, and the insult and agony inflicted upon the veiled women of the Punjab?[9]

The minions of Lord Chelmsford, the Viceroy, and his martial author-ities rent the veil from the faces of the women of the Punjab. Not only were men mown down as if they were grass that is born to wither; but they tore asunder the cherished Purdah,[10] that innermost privacy of the chaste womanhood of India. My sisters were stripped naked, they were flogged, they were outraged. These policies left your British democracy betrayed, dishonored, for no dishonor clings to the martyrs who suffered, but to the tyrants who inflicted the tyranny and pain. Should they hold their Empire by dishonoring the women of another nation or lose it out of chivalry for their honor and chastity? The Bible asked, "What shall it profit a man to gain the whole world and lose his own soul?" You deserve no Empire. You have lost your soul; you have the stain of blood-guiltiness upon you; no nation that rules by tyranny is free; it is the slave of its own despotism.

READING AND DISCUSSION QUESTIONS

1. Why is Naidu angry?
2. According to Naidu, how does the treatment of Indian women by British officials differ from their treatment of English women?
3. Why does she say that the English "deserve no Empire"? What might this reveal about Indian values at the time?

[9] **veiled women of the Punjab:** Punjab was a region in the northwestern portion of India. In 1919 the local British authority sent troops to fire into a crowd that was meeting to celebrate a Sikh religious festival. The group did not know that the British authority had banned such meetings. This became known as the Amritsar Massacre and according to official records, 378 people were killed and more than 1,000 were injured.

[10] **Purdah:** Practice in which Indian women hide themselves from view behind veils or in special building enclosures.

DOCUMENT 28-5

HU SHI
The Chinese Attitude Toward Modern Civilization of the West
1926

Chinese nationalism during the World War I era had an intellectual com-
ponent embodied in what became known as the New Culture Movement.
Beginning about 1916, young intellectuals educated in the West and those
who embraced Western ideals questioned China's traditionalism — especially
Confucianism — and sought to move the country into the modern era. Hu
Shi, a movement leader and Beijing University professor who received his
Ph.D. from Columbia University, denied that traditional Chinese ideals
were more spiritual than the materialism and individualism of the West. He
embraced the West's practical and scientific approaches and urged educated
Chinese to adopt a simpler, modern version of the written Chinese language.

"OUR ATTITUDE TOWARD MODERN CIVILIZATION OF THE WEST"

[The "Materialism" of Western Societies]
One of the most baseless, most harmful statements has to do with the
condemnation of Western civilization as "materialistic" and the praise of
Oriental civilization as "spiritual." . . . In the past it was used to provide
some kind of psychological lift, or self-congratulatory consolation, when
we, the Oriental people, were cruelly oppressed and badly humiliated by
the Occidentals [people of European descent]. During the past few years
when the Westerners themselves, in reaction to the disastrous World
War I, became increasingly disillusioned with a modern civilization based
upon the advance of science and technology, we have often heard from
their scholars the praise of the so-called spiritual civilization of the East.
Though this praise results from an abnormal, though understandable,
mentality of a temporary nature, it is more than welcome to the culturally
chauvinistic Orientals. It strengthens the bias about the alleged superiority
of Oriental civilization. . . .

Hu Shi, "Our Attitude Toward Modern Civilization of the West," in Dun J. Li, *Mod-*
ern China from Mandarin to Commissar (New York: Scribner, 1978).

While a man in an ocean liner should not look down upon another man sailing a junk [a traditional Chinese ship with sails], it is ridiculous for the latter to brag about his spiritual superiority simply because his junk is more primitive and less convenient than the ocean liner. Technological backwardness is not synonymous with spiritual advancement. . . .

Throughout history the greatest tragedy has always been man's inability to ward off hunger and cold despite his hard labor. How can we in good conscience lecture a man about to be starved to death on the virtue of contentment, fate, and self-satisfaction? A man who condemns material comfort for no other reason than its unavailability to him can be compared to the fox in a Western fable who announces proudly that it does not like sour grapes when the grapes, ripe and sweet, are too high for it to reach. Poverty is not something to be proud of: those who state otherwise are either indulging in self-deception or too lazy to do something about it. More pathetic still are those who fast, mutilate their bodies, or commit suicide by fire, all in the name of "spiritual civilization." All these people — the self-congratulators, the self-deceivers, the self-mutilators, and the suicides — are mentally ill, really, since their attitude toward life is that of a dying man. . . .

Unlike its Oriental counterpart, the modern civilization of the West takes into full consideration the importance of material enjoyment. It has as its foundation two basic concepts. First, the purpose of life is the pursuit of happiness. Second, poverty is a sin; so is physical weakness or illness. The second concept, logically, is a derivative of the first. The goal of this civilization is, in short, the enrichment of life. As poverty is a sin, the Westerners devote their energy to the opening up of natural resources, the promotion of industry, the improvement of manufactured products, and the expansion of commerce. As physical weakness or illness is also a sin, they spare no effort in the study and improvement of medical care, the promotion of sanitation, hygiene, physical fitness and sports, the prevention of contagious disease, and the improvement of heredity. Since the pursuit of happiness is the purpose of life, they busy themselves with the enhancement of comfort in their living quarters, the improvement of transportation and communication, the beautification of their cities, the promotion of the arts, the assurance of safety in their streets, and finally, the security of incorruptibility in government and among government officials. To be sure, Western civilization contains in it certain elements that sometimes prompt its adherents to commit aggression, pillage, or even mass murder, which has to be condemned, of course. Neither can it be denied that it has brought benefit to those who embrace it.

The New Religion

Though modern civilization of the West has not yet dissociated itself from the religion of the past [Christianity], one nevertheless senses that a new religion has been slowly developing. . . . Not surprisingly, the first characteristic of the new religion is its logic and rationality. As modern science enables man to discover new knowledge, to conquer nature for his own benefit, and to do a multitude of things that historically have been regarded as unattainable or even inconceivable, man's confidence in himself has increased enormously, and he believes, for the first time, that he can shape the future in accordance with his own wishes. Not surprisingly, the second characteristic of the new religion is its humanism. The acquisition of more and more knowledge not only enhances man's ability to cope with his environment but also broadens his social perspective, thus increasing his empathy with his fellow men. Not surprisingly, the third characteristic of the new religion is its social ethics. . . .

All the old religions stress salvation on an individual basis, and all the old ethics centers on the civilization of moral worth, again of a personal nature. The adherents of old religions do occasionally speak of the necessity of "saving" others, but they are more than satisfied if they can somehow save themselves. Forever looking inward and, as a result, becoming more and more involved with no one except themselves, they lose contact with the outside world. They do not understand worldly problems, let alone resolve them. . . . What is the use of this so-called self-cultivation of virtues if the net result is a mummy-like parasite, totally ignorant of practical matters and insensitive to the suffering of others? . . .

Occidental and Oriental Civilizations Compared

As "discontent" characterizes the modern civilization of the West, "content" characterizes the traditional civilization of the East. Being content, we Orientals do not strive for the improvement of our living standard, do not pay much attention to new discoveries and new inventions, and do not, even remotely, contemplate upon such "strange" ideas as the conquest of nature. We relish our ignorance, find satisfaction with the status quo, however unpleasant, and speak resignedly about our "fate." We are not even reformers, let alone revolutionaries. We are, in fact, the obedient servants of our rulers, whomever they happen to be.

READING AND DISCUSSION QUESTIONS

1. Why is Hu Shi uncomfortable with the comparisons between Eastern spirituality and Western materialism? How does he think such comparisons function?

2. What does Hu Shi say is the goal of modern Western civilization?

3. What are the two main characteristics of the so-called new religion of the West?

4. What does the author see as the deficits of the "old religions"?

COMPARATIVE QUESTIONS

1. Why did some nationalist movements become more violent than others? Support your argument with evidence from at least two accounts.

2. Based on the account by Graffam, the Balfour Declaration correspondence, and the Iranian letters, in what ways did Turks, Jews, and Arabs seek to reinforce their unique notions of cultural identity?

3. How did nationalist movements throughout Asia address the issue of Western influence? What counterarguments did they face?

4. What tension between modernism and tradition do Hu Shi and the Arab writers express?

CHAPTER 29

The Age of Anxiety in the West

The return to normalcy, stability, and prosperity that most leaders sought after the 1919 Paris peace talks proved to be elusive. Instead, the schisms wrought by the Great War, Russian Revolution, and Asian nationalist movements sparked considerable change worldwide that left Western countries anxious about their place in the diplomatic arena and concerned about ongoing crises around the globe. During this time of uncertainty, many philosophers and writers began to question the long-held ideals that drove development in the Western world — specifically the emphasis on progress, rationality, and individual rights. The onset of the Great Depression only validated and escalated their concerns about the fate of the world. Such doubts and anxieties, however, also led to a flowering of ideas in art, literature, philosophy, religion, and the sciences, as well as the rise of commercial entertainment.

DOCUMENT 29-1

JOHN MAYNARD KEYNES

From The Economic Consequences of the Peace: *An Analysis of the Versailles Treaty*

1920

Though leaders at the Paris Peace Conference hoped that the Treaty of Versailles would establish a lasting peace and economic prosperity for the Allied nations, the agreement they reached laid the groundwork for ongoing tensions. Germany received sole blame for the war and was penalized with

John Maynard Keynes, *The Economic Consequences of the Peace* (New York: Harcourt, Brace and Howe, 1920), 226–227, 296–297.

harsh financial reparations. Economist John Maynard Keynes, an advisor to the British prime minister at the peace talks, astutely recognized the long-term problems inherent in the treaty and warned that, unless it were revised to allow Germany to prosper as well, Europe was doomed to economic collapse. His predictions proved correct when Germany's economy faltered in 1923 and when the Great Depression rocked the world economy after 1929.

The Treaty includes no provisions for the economic rehabilitation of Europe, — nothing to make the defeated Central Empires[1] into good neighbors, nothing to stabilize the new States of Europe,[2] nothing to reclaim Russia; nor does it promote in any way a compact of economic solidarity amongst the Allies themselves; no agreement was reached at Paris for restoring the disordered finances of France and Italy, or to adjust the systems of the Old World and the New.

The Council of Four[3] paid no attention to these issues, being preoccupied with others, — Clemenceau to crush the economic life of his enemy, Lloyd George to do a deal and bring home something which would pass muster for a week, the President to do nothing that was not just and right. It is an extraordinary fact that the fundamental economic problems of a Europe starving and disintegrating before their eyes, was the one question in which it was impossible to arouse the interest of the Four. Reparation was their main excursion into the economic field, and they settled it as a problem of theology, of politics, of electoral chicane, from every point of view except that of the economic future of the States whose destiny they were handling. . . .

For the immediate future events are taking charge, and the near destiny of Europe is no longer in the hands of any man. The events of the coming year will not be shaped by the deliberate acts of statesmen, but by the hidden currents, flowing continually beneath the surface of political history, of which no one can predict the outcome. In one way only can we influence these hidden currents, — by setting in motion those forces of

---

[1] **Central Empires**: Germany, Austria-Hungary, and the Ottoman Empire — the losing alliance in the Great War.

[2] **new States of Europe**: The Treaty of Versailles dismembered the Austro-Hungarian and German Empires, in the process creating newly independent states including Czechoslovakia, Hungary, Yugoslavia, Lithuania, Latvia, and Estonia.

[3] **Council of Four**: Representatives of the four Allied powers that were the driving force behind the treaty: Woodrow Wilson of the United States, Georges Clemenceau of France, David Lloyd George of Great Britain, and Vittorio Orlando of Italy.

instruction and imagination which change *opinion*. The assertion of truth, the unveiling of illusion, the dissipation of hate, the enlargement and instruction of men's hearts and minds, must be the means.

In this autumn of 1919, in which I write, we are at the dead season of our fortunes. The reaction from the exertions, the fears, and the sufferings of the past five years is at its height. Our power of feeling or caring beyond the immediate questions of our own material well-being is temporarily eclipsed. The greatest events outside our own direct experience and the most dreadful anticipations cannot move us.

We have been moved already beyond endurance, and need rest. Never in the lifetime of men now living has the universal element in the soul of man burnt so dimly.

READING AND DISCUSSION QUESTIONS

1. What does Keynes believe is missing from the Treaty of Versailles?
2. According to Keynes, what were the Allied powers' primary concerns in crafting the treaty?
3. What crucial analysis does the author say is missing from the economic plan established in the treaty?
4. How does Keynes think countries can influence the future?

DOCUMENT 29-2

SENATOR HENRY L. MYERS
U.S. Senate Speech on Censorship
June 29, 1922

In the United States, rising concerns about the corrupting influence of the burgeoning motion picture industry fueled a movement among political leaders toward federal regulation that reached a critical mass in the early 1920s. This was due partly to the industry's increasing focus on sex and

Senator Henry L. Meyers, U.S. Senate Speech, June 29, 1922.

violence to lure audiences, and partly to various public scandals (from divorce to murder) involving Hollywood actors. In a speech before the Senate, Montana senator Henry L. Myers supported federal legislation that would establish a national censorship board to oversee the content of films in an effort to safeguard public morals. The measure failed.

The motion picture is a great invention, and it has become a powerful factor for good or bad in our civilization. . . .

Through motion pictures the young and the old may see depicted every good motive, laudable ambition, commendable characteristic, ennobling trait of humanity. They may be taught that honesty is the best policy; that virtue and worth are rewarded; that industry leads to success. . . .

However, from all accounts, the business has been conducted, generally speaking, upon a low plane and in a decidedly sordid manner. Those who own and control the industry seem to have been of the opinion that the sensual, the sordid, the prurient, the phases of fast life, the ways of extravagance, the risqué, the paths of shady life, drew the greatest attendance and coined for them the most money, and apparently they have been out to get the coin, no matter what the effect upon the public, young or old; and when thoughtful people have suggested or advocated official censorship, in the interest of good citizenship and wholesome morals, the owners of the industry have resented it and, in effect, declared that it was nobody's business other than theirs and concerned nobody other than them what kind of shows they produced; that if people did not like their shows they could stay away from them; that it was their business, and they would conduct it as they might please. . . .

In that they are mistaken. The State has an interest in citizenship and a concern in the education of the young. The State has an interest in good morals. It regulates in many ways all of those things. The motion-picture industry vitally concerns all of those things — citizenship, education, morals — and is therefore subject to regulation by the State. It has become a public utility, and is therefore the legitimate subject of State regulation. . . .

The industry has gone so far in defying public sentiment, and has been so flagrant in its abuse of its privileges that a public sentiment for censorship has been aroused which will not be brooked. It may be temporarily checked; it may be temporarily lulled by fair promises, but it is bound to grow, because censorship is needed and would be a good thing. . . .

I believe that a great deal of the extravagance of the day, a great deal of the disposition to live beyond one's means, yea, a great deal of the crime of the day comes from moving pictures. Through them young people gain ideas of fast life, shady ways, laxity of living, loose morals. Crime is freely depicted in alluring colors. Lax morals are held up lightly before them. The sensual is strongly appealed to. Many of the pictures are certainly not elevating; some, at least, are not fit to be seen.

About 18 months ago, in this city, there occurred a foul and most shocking murder. . . . Four youths of this city, in age from 15 to 20 years, as I recollect, stole an automobile, and in it followed an honest, peaceable, industrious barber as he was going to his loving family and quiet home after a day's work, and overtaking him, one of the youths jumped out of the automobile, in a residential section of the city, and murdered him by firing a pistol at him at close range. The victim dropped dead. The youths became panic-stricken on account of close-at-hand pedestrians and fled in the stolen machine. . . .

I have no doubt those young criminals got their ideas of the romance of crime from moving pictures. I believe moving pictures are doing as much harm to-day as saloons did in the days of the open saloon — especially to the young. They are running day and night, Sunday and every other day, the year round, and in most jurisdictions without any regulation by censorship. I would not abolish them. . . . I would close them on Sunday and regulate them week days by judicious censorship. . . .

When we look to the source of the moving pictures, the material for them, the personnel of those who pose for them, we need not wonder that many of the pictures are pernicious. . . .

At Hollywood, Calif., is a colony of these people, where debauchery, riotous living, drunkenness, ribaldry, dissipation, free love, seem to be conspicuous. Many of these "stars," it is reported, were formerly bartenders, butcher boys [street vendors], sopers [drug addicts], swampers [truck drivers], variety actors and actresses, who may have earned $10 or $20 a week, and some of whom are now paid, it is said, salaries of something like $5,000 a month or more, and they do not know what to do with their wealth, extracted from poor people, in large part, in 25 or 50 cent admission fees, except to spend it in riotous living, dissipation, and "high rolling" [likely gambling].

There are some of the characters from whom the young people of to-day are deriving a large part of their education, views of life, and character-forming habits. From these sources our young people gain much of their views of life, inspirations, and education. Rather a poor source, is it not? Looks like there is some need for censorship, does it not? . . .

There was recently some reference in Washington papers to a suggested effort by the Washington Chamber of Commerce or Board of Trade, one or the other, I do not recall which, to induce the Hollywood motion-picture colony to move to this community and establish itself at Great Falls, near this city. I hope it may not be done. From all accounts the Washington Chamber of Commerce or Board of Trade would better invite here a colony of lepers or an institution for the propagation and dissemination of smallpox. . . .

READING AND DISCUSSION QUESTIONS

1. What does Myers see as the potentially positive impact of motion pictures?

2. Why does he think filmmakers have chosen to focus on certain themes?

3. How does Myers explain the role of government and the need for censorship?

4. What social problems does he attribute to the film industry?

DOCUMENT 29-3

ADOLF HITLER
From Mein Kampf
1925

Adolf Hitler (1889–1945) was a relatively anonymous player on the world political stage until an ill-fated attempt to seize control of the German government in 1923 landed him in jail. In prison, he wrote Mein Kampf, *in which he outlined his theories about national socialism as a preferred system of government and how best to achieve this political revolution. Hitler explained his hatred for Jews, who he believed sought world domination; and who, through intermarriage, were "polluting" the purity of the German race;*

Adolf Hitler, *Mein Kampf*, trans. Ralph Manheim (Boston: Houghton Mifflin, 1971), 293–296, 300–303.

and he linked Germany's future to extermination of the Jews. Initially, Mein Kampf sold poorly, but a few years before Hitler came to power, sales increased and it later became a best seller. It is now banned in several countries — a measure of the volatility of the "Nazi bible."

It is idle to argue which race or races were the original representative of human culture and hence the real founders of all that we sum up under the word "humanity." It is simpler to raise this question with regard to the present, and here an easy, clear answer results. All the human culture, all the results of art, science, and technology that we see before us today, are almost exclusively the creative product of the Aryan.[4] This very fact admits of the not unfounded inference that he alone was the founder of all higher humanity, therefore representing the prototype of all that we understand by the word "man." He is the Prometheus of mankind from whose bright forehead the divine spark of genius has sprung at all times, forever kindling anew that fire of knowledge which illumined the night of silent mysteries and thus caused man to climb the path to mastery over the other beings of this earth. Exclude him — and perhaps after a few thousand years darkness will again descend on the earth, human culture will pass, and the world turn to a desert.

If we were to divide mankind into three groups, the founders of culture, the bearers of culture, the destroyers of culture, only the Aryan could be considered as the representative of the first group. From him originate the foundations and walls of all human creation, and only the outward form and color are determined by the changing traits of character of the various peoples. He provides the mightiest building stones and plans for all human progress and only the execution corresponds to the nature of the varying men and races. . . .

The progress of humanity is like climbing an endless ladder; it is impossible to climb higher without first taking the lower steps. Thus, the Aryan had to take the road to which reality directed him and not the one that would appeal to the imagination of a modern pacifist. The road of reality is hard and difficult, but in the end it leads where our friend would like to bring humanity by dreaming, but unfortunately removes more than bringing it closer.

---

[4] **Aryan**: Term used by Hitler and the Nazis to refer to a white, non-Jewish person, typically with Nordic features, who was allegedly a member of a superior (so-called master) race.

Hence it is no accident that the first cultures arose in places where the Aryan, in his encounters with lower peoples, subjugated them and bent them to his will. They then became the first technical instrument in the service of a developing culture.

Thus, the road which the Aryan had to take was clearly marked out. As a conqueror he subjected the lower beings and regulated their practical activity under his command, according to his will and for his aims. Bit in directing them to a useful, though arduous activity, he not only spared the life of those he subjected; perhaps he gave them a fate that was better than their previous so-called "freedom." As long as he ruthlessly upheld the master attitude, not only did he really remain master, but also the preserver and increaser of culture. For culture was based exclusively on his abilities and hence on his actual survival. As soon as the subjected people began to raise themselves up and probably approached the conqueror in language, the sharp dividing wall between master and servant fell. The Aryan gave up the purity of his blood and, therefore, lost his sojourn in the paradise which he had made for himself. He became submerged in the racial mixture, and gradually, more and more, lost his cultural capacity, until at last, not only mentally but also physically, he began to resemble the subjected aborigines more than his own ancestors. For a time he could live on the existing cultural benefits, but then petrifaction set in and he fell a prey to oblivion.

Thus cultures and empires collapsed to make place for new formations.

Blood mixture and the resultant drop in the racial level is the sole cause of the dying out of old cultures; for men do not perish as a result of lost wars, but by the loss of that force of resistance which is contained only in pure blood.

All who are not of good race in this world are chaff.

And all occurrences in world history are only the expression of the races' instinct of self-preservation, in the good or bad sense. . . .

The mightiest counterpart to the Aryan is represented by the Jew. In hardly any people in the world is the instinct of self-preservation developed more strongly than in the so-called "chosen." Of this, the mere fact of the survival of this race may be considered the best proof. Where is the people which in the last two thousand years has been exposed to so slight changes of inner disposition, character, etc., as the Jewish people? What people, finally, has gone through greater upheavals than this one — and nevertheless issued from the mightiest catastrophes of mankind unchanged? What an infinitely tough will to live and preserve the species speaks from these facts!

The mental qualities of the Jew have been schooled in the course of many centuries. Today he passes as "smart," and this in a certain sense he has been at all times. But his intelligence is not the result of his own development, but of visual instruction through foreigners. For the human mind cannot climb to the top without steps; for every step upward he needs the foundation of the past, and this in the comprehensive sense in which it can be revealed only in general culture. All thinking is based only in small part on man's own knowledge, and mostly on the experience of the time that has preceded. The general cultural level provides the individual man, without his noticing it as a rule, with such a profusion of preliminary knowledge that, thus armed, he can more easily take further steps of his own. The boy of today, for example, grows up among a truly vast number of technical acquisitions of the last centuries, so that he takes for granted and no longer pays attention to much that a hundred years ago was a riddle to even the greatest minds, although for following and understanding our progress in the field in question it is of decisive importance to him. If a very genius from the twenties of the past century should suddenly leave his grave today, it would be harder for him even intellectually to find his way in the present era than for an average boy of fifteen today. For he would lack all the infinite preliminary education which our present contemporary unconsciously, so to speak, assimilates while growing up amidst the manifestations of our present general civilization.

Since the Jew — for reasons which will at once become apparent — was never in possession of a culture of his own, the foundations of his intellectual work were always provided by others. His intellect at all times developed through the cultural world surrounding him.

The reverse process never took place.

For if the Jewish people's instinct of self-preservation is not smaller but larger than that of other peoples, if his intellectual faculties can easily arouse the impression that they are equal to the intellectual gifts of other races, he lacks completely the most essential requirement for a cultured people, the idealistic attitude.

In the Jewish people the will to self-sacrifice does not go beyond the individual's naked instinct of self-preservation. Their apparently great sense of solidarity is based on the very primitive herd instinct that is seen in many other living creatures in this world. It is a noteworthy fact that the herd instinct leads to mutual support only as long as a common danger makes this seem useful or inevitable. The same pack of wolves which has just fallen on its prey together disintegrates when hunger abates into its individual beasts. The same is true of horses which try to defend themselves against an assailant in a body, but scatter again as soon as the danger is past.

It is similar with the Jew. His sense of sacrifice is only apparent. It exists only as long as the existence of the individual makes it absolutely necessary. However, as soon as the common enemy is conquered, the danger threatening all averted and the booty hidden, the apparent harmony of the Jews among themselves ceases, again making way for their old causal tendencies. The Jew is only united when a common danger forces him to be or a common booty entices him; if these two grounds are lacking, the qualities of the crassest egoism come into their own, and in the twinkling of an eye the united people turns into a horde of rats, fighting bloodily among themselves.

If the Jews were alone in this world, they would stifle in filth and offal; they would try to get ahead of one another in hate-filled struggle and exterminate one another, in so far as the absolute absence of all sense of self-sacrifice, expressing itself in their cowardice, did not turn battle into comedy here too.

So it is absolutely wrong to infer any ideal sense of sacrifice in the Jews from the fact that they stand together in struggle, or, better expressed, in the plundering of their fellow men.

Here again the Jew is led by nothing but the naked egoism of the individual.

That is why the Jewish state — which should be the living organism for preserving and increasing a race — is completely unlimited as to territory. For a state formation to have a definite spatial setting always presupposes an idealistic attitude on the part of the state-race, and especially a correct interpretation of the concept of work. In the exact measure in which this attitude is lacking, any attempt at forming, even of preserving, a spatially delimited state fails. And thus the basis on which alone culture can arise is lacking.

Hence the Jewish people, despite all apparent intellectual qualities, is without any true culture, and especially without any culture of its own. For what sham culture the Jew today possesses is the property of other peoples, and for the most part it is ruined in his hands.

READING AND DISCUSSION QUESTIONS

1. What does Hitler say led to the downfall of Aryan culture?
2. According to Hitler, what is the source of the Jewish intellect?

3.   How does he argue against the notion of a unified Jewish community and an identity built on sacrifice?

4.   Based on your reading, how does Hitler conceptualize his own role and responsibilities regarding the maintenance of the Aryan race?

DOCUMENT 29-4

SIGMUND FREUD

From Civilization and Its Discontents

1929

In the 1920s, Austrian psychologist Sigmund Freud (1856–1939) joined other thinkers in exploring human nature, culture, and society. In Civilization and Its Discontents, *he noted that civilization was the product of ongoing tensions between the greater good and the individual. Rejecting notions of man's rationality that had prevailed since the Enlightenment, Freud argued that men were irrational, driven by baser instincts (sexual desire and aggression) and the drive for pleasure that were incompatible with civilization's need for order and community. As such, even utopian social models (which he believed communism to be) could not succeed. One of his last books,* Civilization *was an instant hit, selling 12,000 copies its first year, and it has remained popular.*

The element of truth behind all this, which people are so ready to disavow, is that men are not gentle creatures who want to be loved, and who at the most can defend themselves if they are attacked; they are, on the contrary, creatures among whose instinctual endowments is to be reckoned a powerful share of aggressiveness. As a result, their neighbor is for them not only a potential helper or sexual object, but also someone who tempts them to satisfy their aggressiveness on him, to exploit his capacity for work without compensation, to use him sexually without his consent, to seize his possessions, to humiliate him, to cause him pain, to torture and to kill him.

Sigmund Freud, *Civilization and Its Discontents*, trans. and ed. James Strachey (New York: Norton, 2005), 103–108.

Homo homini lupus.[5] Who, in the face of all his experience of life and of history, will have the courage to dispute this assertion? As a rule this cruel aggressiveness waits for some provocation or puts itself at the service of some other purpose, whose goal might also have been reached by milder measures. In circumstances that are favorable to it, when the mental counterforces which ordinarily inhibit it are out of action, it also manifests itself spontaneously and reveals man as a savage beast to whom consideration towards his own kind is something alien. Anyone who calls to mind the atrocities committed during the racial migrations or the invasions of the Huns, or by the people known as Mongols under Jenghiz Khan and Tamerlane, or at the capture of Jerusalem by the pious Crusaders, or even, indeed, the horrors of the recent World War — anyone who calls these things to mind will have to bow humbly before the truth of this view.

The existence of this inclination to aggression, which we can detect in ourselves and justly assume to be present in others, is the factor which disturbs our relations with our neighbor and which forces civilization into such a high expenditure [of energy]. In consequence of this primary mutual hostility of human beings, civilized society is perpetually threatened with disintegration. The interest of work in common would not hold it together; instinctual passions are stronger than reasonable interests. Civilization has to use its utmost efforts in order to set limits to man's aggressive instincts and to hold the manifestations of them in check by psychical reaction-formations. Hence, therefore, the use of methods intended to incite people into identifications and aim-inhibited relationships of love, hence the restriction upon sexual life, and hence too the ideal's commandment to love one's neighbor as oneself — a commandment which is really justified by the fact that nothing else runs so strongly counter to the original nature of man. In spite of every effort, these endeavors of civilization have not so far achieved very much. It hopes to prevent the crudest excesses of brutal violence by itself assuming the right to use violence against criminals, but the law is not able to lay hold of the more cautious and refined manifestations of human aggressiveness. The time comes when each one of us has to give up as illusions the expectations which, in his youth, he pinned upon his fellow-men, and when he may learn how much difficulty and pain has been added to his life by their ill-will. At the same time, it would be unfair to reproach civilization with trying to eliminate strife and competition from human activity. These things are

---

[5] *Homo homini lupus*: A Latin phrase that translates loosely to "man is a wolf to man," meaning that men prey upon each other.

undoubtedly indispensable. But opposition is not necessarily enmity; it is merely misused and made an *occasion* for enmity.

The communists believe that they have found the path to deliverance from our evils. According to them, man is wholly good and is well-disposed to his neighbor; but the institution of private property has corrupted his nature. The ownership of private wealth gives the individual power, and with it the temptation to ill-treat his neighbor; while the man who is excluded from possession is bound to rebel in hostility against his oppressor. If private property were abolished, all wealth held in common, and everyone allowed to share in the enjoyment of it, ill-will and hostility would disappear among men. Since everyone's needs would be satisfied, no one would have any reason to regard another as his enemy; all would willingly undertake the work that was necessary. I have no concern with any economic criticisms of the communist system; I cannot inquire into whether the abolition of private property is expedient or advantageous. But I am able to recognize that the psychological premises on which the system is based are an untenable illusion. In abolishing private property we deprive the human love of aggression of one of its instruments, certainly a strong one, though certainly not the strongest; but we have in no way altered the differences in power and influence which are misused by aggressiveness, nor have we altered anything in its nature. Aggressiveness was not created by property. It reigned almost without limit in primitive times, when property was still very scanty, and it already shows itself in the nursery almost before property has given up its primal, anal form, it forms the basis of every relation of affection and love among people (with the single exception, perhaps, of the mother's relation to her male child). If we do away with personal rights over material wealth, there still remains prerogative in the field of sexual relationships, which is bound to become the source of the strongest dislike and the most violent hostility among men who in other respects are on an equal footing. If we were to remove this factor, too, by allowing complete freedom of sexual life and thus abolishing the family, the germ-cell of civilization, we cannot, it is true, easily foresee what new paths the development of civilization could take; but one thing we can expect, and that is that this indestructible feature of human nature will follow it there.

It is clearly not easy for men to give up the satisfaction of this inclination to aggression. They do not feel comfortable without it. The advantage which a comparatively small cultural group offers of allowing this instinct an outlet in the form of hostility against intruders is not to be despised. It is always possible to bind together a considerable number of people in love, so long as there are other people left over to receive the manifestations of their aggressiveness. I once discussed the phenomenon that it is precisely communities with adjoining territories, and related to each other in other ways as well, who are engaged in constant feuds and in ridiculing each other — like the Spaniards and Portuguese, for instance, the North Germans and South Germans, the English and Scotch, and so on. I gave this phenomenon the name of "the narcissism of minor differences," a name which does not do much to explain it. We can now see that it is a convenient and relatively harmless satisfaction of the inclination to aggression, by means of which cohesion between the members of the community is made easier. In this respect the Jewish people, scattered everywhere, have rendered most useful services to the civilizations of the countries that have been their hosts; but unfortunately all the massacres of the Jews in the Middle Ages did not suffice to make that period more peaceful and secure for their Christian fellows. When once the apostle Paul had posited universal love between men as the foundation of his Christian community, extreme intolerance on the part of Christendom towards those who remained outside it became the inevitable consequence. To the Romans, who had not founded their communal life as a State upon love, religious intolerance was something foreign, although with them religion was a concern of the State and the State was permeated by religion. Neither was it an unaccountable chance that the dream of a Germanic world-dominion called for antisemitism as its complement; and it is intelligible that the attempt to establish a new, communist civilization in Russia should find its psychological support in the persecution of the bourgeois. One only wonders, with concern, what the Soviets will do after they have wiped out their bourgeois.[6]

READING AND DISCUSSION QUESTIONS

1. What does Freud see as the main threat to civilization?

2. Why does he disagree with the communists who believe that doing away with private ownership of property will end aggression?

3. What does Freud consider to be the root of human aggression?

4. According to Freud how does the concept of "the other" or "the outsider" factor into the establishment of political and social power?

---

[6] **bourgeois**: A term used by Marxists to denote a person of the property-owning or middle class, whose attitudes, values, and political behavior are dictated by concern for property ownership.

COMPARATIVE QUESTIONS

1. How did each of these writers' anxieties about the post–World War I era shape the policies and ideas they sought to develop?

2. In what way is Senator Myers's argument for censoring films in keeping with Freud's discussion of civilization and human nature?

3. Both Myers and Hitler fear a "corrupting" influence on society. Based on your readings, how do they each define that influence?

4. Given his concept of human nature, would Freud agree or disagree with Keynes's predictions about the Treaty of Versailles, as well as his thoughts about how it was crafted?

CHAPTER 30

Dictatorships and the Second World War

The political and economic crises of the interwar years fueled global anxieties and contributed to the rise of ruthless authoritarian regimes, especially in hard-hit countries such as Germany and the Soviet Union. Joseph Stalin sought to consolidate Soviet government power in the name of socialism, while Adolf Hitler built his empire in Germany on a foundation of racial hatred against the Jews and territorial expansion across Europe. Both regimes fostered distinct ideas about citizenship and what contributions citizens — men *and* women — were expected to make. Hitler's seizure of Poland in 1939 sparked World War II. Japan hoped to capitalize on the resulting upheaval and expand its empire across Asia into territories controlled by Europe and the United States. The Japanese attack on Pearl Harbor in 1941 pulled the United States into the conflict, which finally ended when the United States dropped the first atomic bombs on the Japanese cities of Hiroshima and Nagasaki.

DOCUMENT 30-1

GERTRUD SCHOLTZ-KLINK
Speech to the National Socialist Women's Association
1935

Adolf Hitler rose to power on the promise of economic recovery, but he also sought a social revolution. Along with his attacks on Jews, communists,

From Susan Groag Bell, and Karen M. Offen, eds., *Women, the Family, and Freedom: The Debate in Documents*, Volume II, 1750–1880 (Stanford, Calif.: Board of Trustees of the Leland Stanford Junior University, 1983).

Gypsies, and homosexuals, Hitler took aim at feminists and proponents of women's equality. He believed a woman's place was in the home, subordinate to her husband, and not in the workforce, government, or Nazi politics. Toward that end, all women's organizations were consolidated under the National Socialist Women's Association. In 1935, Gertrud Scholtz-Klink, newly appointed by party and government officials as national women's leader, delivered a speech to the organization on how she planned to help women combine work with motherhood and learn to embrace national socialism.

A year has passed since the day we met here for the first time as a unified group of German women, to demonstrate our willingness to cooperate in our Führer's [Hitler's] work of reconstruction.

This year has been inspired by the desire to mark our times with our best efforts so that our descendants will be able to forget our nation's fourteen years of weakness and sickness.[1] We women knew, quite as well as German men, that we had to teach a people, partially sunk in self-despair, attitudes requiring those very qualities that had been deliberately suppressed in our nation. In order to carry out our intentions to unite and to march shoulder to shoulder, we demanded honor and loyalty, strength and sincerity, humility and respect — such virtues appeal to the soul of a people. In matters of the soul, however, it is no longer the majority who decide, but the strength and inner freedom of upright individuals. Therefore, we could only fulfill our task if it enabled us to penetrate the soul of the individual. . . .

When we came to the point of recognizing that the human eye reflected a nation's soul, we had to reach the women of our nation, once and for all, through our labor on women's behalf. Because as mothers our women have carried the heavy burden of the past fourteen years — and the ruins of the war and post-war period — in their hearts; and as future mothers other women must presently develop an understanding of the demands of our times — to both of these groups we dedicated the first important path that we built to the hearts of German women: our Reichs-Maternity Service.

Urged on by the tired eyes of many over-burdened mothers and the responsibility for the coming generation of mothers, we joined together

---

[1] **fourteen years of weakness and sickness**: A likely reference to Germany's economic hardship following World War I and the terms of the Treaty of Versailles.

under the leadership of the National Socialist Women's Association . . . and appealed to the German women especially trained for this work. When I tell you today that, between the 1st of October 1934 and the 1st of April 1935, we enrolled more than 201,700 women in 7,653 maternity school courses in about 2,000 locations throughout the German Reich, it may not seem much at first glance. But we must not forget that we had no funds and met with much opposition, and that we had no patronage since we were quite unknown. But we did have absolute and unshakable faith. None of our traveling teachers asked: How much will I earn? Or, What are my pension rights? We have done this work out of a sense of duty to our nation — and our nation has responded. On Mothers' Day this year we were presented with 3.5 million marks for this work of maternity training. Moreover, on this day of honor for the mothers of Germany, when we all collected money in the streets, we found that our humblest fellow-countrymen were the most generous. This was surely the most wonderful reward for all of us, but it also gave practical evidence of where our major efforts must be directed. And when, only one or two months from now, we open our Reichs-Maternity School in Wedding, formerly one of the most solidly "red" [communist] quarters of Berlin, we will be able to congratulate ourselves on having prepared a place, on behalf of our Party and our State, that will reveal to all of you how we are solving our problems.

In this place, mothers of all ages and classes discuss their problems and their needs. Here they will become acquainted with the aims of a National Socialist state and will receive inspiration to pass them on from woman to woman, and thus to recover our national faith in ourselves. If by means of the Reichs-Maternity Service we gradually succeed in brightening the eyes of our mothers and in bringing some joy into their often difficult lives, perhaps even a song to their lips, we may consider that we have accomplished our task, because happy mothers will raise happy children. But our Reichs-Maternity Service must also make a point of teaching our young and future mothers those things that a liberal era did not teach them — for the omission of which our nation has had to pay dearly — namely, that through marriage we consciously become mothers of the nation; that is, we understand and share every national requirement laid upon German men, and that, therefore, as wives we must unconditionally become the companions of our men — not merely in personal terms, but in all national requirements.

First we pursued our task by appealing to the mothers of the nation, and then to that generation closest to the mothers, the girls between eighteen and twenty-five years of age. We called upon them to join voluntarily in the chain of helping hands and to create a relationship of unbreakable trust among German women. And they came, our girls of the German Women's Labor Service.[2]

You, my girls, who have now spent two years with me in the struggle for the autonomy of the German people, have learned to carry every responsibility and have become the inspiration of our mothers. No matter whether our girls are cheerfully helping German settlers on the moors in their difficult work of creating new homes; or whether they are working in Rhön, Spessart, or in eastern Bavaria, hand in hand with the National Socialist Welfare Organization in giving help to careworn adults and joyless children, in reawakening a taste for beauty and a belief in themselves; or whether they are helping German peasant women harvest from dawn to dusk — one thing unites them all, for they know: We are needed, we are of some use, and we are playing our parts in the rebirth of our nation. . . .

Since at present we cannot satisfy all these demands [for compulsory labor service], owing to financial and organizational difficulties, we have begun by making only those demands that professional and university women can take the lead in supporting. . . . At one time, it was considered the height of achievement in Germany to know everything and thereby to lose the simple-mindedness of childhood. We wish to impress on our women at the universities that, as university students, they must place the intellectual abilities entrusted to them at the disposal of their nation with the same humility as that with which women workers and mothers fulfill their duties. . . . This summer our women students began to live in this manner and thereby joined the chain of helping hands we have created among ourselves. They went to German factories and replaced working women and mothers, enabling them to have a real vacation in order to regain strength for their hard day-to-day existence. For it is these women, these mothers of families, who are hardest hit by the short working hours or unemployment of their husbands, because at home their children sap their strength. . . .

This brings us to the point where we must consider the millions of German women who perform heavy labor in factories day in and day out. If we consider the human eye as the measure of people's soul, it is here that we find the deepest imprints of that fourteen-year-long attempt to strangle our national soul. We know that a great deal of industrial work

---

[2] **German Women's Labor Service**: A program in which women worked on various public works projects. Participation became mandatory in 1939.

must always be done by women, but it is essential that the woman at the machine should feel that she, in her position, represents her nation, in common with all other women. That is to say, we awaken her consciousness so that she will say to herself: "This is my responsibility, my attitude determines the attitude of the nation." . . .

I must deal briefly with a question that is constantly brought to our attention, that is, how our present attitude toward life differs from that of the previous women's movement. First, in principle we permit only Germans to be leaders of German women and to concern themselves with matters of importance to Germans. Second, as a matter of principle we never have demanded, nor shall we ever demand, equal rights for women with the men of our nation. Instead we shall always make women's special interests dependent upon the needs of our entire nation. All further considerations will follow from this unconditional intertwining of the collective fate of the nation.

READING AND DISCUSSION QUESTIONS

1. In what ways does Scholtz-Klink believe women have played and will continue to play an important role in the nation?

2. What lessons must the Maternity Service teach future mothers that the liberal era did not?

3. What does the author have to say on the subject of women and paid employment?

4. How do the ideas that Scholtz-Klink outlines differ from those of past women's movements?

The Nuremberg Laws: The Centerpiece of Nazi Racial Legislation

1935

Adolf Hitler's beliefs about Germanic racial superiority, first articulated in his 1925 book Mein Kampf *(see Document 29-3), became the foundation for the Nuremberg Laws, enacted after Hitler seized power as German chancellor in 1933. Designed to preserve the purity of the German race, the laws — which were a manifestation of Hitler's fierce anti-Semitism — deemed Jews inferior, defined who was a Jew, and prohibited intermarriage between Germans and non-Germans (especially Jews). In the end, Jews lost not only citizenship rights and jobs but also their freedom and lives; ultimately, six million perished in the Holocaust.*

ARTICLE 5

1. A Jew is anyone who descended from at least three grandparents who were racially full Jews. Article 2, par. 2, second sentence will apply.
2. A Jew is also one who descended from two full Jewish parents, if: (a) he belonged to the Jewish religious community at the time this law was issued, or who joined the community later; (b) he was married to a Jewish person, at the time the law was issued, or married one subsequently; (c) he is the offspring from a marriage with a Jew, in the sense of Section 1, which was contracted after the Law for the Protection of German Blood and German Honor became effective . . . ; (d) he is the offspring of an extramarital relationship, with a Jew, according to Section 1, and will be born out of wedlock after July 31, 1936. . . .

LAW FOR THE PROTECTION OF GERMAN BLOOD AND GERMAN HONOR OF SEPTEMBER 15, 1935

Thoroughly convinced by the knowledge that the purity of German blood is essential for the further existence of the German people and animated by the inflexible will to safe-guard the German nation for the entire future,

---

U.S. Chief of Counsel for the Prosecution of Axis Criminality, Nazi Conspiracy and Aggression *(Washington, D.C.: U.S. Government Printing Office, 1946), vol. 4, doc. no. 1417-PS, 8–10; vol. 4, doc. no. 2000-PS, 636–638.*

the Reichstag[3] has resolved upon the following law unanimously, which is promulgated herewith:

Section 1

1. Marriages between Jews and nationals of German or kindred blood are forbidden. Marriages concluded in defiance of this law are void, even if, for the purpose of evading this law, they are concluded abroad. . . .

Section 2

Relation[s] outside marriage between Jews and nationals of German or kindred blood are forbidden.

Section 3

Jews will not be permitted to employ female nationals of German or kindred blood in their household.

Section 4

1. Jews are forbidden to hoist the Reich and national flag and to present the colors of the Reich. . . .

Section 5

1. A person who acts contrary to the prohibition of Section 1 will be punished with hard labor.
2. A person who acts contrary to the prohibition of Section 2 will be punished with imprisonment or with hard labor.
3. A person who acts contrary to the provisions of Sections 3 or 4 will be punished with imprisonment up to a year and with a fine or with one of these penalties. . . .

READING AND DISCUSSION QUESTIONS

1. What makes someone a Jew, according to the Nuremberg Laws?
2. Why do you think so much is attention paid to "relations" between Germans and Jews in these laws?
3. Within the laws, what restrictions render Jews different from and inferior to other Germans?
4. What punishments are promised to those who break these laws?

---

[3] **Reichstag**: The German legislative assembly.

DOCUMENT 30-3

Letters to Izvestiya: On the Issue of Abortion

1936

As Joseph Stalin (1879–1953) rose to absolute power in the Soviet Union between 1922 and 1927, he launched an ambitious and strict campaign to solidify socialism by placing all economic development under government control and promoting new cultural values. Women, who had gained greater equality after the 1917 Bolshevik Revolution, became a key focus. As birthrates dropped by up to 50 percent from 1930 to 1935, Stalin's government released propaganda celebrating women's traditional roles as wives and mothers and enacted legislation outlawing abortion except to save the mother's life. The public's thoughts on this legal change ran in newspapers such as Pravda *and* Izvestiya.

LETTER FROM A STUDENT [K.B.]

I have read in the press the draft law on the prohibition of abortion, aid to expectant mothers, etc., and cannot remain silent on this matter.

There are thousands of women in the same position as myself. I am a student reading the first course of the second Moscow Medical Institute. My husband is also a student reading the same course at our Institute. Our scholarships amount jointly to 205 rubles. Neither he nor I have a room of our own. Next year we intend to apply for admission to a hostel, but I do not know whether our application will be granted. I love children and shall probably have some in four or five years' time. But can I have a child now? Having a child now would mean leaving the Institute, lagging behind my husband, forgetting everything I have learnt and probably leaving Moscow because there is nowhere to live.

There is another married couple in our Institute, Mitya and Galya, who live in a hostel. Yesterday Galya said to me: "If I become pregnant I shall have to leave the Institute; one cannot live in a hostel with children."

I consider that the projected law is premature because the housing problem in our towns is a painful one. Very often it is the lack of living quarters that is the reason behind an abortion. If the draft included an

"Letters to *Izvestiya* on the Abortion Issues," May–June 1936, in Rudolf Schlesinger, ed., *The Family in the U.S.S.R.* (London: Routledge, 1947), 255–259, 263–265.

article assuring married couples, who are expecting a baby, of a room — that would be a different matter.

In five years' time when I am a doctor and have a job and a room I shall have children. But at present I do not want and cannot undertake such a responsibility. . . .

Answer to the Student K.B.

Your paper recently published a letter from a student, K.B., in which she raised objections to the prohibition of abortions. I think the author of the letter . . . has not grasped the full significance of the projected law. The difficulties about which K.B. writes and which, according to her, justify abortion are, she thinks, the difficulties of to-day which will have disappeared to-morrow. The writer of that letter completely ignored the fact that the government, by widening the network of child-welfare institutions, is easing the mother's task in looking after the child. The main mistake K.B. makes is, in my view, that she approaches the problem of childbearing as though it were a private matter. This would explain why she writes: "I shall have them (children) in four or five years' time." She hopes by that time to have completed her studies, obtained a medical diploma and found both a job and a room. But one must be logical! If during these years, K.B. intends to have recourse to abortions, who can vouch that by the time when she desires to have children she will still be able to do so? And for a normal woman to be deprived of the possibility of having children is as great a misfortune as the loss of a dear one.

I used to study in a factory and received a very small allowance while bringing up my small son whom I had to bring up on my own. (His father was dead.) It was a hard time. I had to go and unload trains or look for similar work that would bring in some money . . . that was in 1923. Now my son is a good, rough Komsomol[4] and a Red Army[5] soldier in the Far East. How great are my joy and pride that I did not shun the difficulties and that I managed to bring up such a son.

Letter from an Engineer [E.T.]

I am non-party [not Communist], married, with a 5-year-old son. I work as an engineer and have been and still am in a responsible position. I regard myself as a good citizen of the U.S.S.R.

---

[4] **Komsomol**: Member of the Communist Youth Organization.
[5] **Red Army**: The reconstituted Soviet army founded by Commissar of Military and Naval Affairs Leon Trotsky (1879–1940) after the 1917 Bolshevik Revolution.

I cannot agree with the prohibition of abortions. And I am very glad that this law has not entered into force but has been submitted to the workers for discussion.

The prohibition of abortion means the compulsory birth of a child to a woman who does not want children. The birth of a child ties married people to each other. Not everyone will readily abandon a child, for alimony is not all that children need. Where the parents produce a child of their own free will, all is well. But where a child comes into the family against the will of the parents, a grim personal drama will be enacted which will undoubtedly lower the social value of the parents and leave its mark on the child.

A categorical prohibition of abortion will confront young people with a dilemma: either complete sexual abstinence or the risk of jeopardizing their studies and disrupting their life. To my mind any prohibition of abortion is bound to mutilate many a young life. Apart from this, the result of such a prohibition might be an increase in the death-rate from abortions because they will then be performed illegally.

LETTER FROM PROFESSOR K. BOGOREKOV, LENINGRAD

Abortions are harmful. One cannot disagree with that. But situations in life do exist when this harmful remedy will allow a woman to preserve normal conditions of life.

If a single child already ties a woman down, two, three, or four children leave her no possibility at all of participating in social life and having a job. A man suffers less. He gives the family his salary irrespective of the number of children — and the whole burden falls upon the mother.

Sometimes abortion is an extreme but decisive means of averting the disruption of a young woman's life. It may become imperative, through the accident of an unlucky liaison for a young girl-student without means for whom a child would be a heavy penalty, or through bad heredity of the parents or a number of other contingencies which play an important part in life and can often lead to its mutilation. All this must be taken into account.

It must not be thought that the majority of abortions are the result of irresponsible behavior. Experience shows that a woman resorts to abortion as a last resource when other methods of safeguard against pregnancy have failed and the birth of a child threatens to make her life more difficult.

Simple statistics show that in spite of this the birth-rate of our country is increasing rapidly.[6] And what is needed is not pressure, but a stimulation

---

[6] **Birth-rate . . . increasing rapidly:** From what is known, this is a false statement.

of the birth-rate by means of financial assistance, improved housing conditions, legal action against those who fail to pay alimony, etc. . . .

Abortions will become obsolete by themselves when knowledge of human anatomy spreads, methods of birth-control are more widely used and — last but not least — when housing conditions are improved. . . .

LETTER FROM PROFESSOR M. MALINOVSKY

Performing an abortion is an operation undoubtedly involving great risks. There are few operations so dangerous as the cleaning out of the womb during pregnancy. Under the best of conditions and in the hands of the most experienced specialist this operation still has a "normal" percentage of fatal cases. It is true that the percentage is not very high. Our surgeons have brought the technique of performing abortions to perfection. The foreign doctors who have watched operations in our gynæcological hospitals have unanimously testified that their technique is irreproachable. And yet . . . here are still cases in which it is fatal. This is understandable. The operation is performed in the dark and with instruments which, so far as their effect on so tender an organ as the womb is concerned, remind one of a crowbar. And even the most gifted surgeons, virtuosi at their job, occasionally cause great and serious injuries for which the woman often pays with her life. . . .

The slave-like conditions of hired labor, together with unemployment and poverty, deprive women in capitalist countries of the impulse for childbearing. Their "will to motherhood" is paralyzed. In our country all the conditions for giving birth to and bringing up a healthy generation exist. The "fear of motherhood," the fear of the morrow, the anxiety over the child's future are gone.

The lighthearted attitude towards the family, the feeling of irresponsibility which is still quite strong in men and women, the disgusting disrespect for women and children — all these must come before our guns. Every baseness towards women and every form of profligacy [extravagance] must be considered as serious antisocial acts. . . .

READING AND DISCUSSION QUESTIONS

1. Why does K.B. argue that abortion must remain legal? What solution for reducing the number of abortions does she propose? What generational differences do you notice between K.B.'s position and the woman who responded to her?

2. Why does E. T. oppose the ban on abortion?

3. Professor K. Bogorekov says that abortion will cease when what happens?

4. What comparison does Professor Malinovsky make between socialist and capitalist countries?

DOCUMENT 30-4

RUDOLF HÖSS

From the Memoirs of the SS Kommandant at Auschwitz

1946

In fewer than ten years, Rudolf Höss rose through the ranks of the Nazi SS (Guard Detachment) to become commandant of Auschwitz concentration camp in Poland and, ultimately, head of all of Hitler's concentration camps. At Auschwitz, one of several sites to which Jews were sent to serve as forced factory workers, Höss oversaw the killing of more than one million Jews in gas chambers. After the war, Höss was captured and tried for crimes against humanity by the international tribunal at Nuremberg. Before his execution in 1947, he wrote an account of his wartime experiences, including his feelings about Jews and his role in the Holocaust.

Since I was a fanatic National Socialist, I was firmly convinced that our idea would take hold in all countries, modified by the various local customs, and would gradually become dominant. This would then break the dominance of international Jewry. Anti-Semitism was nothing new throughout the whole world. It always made its strongest appearance when the Jews had pushed themselves into positions of power and when their evil actions became known to the general public. . . . I believed that because our ideas were better and stronger, we would prevail in the long run. . . .

I want to emphasize here that I personally never hated the Jews. I considered them to be the enemy of our nation. However, that was precisely the reason to treat them the same way as the other prisoners. I never made

Death Dealer: The Memoirs of the SS Kommandant at Auschwitz, ed. Steven Paskuly (Amherst, N.Y.: Prometheus Books, 1992).

a distinction concerning this. Besides, the feeling of hatred is not in me, but I know what hate is, and how it manifests itself. I have seen it and I have felt it.

The original order . . . to annihilate all the Jews stated, "All Jews without exception are to be destroyed." It was later changed by Himmler[7] so that those able to work were to be used in the arms factories. This made Auschwitz the assembly point for the Jews to a degree never before known. . . .

When he gave me the order personally . . . to prepare a place for mass killings and then carry it out, I could never have imagined the scale, or what the consequences would be. Of course, this order was something extraordinary, something monstrous. However, the reasoning behind the order of this mass annihilation seemed correct to me. At the time I wasted no thoughts about it. I had received an order; I had to carry it out. I could not allow myself to form an opinion as to whether this mass extermination of the Jews was necessary or not. At the time it was beyond my frame of mind. Since the Führer himself had ordered "The Final Solution of the Jewish Question," there was no second guessing for an old National Socialist, much less an SS officer. "Führer, you order. We obey"[8] was not just a phrase or a slogan. It was meant to be taken seriously.

Since my arrest I have been told repeatedly that I could have refused to obey this order, and even that I could have shot Himmler dead. I do not believe that among the thousands of SS officers there was even one who would have had even a glimmer of such a thought. . . . Of course, many SS officers moaned and groaned about the many harsh orders. Even then, they carried out every order. . . . As leader of the SS, Himmler's person was sacred. His fundamental orders in the name of the Führer were holy. There was no reflection, no interpretation, no explanation about these orders. They were carried out ruthlessly, regardless of the final consequences, even if it meant giving your life for them. Quite a few did that during the war.

It was not in vain that the leadership training of the SS officers held up the Japanese as shining examples of those willing to sacrifice their lives for the state and for the emperor, who was also their god. SS education was not just a series of useless high school lectures. It went far deeper, and Himmler knew very well what he could demand of his SS. . . .

---

[7] **Himmler**: Heinrich Himmler; head of the Nazi SS under Hitler and Höss's superior.
[8] **"Führer . . . We obey"**: All SS members swore the following oath: "I swear to you Adolf Hitler, as Führer and Chancellor of the Reich, loyalty and bravery. I vow to you and to the authorities appointed by you obedience onto death, so help me God."

Whatever the Führer or Himmler ordered was always right. Even democratic England has its saying, "My country, right or wrong," and every patriotic Englishman follows it.

* * *

Before the mass destruction of the Jews began, all the Russian politruks [communists] and political commissars[9] were killed in almost every camp during 1941 and 1942. According to the secret order given by Hitler, the Einsatzgruppe[10] searched for and picked up the Russian politruks and commissars from all the POW camps. They transferred all they found to the nearest concentration camp for liquidation. . . . The first small transports were shot by firing squads of SS soldiers.

While I was on an official trip, my second in command, Camp Commander Fritzsch, experimented with gas for killings. He used a gas called Cyclon B,[11] prussic acid, which was often used as an insecticide in the camp to exterminate lice and vermin. There was always a supply on hand. When I returned Fritzsch reported to me about how he had used the gas. We used it again to kill the next transport.

The gassing was carried out in the basement of Block 11. I viewed the killings wearing a gas mask for protection. Death occurred in the crammed-full cells immediately after the gas was thrown in. Only a brief choking outcry and it was all over. . . .

At the time I really didn't waste any thoughts about the killing of the Russian POWs. It was ordered; I had to carry it out. But I must admit openly that the gassings had a calming effect on me, since in the near future the mass annihilation of the Jews was to begin. Up to this point it was not clear to me . . . how the killing of the expected masses was to be done. Perhaps by gas? But how, and what kind of gas? Now we had discovered the gas and the procedure. I was always horrified of death by firing squads, especially when I thought of the huge numbers of women and children who would have to be killed. I had had enough of hostage executions, and the mass killings by firing squad order by Himmler and Heydrich.[12]

Now I was at ease. We were all saved from these bloodbaths, and the victims would be spared until the last moment. That is what I worried

---

[9] **political commissars**: Communist officials whose duty was to teach party principles to members of the military.

[10] **Einsatzgruppe**: Special German military units with orders to kill Jews, communists, and other undesirables.

[11] **Cyclon B**: A poisonous substance use to kill victims in the gas chambers.

[12] **Heydrich**: Reinhard Heydrich (1904–1942) was Himmler's chief lieutenant in the SS, who organized the mass execution of Jews in Eastern Europe in 1941.

about the most when I thought of Eichmann's[13] accounts of the mowing down of the Jews with machine guns and pistols by the Einsatzgruppe. Horrible scenes were supposed to have occurred: people running away even after being shot, the killing of those who were only wounded, especially the women and children. Another thing on my mind was the many suicides among the ranks of the SS Special Action Squads who could no longer mentally endure wading in the bloodbath. Some of them went mad. Most of the members of the Special Action Squads drank a great deal to help get through this horrible work. According to [Captain] Höffle's accounts, the men of Globocnik's extermination section drank tremendous quantities of alcohol.

In the spring of 1942 the first transports of Jews arrived from Upper Silesia. All of them were to be exterminated. They were led from the ramp across the meadow, later named section B-II of Birkenau,[14] to the farmhouse called Bunker I. Aumeier, Palitzsch, and a few other block leaders led them and spoke to them as one would in casual conversation, asking them about their occupations and their schooling in order to fool them. After arriving at the farmhouse they were told to undress. At first they went very quietly into the rooms where they were supposed to be disinfected. At that point some of them became suspicious and started talking about suffocation and extermination. Immediately a panic started. Those still standing outside were quickly driven into the chambers, and the doors were bolted shut. In the next transport those who were nervous or upset were identified and watched closely at all times. As soon as unrest was noticed these troublemakers were inconspicuously led behind the farmhouse and killed with a small-caliber pistol, which could not be heard by the others. . . .

I also watched how some women who suspected or knew what was happening, even with the fear of death all over their faces, still managed enough strength to play with their children and to talk to them lovingly. Once a woman with four children, all holding each other by the hand to help the smallest ones over the rough ground, passed by me very slowly. She stepped very close to me and whispered, pointing to her four children, "How can you murder these beautiful, darling children? Don't you have any heart?"

---

[13] **Eichmann:** Adolf Eichmann (1906–1962) organized the deportation of approximately three million Jews to the death camps.

[14] **Birkenau:** German town where a large addition to the Auschwitz complex was built.

Another time an old man hissed while passing me, "Germany will pay a bitter penance for the mass murder of the Jews." His eyes glowed with hatred as he spoke. In spite of this he went bravely into the gas chamber without worrying about the others. . . .

Occasionally some women would suddenly start screaming in a terrible way while undressing. They pulled out their hair and acted as if they had gone crazy. Quickly they were led behind the farmhouse and killed by a bullet in the back of the neck from a small-caliber pistol. . . . As the doors were being shut, I saw a woman trying to shove her children out the chamber, crying out, "Why don't you at least let my precious children live?" There were many heart-breaking scenes like this which affected all who were present.

In the spring of 1942 hundreds of people in the full bloom of life walked beneath the budding fruit trees of the farm into the gas chamber to their death, most of them without a hint of what was going to happen to them. To this day I can still see these pictures of the arrivals, the selections, and the procession to their death. . . .

The mass annihilation with all the accompanying circumstances did not fail to affect those who had to carry it out. They just did not watch what was happening. With very few exceptions all who performed this monstrous "work" had been ordered to this detail. All of us, including myself, were given enough to think about which left a deep impression. Many of the men often approached me during my inspection trips through the killing areas and poured out their depression and anxieties to me, hoping that I could give them some reassurance. During these conversations the question arose again and again, "Is what we have to do here necessary? Is it necessary that hundreds of thousands of women and children have to be annihilated?" And I, who countless times deep inside myself had asked the same question, had to put them off by reminding them that it was Hitler's order. I had to tell them that it was necessary to destroy all the Jews in order to forever free Germany and the future generations from our toughest enemy.

It goes without saying that the Hitler order was a firm fact for all of us, and also that it was the duty of the SS to carry it out. However, secret doubts tormented all of us. Under no circumstances could I reveal my secret doubts to anyone. I had to convince myself to be like a rock when faced with the necessity of carrying out this horribly severe order, and I had to show this in every way, in order to force all those under me to hang on mentally and emotionally. . . .

Hour upon hour I had to witness all that happened. I had to watch day and night, whether it was the dragging and burning of the bodies, the teeth being ripped out, the cutting of the hair,[15] I had to watch all this horror. For hours I had to stand in the horrible, haunting stench while the mass graves were dug open, and the bodies were dragged out and burned. I also had to watch the procession of death itself through the peephole of the gas chamber because the doctors called my attention to it. I had to do all of this because I was the one to whom everyone looked, and because I had to show everybody that I was not only the one who gave the orders and issued the directives, but that I was also willing to be present at whatever task I ordered my men to perform. . . .

And yet, everyone in Auschwitz believed the Kommandant really had a good life. Yes, my family had it good in Auschwitz, every wish that my wife or my children had was fulfilled. The children could live free and easy. My wife had her flower paradise. The prisoners tried to give my wife every consideration and tried to do something nice for the children. By the same token no former prisoner can say that he was treated poorly in any way in our house. My wife would have loved to give a present to every prisoner who performed a service for us. The children constantly begged me for cigarettes for the prisoners. The children especially loved the gardeners. In our entire family there was a deep love for farming and especially for animals. Every Sunday I had to drive with them across all the fields, walk them through the stables, and we could never skip visiting the dog kennels. Their greatest love was for our two horses and our colt. The prisoners who worked in the household were always dragging in some animal the children kept in the garden. Turtles, martens, cats, or lizards; there was always something new and interesting in the garden. The children splashed around in the summertime in the small pool in the garden or the Sola River. Their greatest pleasure was when daddy went into the water with them. But he had only a little time to share all the joys of childhood.

Today I deeply regret that I didn't spend more time with my family. I always believed that I had to be constantly on duty. Through this exaggerated sense of duty I always had made my life more difficult than it actually was. My wife often urged me, "Don't always think of your duty, think of your family too." But what did my wife know about the things that depressed me? She never found out.[16]

---

[15] teeth . . . hair: Teeth extracted from corpses were soaked in acid to remove muscle and bone before the gold fillings were extracted. Hair from victims was used to make felt and thread.

[16] She never found out: Höss later stated that his wife actually did learn of his participation in the mass executions at the camp.

READING AND DISCUSSION QUESTIONS

1. How does Höss explain his anti-Semitism? What specific examples does he cite?

2. According to Höss, why didn't he and other SS officers rebel against the order to kill the Jews?

3. How did viewing the mass deaths by gas affect Höss? How were other officers affected?

4. How does Höss describe the reaction of Jews in the camp to what was about to happen to them?

DOCUMENT 30-5

HENRY L. STIMSON

On the Decision to Use the Atomic Bomb

1947

Secretary of War Henry L. Stimson, chair of the atomic advisory board, the Interim Committee, was the person who advised President Harry S Truman (1945–1953) to drop the atomic bomb on Hiroshima and Nagasaki, Japan — the first use of atomic weapons. These bombings claimed roughly 200,000 lives, wreaked unprecedented devastation, and transformed the nature and practice of war. The use of atomic weapons, although successful in bringing the Pacific conflict to an end, has remained the subject of much debate. In February 1947, Stimson published this article in Harper's Magazine *explaining why he recommended the use of atomic bombs against the Japanese.*

GOALS OF THE MANHATTAN PROJECT[17]

The original experimental achievement of atomic fission had occurred in Germany in 1938, and it was known that the Germans had continued their

---

Henry L. Stimson, "The Decision to Use the Atomic Bomb," *Harper's Magazine*, February, 1947.

[17] **Manhattan Project**: Secret U.S. effort launched in 1939 to develop nuclear energy and weapons, which grew partly out of the fear that Germany had already begun researching atomic weapons.

experiments. In 1941 and 1942 they were believed to be ahead of us, and it was vital that they should not be the first to bring atomic weapons into the field of battle. Furthermore, if we should be the first to develop the weapon, we should have a great new instrument for shortening the war and minimizing destruction. At no time, from 1941 to 1945, did I ever hear it suggested by the President, or by any other responsible member of the government, that atomic energy should not be used in the war. All of us of course understood the terrible responsibility involved in our attempt to unlock the doors to such a devastating weapon; President Roosevelt particularly spoke to me many times of his own awareness of the catastrophic potentialities of our work. But we were at war, and the work must be done. . . .

RECOMMENDATION OF THE INTERIM COMMITTEE AND THE SECRETARY OF WAR

The discussions of the committee ranged over the whole field of atomic energy, in its political, military, and scientific aspects. . . . The committee's work included the drafting of the statements which were published immediately after the first bombs were dropped, the drafting of a bill for the domestic control of atomic energy, and recommendations looking toward the international control of atomic energy. . . .

On June 1, after its discussions with the Scientific Panel, the Interim Committee unanimously adopted the following recommendations:

1. The bomb should be used against Japan as soon as possible.
2. It should be used on a dual target — that is, a military installation or war plant surrounded by or adjacent to houses and other buildings most susceptible to damage, and
3. It should be used without prior warning [of the nature of the weapon]. One member of the committee, Mr. Bard,[18] later changed his view and dissented from recommendation. . . .

In reaching these conclusions the Interim Committee carefully considered such alternatives as a detailed advance warning or a demonstration in some uninhabited area. Both of these suggestions were discarded as impractical. They were not regarded as likely to be effective in compelling a surrender of Japan, and both of them involved serious risks. Even the New Mexico test would not give final proof that any given bomb was certain to explode when dropped from an airplane. Quite apart from the

---

[18] **Mr. Bard**: Ralph Bard; undersecretary of the navy and Interim Committee member.

generally unfamiliar nature of atomic explosives, there was the whole problem of exploding a bomb at a predetermined height in the air by a complicated mechanism which could not be tested in the static test of New Mexico. Nothing would have been more damaging to our effort to obtain surrender than a warning or a demonstration followed by a dud — and this was a real possibility. Furthermore, we had no bombs to waste. It was vital that a sufficient effect be quickly obtained with the few we had. . . .

The committee's function was, of course, entirely advisory. The ultimate responsibility for the recommendation to the President rested upon me, and I have no desire to veil it. The conclusions of the committee were similar to my own, although I reached mine independently. I felt that to extract a genuine surrender from the [Japanese] Emperor and his military advisers, they must be administered a tremendous shock which would carry convincing proof of our power to destroy the Empire. Such an effective shock would save many times the number of lives, both American and Japanese, that it would cost.

The facts upon which my reasoning was based and steps taken to carry it out now follow.

The principal political, social, and military objective of the United States in the summer of 1945 was the prompt and complete surrender of Japan. Only the complete destruction of her military power could open the way to lasting peace. . . .

As we understood it in July, there was a very strong possibility that the Japanese government might determine upon resistance to the end, in all the areas of the Far East under its control. In such an event the Allies would be faced with the enormous task of destroying an armed force of five million men and five thousand suicide aircraft, belonging to a race which had already amply demonstrated its ability to fight literally to the death.

The strategic plans of our armed forces for the defeat of Japan, as they stood in July, had been prepared without reliance upon the atomic bomb, which had not yet been tested in New Mexico. We were planning an intensified sea and air blockade, and greatly intensified strategic air bombing, through the summer and early fall, to be followed on November 1 by an invasion of the southern island of Kyushu. This would be followed in turn by an invasion of the main island of Honshu in the spring of 1946. The total U.S. military and naval force involved in this grand design was of the order of 5,000,000 men; if all those indirectly concerned are included, it was larger still.

We estimated that if we should be forced to carry this plan to its conclusion, the major fighting would not end until the latter part of 1946, at the earliest. I was informed that such operations might be expected to cost over a million casualties to American forces alone. Additional large losses might be expected among our allies, and, of course, if our campaign were successful and if we could judge by previous experience, enemy casualties would be much larger than our own. . . .

After Japan on July 28 rejected the Potsdam ultimatum,[19] which gave their leaders the choice of immediate surrender or the "utter destruction of the Japanese homeland," plans went forward for using the atomic bombs.

Because of the importance of the atomic mission against Japan, the detailed plans were brought to me by the military staff for approval. With President Truman's warm support I struck off the list of suggested targets the city of Kyoto. Although it was a target of considerable military importance, it had been the ancient capital of Japan and was a shrine of Japanese art and culture. We determined that it should be spared. I approved four other targets including the cities of Hiroshima and Nagasaki.

Hiroshima was bombed on August 6, and Nagasaki on August 9. These two cities were active working parts of the Japanese war effort. One was an army center; the other was naval and industrial. Hiroshima was the headquarters of the Japanese Army defending southern Japan and was a major military storage and assembly point. Nagasaki was a major seaport and it contained several large industrial plants of great wartime importance. We believed that our attacks had struck cities which must certainly be important to the Japanese military leaders, both Army and Navy, and we waited for a result. We waited one day.

FINAL REFLECTIONS

As I look back over the five years of my service as Secretary of War, I see too many stern and heartrending decisions to be willing to pretend that war is anything else than what it is. The face of war is the face of death; death is an inevitable part of every order that a wartime leader gives. The decision to use the atomic bomb was a decision that brought death to over a hundred thousand Japanese. No explanation can change that fact and I do not wish to gloss it over. But this deliberate, premeditated destruction was our least abhorrent choice. The destruction of Hiroshima and Nagasaki put an end to the Japanese war. It stopped the fire raids and the strangling blockade; it ended the ghastly specter of a clash of great land armies.

---

[19] **Potsdam ultimatum**: The Potsdam Declaration was a U.S. ultimatum demanding Japan's surrender and outlining the conditions of that surrender.

READING AND DISCUSSION QUESTIONS

1. According to Stimson, why was it strategically important for the United States to be the first country to develop atomic weapons?

2. Why did the Interim Committee reject the suggestion to drop bombs on uninhabited or less congested areas?

3. According to Stimson, what were the military's plans in July 1945? Why does he think the use of the bomb was ultimately a better option?

4. Why were Hiroshima and Nagasaki selected as targets over Kyoto and other locations?

COMPARATIVE QUESTIONS

1. What connections can you make between the Nuremberg Laws and the actions taken by men like Höss?

2. How did leaders such as Höss and Stimson reconcile their roles in the devastating aspects of World War II?

3. How did ideas of national identity and race influence the actions taken by Germany and the United States during the war?

4. How are roles for women linked to larger national objectives in Germany and Russia, as evidenced in the letters to *Izvestiya* and Scholtz-Klink's speech?

CHAPTER 31

Global Recovery and Division Between Superpowers

D espite great hopes for world peace after World War II, stark differences in economic and political ideologies emerged that sharply divided the United States and its European allies from the Soviet Union and its allies. The result was a "cold war" that lasted more than forty years. In the first postwar decade, efforts to rebuild war-torn regions and prevent future wars were the main concern, though at times such efforts took the form of militaristic actions. While the United States did not face outright war on its home soil, it nonetheless entered a period of significant change and internal and external conflict. Postwar economic prosperity contributed to the rise of an international youth culture and movements for social and political (including race and gender) equality. In 1989, the collapse of the Soviet Union raised new hopes for the spread of democracy worldwide and sent a clear message: old ideas had no place in the modern post–cold war world.

DOCUMENT 31-1

HARRY S TRUMAN
The Truman Doctrine
March 12, 1947

Not long after World War II ended, tensions heated up between leaders of the United States and the Soviet Union. Each country feared the other's influence on smaller nations and world politics. Joseph Stalin, who ruled the Soviet Union from 1927 to 1953, renewed efforts to spread communism,

President Harry S Truman, Address Before a Joint Session of Congress, March 12, 1947.

prompting U.S. fears that if one nation fell to communism, others would surely follow. As the Soviet Union intensified its efforts to spread communism to countries such as Greece, Turkey, and Iran, President Harry S Truman (1945–1953) urged congressional approval for financial and military assistance to those same countries and others that sought to maintain free and democratic forms of government. This policy of containing communism became known as the Truman Doctrine.

Mr. President, Mr. Speaker, Members of the Congress of the United States: The gravity of the situation which confronts the world today necessitates my appearance before a joint session of the Congress. The foreign policy and the national security of this country are involved. . . .

The very existence of the Greek state is today threatened by the terrorist activities of several thousand armed men, led by Communists, who defy the government's authority at a number of points, particularly along the northern boundaries. A Commission appointed by the United Nations Security Council is at present investigating disturbed conditions in northern Greece and alleged border violations along the frontier between Greece on the one hand and Albania, Bulgaria, and Yugoslavia on the other.

Meanwhile, the Greek Government is unable to cope with the situation. The Greek army is small and poorly equipped. It needs supplies and equipment if it is to restore the authority of the government throughout Greek territory. Greece must have assistance if it is to become a self-supporting and self-respecting democracy.

The United States must supply that assistance. We have already extended to Greece certain types of relief and economic aid but these are inadequate.

There is no other country to which democratic Greece can turn.

No other nation is willing and able to provide the necessary support for a democratic Greek government. . . .

Greece's neighbor, Turkey, also deserves our attention.

The future of Turkey as an independent and economically sound state is clearly no less important to the freedom-loving peoples of the world than the future of Greece. The circumstances in which Turkey finds itself today are considerably different from those of Greece. Turkey has been spared the disasters that have beset Greece. And during the war, the United States and Great Britain furnished Turkey with material aid.

Nevertheless, Turkey now needs our support.

Since the war Turkey has sought financial assistance from Great Britain and the United States for the purpose of effecting that modernization necessary for the maintenance of its national integrity.

That integrity is essential to the preservation of order in the Middle East.

The British government has informed us that, owing to its own difficulties can no longer extend financial or economic aid to Turkey.

As in the case of Greece, if Turkey is to have the assistance it needs, the United States must supply it. We are the only country able to provide that help.

I am fully aware of the broad implications involved if the United States extends assistance to Greece and Turkey, and I shall discuss these implications with you at this time.

One of the primary objectives of the foreign policy of the United States is the creation of conditions in which we and other nations will be able to work out a way of life free from coercion. This was a fundamental issue in the war with Germany and Japan. Our victory was won over countries which sought to impose their will, and their way of life, upon other nations.

To ensure the peaceful development of nations, free from coercion, the United States has taken a leading part in establishing the United Nations, The United Nations is designed to make possible lasting freedom and independence for all its members. We shall not realize our objectives, however, unless we are willing to help free peoples to maintain their free institutions and their national integrity against aggressive movements that seek to impose upon them totalitarian regimes. This is no more than a frank recognition that totalitarian regimes imposed on free peoples, by direct or indirect aggression, undermine the foundations of international peace and hence the security of the United States.

The peoples of a number of countries of the world have recently had totalitarian regimes forced upon them against their will. The Government of the United States has made frequent protests against coercion and intimidation, in violation of the Yalta agreement,[1] in Poland, Rumania, and Bulgaria. I must also state that in a number of other countries there have been similar developments.

---

[1] **Yalta agreement**: The 1945 accord reached by U.S. president Franklin Roosevelt, British prime minister Winston Churchill, and Soviet premier Joseph Stalin containing agreements to divide the peacetime world into three zones of occupation, to require an unconditional surrender from Germany, and to force Germany to make reparations to the Soviet Union.

At the present moment in world history nearly every nation must choose between alternative ways of life. The choice is too often not a free one.

One way of life is based upon the will of the majority, and is distinguished by free institutions, representative government, free elections, guarantees of individual liberty, freedom of speech and religion, and freedom from political oppression.

The second way of life is based upon the will of a minority forcibly imposed upon the majority. It relies upon terror and oppression, a controlled press and radio, fixed elections, and the suppression of personal freedoms.

I believe that it must be the policy of the United States to support free peoples who are resisting attempted subjugation by armed minorities or by outside pressures.

I believe that we must assist free peoples to work out their own destinies in their own way.

I believe that our help should be primarily through economic and financial aid which is essential to economic stability and orderly political processes.

It is necessary only to glance at a map to realize that the survival and integrity of the Greek nation are of grave importance in a much wider situation. If Greece should fall under the control of an armed minority, the effect upon its neighbor, Turkey, would be immediate and serious. Confusion and disorder might well spread throughout the entire Middle East.

Moreover, the disappearance of Greece as an independent state would have a profound effect upon those countries in Europe whose peoples are struggling against great difficulties to maintain their freedoms and their independence while they repair the damages of war.

It would be an unspeakable tragedy if these countries, which have struggled so long against overwhelming odds, should lose that victory for which they sacrificed so much. Collapse of free institutions and loss of independence would be disastrous not only for them but for the world. Discouragement and possibly failure would quickly be the lot of neighboring peoples striving to maintain their freedom and independence.

Should we fail to aid Greece and Turkey in this fateful hour, the effect will be far reaching to the West as well as to the East.

We must take immediate and resolute action.

I therefore ask the Congress to provide authority for assistance to Greece and Turkey in the amount of $400,000,000 for the period ending June 30, 1948. In requesting these funds, I have taken into consideration the maximum amount of relief assistance which would be furnished to

Greece out of the $350,000,000 which I recently requested that the Congress authorize for the prevention of starvation and suffering in countries devastated by the war.

In addition to funds, I ask the Congress to authorize the detail of American civilian and military personnel to Greece and Turkey, at the request of those countries, to assist in the tasks of reconstruction, and for the purpose of supervising the use of such financial and material assistance as may be furnished. . . .

This is a serious course upon which we embark.

I would not recommend it except that the alternative is much more serious. The United States contributed $341,000,000,000 toward winning World War II. This is an investment in world freedom and world peace.

The seeds of totalitarian regimes are nurtured by misery and want. They spread and grow in the evil soil of poverty and strife. They reach their full growth when the hope of a people for a better life has died. We must keep that hope alive.

The free peoples of the world look to us for support in maintaining their freedoms.

If we falter in our leadership, we may endanger the peace of the world — and we shall surely endanger the welfare of our own nation.

Great responsibilities have been placed upon us by the swift movement of events.

I am confident that the Congress will face these responsibilities squarely.

READING AND DISCUSSION QUESTIONS

1. What reasons does Truman give to convince Congress to provide aid to Greece and Turkey? What consequences does he fear will result from not helping them?

2. How does Truman reconcile providing aid to Turkey and Greece with U.S. foreign policy goals?

3. What alternative forms of government does he say people around the world must now choose between?

4. What conditions does Truman believe make the world ripe for totalitarian regimes?

DOCUMENT 31-2

UNITED NATIONS GENERAL ASSEMBLY
Declaration on the Granting of Independence to Colonial Countries and Peoples
December 14, 1960

After centuries of empire building and colonization, in the decades after World War II, European countries began to move toward decolonization. Many former colonies obtained their freedom after 1945, driven in large part by Africa and Asia's increasing quest for self-government. In 1960, the United Nations formalized the gradual process of granting independence to these once-colonized peoples, outlining its basic assumptions about human rights and self-rule that would guide much of the decolonization process. Most UN member nations voted in favor of the declaration; the nine that abstained, however, were all imperialist nations, including the United States, Great Britain, France, Spain, and Portugal.

General Assembly Resolution 1514 (XV) of 14 December 1960
The General Assembly,

Mindful of the determination proclaimed by the peoples of the world in the Charter of the United Nations to reaffirm faith in fundamental human rights, in the dignity and worth of the human person, in the equal rights of men and women and of nations large and small and to promote social progress and better standards of life in larger freedom,

Conscious of the need for the creation of conditions of stability and well-being and peaceful and friendly relations based on respect for the principles of equal rights and self-determination of all peoples, and of universal respect for, and observance of, human rights and fundamental freedoms for all without distinction as to race, sex, language, or religion,

Recognizing the passionate yearning for freedom in all dependent peoples and the decisive role of such peoples in the attainment of their independence,

General Assembly of the United Nations, Resolution 1514 (XV), December 14, 1960.

Aware of the increasing conflicts resulting from the denial of or impediments in the way of the freedom of such peoples, which constitute a serious threat to world peace,

Considering the important role of the United Nations in assisting the movement for independence in Trust and Non-Self-Governing Territories,

Recognizing that the peoples of the world ardently desire the end of colonialism in all its manifestations,

Convinced that the continued existence of colonialism prevents the development of international economic co-operation, impedes the social, cultural, and economic development of dependent peoples and militates against the United Nations ideal of universal peace,

Affirming that peoples may, for their own ends, freely dispose of their natural wealth and resources without prejudice to any obligations arising out of international economic co-operation, based upon the principle of mutual benefit, and international law,

Believing that the process of liberation is irresistible and irreversible and that, in order to avoid serious crises, an end must be put to colonialism and all practices of segregation and discrimination associated therewith,

Welcoming the emergence in recent years of a large number of dependent territories into freedom and independence, and recognizing the increasingly powerful trends towards freedom in such territories which have not yet attained independence,

Convinced that all peoples have an inalienable right to complete freedom, the exercise of their sovereignty, and the integrity of their national territory,

Solemnly proclaims the necessity of bringing to a speedy and unconditional end colonialism in all its forms and manifestations;

And to this end

Declares that:

1. The subjection of peoples to alien subjugation, domination, and exploitation constitutes a denial of fundamental human rights, is contrary to the Charter of the United Nations, and is an impediment to the promotion of world peace and co-operation.

2. All peoples have the right to self-determination; by virtue of that right they freely determine their political status and freely pursue their economic, social, and cultural development.
3. Inadequacy of political, economic, social or educational preparedness should never serve as a pretext for delaying independence.
4. All armed action or repressive measures of all kinds directed against dependent peoples shall cease in order to enable them to exercise peacefully and freely their right to complete independence, and the integrity of their national territory shall be respected.
5. Immediate steps shall be taken, in Trust and Non-Self-Governing Territories or all other territories which have not yet attained independence, to transfer all powers to the peoples of those territories, without any conditions or reservations, in accordance with their freely expressed will and desire, without any distinction as to race, creed, or color, in order to enable them to enjoy complete independence and freedom.
6. Any attempt aimed at the partial or total disruption of the national unity and the territorial integrity of a country is incompatible with the purposes and principles of the Charter of the United Nations.
7. All States shall observe faithfully and strictly the provisions of the Charter of the United Nations, the Universal Declaration of Human Rights and the present Declaration on the basis of equality, non-interference in the internal affairs of all States, and respect for the sovereign rights of all peoples and their territorial integrity.

READING AND DISCUSSION QUESTIONS

1. According to this declaration, what goals do the peoples of the world share?
2. What problems would continued colonialism pose?
3. According to the declaration, what constitutes basic human rights?
4. How does the General Assembly project its own role in decolonization?

DOCUMENT 31-3

JOHN F. KENNEDY
On the "Space Race" to the Moon
September 12, 1962

Early in his presidency, John F. Kennedy set out to beat the Soviet Union in the latest phase of the two nations' ongoing cold war rivalry: the so-called space race. Frustrated that the Soviets had already launched the first human into space with Sputnik in 1957, Kennedy unveiled his ambitious goal to land the first man on the moon by the end of the decade first to Congress in 1961 and then in public speeches such as this one given at Rice University. The United States reached that goal nearly six years after JFK's assassination in 1963.

[M]an, in his quest for knowledge and progress, is determined and cannot be deterred. The exploration of space will go ahead, whether we join in it or not, and it is one of the great adventures of all time, and no nation which expects to be the leader of other nations can expect to stay behind in the race for space.

Those who came before us made certain that this country rode the first waves of the industrial revolutions, the first waves of modern invention, and the first wave of nuclear power, and this generation does not intend to founder in the backwash of the coming age of space. We mean to be a part of it — we mean to lead it. For the eyes of the world now look into space, to the moon and to the planets beyond, and we have vowed that we shall not see it governed by a hostile flag of conquest, but by a banner of freedom and peace. We have vowed that we shall not see space filled with weapons of mass destruction, but with instruments of knowledge and understanding.

Yet the vows of this Nation can only be fulfilled if we in this Nation are first, and, therefore, we intend to be first. In short, our leadership in science and in industry, our hopes for peace and security, our obligations to ourselves as well as others, all require us to make this effort, to solve these mysteries, to solve them for the good of all men, and to become the world's leading space-faring nation.

President John F. Kennedy, Speech at Rice University, September 12, 1962.

We set sail on this new sea because there is new knowledge to be gained, and new rights to be won, and they must be won and used for the progress of all people. For space science, like nuclear science and all technology, has no conscience of its own. Whether it will become a force for good or ill depends on man, and only if the United States occupies a position of pre-eminence can we help decide whether this new ocean will be a sea of peace or a new terrifying theater of war. I do not say the we should or will go unprotected against the hostile misuse of space any more than we go unprotected against the hostile use of land or sea, but I do say that space can be explored and mastered without feeding the fires of war. . . .

There is no strife, no prejudice, no national conflict in outer space as yet. Its hazards are hostile to us all. Its conquest deserves the best of all mankind, and its opportunity for peaceful cooperation many never come again. But why, some say, the moon? Why choose this as our goal? And they may well ask why climb the highest mountain? Why, 35 years ago, fly the Atlantic? Why does Rice play Texas?

We choose to go to the moon. We choose to go to the moon in this decade and do the other things, not because they are easy, but because they are hard, because that goal will serve to organize and measure the best of our energies and skills, because that challenge is one that we are willing to accept, one we are unwilling to postpone, and one which we intend to win, and the others, too.

It is for these reasons that I regard the decision last year to shift our efforts in space from low to high gear as among the most important decisions that will be made during my incumbency in the office of the Presidency.

In the last 24 hours we have seen facilities now being created for the greatest and most complex exploration in man's history. We have felt the ground shake and the air shattered by the testing of a Saturn C-1 booster rocket, many times as powerful as the Atlas which launched John Glenn, generating power equivalent to 10,000 automobiles with their accelerators on the floor. We have seen the site where the F-1 rocket engines, each one as powerful as all eight engines of the Saturn combined, will be clustered together to make the advanced Saturn missile, assembled in a new building to be built at Cape Canaveral as tall as a 48 story structure, as wide as a city block, and as long as two lengths of this field.

Within these last 19 months at least 45 satellites have circled the earth. Some 40 of them were "made in the United States of America" and they were far more sophisticated and supplied far more knowledge to the people of the world than those of the Soviet Union.

The Mariner spacecraft now on its way to Venus is the most intricate instrument in the history of space science. The accuracy of that shot is comparable to firing a missile from Cape Canaveral and dropping it in this stadium between the 40-yard lines.

Transit satellites are helping our ships at sea to steer a safer course. Tiros satellites have given us unprecedented warnings of hurricanes and storms, and will do the same for forest fires and icebergs.

We have had our failures, but so have others, even if they do not admit them. And they may be less public.

To be sure, we are behind, and will be behind for some time in manned flight. But we do not intend to stay behind, and in this decade, we shall make up and move ahead.

The growth of our science and education will be enriched by new knowledge of our universe and environment, by new techniques of learning and mapping and observation, by new tools and computers for industry, medicine, the home as well as the school. Technical institutions, such as Rice, will reap the harvest of these gains.

And finally, the space effort itself, while still in its infancy, has already created a great number of new companies, and tens of thousands of new jobs. Space and related industries are generating new demands in investment and skilled personnel, and this city and this State, and this region, will share greatly in this growth. What was once the furthest outpost on the old frontier of the West will be the furthest outpost on the new frontier of science and space. Houston, your City of Houston, with its Manned Spacecraft Center, will become the heart of a large scientific and engineering community. During the next 5 years the National Aeronautics and Space Administration expects to double the number of scientists and engineers in this area, to increase its outlays for salaries and expenses to $60 million a year; to invest some $200 million in plant and laboratory facilities; and to direct or contract for new space efforts over $1 billion from this Center in this City.

To be sure, all this costs us all a good deal of money. This year's space budget is three times what it was in January 1961, and it is greater than the space budget of the previous eight years combined. That budget now stands at $5,400 million a year — a staggering sum, though somewhat less than we pay for cigarettes and cigars every year. Space expenditures will soon rise some more, from 40 cents per person per week to more than 50 cents a week for every man, woman and child in the United Stated, for we have given this program a high national priority — even though I realize that this is in some measure an act of faith and vision, for we do not now know what benefits await us.

But if I were to say, my fellow citizens, that we shall send to the moon, 240,000 miles away from the control station in Houston, a giant rocket more than 300 feet tall, the length of this football field, made of new metal alloys, some of which have not yet been invented, capable of standing heat and stresses several times more than have ever been experienced, fitted together with a precision better than the finest watch, carrying all the equipment needed for propulsion, guidance, control, communications, food and survival, on an untried mission, to an unknown celestial body, and then return it safely to earth, re-entering the atmosphere at speeds of over 25,000 miles per hour, causing heat about half that of the temperature of the sun — almost as hot as it is here today — and do all this, and do it right, and do it first before this decade is out — then we must be bold. . . .

READING AND DISCUSSION QUESTIONS

1. According to President Kennedy, why is it important that the United States be the first country to master space?

2. What reasons does he give for making the moon the centerpiece of the space program?

3. What are the economic and educational benefits of the space program for the United States?

4. How does Kennedy link space exploration with U.S. foreign policy?

DOCUMENT 31-4

Feminist Manifestos from the Late 1960s

ca. 1968

In the postwar United States, young people began to question long-held social and political values, including those concerning gender roles. The women's movement that emerged in the 1960s split into liberal groups that

---

"No More Miss America," from *Sisterhood Is Powerful: An Anthology of Writings from the Women's Liberation Movement*, ed. Robin Morgan (New York: Vintage, 1970), 584–588. "Statement of Purpose (1972)" from Anne Koedt, Ellen Levine, and Anita Rapone, eds., *Radical Feminism* (New York: Quadrangle Books, 1973), 384–387.

sought equality within the existing system and radical (typically younger)
feminists who believed the system of patriarchal power and domination was
beyond repair. In 1968, radical feminists leapt onto the national stage with
a protest at the Miss America Pageant in Atlantic City, New Jersey, and
threw symbols of women's oppression such as cosmetics, girdles, and bras
into a trash can, crowned a sheep as Miss America, and issued a manifesto
calling for women's liberation. Other women, like those from suburban
Westchester County in New York, shared their vision of a radical new gender
order, as outlined in their manifesto.

No More Miss America

On September 7th in Atlantic City, the Annual Miss America Pageant will
again crown "your ideal." But this year, reality will liberate the contest
auction-block in the guise of "genyooine" [i.e., genuine] de-plasticized,
breathing women. Women's Liberation Groups, black women, high-
school and college women, women's peace groups, women's welfare and
social-work groups, women's job-equality groups, pro-birth control and
pro-abortion groups — women of every political persuasion — all are invited to join us in a daylong boardwalk-theater event, starting at 1:00 P.M.
on the boardwalk in front of Atlantic City's Convention Hall. . . .

Male reporters will be refused interviews. We reject patronizing re-
portage. *Only newswomen will be recognized.*

The Ten Points
We Protest:

1. The *Degrading Mindless-Boob-Girlie Symbol.* The Pageant contest-
   ants epitomize the roles we are all forced to play as women. The
   parade down the runway blares the metaphor of the 4-H Club county
   fair, where the nervous animals are judged for teeth, fleece, etc.,
   and where the best "specimen" gets the blue ribbon. So are women in
   our society forced daily to compete for male approval, enslaved by
   ludicrous "beauty" standards we ourselves are conditioned to take
   seriously.
2. *Racism with Roses.* Since its inception in 1921, the Pageant has not
   had one Black finalist, and this has not been for a lack of test-case con-
   testants. There has never been a Puerto Rican, Alaskan, Hawaiian,
   or Mexican-American winner. Nor has there ever been a *true* Miss
   America — an American Indian.

3. *Miss America as Military Death Mascot.* The highlight of her reign each year is a cheerleader-tour of American troops abroad — last year she went to Vietnam to pep talk our husbands, fathers, sons, and boyfriends into dying and killing with a better spirit. She personifies the "unstained patriotic American womanhood our boys are fighting for." The Living Bra and the Dead Soldier. We refuse to be used as Mascots for Murder.

4. *The Consumer Con-Game.* Miss America is a walking commercial for the Pageant's sponsors. Wind her up and she plugs your product on promotion tours and TV — all in an "honest, objective" endorsement. What a shill.

5. *Competition Rigged and Unrigged.* We deplore the encouragement of an American myth that oppresses men as well as women: the win-or-you're-worthless competitive disease. The "beauty contest" creates only one winner to be "used" and forty-nine losers who are "useless."

6. *The Woman as Pop Culture Obsolescent Theme.* Spindle, mutilate, and then discard tomorrow. What is so ignored as last year's Miss America? This only reflects the gospel of our society, according to Saint Male: women must be young, juicy, malleable — hence age discrimination and the cult of youth. And we women are brainwashed into believing this ourselves!

7. *The Unbeatable Madonna-Whore Combination.* Miss America and Playboy's centerfold are sisters over the skin. To win approval, we must be both sexy and wholesome, delicate but able to cope, demure yet titillatingly bitchy. Deviation of any sort brings, we are told, disaster: "You won't get a man!!"

8. *The Irrelevant Crown on the Throne of Mediocrity.* Miss America represents what women are supposed to be: unoffensive, bland, apolitical. If you are tall, short, over or under what weight The Man prescribes you should be, forget it. Personality, articulateness, intelligence, commitment — unwise. Conformity is the key to the crown — and, by extension, to success in our society.

9. *Miss America as Dream Equivalent to — ?* In this reputedly democratic society, where every little boy supposedly can grow up to be President, what can every little girl hope to grow up to be? Miss America. That's where it's at. Real power to control our own lives is restricted to men, while women get patronizing pseudopower, an ermine cloak and a bunch of flowers; men are judged by their actions, women by their appearance.

10. *Miss America as Big Sister Watching You.* The Pageant exercises Thought Control, attempts to sear the Image onto our minds, to fur-

ther make women oppressed and men oppressors; to enslave us all the more in high-heeled, low-status roles; to inculcate false values in young girls; to use women as beasts of buying; to seduce us to prostitute ourselves before our own oppression.

WESTCHESTER RADICAL FEMINISTS' MANIFESTO

Suburban women, in common with all women, have lived in intimacy with and dependence on our oppressor. In isolation and tightly bound to our families, we have viewed the world and our condition from the level of patriarchal ideas of money and power. We now recognize that these patriarchal concepts have and still do dominate and control our lives, but our thinking, hopes, and aspirations are changing. . . .

As suburban women, we recognize that many of us live in more economic and material comfort than our urban sisters, but we have come to realize through the woman's movement, feminist ideas and consciousness raising,[2] that this comfort only hides our essential powerlessness and oppression. . . . Like dogs on a leash, our own status and power will reach as far as our husbands and their income and prestige will allow. As human beings, as individuals, we, in fact, own very little and should our husbands leave us or us them, we will find ourselves with the care and responsibility of children and without money, jobs, credit or power. For this questionable condition, we have paid the price of isolation and exploitation by the institutions of marriage, motherhood, psychiatry, and consumerism. Although our life styles may appear materially better, we are, as all women, dominated by men at home, in bed and on the job; emotionally, sexually, domestically and financially. . . .

We believe that:

1. The notion of fixed sex roles is arbitrary and unjust.
2. That suburbia is a wasteland; a human ghetto for women minimizing their opportunity for growth.
3. That diverse forms of sexual relationships based on mutual consent are a matter of individual choice and right.

---

[2] **consciousness raising:** Practice created by women's liberation groups in which women would meet and make connections between the gender disparities they experienced in their own lives and women's broader social status. It led to the idea that "the personal is political" — the notion that the problems women experienced privately were often shared by other women, and therefore provided the basis for political change.

4. The institution of marriage presumes and establishes the lifelong servitude of women.

5. All economic institutions subject and deprive the suburban women, as well as all women, of economic power; even her power as a consumer is a myth since she spends and buys no more than her husband will allow.

6. Women are no more inherently suited to child rearing than men and men must be held responsible also for the emotional, educational, and physical development of children.

7. The mutual dependence of mothers and children is in essence an act of tyranny which serves to thwart, retard, and immobilize both mother and children.

8. The adjustment theories adhered to by most psychologists and psychiatrists and their institutions perpetuate destructive attitudes towards women, undermine their self value and self esteem, and are generally harmful to the wholesome development and welfare of women.

9. The fact that we live with and even support some of these institutions which are sexist does not in any way alter our basic beliefs. We presently live the way we do because there are no good alternatives.

10. Women's liberation is not human liberation and we place the cause of women above all other causes.

11. We are committed to the understanding of our condition as women so that we may create and invent new ways to live and to find both collective and individual realization and strength.

READING AND DISCUSSION QUESTIONS

1. Why would the pageant protesters refuse to cooperate with male reporters?

2. What image of femininity does the Miss America Pageant project according to the feminists, and why do the protesters oppose this image?

3. According to the protesters, how does the pageant reinforce limited gender roles for all women?

4. According to the authors of the Westchester manifesto, how do institutions, particularly marriage, deprive women of economic power?

MIKHAIL GORBACHEV

From Perestroika: New Thinking for Our Country and the World

1986

When Mikhail Gorbachev came to power in the Soviet Union in 1985, his country faced serious challenges. The economy was suffering under the weight of the arms race with the United States, and due to worker absenteeism and declining productivity. An ardent socialist, Gorbachev recognized that the system needed an overhaul if it were to succeed. He also believed that political changes — including negotiations with the West and a democratization of socialism — were crucial. In his 1987 book, Perestroika, *Gorbachev outlined his solutions for reforming the Soviet Union, which included perestroika (economic restructuring) and glasnost (greater openness and expanded freedom of expression and speech).*

Perestroika[3] is an urgent necessity arising from the profound processes of development in our socialist society. This society is ripe for change. It has long been yearning for it. Any delay in beginning perestroika could have led to an exacerbated internal situation in the near future, which, to put it bluntly, would have been fraught with serious social, economic, and political crises. . . .

In the latter half of the seventies — something happened that was at first sight inexplicable. The country began to lose momentum. Economic failures became more frequent. Difficulties began to accumulate and deteriorate, and unresolved problems to multiply. Elements of what we call stagnation and other phenomena alien to socialism began to appear in the life of society. A kind of "braking mechanism" affecting social and economic development formed. And all this happened at a time when

---

Mikhail Gorbachev, *Perestroika: New Thinking for Our Country and the World* (New York: Harper & Row, 1987).

[3] **Perestroika**: Gorbachev's economic restructuring reform included an easing of government price controls on some goods, more independence for state enterprises, and the establishment of profit-seeking private cooperatives to provide personal services for consumers.

scientific and technological revolution opened up new prospects for economic and social progress. . . .

An absurd situation was developing. The Soviet Union, the world's biggest producer of steel, raw materials, fuel and energy, has shortfalls in them due to wasteful or inefficient use. One of the biggest producers of grain for food, it nevertheless has to buy millions of tons of grain a year for fodder. We have the largest number of doctors and hospital beds per thousand of the population and, at the same time, there are glaring shortcomings in our health services. Our rockets can find Halley's comet and fly to Venus with amazing accuracy, but side by side with these scientific and technological triumphs is an obvious lack of efficiency in using scientific achievements for economic needs, and many Soviet household appliances are of poor quality.

This, unfortunately, is not all. A gradual erosion of the ideological and moral values of our people began.

It was obvious to everyone that the growth rates were sharply dropping and that the entire mechanism of quality control was not working properly; there was a lack of receptivity to the advances in science and technology; the improvement in living standards was slowing down and there were difficulties in the supply of foodstuffs, housing, consumer goods, and services.

On the ideological plane as well, the braking mechanism brought about ever greater resistance to the attempts to constructively scrutinize the problems that were emerging and to the new ideas. Propaganda of success — real or imagined — was gaining the upper hand. Eulogizing and servility were encouraged; the needs and opinions of ordinary working people, of the public at large, were ignored. . . .

The presentation of a "problem-free" reality backfired: a breach had formed between word and deed, which bred public passivity and disbelief in the slogans being proclaimed. It was only natural that this situation resulted in a credibility gap: everything that was proclaimed from the rostrums and printed in newspapers and textbooks was put in question. Decay began in public morals; the great feeling of solidarity with each other that was forged during the heroic times of the Revolution [1917], the first five-year plans,[4] the Great Patriotic War,[5] and postwar rehabilitation was weakening; alcoholism, drug addiction, and crime were growing; and the penetration

---

[4] **five-year plans**: Stalin's attempts to transform the rural, agrarian Soviet Union into an industrial state. The first plan began in 1928, the second in 1932 (a year early), and succeeded at tremendous human cost.

[5] **Great Patriotic War**: Soviet name for World War II, in which the Soviets lost at least 20 million people.

of the stereotypes of mass culture alien to us, which bred vulgarity and low tastes and brought about ideological barrenness increased. . . .

An unbiased and honest approach led us to the only logical conclusion that the country was verging on crisis. . . .

I would like to emphasize here that this analysis began a long time before the April Plenary Meeting[6] and that therefore its conclusions were well thought out. It was not something out of the blue, but a balanced judgment. It would be a mistake to think that a month after the Central Committee Plenary Meeting in March 1985, which elected me General Secretary, there suddenly appeared a group of people who understood everything and knew everything, and that these people gave clear-cut answers to all questions. Such miracles do not exist.

The need for change was brewing not only in the material sphere of life but also in public consciousness. People who had practical experience, a sense of justice and commitment to the ideals of Bolshevism[7] criticized the established practice of doing things and noted with anxiety the symptoms of moral degradation and erosion of revolutionary ideals and socialist values. . . .

Perestroika is closely connected with socialism as a system. That side of the matter is being widely discussed, especially abroad, and our talk about perestroika won't be entirely clear if we don't touch upon that aspect.

Does perestroika mean that we are giving up socialism or at least some of its foundations? Some ask this question with hope, others with misgiving.

There are people in the West who would like to tell us that socialism is in a deep crisis and has brought our society to a dead end. That's how they interpret our critical analysis of the situation at the end of the seventies and beginning of the eighties. We have only one way out, they say: to adopt capitalist methods of economic management and social patterns, to drift toward capitalism.

They tell us that nothing will come of perestroika within the framework of our system. They say we should change this system and borrow from the experience of another socio-political system. To this they add that, if the Soviet Union takes this path and gives up its socialist choice, close links with the West will supposedly become possible. They go so far as to claim that the October 1917 Revolution was a mistake which almost completely cut off our country from world social progress.

To put an end to all the rumors and speculations that abound in the West about this, I would like to point out once again that we are conducting

---

[6] **April Plenary Meeting**: Regular meeting of the Communist Party's officials.

[7] **Bolshevism**: Lenin's program of Soviet communism that came to power in Russia after the October Revolution of 1917 (see Document 27-2).

all our reforms in accordance with the socialist choice. We are looking within socialism, rather than outside it, for the answers to all the questions that arise. We assess our successes and errors alike by socialist standards. Those who hope that we shall move away from the socialist path will be greatly disappointed. Every part of our program of perestroika — and the program as a whole, for that matter — is fully based on the principle of more socialism and more democracy. . . .

We will proceed toward better socialism rather than away from it. We are saying this honestly, without trying to fool our own people or the world. Any hopes that we will begin to build a different, nonsocialist society and go over to the other camp are unrealistic and futile. Those in the West who expect us to give up socialism will be disappointed. It is high time they understood this, and, even more importantly, proceeded from that understanding in practical relations with the Soviet Union. . . .

We want more socialism and, therefore, more democracy. . . .

READING AND DISCUSSION QUESTIONS

1. What does Gorbachev believe caused the Soviet Union's difficulties?

2. Why is the "credibility gap" such a key factor?

3. What do critics outside the Soviet Union have to say about perestroika?

4. Is perestroika meant to move the Soviet Union away from socialism? What is Gorbachev's vision of perestroika as a solution to his country's woes?

COMPARATIVE QUESTIONS

1. What egalitarian notions are expressed in the UN declaration and the U.S. feminist manifestos?

2. What cold war objectives are clear in both Kennedy's and Truman's missions and ideals? What seems to have changed in the fifteen years separating their speeches?

3. Does Gorbachev's notion of perestroika symbolize a victory in terms of the Truman Doctrine?

4. How would you summarize the dramatic global changes in the decades after World War II? Cite at least one example from each document.

CHAPTER 32

Latin America, Asia, and Africa in the Contemporary World

During the mid twentieth century, the nations of Latin America, Asia, and Africa sought to end Western colonial rule and regain control of the vast resources that Western colonizers and multinational corporations had exploited as their own. Nationalist movements seeking to end oppression and gain independence built momentum during the economic hardships of the Great Depression and the aftermath of World War II. Some moved toward the capitalist democratic model of the United States; others, such as China, firmly embraced communism. In the Middle East, nationalism had vastly different meanings for Arabs and Jews, particularly in Palestine and especially after the creation of Israel as a Jewish homeland in 1948. Taken together, movements for national identity and self-determination ultimately sought to break away from the politics and controls of the so-called First World, and in doing so, reshaped the global economy and international relationships.

DOCUMENT 32-1

LÁZARO CÁRDENAS
Speech to the Nation
March 18, 1938

Faced with a global depression, Latin American leaders looked inward for ways to increase their economic viability and facilitate independence from Western interests. One possible solution was to nationalize industries and agricultural production that had been controlled and financially exploited by First World colonial interests. By 1921, Mexico was the world's second

President Lázaro Cárdenas, Radio Address, March 18, 1938.

largest oil producer, but its workforce and petroleum assets were controlled by British and U.S. companies. In this speech, Mexican president Lázaro Cárdenas outlines his decision to seize the oil companies within Mexico and nationalize them under the Mexican government. Following his radio address, a six-hour parade wound through the streets of Mexico. In response, Britain and the United States boycotted Mexican oil.

In each and every one of the various attempts of the Executive to arrive at a final solution of the conflict within conciliatory limits . . . the intransigence of the companies was clearly demonstrated.

Their attitude was therefore premeditated and their position deliberately taken, so that the Government, in defense of its own dignity, had to resort to application of the Expropriation Act,[1] as there were no means less drastic or decision less severe that might bring about a solution of the problem.

For additional justification of the measure herein announced, let us trace briefly the history of the oil companies' growth in Mexico and of the resources with which they have developed their activities.

It has been repeated *ad nauseam* that the oil industry has brought additional capital for the development and progress of the country. This assertion is an exaggeration. For many years throughout the major period of their existence, the oil companies have enjoyed great privileges for development and expansion, including customs and tax exemptions and innumerable prerogatives; it is these factors of special privilege, together with the prodigious productivity of the oil deposits granted them by the Nation [Mexico] often against public will and law, that represent almost the total amount of this so-called capital.

Potential wealth of the Nation; miserably underpaid native labor; tax exemptions; economic privileges; governmental tolerance — these are the factors of the boom of the Mexican oil industry.

Let us now examine the social contributions of the companies. In how many of the villages bordering on the oil fields is there a hospital, or school or social center, or a sanitary water supply, or an athletic field, or even an electric plant fed by the millions of cubic meters of natural gas allowed to go to waste?

---

[1] **Expropriation Act**: Passed by the Mexican congress in 1936, the act gave President Cárdenas the power to seize (expropriate) foreign property for the national good.

What center of oil production, on the other hand, does not have its company police force for the protection of private, selfish, and often illegal interests? These organizations, whether authorized by the Government or not, are charged with innumerable outrages, abuses, and murders, always on behalf of the companies that employ them.

Who is not aware of the irritating discrimination governing construction of the company camps? Comfort for the foreign personnel; misery, drabness, and insalubrity [unhealthiness] for the Mexicans. Refrigeration and protection against tropical insects for the former; indifference and neglect, medical service and supplies always grudgingly provided, for the latter; lower wages and harder more exhausting labor for our people.

The tolerance which the companies have abused was born, it is true, in the shadow of the ignorance, betrayals, and weakness of the country's rulers; but the mechanism was set in motion by investors lacking in the necessary moral resources to give something in exchange for the wealth they have been exploiting.

Another inevitable consequence of the presence of the oil companies, strongly characterized by their anti-social tendencies, and even more harmful than all those already mentioned, has been their persistent and improper intervention in national affairs.

The oil companies' support to strong rebel factions against the constituted government in the Huasteca region of Veracruz and in the Isthmus of Tehuantepec during the years 1917 to 1920 is no longer a matter for discussion by anyone. Nor is anyone ignorant of the fact that in later periods and even at the present time, the oil companies have almost openly encouraged the ambitions of elements discontented with the country's government, every time their interests were affected either by taxation or by the modification of their privileges or the withdrawal of the customary tolerance. They have had money, arms, and munitions for rebellion, money for the anti-patriotic press which defends them, money with which to enrich their unconditional defenders. But for the progress of the country, for establishing an economic equilibrium with their workers through a just compensation of labor, for maintaining hygienic conditions in the districts where they themselves operate, or for conserving the vast riches of the natural petroleum gases from destruction, they have neither money, nor financial possibilities, nor the desire to subtract the necessary funds from the volume of their profits.

Nor is there money with which to meet a responsibility imposed upon them by judicial verdict, for they rely on their pride and their economic power to shield them from the dignity and sovereignty of a Nation which has generously placed in their hands its vast natural resources and now finds itself unable to obtain the satisfaction of the most elementary obligations by ordinary legal means.

As a logical consequence of this brief analysis, it was therefore necessary to adopt a definite and legal measure to end this permanent state of affairs in which the country sees its industrial progress held back by those who hold in their hands the power to erect obstacles as well as the motive power of all activity and who, instead of using it to high and worthy purposes, abuse their economic strength to the point of jeopardizing the very life of a Nation endeavoring to bring about the elevation of its people through its own laws, its own resources, and the free management of its own destinies.

With the only solution to this problem thus placed before it, I ask the entire Nation for moral and material support sufficient to carry out so justified, important, and indispensable a decision.

The Government has already taken suitable steps to maintain the constructive activities now going forward throughout the Republic, and for that purpose it asks the people only for its full confidence and backing in whatever dispositions the Government may be obliged to adopt.

Nevertheless, we shall, if necessary, sacrifice all the constructive projects on which the Nation has embarked during the term of this Administration in order to cope with the financial obligations imposed upon us by the application of the Expropriation Act to such vast interests; and although the subsoil of the country will give us considerable economic resources with which to meet the obligation of indemnization [compensation] which we have contracted, we must be prepared for the possibility of our individual economy also suffering the indispensable readjustments, even to the point, should the Bank of Mexico deem it necessary, of modifying the present exchange rate of our currency, so that the whole country may be able to count on sufficient currency and resources with which to consolidate this act of profound and essential economic liberation of Mexico.

It is necessary that all groups of the population be imbued with a full optimism and that each citizen, whether in agricultural, industrial, commercial, transportation, or other pursuits, develop a greater activity from this moment on, in order to create new resources which will reveal that the spirit of our people is capable of saving the nation's economy by the efforts of its own citizens.

And, finally, as the fear may arise among the interests now in bitter conflict in the field of international affairs[2] that a deviation of raw materials fundamentally necessary to the struggle in which the most powerful nations are engaged might result from the consummation of this act of national sovereignty and dignity, we wish to state that our petroleum operations will not depart a single inch from the moral solidarity maintained by Mexico with the democratic nations, whom we wish to assure that the expropriation now decreed has as its only purpose the elimination of obstacles erected by groups who do not understand the evolutionary needs of all peoples and who would themselves have no compunction in selling Mexican oil to the highest bidder, without taking into account the consequences of such action to the popular masses and the nations in conflict.

READING AND DISCUSSION QUESTIONS

1. What privileges does Cárdenas claim that foreign-owned oil companies have enjoyed in Mexico? And at what expense to his country?

2. What are some of the abuses and grievances that Cárdenas outlines about the conduct of foreign oil companies?

3. What does the president ask citizens listening to this radio address to do to support his action?

4. Based on Cárdenas's speech, what political reason might motivate him to expropriate the foreign companies?

---

[2] **international affairs:** World War II in Europe was still more than a year away, but the Japanese invasion of China was in full swing; Spain was in the midst of its civil war; and Nazi Germany had just annexed Austria.

DOCUMENT 32-2

JAMES AGGREY, LÉON G. DAMAS, AND LÉOPOLD SÉDAR SENGHOR
From "Parable of the Eagle," "Limbo," and "Prayer for Peace"
1929, 1962, 1991

In response to centuries of European colonization, black African intellectuals in the twentieth century began to articulate strong messages of national and cultural pride. Often educated in the West, these intellectuals formed the ideological movement known as Diaspora. Concurrently, mass protests sought to wrest control of the continent's economic destiny and resources (such as cocoa production) from European hands. This movement accelerated dramatically after World War II. In the works that are excerpted here, the authors describe the devastating impact of colonization on the African psyche, culture, and identity, and offer distinctive visions of future African independence and the steps necessary to achieve it.

James Aggrey, "Parable of the Eagle"

A certain man went through a forest seeking any bird of interest he might find. He caught a young eagle, brought it home and put it among his fowls and ducks and turkeys, and gave it chickens' food to eat even though it was an eagle, the king of birds.

Five years later a naturalist came to see him and, after passing through his garden, said: "That bird is an eagle, not a chicken."

"Yes," said its owner, "but I have trained it to be a chicken. It is no longer an eagle, it is a chicken, even though it measures fifteen feet from tip to tip of its wings."

"No," said the naturalist, "it is an eagle still: it has the heart of an eagle, and I will make it soar high up to the heavens."

James Aggrey, "Parable of the Eagle," in Edward W. Smith, *Aggrey of Africa* (London: SCM Press, 1929); Léon G. Damas, "Limbo," *Pigments* (Paris: Presence Africaine, 1962); Léopold Sédar Senghor, "Prayer for Peace," in Melvin Dixon, ed. and trans., *The Collected Poetry of Léopold Sédar Senghor* (Charlottesville, VA: University of Virginia Press, 1991).

"No," said the owner, "it is a chicken, and it will never fly."

They agreed to test it. The naturalist picked up the eagle, held it up, and said with great intensity: "Eagle, thou art an eagle; thou dost belong to the sky and not to this earth; stretch forth thy wings and fly."

The eagle turned this way and that, and then, looking down, saw the chickens eating their food, and down he jumped.

The owner said: "I told you it was a chicken."

"No," said the naturalist, "it is an eagle. Give it another chance tomorrow."

So the next day he took it to the top of the house and said: "Eagle, thou art an eagle; stretch forth thy wings and fly." But again the eagle, seeing the chickens feeding, jumped down and fed with them.

Then the owner said: "I told you it was a chicken."

"No," asserted the naturalist, "it is an eagle, and it still has the heart of an eagle; only give it one more chance, and I will make it fly tomorrow."

The next morning he rose early and took the eagle outside the city, away from the houses, to the foot of a high mountain. The sun was just rising, gilding the top of the mountain with gold, and every crag was glistening in the joy of that beautiful morning.

He picked up the eagle and said to it: "Eagle, thou art an eagle; thou dost belong to the sky and not to this earth; stretch forth thy wings and fly!"

The eagle looked around and trembled as if new life were coming to it; but it did not fly. The naturalist then made it look straight at the sun. Suddenly it stretched out its wings and, with the screech of an eagle, it mounted higher and higher and never returned. It was an eagle, though it had been kept and tamed as a chicken!

My people of Africa, we were created in the image of God, but men have made us think that we are chickens, and we still think we are; but we are eagles. Stretch forth your wings and fly! Don't be content with the food of chickens!

Léon G. Damas, "Limbo"

Give me back my black dolls. I want to play with them,
Play the ordinary games that come naturally to me,
Stay in the shadow of their rules,
Get back my courage and my boldness,
Feel myself, what I was yesterday,
Without complexity.
Yesterday, when I was torn up by the roots.
Will they ever know the rancor eating at my heart,

My mistrustful eye open too late?
They have stolen the space that was mine
The customs, the days of my life
The singing, the rhythm, the strain,
The path, the water, the hut
The earth, gray, smoky
And wisdom, the words, the palavers,[3]
The ancients.
And the beat, the hands, the beating of the hands
And the stamping of feet on the ground.
Give them back to me, my black dolls,
My black dolls,
Black dolls
Black.

LÉOPOLD SÉDAR SENGHOR, "PRAYER FOR PEACE"

[For grand organ]

To Georges and Claude Pompidou

". . . Sicut et nos dimittimus debitoribus nostris" ["As we forgive those who trespass against us"][4]

   Lord Jesus, at the end of this book, which I offer You as a ciborium[5] of sufferings

   At the beginning of the Great Year, in the sunlight of Your peace on the snowy roofs of Paris

   — Yet I know that my brothers' blood will redden once more the Yellow East, on the shores of the Pacific Ocean ravaged by storms and hatreds[6]

   I know that this blood is the spring libation[7] with which the Great Publicans[8] have been fertilizing the Empire's lands for seventy years

---

[3] palavers: Long, rambling discussions.
[4] Sicut et nos . . . against us: A line from the Lord's Prayer.
[5] ciborium: Goblet-shaped vessel that holds the communion wafers in the Catholic mass.
[6] my brothers' blood . . . hatreds: Senghor does not expect a quick end to the war against Japan, in which African soldiers were involved in combat.
[7] spring libation: Ritual pouring of wine or oil on the ground as a sacrifice to a god.
[8] Great Publicans: Tax collectors of the Roman Empire who were known for their greed and extortion.

Lord, at the foot of this cross — and it is no longer You who are the tree of sorrow, but above the Old and New Worlds, Crucified Africa

And her right arm stretches over my land, and her left side shades America

And her heart is beloved Haiti, Haiti[9] who dared to proclaim Man before the Tyrant

At the feet of my Africa crucified for four hundred years and yet still breathing

Let me recite to you Lord, her prayer of peace and pardon.

II

Lord God, forgive white Europe!

And it is true, Lord, that for four enlightened centuries, she has thrown the spit and baying of her watch-dogs on my lands

And Christians, renouncing Your light and the gentleness of Your heart

Lighted their campfires with my parchments, tortured my disciples, deported my doctors and my masters of science.

Their gunpowder crumbled in a flash our proud fortresses and the hills

And their cannon balls blasted through the loins of vast empires as a bright day, from the Western Horn to the Eastern horizon

And as though they were hunting grounds, they burned the intangible forests, dragging Ancestors and spirits by their peaceful beards.

And they made their sacred mystery the Sunday diversion of sleep-walking bourgeoisie[10]

Lord, forgive those who made guerrilla fighters of the Askia,[11] sergeants of my princes

Boys of my servants and wage-earners of my peasants, a race of proletarians of my people.

For you must forgive those who hunted my children as though they were wild elephants

And they disciplined them with whiplashes and made them the black hands of those whose hands were white.

---

[9] **Haiti:** In 1801, the overwhelmingly black population of the French sugar colony Saint-Domingue rebelled against French rule and won their independence (see Document 21-5).

[10] **Sunday diversion . . . bourgeoisie:** Reference to African religious art on display in European museums.

[11] **Askia:** Ruling house of the West African empire of Songhai in the 1500s.

For you must forget those who exported ten million of my sons in the leper camps of their ships

Who killed two hundred million of them.[12]

And they made a lonely old age for me in the forest of my nights and the savannah of my days.

Lord, the mirror of my eyes grows cloudy

And now the serpent of hate rears its head in my heart, that serpent I had thought dead . . .

III

Kill it Lord, for I must continue my journey, and I want to pray especially for France.

Lord, among the white nations, place France at the Father's right hand.

Oh! I do know that she too is Europe, that she snatched my children from me like a cattle-stealing brigand from the North, to fertilize her fields of cane and cotton, for black sweat is manure.

That she too brought death and guns to my blue villages, that she set my people against one another like dogs fighting over a bone

That she treated those who resisted like bandits and spat on the heads harboring great plans.

Yes Lord, forgive France who speaks for the right way and treads the devious paths

Who invites me to her table and bids me bring my own bread, who gives with her right hand and takes back half with her left.

Yes Lord, forgive France who hates her occupiers [the Germans] and yet imposes such grave occupation on me

Who opens triumphal ways to heroes and treats her Senegalese like mercenaries, making them the black watchdogs of the Empire

Who is the Republic and hands over countries to big business

And of my Mesopotamia, of my Congo, they have made a vast cemetery under the white sun.

IV

Oh! Lord, erase from my memory the France that is not France, that mask of meanness and of hate on France's face

That mask of meanness and of hate for which I have but hate — but I can surely hate Evil

---

[12] **Who killed . . . them:** If Senghor implies that the transatlantic slave trade resulted in 200 million deaths, this would be an exaggeration. Perhaps he means that colonialism killed 200 million Africans in a figurative sense.

For I have a great weakness for France.

Bless this shackled nation who has twice succeeded in freeing her hands and dared proclaim the accession of the poor to the royal throne

Who changed slaves of the day into men who were free, equal, brothers[13]

Bless this nation who brought me Your Good News [the Christian Gospel], Lord, and opened my heavy eyelids to the light of faith.

She opened my heart to the knowledge of the world, showing me the rainbow of the new faces that are my brothers.

I greet you my brothers: you Mohamed Ben Abdallah, you Razafymahatratra, and then you out there Pham-Manh-Tuong,[14] you from the pacific seas and you from the enchanted forests

I greet you all with a catholic heart.

Ah! I know well that more than one of Your messengers hunted my priests like game and made great carnage of pious images.

And yet we could have lived in harmony, for these very images were the Jacob's ladder[15] from the earth to Your heaven

The clear oil lamp that helps us wait for dawn, the stars that foreshadow the sun.

I know that many of Your missionaries blessed the arms of violence and made compacts with the bankers' gold

But there must always be traitors and fools.

V

Oh bless this nation, Lord, who seeks her own face under the mask and finds it hard to recognize

Who seeks You in the cold, in the hunger that gnaws at her bones and entrails

And the betrothed mourns her widowhood, and the young man sees his youth stolen away

And the wife laments the absent eye of her husband, and the mother seeks the dream of her child amidst the rubble.

Oh! bless this nation who breaks her bonds, bless this nation at bay who defies the ravenous pack of bullies and torturers.

And with her all the peoples of Europe, all the peoples of Asia all the peoples of Africa and all the peoples of America

---

[13] **Who changed slaves . . . brothers**: Reference to the French Revolution.

[14] **my brothers . . . Pham-Manh-Tuong**: Other peoples under French colonial rule.

[15] **Jacob's ladder**: Bibical reference to the ladder from earth to heaven that Jacob saw in a dream.

Who sweat blood and sufferings. And in the midst of these millions of waves, see the surging heads of my people.

And grant that their warm hands embrace the earth in a band of brotherly hands

UNDER THE RAINBOW OF YOUR PEACE.

Paris, January 1945[16]

READING AND DISCUSSION QUESTIONS

1. What do each of these poets claim was taken from Africa and Africans? How do these poets differ in their responses to colonization and their suggestions to their fellow countrymen?

2. According to Aggrey, how is Africa like the eagle? What does he see as his country's first step toward independence?

3. Why does Sédar Senghor want to forgive France?

4. Who do you believe is the imagined audience for the "Parable of the Eagle"? For "Limbo"? Do you think the intended audiences are the same? Why or why not?

DOCUMENT 32-3

CHARLES DE GAULLE
Comments on Algeria
April 11, 1961

The lengthy Algerian War (1954–1962) was actually a series of conflicts rooted in the movement for Algerian independence from France. A Muslim West African country, Algeria provided colonial France with access to Saharan oil reserves as well as a base for commerce and industry. In return,

---

"Fourth Press Conference Held by General Charles de Gaulle as President of the French Republic in Paris and the Elysee Palace on April 11, 1961," in *Major Addresses, Statements, and Press Conferences of General Charles de Gaulle, May 19, 1958–January 31, 1964* (New York: French Embassy Press and Information Division, 1964), 113–118.

[16] **Paris, January 1945**: This work is set in 1945 Paris, after the city is liberated from Nazi occupation.

France offered Algeria ongoing economic aid. However, years of violent Algerian resistance to colonial rule had drained France's resources. Pulled in both directions, French president Charles de Gaulle (1958–1969) devised the controversial strategy to issue a referendum to the Algerian people. If they chose independence — as they ultimately did — he would end France's hold on the country. At a 1961 press conference, de Gaulle explained his willingness to accept Algerian independence.

I should like it to be well understood that in France's policy toward Algeria, the following essential idea must be faced squarely: in the world of today and in the times in which we live, France has no interest whatsoever in maintaining under her jurisdiction and under her dependence an Algeria which would choose another destiny, and it would not be in France's interest to be responsible for the population of an Algeria which would have become master of its own fate and would have nothing to offer in exchange for what it would ask. The fact is that, to say the least, Algeria costs us much more than it is worth to us. Whether in the matter of administrative expenses, economic investments, social welfare, cultural development, or the many obligations with regard to the maintenance of law and order — what we furnished to it in effort, money, and human ability has no counterpart that anywhere nearly approaches it.

It must in the same way be realized that France's present responsibilities in Algeria constitute heavy military and diplomatic burdens for her. And that is why France would consider today with the greatest calm a solution whereby Algeria would cease to be a part of France — a solution which in former times might have seemed disastrous for us but which, I say it again, we consider with a perfectly calm mind. . . .

There are people who will say: "But it is the rebellion which leads you to think in this way." . . . It is not this that makes me speak as I do; I do not deny that the events which have occurred, which are occurring in Algeria have confirmed what I have thought and demonstrated for more than twenty years, without any joy of course — and you can well understand why — but with the certainty of serving France well.

Since Brazzaville,[17] I have not ceased to affirm that the populations dependent on us should have the right to self-determination. In 1941, I

---

[17] **Brazzaville**: De Gaulle and some forty colonial administrators attended the Brazzaville Conference in French West Africa in 1944. No Africans participated and independence was not discussed. The conference proposed a number of reforms in the French African colonies.

granted independence to the mandated States of Syria and Lebanon. In 1945, I gave all Africans, including Algerian Moslems, the right to vote. In 1947, I approved the Statute of Algeria which, if it had been applied, would probably have led to the progressive institution of an Algerian State Associated with France.[18] . . . I agreed that the protectorate treaties concerning Tunisia and Morocco should be approved. . . . In 1958, having resumed leadership,[19] I, along with my Government, created the Community[20] and later recognized and aided the independence of the young States in Black Africa and Madagascar. Not having returned to power in time to prevent the Algerian insurrection, immediately upon my return I proposed to its leader to conclude the peace of the brave and to open political talks . . . and I and my government have not ceased to act in order to promote a Moslem leadership in Algeria and to put the Moslems in a position to take local affairs into their own hands, until such time as they are able to take over on the government level. . . .

In conclusion, what does this add up to: to decolonization. But if I have undertaken and pursued this task for a long time, it is not only because we could foresee and later because we witnessed the vast movement toward freedom which the world war and its aftermath unleashed in every corner of the globe, and which the rival bids of the Soviet Union and America did not fail to emphasize. I have done it also, and especially, because it seemed to me contrary to France's present interests and new ambition to remain bound by obligations and burdens which are no longer in keeping with the requirements of her strength and influence. . . .

Moreover, this is true for others as well. It must be recognized that in the great transformation which is taking place from one end of the universe to the other, the itching for independence of erstwhile dominated peoples and also the incitements thrown out by all the demagogues of the world are not the only motivating forces. There is another which is not always very clearly perceived. . . . We French built our empire at a time

---

[18] **Statute of Algeria . . . France**: Algerians were given the right to vote for members of the three assemblies that met in 1946 to determine the constitutional framework of postwar Algeria. However, voting was weighted in such a way as to guarantee French dominance of the assemblies.

[19] **having resumed leadership**: In June 1958, French president Rene Coty asked de Gaulle to handle the Algerian situation.

[20] **the Community**: The French Community was a plan proposed by de Gaulle in 1958, according to which French colonies, primarily in Africa, would continue to receive French economic and technical aid and would gain control of their internal affairs.

when our internal activities had reached a sort of ceiling — an industry which was not breaking any new ground, an agriculture which was not making any changes, trade channels which were fixed, salaries and wages unchanged, practically stereotyped budgets, gold currency, interest rates at 3%, etc. On the other hand, our old ambitions of European hegemony and natural frontiers were countered by the treaties of 1815 and, after 1870,[21] by the unity and strength of a threatening Germany. Then we sought in distant extensions a new role for the surplus of our enterprising abilities, a complement to our prestige and soldiers for our defense.

France does not have to be at all sorry for what she has achieved overseas in this capacity and in this form. I have said it often and I repeat: it constitutes a great human accomplishment which — notwithstanding certain abuses and errors and despite all the endless spouting of all sorts of worthless demagogues — will forever be a credit to France. But how many things have changed today.

Now our great national ambition is our own national progress, constituting a real source of power and influence. Now the modern era permits us, compels us, to undertake a vast development. Now for this development to succeed we must first of all employ the means and resources at our disposal on our own behalf, in our own country. All the more so as we need these means and resources to ensure our own defense and that of our neighbors against the greatest imperialism that the world has ever known — the imperialism of the Soviet Union. We also need these means to win out in the tremendous economic, technical, and social struggle now under way between the forces of humanity and the forces of slavery [i.e., the cold war].

It is a fact: our interest, and consequently our policy, lies in decolonization. Why should we continue to cling to costly, bloody, and fruitless domination when our country has to undergo complete renovation, when all the underdeveloped countries, beginning with those which yesterday were our dependencies and which today are our favorite friends, ask for our aid and our assistance? But this aid and this assistance — why should we extend them if it is not worthwhile, if there is no cooperation, if what we give finds no return? Yes, it is a matter of exchange, because of what is due us, but also because of the dignity of those with whom we are dealing. . . .

---

[21] **treaties of 1815 . . . 1870**: A treaty approved at the Congress of Vienna (1815) essentially returned France to its pre-revolutionary borders. The Treaty of Paris (1870), which followed the French defeat by the Germans in the Franco-Prussian War, resulted in the French loss of the border region of Alsace and most of Lorraine.

Some people say, "What would happen to these territories if France withdrew? They would straightaway fall into misery and chaos, until Communism took over." That is, no doubt, what would happen to them; but then we would no longer have any duty toward them other than to pity them.

Some people say also, "Either the Soviet Union or the United States — or both at once — would try to take France's place in the territories from which she withdrew." My answer is: I wish both of them a lot of fun.

But it is also possible that the Algerian populations — through self-determination, while deciding on the institution of a sovereign State — will express their desire to see the new Algeria associated with the new France. In such an event, it would have to be known on both sides what this actually meant. That is why a solution should be submitted to the vote of the Algerian people — pending ratification by the French people — a solution agreed upon beforehand by the Government and the different political elements in Algeria, the rebels in particular. France would undoubtedly be willing to lend her economic, administrative, financial, cultural, military, and technical aid to the young Mediterranean State, provided the organic cooperation between the Algerian communities, preferential conditions for economic and cultural exchange, and finally the bases and facilities necessary for our defense, are assured and guaranteed. . . .

Naturally we are anxious that, once peace has been re-established and civil liberties restored, the populations may sincerely choose their destiny. After which, if it is not in vain, France will undoubtedly be led, by her heart and her reason, to give her aid and friendship.

That is what I wanted to say about Algeria.

READING AND DISCUSSION QUESTIONS

1. What reasons does de Gaulle present to support his statement that it is not in France's interest to hold on to Algeria?

2. How does de Gaulle counter charges that his decision to support independence was prompted by Algerian insurrections?

3. What role does de Gaulle say World War II played in decolonization?

4. According to de Gaulle, what are the differences between France's goals in building its overseas empire and the country's present-day (1961) goals?

DOCUMENT 32-4

NELSON MANDELA

The Rivonia Trial Speech to the Court

April 20, 1964

Following World War II, the white Afrikaner government that came to power in South Africa enacted extreme forms of legal segregation — known as apartheid — that relegated blacks to the lowest paid jobs and poorest regions of the country. In the 1950s and 1960s, the African National Congress (ANC), led by young attorney Nelson Mandela, protested these racist policies first peacefully and later violently. The organization was outlawed in 1961, but Mandela continued to run the ANC while in hiding for seventeen months before he was arrested, tried, and found guilty of treason. He was imprisoned until 1990. Mandela first presented this defense following the 1963 arrest of ANC leaders at Liliesleaf Farm, Rivonia, and later included it in reports he released after becoming the first democratically elected president of South Africa in 1994.

In my youth . . . I listened to the elders of my tribe telling stories of the old days. Amongst the tales they related to me were those of wars fought by our ancestors in defense of the father-land. . . . I hoped then that life might offer me the opportunity to serve my people and make my own humble contribution to their freedom struggle. This is what has motivated me in all that I have done in relation to the charges made against me in this case. . . .

I have already mentioned that I was one of the persons who helped to form Umkonto.[22] I, and the others who started the organization, did so for two reasons. Firstly, we believed that as a result of Government policy, violence by the African people had become inevitable, and that unless responsible leadership was given to canalize and control the feelings of our people, there would be outbreaks of terrorism which would produce an

Nelson Mandela, *No Easy Walk to Freedom*, ed. Ruth First (New York: Basic Books, 1965), 163–168.

[22] **Umkonto**: Short for "Umkonto we Sizwe," or Spear of the Nation, a militant subgroup of the African National Congress that Mandela founded while in hiding in 1961.

intensity of bitterness and hostility between the various races of this country which is not produced even by war. Secondly, we felt that without violence there would be no way open to the African people to succeed in their struggle against the principle of White supremacy. All lawful modes of expressing opposition to this principle had been closed by legislation, and we were placed in a position in which we had either to accept a permanent state of inferiority, or to defy the Government. . . .

But the violence which we chose to adopt was not terrorism. We who formed Umkonto were all members of the African National Congress, and had behind us the ANC tradition of non-violence and negotiation as a means of solving political disputes. We believed that South Africa belonged to all the people who lived in it, and not to one group, be it Black or White. We did not want an interracial war, and tried to avoid it to the last minute. . . .

The African National Congress was formed in 1912 to defend the rights of the African people. . . . For thirty-seven years — that is until 1949 — it adhered strictly to a constitutional struggle. It put forward demands and resolutions; it sent delegations to the Government in the belief that African grievances could be settled through peaceful discussion and that Africans could advance gradually to full political rights. But White Governments remained unmoved, and the rights of Africans became less instead of becoming greater. . . .

Even after 1949, the ANC remained determined to avoid violence. At this time, however, there was a change from the strictly constitutional means of protest which had been employed in the past. The change was embodied in a decision which was taken to protest against apartheid legislation by peaceful, but unlawful, demonstrations against certain laws. Pursuant to this policy the ANC launched the Defiance Campaign, in which I was placed in charge of volunteers. This campaign was based on the principles of passive resistance.[23] More than 8,500 people defied apartheid laws and went to jail. Yet there was not a single instance of violence in the course of this campaign on the part of any defier. . . .

In 1960 there was the shooting at Sharpeville,[24] which resulted in the proclamation of a state of emergency and the declaration of the ANC as an unlawful organization. My colleagues and I, after careful consideration,

---

[23] **passive resistance**: Form of nonviolent political protest used and popularized by Indian leader Mohandas Gandhi (1869–1948).
[24] **Sharpeville**: The Sharpeville Massacre of 1960, in which police killed 69 and wounded 178 anti-apartheid demonstrators.

decided that we would not obey this decree. The African people were not part of the Government and did not make the laws by which they were governed. We believed in the words of the Universal Declaration of Human Rights,[25] that "the will of the people shall be the basis of authority of the Government," and for us to accept the banning was equivalent to accepting the silencing of the Africans for all time. The ANC refused to dissolve, but instead went underground. . . .

Each disturbance pointed clearly to the inevitable growth among Africans of the belief that violence was the only way out — it showed that a Government which uses force to maintain its rule teaches the oppressed to use force to oppose it. . . .

The avoidance of civil war had dominated our thinking for many years, but when we decided to adopt violence as part of our policy, we realized that we might one day have to face the prospect of such a war. . . . We did not want to be committed to civil war, but we wanted to be ready if it became inevitable.

Four forms of violence were possible. There is sabotage, there is guerrilla warfare, there is terrorism, and there is open revolution. We chose to adopt the first method and to exhaust it before taking any other decision.

In the light of our political background the choice was a logical one. Sabotage did not involve loss of life, and it offered the best hope for future race relations. Bitterness would be kept to a minimum and, if the policy bore fruit, democratic government could become a reality. . . .

Attacks on the economic lifelines of the country were to be linked with sabotage on Government buildings and other symbols of apartheid. These attacks would serve as a source of inspiration to our people. In addition, they would provide an outlet for those people who were urging the adoption of violent methods and would enable us to give concrete proof to our followers that we had adopted a stronger line and were fighting back against Government violence. . . .

Another of the allegations made by the State is that the aims and objects of the ANC and the Communist Party are the same. . . .

It is true that there has often been close cooperation between the ANC and the Communist Party. But cooperation is merely proof of a common goal — in this case the removal of White supremacy — and is not proof of a complete community of interests. . . .

---

[25] **Universal Declaration of Human Rights**: A declaration of the rights entitled to every human being, adopted by the United Nations on December 10, 1948.

It is perhaps difficult for White South Africans, with an ingrained prejudice against communism, to understand why experienced African politicians so readily accept communists as their friends. But to us the reason is obvious. Theoretical differences amongst those fighting against oppression is a luxury we cannot afford at this stage. What is more, for many decades communists were the only political group in South Africa who were prepared to treat Africans as human beings and their equals; who were prepared to eat with us, talk with us, live with us, and work with us. They were the only political group which was prepared to work with the Africans for the attainment of political rights and a stake in society. Because of this, there are many Africans who, today, tend to equate freedom with communism. . . .

Our fight is against real, and not imaginary, hardships or, to use the language of the State prosecutor, "so-called hardships." Basically, we fight against two features which are the hallmarks of African life in South Africa and which are entrenched by legislation which we seek to have repealed. These features are poverty and lack of human dignity. . . .

South Africa is the richest country in Africa, and could be one of the richest countries in the world. But it is a land of extremes and remarkable contrasts. The Whites enjoy what may well be the highest standard of living in the world, whilst Africans live in poverty and misery. Forty percent of the Africans live in hopelessly overcrowded and, in some cases, drought-stricken Reserves, where soil erosion and the overworking of the soil make it impossible for them to live properly off the land. Thirty percent are laborers, labor tenants, and squatters on White farms and work and live under conditions similar to those of the serfs of the Middle Ages. The other 30 percent live in towns where they have developed economic and social habits which bring them closer in many respects to White standards. Yet most Africans, even in this group, are impoverished by low incomes and [the] high cost of living. . . .

The lack of human dignity experienced by Africans is the direct result of the policy of White supremacy. White supremacy implies Black inferiority. Legislation designed to preserve White supremacy entrenches this notion. Menial tasks in South Africa are invariably performed by Africans. When anything has to be carried or cleaned the White man will look around for an African to do it for him, whether the African is employed by him or not. Because of this sort of attitude, Whites tend to regard Africans as a separate breed. They do not look upon them as people with families of their own; they do not realize that they have emotions — that they fall in love like White people do; that they want to be with their wives and children like White people want to be with theirs; that they want to earn enough money to support their families properly, to feed and clothe them and send them to school. And what "house-boy" or "garden-boy" or laborer can ever hope to do this? . . .

Poverty and the breakdown of family life have secondary effects. Children wander about the streets of the townships because they have no schools to go to, or no money to enable them to go to school, or no parents at home to see that they go to school, because both parents (if there be two) have to work to keep the family alive. This leads to a breakdown in moral standards, to an alarming rise in illegitimacy, and to growing violence which erupts, not only politically, but everywhere. Life in the townships is dangerous. There is not a day that goes by without somebody being stabbed or assaulted. And violence is carried out of the townships in the White living areas. People are afraid to walk alone in the streets after dark. Housebreakings and robberies are increasing, despite the fact that the death sentence can now be imposed for such offenses. Death sentences cannot cure the festering sore. . . .

During my lifetime I have dedicated myself to this struggle of the African people. I have fought against White domination, and I have fought against Black domination. I have cherished the ideal of a democratic and free society in which all persons live together in harmony and with equal opportunities. It is an ideal which I hope to live for and to achieve. But if needs be, it is an ideal for which I am prepared to die.

READING AND DISCUSSION QUESTIONS

1. What reason does Mandela give for the ANC's decision to defy the government decree that outlawed their group?

2. What form of violence does the formerly nonviolent ANC adopt, and how does Mandela justify this decision?

3. How does Mandela describe the experience of blacks under apartheid?

4. Why does Mandela believe that the fundamental theories of communism hold a certain appeal to black South African politicians, while white South Africans reject it?

DOCUMENT 32-5

UNYA SHAVIT

Arab and Israeli Soccer Players Discuss Ethnic Relations in Israel

November 3, 2000

Since the creation of the state of Israel in 1948, tensions between Arabs and Jews in the region have continued to generate conflict and inspire fierce loyalty within each group. Jews consider the region their rightful homeland, while Arabs see it as part of their home of Palestine. In September of 2000, following failed negotiations between Yasir Arafat, the leader of the Palestinian Liberation Organization (PLO), and Israeli prime minister Ehud Barak, violence surged in Israel, the West Bank, and the Gaza Strip. Writing for the Hebrew daily paper Ha'aretz, *journalist Unya Shavit explored the complex issues of nationalism and discrimination among Arab and Jewish soccer teammates.*

Two weeks ago, having suffered three losses and four ties, Maccabi Ahi Nazareth found itself last in the National League. The team's lackluster performance did little to improve the atmosphere in Nazareth,[26] its mood already dampened by the recent rioting and its harsh economic consequences. In an effort to keep from sinking to a lower league, the team's management fired coach Samir Issa and appointed Eli Mahpoud in his place. Surprisingly, the replacement of an Arab coach with a Jewish one, even in these tense times, was accepted in Nazareth without protest. The Ahi Nazareth fans, it seems, just want their team to stay in the National League, the second of the six divisions in Israeli soccer, under the Premier League. If nothing else, at least that. This is Mahpoud's second stint in Nazareth. Last season, when Maccabi Ahi Nazareth found itself in similar straits, Mahpoud came on as its coach and succeeded in keeping it in the National League. When the season ended, he accepted the better contract offered by Maccabi Kiryat Gat. But the relationship with Kiryat Gat

---

Unya Shavit, "Playing for Keeps," *Ha'aretz*, November 3, 2000.

[26] **Nazareth**: City in northern Israel.

proved short-lived, and Mahpoud found himself out of a job — a common enough occurrence in the dizzying game of musical chairs that is Israeli soccer. When the offer from Nazareth came, Mahpoud agreed almost immediately.

The recent outbreak of violence, he says, had little influence on his deliberations on whether or not to accept the job. "I was worried only that the roads might be closed, and I would not be able to make it to practice. Those around me were more concerned than I was. I did not give much thought to what happened in Nazareth. I like to think positive. There are radical minorities everywhere. I don't know the city, but I do know the team and its fans, and they're wonderful people. They welcomed me warmly when I signed back on." . . . .

Driving to practice from his home in Petah Tikva last week, Mahpoud was unwilling to talk politics. His radio was tuned to the all-music station Galgalatz throughout the two-hour trip to Nazareth and to local sports news on the 90-minute drive back. The fact that he coaches an Arab team is mere coincidence, as far as he is concerned. People who work in sports, he believes, should worry only about sports.

Mahpoud claims that the team's four Jewish players — Sagi Strauss, Shlomi Ben-Hamu, Arik Hangali, and Emil Castiel — were similarly un-affected by the current crisis. "The rioting in Nazareth had no effect on anyone in the team, Jewish or Arab," he says. "None of the Jewish play-ers came and said they wanted to leave. Soccer players are soccer players: they want to play." . . .

Issam Issami, the team's striker, is a Druze[27] who served in the Israeli army. He spent last season playing for Maccabi Netanya and had hoped to move to Betar Jerusalem for the current season. "I was at the Betar tryouts this summer. By the end of the first week, I felt I was not welcome there. Fans yelled curses at me during the first practice. The players didn't say anything to my face, but I knew that behind my back they were asking, 'Why did they have to bring the Arab player?' I knew what would happen if I made a mistake during the first game, that the crowd would call me a dirty Arab. Jerusalem has Jews and goys [non-Jews]. I'm a goy to them. I spent three years in the army, and I'm a goy to them."

---

[27] **Druze:** Member of a religious community in parts of Israel and the Middle East that incorporates some Islamic symbolism with a belief that al-Hakim, a tenth-century Islamic leader and successor to Muhammad, represented God's earthly form. The Druze are considered a legal nationality in Israel.

Is it possible that you simply weren't good enough for Betar?
"Of course that's what they'd say. But that's not what I feel. Look, it's my country. I feel that it's my country. But you won't give me the space to feel that. You act like it's not my country, not in soccer, and not in other areas."

LIFE AS AN ARAB PLAYER

Mahpoud, once a star player in Hapoel Petah Tikva, was first recommended for the job by his friend Azmi Nassar, who two years ago led the Palestinian national team to third place in the Pan Arab Games. Nassar says he thought Mahpoud would work well with an Arab team. "He's an honest person, understands a lot about soccer. He has this restaurant in Petah Tikva where he works with Arab employees, and he gets along with them. I was sure he would not be patronizing or dismissive toward the Arab players."

Nassar is now coach of Bnei Sakhnin, the National League's other Arab team. Bnei Sakhnin now faces a double challenge. It is struggling not only to remain in the league, but also to maintain its status as "Israel's leading Arab team." Maccabi Ahi Nazareth is its arch-enemy. Last week the two teams played each other; Bnei Sakhnin won 2–1.

In the days preceding this much-awaited match, Mahpoud and Nassar's friendship helped take some of the sting out of the fierce rivalry. There was, however, another reason why passions did not quite rise to their expected frenzy: up until the last minute, it was not clear whether the game would even take place.

The police refused to allow the match to be held in Nazareth. When Kiryat Eliezer was suggested as an alternative site, the insurance company demanded an exorbitant security deposit. "It's hard to prepare a team for a match this way," Mahpoud said last Tuesday, during the break between morning and afternoon practice. "You have to divide up the practice load, follow a plan, and you can't do that under these conditions. The Arab teams are harmed through no fault of their own."

Do you support the Arab players' claims that they suffer from discrimination?
"People in Ahi Nazareth say that the referees are prejudiced against them. In some games I feel that it's true. I think it's mostly because we're a small team, even for the second league. But it's also true that the life of an Arab player is much harder.

"They tell me that players on rival teams curse them, calling them 'dirty Arab' and names like that. That infuriates me. I always tell them that you can't allow yourself to be affected by these provocations. This is their

job, their livelihood, and they have to keep it. I also get sworn at by the fans
of rival teams. When I was coaching a Jewish team, the curses were much
softer. Here people yell, 'You son of a bitch, why are you coaching Arabs?' "

What about your friend Azmi Nassar?

"Azmi did not get a single offer from a Jewish team, despite his many successes. I don't know why that is. He's an excellent coach. Speaking in
purely professional terms, he has what it takes to coach a Premier League
team. Maybe it's because soccer is such an emotional business. If his team
failed, well, you know the kind of position the administration would then
be in, having hired an Arab coach." . . .

CARPOOLS AND MUSIC

Having finished their lunch, four of the Ahi Nazareth players [Shomi Ben
Hamu, Arik Hangali, Ashraf Suliman, and Abed Titi] sit around a table in
a downtown restaurant and talk. . . .

The four are friends, and not only on the soccer field. Titi, Ben Hamu
and Hangali carpool to practice, meeting each day at the Netanya junc-
tion. Whoever is driving gets to choose the music, so that Ben Hamu and
Hangali are constantly exposed to the latest Arab hits.

SULIMAN: We in Nazareth want good players. We don't care if they're Jewish, Arab or foreign, as long as they play well.

HANGALI: I never thought I'd end up playing for an Arab team, but from
 the moment I got here, I felt at home. I was treated very warmly, and
 I knew I was staying. You have to know how to keep sports and politics
 apart. We're in sports, we all have the same goal. I feel that I represent
 the city of Nazareth. I have no problem with that. But I also represent
 myself — if I don't play well, I'll disgrace myself, too. We're not
 repressing reality. Titi and Suliman are really our friends. If a few
 extremists raised some hell, is that any reason to be mad at them?

TITI: We only want peace and quiet. What does anyone, Jewish or Arab,
 have to gain from people being killed? Why can't we all have fun
 together?

SULIMAN: Iad Lawabneh, the first casualty from Nazareth, was a big fan of
 ours. He was killed 15 minutes before our game against Kiryat Gat
 began. Our management asked to have the game postponed, but it
 wasn't. We lost.

BEN HAMU: I had no problem playing when the riots started. I never
 thought of leaving the team. All in all, I know both the people here

and the administration. People in my family were worried about me, said I should look into other options. But eventually, when things calmed down, those fears disappeared, too.

HANGALI: When we came to practice on the days of the rioting, we found fans waiting. They said they'd look out for us. Today, when people in Tel Aviv ask me whether I'm afraid to go to Nazareth, I laugh. What's there to be afraid of?

BEN HAMU: Joining Nazareth changed something for me. I didn't know any Arabs before, had no Arab friends. I knew nothing about their mentality. Today I get together with friends from the Arab team even after practice. We go out to eat or go bowling. Today all I want is for there to be peace. . . .

READING AND DISCUSSION QUESTIONS

1. How does the author explain the apparent lack of protest when Maccabi Ahi Nazareth replaced its Arab coach with a Jewish one despite the tense political climate and strained Arab-Jewish relations?

2. Do Arab or Jewish players seem to face more discrimination? Why do you think this is so?

3. What are some of the obstacles the coaches and players face in order to play within their league? Where do those obstacles come from?

4. What reasons, if any, might the interviewed players have to downplay ethnic differences and the experiences of playing in sometimes hostile environments and under violent circumstances?

COMPARATIVE QUESTIONS

1. What forces helped inspire the various nationalist movements of the twentieth century?

2. What benefits do Cárdenas and de Gaulle see for their respective nations by ending colonial rule?

3. Would poets Aggrey, Damas, and Sédar Senghor disagree with Mandela's approach to liberating blacks in South Africa? Why or why not?

4. How do shifting national boundaries and political regimes produce discrimination in the Arab-Jewish context and in South Africa?

5. Mandela's trial speech and the works of the three diaspora poets reflect on struggles taking place in African nations. What are those struggles, and what might account for the differences in tone between the documents? Does the period during which the documents were written affect their tone?

CHAPTER 33

A New Era in World History

The 1990s marked the beginning of a new era in world history. The cold war was over, new human rights initiatives were springing up in long-repressed countries, and the so-called age of globalization was under way. By the early twenty-first century, the political and economic systems of all countries were more intricately linked and interdependent than ever before. Booms and busts, environmental issues, terrorism, war, and the spread of multinational corporations had become concerns for all nation-states. The United Nations emerged as an important voice in the global political arena. Western corporations reached into developing nations promising economic improvement on the one hand, and seeking new and cheaper sources of labor on the other. For some, the global economy has led to growth, technological development, and the promise of social and political reform. For others, the greater worldwide interconnectedness has exposed vast differences in values and wealth. One international constant remains — the struggle of people to be responsible global citizens.

DOCUMENT 33-1

OSAMA (USAMA) BIN LADEN
*A Call on Muslims to Take Up Arms
Against America*
1998

Years before Osama bin Laden was linked to the 2001 terrorist attacks on the World Trade Center and the Pentagon he began building a movement to create an Islamic state and oust secular governments in Islamic countries. He shrewdly capitalized on dissatisfaction among Islamic fundamentalists with

---

"Interview with Usama Bin Laden by His Followers," *Nida'ul Islam* 15 (October–November 1996). Translated by Akram Khater.

U.S. foreign policy, which they saw as anti-Arab. Bin Laden's anti-Western and frequently anti-U.S. rhetoric, like that used in this 1998 al-Qaeda call to arms, helped him amass a huge following in the 1990s. In the interview with his followers excerpted below, bin Laden shared his philosophy and foreshadowed his use of terrorism in 2001.

Interview with Usama Bin Laden by His Followers, 1998

Q. What is the meaning of your call for Muslims to take up arms against America in particular, and what is the message that you wish to send to the West in general?

The call to wage war against America was made because America has spearheaded the crusade against the Islamic nation, sending tens of thousands of its troops to the land of the two Holy Mosques, over and above its meddling in its affairs and its politics and its support of the oppressive, corrupt, and tyrannical regime that is in control. These are the reasons behind the singling out of America as a target. And not exempt from responsibility are those Western regimes whose presence in the region offers support to the American troops there. We know at least one reason behind the symbolic participation of the Western forces and that is to support the Jewish and Zionist plans for expansion of what is called the Great Israel. Surely, their presence is not out of concern over their interests in the region. . . . Their presence has no meaning save one and that is to offer support to the Jews in Palestine who are in need of their Christian brothers to achieve full control over the Arab Peninsula, which they intend to make an important part of the so called Greater Israel. . . .

Q. Many of the Arabic as well as the Western mass media accuse you of terrorism and of supporting terrorism. What do you have to say to that?

There is an Arabic proverb that says, "She accused me of having her malady, then snuck away." Besides, terrorism can be commendable and it can be reprehensible. Terrifying an innocent person and terrorizing him is objectionable and unjust, also unjustly terrorizing people is not right.

Whereas, terrorizing oppressors and criminals and thieves and robbers is necessary for the safety of people and for the protection of their property. There is no doubt in this. Every state and every civilization and culture has to resort to terrorism under certain circumstances for the purpose of abolishing tyranny and corruption. Every country in the world has its own security system and its own security forces, its own police, and its own army. They are all designed to terrorize whoever even contemplates an attack on that country or its citizens. The terrorism we practice is of the commendable kind, for it is directed at the tyrants and the aggressors and the enemies of Allah, the tyrants, the traitors who commit acts of treason against their own countries and their own faith and their own prophet and their own nation. Terrorizing those and punishing them are necessary measures to straighten things and to make them right. Tyrants and oppressors who subject the Arab nation to aggression ought to be punished. The wrongs and the crimes committed against the Muslim nation are far greater than can be covered by this interview. America heads the list of aggressors against Muslims. The recurrence of aggression against Muslims everywhere is proof enough. For over half a century, Muslims in Palestine have been slaughtered and assaulted and robbed of their honor and of their property. Their houses have been blasted, their crops destroyed. And the strange thing is that any act by them to avenge themselves or to lift the injustice befalling them causes great agitation in the United Nations, which hastens to call for an emergency meeting only to convict the victim and to censure the wronged and the tyrannized whose children have been killed and whose crops have been destroyed and whose farms have been pulverized. . . .

In today's wars, there are no morals, and it is clear that mankind has descended to the lowest degrees of decadence and oppression. They rip us of our wealth and of our resources and of our oil. Our religion is under attack. They kill and murder our brothers. They compromise our honor and our dignity and if we dare to utter a single word of protest against the injustice, we are called terrorists. This is compounded injustice. And the United Nations insistence to convict the victims and support the aggressors constitutes a serious precedent that shows the extent of injustice that has been allowed to take root in this land. . . .

Q. What is your relationship with the Islamic movements in various regions of the world, such as Chechnya and Kashmir and other Arab countries?

Cooperation for the sake of truth and righteousness is demanded from Muslims. A Muslim should do his utmost to cooperate with his fellow Muslims. But Allah says of cooperation that it is not absolute, for there is cooperation to do good, and there is cooperation to commit aggression and act unjustly. A Muslim is supposed to give his fellow Muslim guidance and support. He [Allah] said, "Stand by your brother be he oppressor or oppressed." When asked how were they to stand by him if he were the oppressor, he answered them, saying, "by giving him guidance and counsel." It all goes to say that Muslims should cooperate with one another and should be supportive of one another, and they should promote righteous-ness and mercy. They should all unite in the fight against polytheism, and they should pool all their resources and their energy to fight the Americans and the Zionists and those with them. They should, however, avoid side issues and rise over the small problems, for these are less detrimental. Their fight should be directed against unbelief and unbelievers. . . .

Q. We heard your message to the American government and later your message to the European governments who participated in the occupation of the Gulf. Is it possible for you to address the people of these countries?

As we have already said, our call is the call of Islam that was revealed to Muhammad. It is a call to all mankind. We have been entrusted with good cause to follow in the footsteps of the Messenger and to communicate his message to all nations. It is an invitation that we extend to all the nations to embrace Islam, the religion that calls for justice, mercy, and fraternity among all nations, not differentiating between black and white or between red and yellow except with respect to their devotedness. All people who worship Allah, not each other, are equal before him. We are entrusted to spread this message and to extend that call to all the people. We nonethe-less fight against their governments and all those who approve of the injus-tice they practice against us. We fight the governments that are bent on attacking our religion and on stealing our wealth and on hurting our feel-ings. And as I have mentioned before, we fight them, and those who are part of their rule are judged in the same manner. . . .

Q. In your last statement, there was a strong message to the American government in particular. What message do you have for the European governments and the West in general?

Praise be to Allah and prayers and peace upon Muhammad. With respect to the Western governments that participated in the attack on the land of the two Holy Mosques regarding it as ownerless, and in the siege against the Muslim people of Iraq,[1] we have nothing new to add to the previous message. What prompted us to address the American government in par-ticular is the fact that it is on the head of the Western and the crusading forces in their fight against Islam and against Muslims. The two explosions that took place in Riyadh and in Khobar recently were but a clear and pow-erful signal to the governments of the countries that willingly participated

---

[1] **siege against the Muslim people of Iraq**: Reference to the U.S. bombing of Iraq during the Gulf War in 1991.

in the aggression against our countries and our lives and our sacrosanct symbols. It might be beneficial to mention that some of those countries have begun to move toward independence from the American government with respect to the enmity that it continues to show toward the Muslim people. We only hope that they will continue to move in that direction, away from the oppressive forces that are fighting against our countries. We, however, differentiate between the Western government and the people of the West. If the people have elected those governments in the latest elections, it is because they have fallen prey to the Western media, which portray things contrary to what they really are. And while the slogans raised by those regimes call for humanity, justice, and peace, the behavior of their governments is completely the opposite. It is not enough for their people to show pain when they see our children being killed in Israeli raids launched by American planes, nor does this serve the purpose. What they ought to do is change their governments that attack our countries. The hostility that America continues to express against the Muslim people has given rise to feelings of animosity on the part of Muslims against America and against the West in general. Those feelings of animosity have produced a change in the behavior of some crushed and subdued groups, who, instead of fighting the Americans inside the Muslim countries, went on to fight them inside the United States of America itself.

The Western regimes and the government of the United States of America bear the blame for what might happen. If their people do not wish to be harmed inside their very own countries, they should seek to elect governments that are truly representative of them and that can protect their interests. . . .

The enmity between us and the Jews goes far back in time and is deeprooted. There is no question that war between the two of us is inevitable. For this reason it is not in the interest of Western governments to expose the interests of their people to all kinds of retaliation for almost nothing. It is hoped that people of those countries will initiate a positive move and force their governments not to act on behalf of other states and other sects. This is what we have to say, and we pray to Allah to preserve the nation of Islam and to help them drive their enemies out of their land.

Q. American politicians have painted a distorted picture of Islam, of Muslims, and of Islamic fighters. We would like you to give us the true picture that clarifies your viewpoint. . . .

The leaders in America and in other countries as well have fallen victim to Jewish Zionist blackmail. They have mobilized their people against Islam and against Muslims. These are portrayed in such a manner as to drive people to rally against them. The truth is that the whole Muslim world is the victim of international terrorism, engineered by America at the United Nations. We are a nation whose sacred symbols have been looted and whose wealth and resources have been plundered. It is normal for us to react against the forces that invade our land and occupy it. . . .

Q. Quite a number of Muslim countries have seen the rise of militant movements whose purpose is to stand up in the face of the pressure exerted on the people by their own governments and other governments. Such is the case in Egypt and Libya and North Africa and Algiers, and such was the case in Syria and in Yemen. There are also other militant groups currently engaged in the fight against the unbelievers and the crusaders, as is the case in Kashmir and Chechnya and Bosnia and the African horn. Is there any message you wish to convey to our brothers who are fighting in various parts of the Islamic World?
Tell the Muslims everywhere that the vanguards of the warriors who are fighting the enemies of Islam belong to them and the young fighters are their sons. Tell them that the nation is bent on fighting the enemies of Islam. Once again, I have to stress the necessity of focusing on the Americans and the Jews, for they represent the spearhead with which the members of our religion have been slaughtered. Any effort directed against America and the Jews yields positive and direct results, Allah willing. It is far better for anyone to kill a single American soldier than to squander his efforts on other activities.

JIHAD[2] AGAINST JEWS AND CRUSADERS: WORLD ISLAMIC FRONT STATEMENT, 23 FEBRUARY 1998

Shaykh Usamah Bin-Muhammad Bin-Ladin
Ayman al-Zawahiri, amir [commander] of the Jihad Group in Egypt
Abu-Yasir Rifa'i Ahmad Taha, Egyptian Islamic Group
Shaykh Mir Hamzah, secretary of the Jamiat-ul-Ulema-e-Pakistan
Fazlur Rahman, amir of the Jihad Movement in Bangladesh

Praise be to God, who revealed the Book [Qur'an], controls the clouds, defeats factionalism, and says in His Book: "But when the forbidden months are past, then fight and slay the pagans wherever ye find them, seize them, beleaguer them, and lie in wait for them in every stratagem (of war)"; and peace be upon our Prophet, Muhammad Bin-'Abdallah, who said: I have been sent with the sword between my hands to ensure that no

---

[2] **Jihad**: Muslim holy war or crusade against infidels (nonbelievers).

one but God is worshiped, God who put my livelihood under the shadow of my spear and who inflicts humiliation and scorn on those who disobey my orders.

The Arabian Peninsula has never — since God made it flat, created its desert, and encircled it with seas — been stormed by any forces like the crusader armies spreading in it like locusts, eating its riches, and wiping out its plantations. All this is happening at a time in which nations are attacking Muslims like people fighting over a plate of food. In the light of the grave situation and the lack of support, we and you are obliged to discuss current events, and we should all agree on how to settle the matter.

No one argues today about three facts that are known to everyone; we will list them, in order to remind everyone:

First, for over seven years the United States has been occupying the lands of Islam in the holiest of places, the Arabian Peninsula, plundering its riches, dictating to its rulers, humiliating its people, terrorizing its neighbors, and turning its bases in the peninsula into a spearhead through which to fight the neighboring Muslim peoples.

If some people have in the past argued about the fact of the occupation, all the people of the peninsula have now acknowledged it. The best proof of this is the Americans' continuing aggression against the Iraqi people using the peninsula as a staging post, even though all its rulers are against their territories being used to that end, but they are helpless.

Second, despite the great devastation inflicted on the Iraqi people by the crusader-Zionist alliance, and despite the huge number of those killed, which has exceeded 1 million. . . . Despite all this, the Americans are once again trying to repeat the horrific massacres, as though they are not content with the protracted blockade imposed after the ferocious war or the fragmentation and devastation.

So here they come to annihilate what is left of this people and to humiliate their Muslim neighbors.

Third, if the Americans' aims behind these wars are religious and economic, the aim is also to serve the Jews' petty state and divert attention from its occupation of Jerusalem and murder of Muslims there. The best proof of this is their eagerness to destroy Iraq, the strongest neighboring Arab state, and their endeavor to fragment all the states of the region — such as Iraq, Saudi Arabia, Egypt, and Sudan — into paper statelets and through their disunion and weakness to guarantee Israel's survival and the continuation of the brutal crusade occupation of the peninsula.

All these crimes and sins committed by the Americans are a clear declaration of war on God, his messenger, and Muslims. And "ulama" [Muslim scholars] have throughout Islamic history unanimously agreed that the jihad is an individual duty if the enemy destroys the Muslim countries. This was revealed by Imam Bin-Qadamah in "Al-Mughni," Imam al-Kisa'i in "Al-Bada'i," al-Qurtubi in his interpretation, and the shaykh [teacher] of al-Islam in his books, where he said: "As for the fighting to repulse [an enemy], it is aimed at defending sanctity and religion, and it is a duty as agreed [by the "ulama"]. Nothing is more sacred than belief except repulsing an enemy who is attacking religion and life."

On that basis, and in compliance with God's order, we issue the following fatwa [legal decree] to all Muslims:

The ruling to kill the Americans and their allies — civilians and military — is an individual duty for every Muslim who can do it in any country in which it is possible to do it, in order to liberate the al-Aqsa Mosque and the holy mosque [Mecca] from their grip, and in order for their armies to move out of all the lands of Islam, defeated and unable to threaten any Muslim. This is in accordance with the words of Almighty God, "and fight the pagans all together as they fight you all together," and "fight them until there is no more tumult or oppression, and there prevail justice and faith in God."

This is in addition to the words of Almighty God: "And why should ye not fight in the cause of God and of those who, being weak, are ill treated (and oppressed)? — women and children, whose cry is: 'Our Lord, rescue us from this town, whose people are oppressors; and raise for us from thee one who will help!' "

We — with God's help — call on every Muslim who believes in God and wishes to be rewarded to comply with God's order to kill the Americans and plunder their money wherever and whenever they find it. We also call on Muslim "ulama," leaders, youths, and soldiers to launch the raid on Satan's U.S. troops and the devil's supporters allying with them, and to displace those who are behind them so that they may learn a lesson.

Almighty God said: "O ye who believe, give your response to God and His Apostle, when He calleth you to that which will give you life. And know that God cometh between a man and his heart, and that it is He to whom ye shall all be gathered."

Almighty God also says: "O ye who believe, what is the matter with you, that when ye are asked to go forth in the cause of God, ye cling so heavily to the earth! Do ye prefer the life of this world to the hereafter? But little is the comfort of this life, as compared with the hereafter. Unless ye go forth, He will punish you with a grievous penalty, and put others in your place; but Him ye would not harm in the least. For God hath power over all things."

Almighty God also says: "So lose no heart, nor fall into despair. For ye must gain mastery if ye are true in faith."

READING AND DISCUSSION QUESTIONS

1. What does bin Laden say is the real motivation for the presence of Western troops in the Middle East?
2. What reasons does he give to justify his version of terrorism?
3. What distinction does bin Laden make between Western people and Western governments? How does he explain the election of Western leaders?
4. What three facts about Americans does he say are indisputable?

DOCUMENT 33-2

GEORGE TARABISHI

A Roundtable Discussion of Globalization and Its Impact on Arab Culture

October 26, 2000

Many leaders and thinkers, particularly those in the East and in smaller countries, worry about globalization's long-term impact. They debate whether globalization will decimate local culture and replace it with that of the West, and whether globalization will make the rich richer and the poor — the vast majority of the world's people — poorer. To address these concerns, Bahrain's Ministry of Culture convened a roundtable of Arab intellectuals. Panel member George Tarabishi, who writes about the world for the French and Arab press, shared highlights of the event and his own views in the article excerpted below.

When Muslim theological scholars used to determine that an issue is con-flictual, they meant that it is permissible to disagree about it, that *ijtihad* [the application of reason] is necessary, and that this conflict and this *ijtihad* cannot be considered heretical. It is within this specific context that I declare that globalization is a conflictual matter. . . .

George Tarabishi, "Globalization and Its Impact on Arab Culture: Globalization as a Matter of Conflict," *al-Bahrain al-Thaqafia* 26 (October 26, 2000). Translated by Akram Khater.

Globalizing the World

There is no doubt that the ability to read globalization as a conflictual matter derives from its seriousness as a phenomenon, from the looseness of its meaning, and from its capacity to be loaded with conflicting meanings and values. In addition, the vastness of this phenomenon and its multiple facets allows it to take as its basis an existential duality and thus a Manichaean[3] reading that depends on feelings and value judgments more than on knowledge. Thus, these approaches to globalization deal with it on the level of the singularities of good and evil, or love and hate, or right and left. Therefore, anyone who speaks of globalization must define first what he means. For me, globalization . . . means nothing more than the world becoming one. Before economy, before media, and before cultural production, the world itself is becoming globalized. We must not forget that the world, in its largest meaning, is a modern concept. Before overcoming the law of distances with modern means of transportation and communication, the world was made of worlds. The borders within these worlds were not merely geographical but also linguistic, religious, and ethnic. It was rare to imagine that each of these partial worlds was the world in its totality.

However, this world, which is being united by globalization — and herein lies the problem — cannot be unified except on the basis of its division into two dualities of a developed world and an underdeveloped world, a world of the rich and a world of the poor, a world that produces information and knowledge and a world where there is not even the means to consume these. According to a famous United Nations description [of the world], 20 percent of the world's population owns 80 percent of its riches, and 80 percent of its people own less than 20 percent of its resources. This places four-fifths of humanity on one side and one-fifth on the other side. According to another report, 20 percent of the world's rich own 85 percent of the global production, while 20 percent of the world's poor own no more than 1.1 percent.

Contrary to a strongly held belief, the globalization of the world — on the basis of this problematic dual division — is not limited to the economic sector alone. . . . In addition to economic globalization — which is without doubt the most obvious and most predisposed to quantification — there is technological globalization, environmental globalization, food globalization, legal globalization, media globalization, and finally cultural globalization.

---

[3] **Manichaean**: A philosophical understanding of the world in terms of good versus evil or dark versus light.

Globalizing the Arab World

If the Arab countries do not have sufficient cultural capacity to absorb globalization, then the concept of counter-globalization, as it is being propounded in the Arab cultural arena today, appears as if it is being activated under an attractive theoretical name — what we have called the mechanism of hegemony [dominance] . . . by a sizable number of intellectuals. It is true that the person who shaped this concept — the Tunisian linguist 'Abd al-Salam al-Masdi, has himself warned against dealing in a utopian fashion with the concept. . . . He clearly stated: "The concept of globalization that we have constructed in our cultural discussion in the book *Globalization and Counter-Globalization* does not mean that we deny the phenomenon of globalization. Nor do we object fundamentally to its existence. Nor are we in any way calling to completely oppose it. Had we done or claimed any of these, then we would be utopian in the absolute sense of the word. What we are calling for is the introduction of a new idea where counter-globalization would be a mentality that eschews negative criticism and embraces positive criticism."

Despite this [warning], it appears that this concept [counter-globalization] . . . has escaped like the genie from the bottle and has acquired an ideological independence that is not related to the rational purpose that produced it. It has imposed itself with incredible speed in the Arab world as a slogan for opposition and resistance, and as an alternative or contrary globalization, which some have defined as "the true globalization as opposed to the fake globalization," others as "the humane versus the monstrous globalization," or, as [Egyptian writer] Mahmud Amin al-'Alam has said, "the globalization of truth not falsehood, the globalization of liberty not enslavement and hegemony, the globalization of science, knowledge and creativity not ignorance, alienation, underdevelopment and dependency."

To draw ourselves away from the intellectually crippling gravitational pull between *globalization* and *counter-globalization*, I believe that we must be armed with both a realistic and critical awareness. This is not meant to confront and counter but to improve our chances of benefiting from its [globalization's] advantages and avoiding its negative aspects. In the large global village that the world is on the verge of becoming, the Arab world — which is more divided than ever — is in need of becoming first a regional singular village. This, I believe, is the shortest path to enter the village of globalization — or its jungle, as its opponents claim — safely.

Since one of the possible definitions of globalization is the erasure of borders, and we are dealing specifically here with cultural globalization, let us then add quickly that the borders that we think we ought to remove in the Arab world are cultural borders. We are realistic enough to realize that the political borders in the Arab world — despite our previous ideological illusions about these borders being artificial — are currently and for the foreseeable future not subject to removal. However, the Arab world is capable, despite the consecration of its divisions and its regional and national characteristics with borders, of representing a singular cultural group. If it was not for this ability, then the Arab world would not have been able to distinguish itself — and be distinguished by others — as an Arab world.

So as not to float in the ethereal world of abstraction, let us say right away that it is new communication technologies that allow for the relatively safe and effective circumvention of Arab cultural borders. The first indication of this penetration is embodied in the Arab satellite television channels, which — regardless of what has been said about their performance or funding and purpose — have succeeded, however partially, in shrinking the Arab world despite its vastness and the invincibility of its political topography.

Another example is presented to us by the capability — which has become a reality in some cases — provided by new communication technologies to publish multiple editions of the same Arabic newspaper or magazine in various Arab capitals and at the same time. If, in the near future, we can develop the spread of the Internet in the Arab world, then another aspect of internal Arab borders — and we mean regional censorship of thought and the means of exchanging it through books, journals, and newspapers — will fall or at least be circumvented. On the Internet the scissors of the censor cannot intrude.

We do not need to view the circumventing or the removal of the cultural borders as solely negative. We can envision a type of positive Arab globalization in which the Arab League — after revising its purpose toward elevating its cultural role — can play an effective role. We can envision, within this context, the establishment of an Arab network that links Arab scientific and university institutions to limit the chaos of Arab research, to lessen duplication and the waste of effort and money, and to allow for a real possibility for coordination of university research and for disseminating that research so that it benefits the Arab world and does not remain locked away collecting dust. Within this context also, we can envision a network to link Arab museums and another network to "revive" Arabic manuscripts in Arab and foreign universities and libraries and thus allow all researchers access without having to travel and waste money and time.

Proponents of the theory of Arab cultural security may object that circumvention of the borders will not be accomplished solely by Arabs but by necessity will be carried out also by "foreign" forces. . . . As is sometimes said in the world of strategy, the best defense is offense. Therefore, we say that the best way to confront globalization is to be present, not absent. In any case, globalization is already here, whether we like it or not. So let us learn how to participate in it. . . . Just as globalization has made possible the emergence of a new economic pole in the world, the Asian pole, and just as it has made possible the crystallization of a European media pole (Euro News in opposition to CNN, for example), there is nothing to keep us from anticipating the emergence of an Arab cultural pole one day. Although light-years separate us from the realization of this dream — whose accomplishment is linked to a chain of democratic, modernizing, and radical changes in the Arab world — we see no reason not to look forward to it. Why? Simply because we refuse to limit ourselves between the jaws of the Fukuyama and Huntington pincers[4]: neither the "end of history" nor the "clash of civilizations" is preordained. We reject the thesis that history is dominated by a singular universal civilization that crushes all else, and we reject the thesis of a history that, through global conflict, reshapes the world along lines of isolated and clashing civilizational islands. We believe that the world is heading toward becoming for the first time in history a single civilization with multiple cultures. Globalization may be the tool for this dialogue between world civilization and national cultures. But this dialogue should take place on the condition — which some may say is utopian — that globalization ceases to be a tool for *hegemony* and instead becomes a tool for *participation*.

To avoid appearing as if I am simply making a play on words, allow me to say that adjusting the equation of globalization from hegemony to participation does not presume absolute equality in the shares of the partners. Globalization is closer to an incorporated company, and our position within the corporation is decided by the size of our stock portfolio. According to our demographic size, our share cannot exceed 3.4 percent; otherwise, we would become hegemonic like others. But even this level is higher than what we can arrive at in the foreseeable future. [This is so] first, because the Arab world does not enter into the company of globalization as a singular stockholder. Its portfolio is distributed among many

---

[4]**Fukuyama and Huntington pincers**: Francis Fukuyama and Samuel Huntington, both academics. Fukuyama wrote *The End of History*, and Huntington took an alternative view in his book *The Clash of Civilizations*.

partners, who in many instances are fighting among themselves. More-over, the Arab world, most of which belongs to the Third World — some parts even belong to the Fourth World[5] — is not equal to the other stock-holders in the globalization company in terms of its capacity for material and intellectual production. This disparity is particularly evident vis-à-vis the large partners who — despite being numerically small — own 80 per-cent of humanity's material production and 95 percent of its intellectual production. We will be realistic if we dream of increasing our share, in stages, from 0.001 to 1 percent within a time frame that is no less than a quarter of a century. This 1 percent is the minimum requirement for "take-off," as the experiences of East and Southeast Asian nations indicate. If we, some or all of us, fail to "take off" in the next quarter of a century, we must not attribute our failure in adjusting the equation of globalization to a fail-ure of globalization itself. The formula for globalization is open and multi-faceted and ever changing in its values, and if there is an unknown that is difficult to determine, it is the Arab unknown, because we are living in a period of high tension between those who support and those who oppose modernity. . . .

The impact of globalization on us and our participation in globaliza-tion, specifically from a cultural perspective, is a matter of *how* in addition to *how much*. If we do not take this into consideration, then we risk our role by falling into the error of separating the tool and the spirit [of global-ization]. Although such a division is possible economically and technolog-ically, and even in the media, it is not possible culturally. From a cultural point of view, globalization is not a neutral phenomenon, for it occurs within a particular culture. At a time when Arab culture, like the other cul-tures of the world, has no option but to engage with it [globalization], then it would appear that this engagement, in the Arab case, will be conflictual rather than cooperative. This is so because the cultural values contained within globalization appear, to a large extent, at odds with predominant Arab values.

We can describe the culture of globalization as being of this world — we do not say secular — while Arab culture is still counted within the reli-gious segment [of cultures] and is still preoccupied with matters of the spiritual world. The culture of globalization, because it is the culture of wealthy society, has a hedonistic tendency to squeeze all pleasure from the present moment and to engage in hyper-consumption. In contrast, Arab

---

[5] **Fourth World**: The countries of the Third World, primarily in Africa and Asia, that have the lowest rates of development.

culture . . . is dominated by the logic of contentment, abstention, and thrift, and spiritual saving for future dark days.

The culture of globalization — by definition a visual culture — depends on the presence of the human body and does not hesitate to uncover and denude it, particularly the female body. Arab culture, in contrast, is a culture of modesty — manifested by covering the body, particularly the female body. The two cultures also diverge greatly on the issue of sexual abstinence and permissiveness. The culture of globalism goes to extremes in allowing for sexual love, while Arab culture goes to extremes in limiting it.

These differences, among others, make the intersection of Arab culture and the culture of globalism a point of painful ruptures. But a certain measure of rupture and pain may be necessary to provide the impetus for what we will call . . . cultural mobility. In our estimation, cultural mobility provides the ideal escape from the dual dangers that threaten the intersection of Arab culture and the culture of globalism. These are (1) the danger of isolationism and cocooning in a suffocating parochial or fundamentalist culture and (2) the danger of being torn away from the self and being swept away by a hegemonic globalizing cultural.

Cultural mobility, which combines the restraint of authenticity and the impetus of globalizing modernity, appears more capable than any other mechanism to control the speed and direction of Arab development and to avoid the pitfalls on either side of its path. . . . As we all know, the discourse about roots is today considered of great value in all of the world's cultures, which feel an undeniable need to hold on to their roots for fear of being uprooted by the winds of globalization, which can also undeniably take the form of a storm. However, holding on to cultural roots does not seem to us to be sufficient or a guarantee of the minimum level — let alone the ideal level — of cultural dynamism. . . . National cultures, including the Arab one, in their march toward integration with the culture of globalization, need wings as much as they need roots.

Nobody can predict what will happen to the Arab world in the next twenty-five years, and how the struggle over the mother of conflicts — which is globalization in our time — will be resolved. However, the study of reality, which does not allow for miraculous transformations — . . . forces us to be more pessimistic about the start of this new era, without being overly pessimistic about its end.

READING AND DISCUSSION QUESTIONS

1. How does Tarabishi define globalization? What was the world like before globalization?

2. In Tarabishi's view, what makes globalization "conflictual" for the Arab world?

3. What does Tarabishi believe the Arab world needs to do if it is to benefit from globalization?

4. Why does he view cultural mobility as the solution to the Arab world's concerns about globalism?

DOCUMENT 33-3

GEORGE W. BUSH

From a Speech to the Joint Session of Congress: "History's Unmarked Grave of Discarded Lies"

September 21, 2001

Ten days after the 2001 attacks on the World Trade Center and Pentagon (and a thwarted attack that resulted in the crash of a hijacked plane in Pennsylvania), President George Bush appeared before Congress. In this televised address, Bush focused on bolstering America's shattered spirit, ascribing responsibity for the attacks, and preparing the nation and the world for the coming U.S. response. While thanking countries that had sent words of support and sympathy, Bush also famously rallied — some say bullied — the rest of the civilized world to unite with him against terrorism.

Mr. Speaker, Mr. President pro tem, members of Congress and fellow Americans,

In the normal course of events, presidents come to this chamber to report on the state of the union. Tonight, no such report is needed. It has already been delivered by the American people.

Collated Media Reports, September 21, 2001.

We have seen it in the courage of passengers who rushed terrorists to save others on the ground. Passengers like an exceptional man named Todd Beamer. And would you please help me welcome his wife, Lisa Beamer, here tonight.

We have seen the state of our union in the endurance of rescuers working past exhaustion. We've seen the unfurling of flags, the lighting of candles, the giving of blood, the saying of prayers in English, Hebrew, and Arabic. We have seen the decency of a loving and giving people who have made the grief of strangers their own.

My fellow citizens, for the last nine days, the entire world has seen for itself the state of our union, and it is strong.

Tonight we are a country awakened to danger and called to defend freedom. Our grief has turned to anger and anger to resolution. Whether we bring our enemies to justice or bring justice to our enemies, justice will be done.

I thank the Congress for its leadership at such an important time. All of America was touched on the evening of the tragedy to see Republicans and Democrats joined together on the steps of this Capitol singing "God Bless America." And you did more than sing. You acted by delivering $40 billion to rebuild our communities and meet the needs of our military. . . .

And on behalf of the American people, I thank the world for its out-pouring of support. . . .

Nor will we forget the citizens of 80 other nations who died with our own: dozens of Pakistanis, more than 130 Israelis, more than 250 citizens of India, men and women from El Salvador, Iran, Mexico, and Japan, and hundreds of British citizens.[6]

America has no truer friend than Great Britain.

Once again we are joined together in a great cause. I'm so honored the British prime minister has crossed an ocean to show his unity with America. Thank you for coming, friend.

On Sept. 11, enemies of freedom committed an act of war against our country. Americans have known wars. But for the past 136 years they have been wars on foreign soil, except for one Sunday in 1941.[7] Americans have known the casualties of war. But not at the center of a great city on a peaceful morning. Americans have known surprise attacks. But never

---

[6] **citizens of 80 other nations . . . British citizens**: Bush lists the nationalities of many of those who died in New York City on 9/11.

[7] **1941**: A reference to the Japanese attack on the U.S. naval base at Pearl Harbor on December 7, 1941, which brought the United States into World War II.

before on thousands of civilians. All of this was brought upon us in a single day. And night fell on a different world, a world where freedom itself is under attack.

Americans have many questions tonight. Americans are asking, "Who attacked our country?"

The evidence we have gathered all points to a collection of loosely affiliated terrorist organizations known as Al Qaeda. They are some of the murderers indicted for bombing American Embassies in Tanzania and Kenya, and responsible for bombing the U.S.S. *Cole*.

Al Qaeda is to terror what the Mafia is to crime. But its goal is not making money; its goal is remaking the world and imposing its radical beliefs on people everywhere.

The terrorists practice a fringe form of Islamic extremism that has been rejected by Muslim scholars and the vast majority of Muslim clerics. A fringe movement that perverts the peaceful teaching of Islam. The terrorists' directive commands them to kill Christians and Jews, to kill all Americans and make no distinctions among military and civilians, including women and children. This group and its leader, a person named Osama bin Laden, are linked to many other organizations in different countries, including the Egyptian Islamic Jihad and the Islamic Movement of Uzbekistan.

There are thousands of these terrorists in more than 60 countries. They are recruited from their own nations and neighborhoods and brought to camps in places like Afghanistan, where they are trained in the tactics of terror. They are sent back to their homes or sent to hide in countries around the world to plot evil and destruction. The leadership of Al Qaeda has great influence in Afghanistan and supports the Taliban regime in controlling most of that country.

In Afghanistan we see Al Qaeda's vision for the world. Afghanistan's people have been brutalized. Many are starving and many have fled. Women are not allowed to attend school. You can be jailed for owning a television. Religion can be practiced only as their leaders dictate. A man can be jailed in Afghanistan if his beard is not long enough.

The United States respects the people of Afghanistan. After all, we are currently its largest source of humanitarian aid. But we condemn the Taliban regime. It is not only repressing its own people; it is threatening people everywhere by sponsoring and sheltering and supplying terrorists. By aiding and abetting murder, the Taliban regime is committing murder.

And tonight the United States of America makes the following demands on the Taliban:

- Deliver to United States authorities all the leaders of Al Qaeda who hide in your land.
- Release all foreign nationals, including American citizens, you have unjustly imprisoned.
- Protect foreign journalists, diplomats, and aid workers in your country.
- Close immediately and permanently every terrorist training camp in Afghanistan and hand over every terrorist and every person in their support structure to appropriate authorities.
- Give the United States full access to terrorist training camps so we can make sure they are no longer operating.

These demands are not open to negotiation or discussion. The Taliban must act and act immediately. They will hand over the terrorists or they will share in their fate.

I also want to speak tonight directly to Muslims throughout the world. We respect your faith. It's practiced freely by many millions of Americans and by millions more in countries that America counts as friends. Its teachings are good and peaceful. And those who commit evil in the name of Allah blaspheme the name of Allah. The terrorists are traitors to their own faith, trying in effect to hijack Islam itself.

The enemy of America is not our many Muslim friends. It is not our many Arab friends. Our enemy is a radical network of terrorists and every government that supports them.

Our war on terror begins with Al Qaeda, but it does not end there. It will not end until every terrorist group of global reach has been found, stopped, and defeated.

Americans are asking, "Why do they hate us?"

They hate what they see right here in this chamber, a democratically elected government. Their leaders are self-appointed. They hate our freedoms, our freedom of religion, our freedom of speech, our freedom to vote and assemble and disagree with each other. They want to overthrow existing governments in many Muslim countries, such as Egypt, Saudi Arabia, and Jordan. They want to drive Israel out of the Middle East. They want to drive Christians and Jews out of vast regions of Asia and Africa.

These terrorists kill not merely to end lives but to disrupt and end a way of life. With every atrocity they hope that America grows fearful, retreating from the world and forsaking our friends. They stand against us because we stand in their way. We're not deceived by their pretenses to piety. We have seen their kind before. They are the heirs of all the murderous ideologies of the 20th century. By sacrificing human life to serve their radical visions, by abandoning every value except the will to power, they follow in the path of fascism, Nazism, and totalitarianism. And they will follow that path all the way to where it ends: in history's unmarked grave of discarded lies.

Americans are asking, "How will we fight and win this war?"

We will direct every resource at our command, every means of diplomacy, every tool of intelligence, every instrument of law enforcement, every financial influence, and every necessary weapon of war to the disruption and to the defeat of the global terror network.

Now, this war will not be like the war against Iraq a decade ago, with the decisive liberation of territory and a swift conclusion. It will not look like the air war above Kosovo two years ago, where no ground troops were used and not a single American was lost in combat.

Our response involves far more than instant retaliation and isolated strikes.

Americans should not expect one battle, but a lengthy campaign unlike any other we have ever seen. It may include dramatic strikes visible on TV and covert operations, secret even in success.

We will starve terrorists of funding, turn them one against another, drive them from place to place until there is no refuge or no rest. And we will pursue nations that provide aid or safe haven to terrorism.

Every nation in every region now has a decision to make. Either you are with us or you are with the terrorists.

From this day forward, any nation that continues to harbor or support terrorism will be regarded by the United States as a hostile regime.

Our nation has been put on notice: We're not immune from attack.

We will take defensive measures against terrorism to protect Americans. Today dozens of federal departments and agencies as well as state and local governments have responsibilities affecting homeland security. These efforts must be coordinated at the highest level.

So tonight I announce the creation of a cabinet-level position reporting directly to me, the Office of Homeland Security. . . .

Many will be involved in this effort, from F.B.I. agents to intelligence operatives to the reservists we have called to active duty. All deserve our thanks and all have our prayers.

And tonight a few miles from the damaged Pentagon, I have a message for our military: be ready. I've called the armed forces to alert and there is a reason. The hour is coming when America will act and you will make us proud.

This is not, however, just America's fight. And what is at stake is not just America's freedom. This is the world's fight, this is civilization's fight, this is the fight of all who believe in progress and pluralism, tolerance, and freedom.

We ask every nation to join us. We will ask and we will need the help of police forces, intelligence service, and banking systems around the world. . . .

Perhaps the NATO charter reflects best the attitude of the world: an attack on one is an attack on all.

The civilized world is rallying to America's side. They understand that if this terror goes unpunished, their own cities, their own citizens, may be next. Terror unanswered can not only bring down buildings, it can threaten the stability of legitimate governments. And you know what? We're not going to allow it.

Americans are asking, "What is expected of us?"

I ask you to live your lives and hug your children. I know many citizens have fears tonight and I ask you to be calm and resolute, even in the face of a continuing threat. I ask you to uphold the values of America and remember why so many have come here.

We're in a fight for our principles and our first responsibility is to live by them. No one should be singled out for unfair treatment or unkind words because of their ethnic background or religious faith.

I ask you to continue to support the victims of this tragedy with your contributions. Those who want to give can go to a central source of information, libertyunites.org, to find the names of groups providing direct help in New York, Pennsylvania, and Virginia. The thousands of F.B.I. agents who are now at work in this investigation may need your cooperation. And I ask you to give it. I ask for your patience with the delays and inconveniences that may accompany tighter security. And for your patience in what will be a long struggle.

I ask your continued participation and confidence in the American economy. Terrorists attacked a symbol of American prosperity. They did not touch its source. America is successful because of the hard work and creativity and enterprise of our people. These were the true strengths of our economy before Sept. 11 and they are our strengths today.

And finally, please continue praying for the victims of terror and their families, for those in uniform, and for our great country. Prayer has comforted us in sorrow and will help strengthen us for the journey ahead.

Tonight I thank my fellow Americans for what you have already done and for what you will do. And ladies and gentlemen of the Congress I thank you, their representatives, for what you have already done and for what we will do together.

Tonight we face new and sudden national challenges. We will come together to improve air safety, to dramatically expand the number of air marshals on domestic flights, and take new measures to prevent hijacking. We will come together to promote stability and keep our airlines flying with direct assistance during this emergency. We will come together to give law enforcement the additional tools it needs to track down terror here at home. We will come together to strengthen our intelligence capabilities to know the plans of terrorists before they act and to find them before they strike. We will come together to take active steps to strengthen America's economy and put our people back to work. . . .

After all that has just passed, all the lives taken and all the possibilities and hopes that died with them, it is natural to wonder if America's future is one of fear. Some speak of an age of terror. I know there are struggles ahead and dangers to face.

But this country will define our times, not be defined by them. As long as the United States of America is determined and strong, this will not be an age of terror. This will be an age of liberty here and across the world.

Great harm has been done to us. We have suffered great loss. And in our grief and anger, we have found our mission and our moment. Freedom and fear are at war. The advance of human freedom, the great achievement of our time and the great hope of every time, now depends on us.

Our nation, this generation, will lift the dark threat of violence from our people and our future. We will rally the world to this cause by our efforts, by our courage. We will not tire. We will not falter and we will not fail. . . .

I will not forget the wound to our country and those who inflicted it. I will not yield. I will not rest. I will not relent in waging this struggle for freedom and security for the American people.

The course of this conflict is not known, yet its outcome is certain. Freedom and fear, justice and cruelty, have always been at war. And we know that God is not neutral between them.

Fellow citizens, we'll meet violence with patient justice, assured of the rightness of our cause and confident of the victories to come. In all that lies before us, may God grant us wisdom and may he watch over the United States of America. Thank you.

READING AND DISCUSSION QUESTIONS

1. What does Bush say is the driving force for al-Qaeda's terrorist attacks on September 11 and beyond?

2. How does Bush link al-Qaeda and Afghanistan?

3. What reasons does the president give for al-Qaeda's hatred of Americans specifically, and her allies generally?

4. What ultimatum does he give the rest of the world?

DOCUMENT 33-4

CAROLINA SIC

From an Interview with Women United for Worker Justice

2005

The increasing influence of multinational corporations in developing countries has been a major component of the rise of a global economy in the late twentieth and early twenty-first centuries. The impact of the multinationals has been hotly debated. Though they bring jobs and technology to poorer countries, they often ally with governments to hold down labor costs and prevent unions from forming. They have also come under scrutiny for worker abuse and substandard working conditions. In late 2003, a group of workers at Korean-based Nobland International, an export apparel manufacturer (maquila) in Guatemala, successfully unionized under the leadership of Carolina Sic, who was only twenty-two when she was interviewed.

I would like to know a little about your background, to get an idea — what was your childhood like? How many siblings do you have?
I was born here in Guatemala, in the capital, and my childhood was difficult. I have two brothers, one older and one younger. The older one isn't doing so well in life, and the other, the same thing. I'm 22 years old, I have a partner and two babies.

Pushing Back: Women Workers Speak Out on Free Trade (Washington D.C.: STITCH: Women United for Worker Justice, 2005), 24–30.

My mother is single because my father left us. My brothers and I used to live in the Children's House, for street kids, until I was seven, when our relatives took us out. Afterwards, I went to a school in zone five. Since my mom was working in a maquila, we would stay with my grandmother. I only got to fifth grade, because my mom didn't have enough money to keep us in school. So then I spent my time helping my grandmother, who made tortillas. By the time I was twelve I was going with my mom to a workshop that had machines. She taught me a lot about the maquila. . . .

When I was 18, I became pregnant and decided to go live with my husband because my mother and I didn't get along. When I went with him, we went through some difficult things. No one in his family was working when I came. My mother-in-law had been fired, and since she had been the only one supporting the family, we didn't know what to do. I sold all my things. These are hard thing — you can get so crazy with it. We would look for wood to make fires. My mother-in-law started making tortillas. Pregnant, I would take in washing, or sell things. My husband finally got a job, but when they found out he was underage, they fired him. By then I was about to have the baby, but I didn't have anything to give the child — since I didn't have a job, I didn't have social security (public healthcare), nothing. So I had the baby. It was a horrible moment, but the baby kept on growing and I decided to go work in this maquila, NB (Nobland), because once again no one in the family was working.

How did you feel when you started in the maquila?
I was nursing at the time. I was worried about my baby, but also excited about having a job and being able to take care of my family. The first two weeks I worked, they paid me the minimum wage, even though I had reached the production goal several days.

So from there I kept working, and as the months went along, I got to know the compañeros and compañeras [male and female coworkers] better. Since a lot of us lived in the same neighborhood, we had a lot of contact and still do. It's really a group of friends that we've had since we were little. Some of us, we met when I was in the streets. We'd get to talking — "What do you think of this?" or, "Why are they treating so-and-so like that?" But since we didn't know what to do, we just kept quiet. There were just five of us.

What were the conditions and treatment like inside the maquila?
It was really hot. The atmosphere was really tense also, because you couldn't leave. They would say, "Hurry up! We've got to make the goal!" They'd scold you. They'd use offensive words. They'd say they weren't

going to give you your salary. We would want to leave, but they would make us stay later and then not pay us overtime — instead they'd just pay like it was regular hours. I wasn't used to being treated like that, because I'd only worked in workshops before, with my mom, and they hadn't treated us like that. In this factory though, the pressure was extreme, but since all of us there needed the job, we dealt with it.

I had been working in the maquila for 10 months when we had finally had enough. By that time, I had one of my friends on each line, and we started talking. So that's how we started the first strike. We formed a group and went to the office and told them what was going on. The company fired us. There were a lot of us — 46. As a result, the majority of us were able to get our jobs back because the company didn't want to pay severance for all of us. They lowered our pay for 15 days for having gone on strike. But we were convinced that what we were doing was right, because we were defending our rights.

We started working again. There were something like five strikes that year. We decided on something, everyone would stop work, and we'd go up to the office. We saw what we were missing — the incentives, the overtime pay. But the management never paid attention to us, never said "Look, let's resolve this problem."

How did you get started with these actions? How did you come to agreement? Were there meetings?
During work hours, we would talk and discuss the things that were going badly, and then one person would take responsibility for telling everyone to stop work, and then we would go to the office to talk. There was a period where they wanted to hit us — they'd say we were like animals. But they couldn't fire us, because if they fired one of us, they'd have to fire everyone. There were over 40 of us, and they didn't want to pay severances, so they decided instead to split us up into two lines, so we couldn't communicate with each other.

We held another strike where we went to the office because the Korean manager had hit a compañera, and we said if they were going to hit one of us, they'd have to hit all of us. They fired all of us that day. I was a month and a half pregnant then, but I didn't know it — I thought I'd been feeling bad because of all the pressure. So I went to the hospital, and they told me that I was pregnant. I saw that as my only opportunity to get my job back, because when you're pregnant, they can't fire you. So I went back to work, but the whole length of the pregnancy was awful: they cut my pay, they cut my overtime, and they took away a bunch of things. They would look at someone who was talking with me and say, "Don't talk with her because she's a troublemaker." They wanted me to quit, but I wasn't going to quit something I had a right to.

When I was eight months pregnant, it was close to the holidays and things got ugly. They made me work at night, but the extra hours didn't show up on my paycheck. They suspended me for a lot of days out of every pay period, and that lowered my salary even more. And since Christmas was coming, I didn't know how I was going to be able to buy anything for my son. I was really confused — I didn't know what to do. On the one hand, I was dealing with so much pressure, and I couldn't take any more. On the other hand, I needed the job and I couldn't lose it. They treated me in such a nasty way, said such nasty things to me — that since I was pregnant, I was useless. They made me cry, but inside I knew that I wasn't the person they were saying I was. They also cut my social security benefits: on my social security certificate they said I earned only 20 quetzales (about US$2.50) a day when really I was earning 70 (about US$8.75). So social security gave me only 1,100 quetzales (about US$136) for my maternity benefit, when my friends had received up to 3,000 (about US$375) for the same three months.

So now I was nine months along, and one Saturday we were working when I felt some pains and knew I was going to have the baby. When I asked for permission to leave, since I might be going into labor, they wouldn't give it to me. They said overtime was obligatory until 4:30 pm. I felt so awful at that point. So I worked that day until 4:30 pm, with labor pains that had started at 1:00 pm. I gave birth early Sunday morning.

Did you know at that time about labor unions?

We didn't know what a union was. Once I saw an ad about a union on TV, and I asked my mom what a union was, and she explained to me that it's something that fights for your rights. But I didn't analyze the issue to the point of joining a union. Also, I had heard that having a union was dangerous because they could even kill you for it.

One time, after being fired after a strike, all of us went to the Labor Ministry. There were about 30 of us, and we said, "Well, either they do right by us or we'll see what happens." For all we'd done at that point, we really didn't know anything about what the laws were or what we could really do. We spoke with a labor inspector. He just talked about reinstatement. He didn't give us any idea to say okay, this, this, and this is going to happen or we're going to strike. We'd hold work stoppages but we didn't get what we wanted. All we got out of it was that they treated us badly and took away everything. We were tired. And while I was suspended for having organized a strike earlier; there was another strike and they fired about 30 workers.

So when these 30 people went to file a complaint because they wouldn't let them return to work, I was already back in the factory. They told me that they had met a girl at the Labor Ministry that worked forming unions. She asked them what the problem was and started talking to them about what a union was. Everyone said to me, "Fine, if you're in a union they kill you and run you out and turn on you, and I don't know — they disappear you." That scared me. But my compañeras said, "Let's do it. Maybe it will work and they'll treat us better." I thought about it and decided to participate. So, several of us started to form the union.

Since I sell things outside the maquila like pants and blouses, everyone comes up to me and I have a lot of people who know me. I know how to interact with them. I know my people, I know how they truly are. Of course when we're with the Koreans, we're not the same people. When we started to have a lot of folks, then we'd meet in my house or in another compañera's house. Every Saturday we would meet with that same organizer to make decisions.

What things changed once the union was formed?

When we got organized, we saw a lot of changes. When we got the injunction and announced that we had a union, we were so proud. We knew that we were going to stand up to defend our compañeras, and we did. When we stood up for a compañera who was being yelled at, the Korean manager didn't believe that we were actually defending her, that we had the right to defend her. That supervisor left. Another supervisor decided to leave too. We got rid of these two supervisors who were really the ones that treated the workers badly. It was such a sense of pride, to be able to say, "I'm going to defend my compañera here and no one can stop me from doing it."

Now, the treatment from the supervisors isn't like it was before. Things are calmer. We had a meeting with the company directly where we were able to say that we weren't going to tolerate mistreatment anymore. And that they couldn't force us to work overtime. And that if we did do one hour of overtime, we would be keeping track, and they would have to pay us. The production goals before, they didn't pay us for reaching them. Now they do. In other words, the whole environment has changed.

How did your family feel about the impact of your union participation on your family life?

Well, with my mom, I didn't have any problems because she was in the same situation in her time. She also worked in a maquila and did the same thing. So she told me it was fine, to stick with it. I did have some trouble with my partner; he didn't accept it. He didn't understand the abuse that took place in the maquila. So he would say that being in a union I could get killed. We had a lot of problems because of it.

They say that with what they call "free trade," the companies will have an easier time leaving any country whenever they want. How does this impact workers?
Oh, like saying "Let's go to Nicaragua" or "Let's go to El Salvador" — it could become a big competition, if in El Salvador they do the same work for less pay. So they'd leave us here without work. I also think that the Labor Ministry takes part, the way that the Labor Ministers say, "Fine, so here the law doesn't apply" so that the maquilas stay put. The businessmen say, "In Guatemala the laws are stricter than in El Salvador, so let's go to El Salvador." I feel the laws are good here. The Labor Ministry should take the role of defending them. If we are on the side of the law, it defends us. If we're not on the side of the law, it can't.

Before we had the union and we'd go to the Labor Ministry, they'd send a labor inspector and when we got to the factory, the legal declaration [formal report] was already signed. We had no idea what it meant to sign a declaration, what it meant to file a complaint. We'd sign the papers, and we didn't even read them. We thought the inspectors had been bought off, because you'd fight, fight, fight, and they wouldn't do anything. If from my very first complaint they had said, "Look, your help will come through this organization," I would have been in the union for three years by now. But they don't give you any information.

And how has it affected the lives of the workers and of their union when the company says it's going to move to another country?
Psychologically, it affects the people because they're afraid of being left without a job. When you form a union, the company starts to say that because of the union they're going to leave. That's when the people start to speak against us, because we're playing a role in fighting for the workers, and then the company takes the line, "Fine, have your union but we're leaving and you'll be out of a job."

What do most people in your community do to try to improve things in their lives?
They work. That, and then a lot of people from my neighborhood have gone to the United States, because they say they pay well there. Even my husband has said that if things don't look up here that we should go to the

U.S. because his brother is there. If the work situation here doesn't improve, what road can you take?

What we would agree with, for the workers of Guatemala, would be to have more work, but not just maquila jobs. Instead, I think there could be other kinds of work, something that gives Guatemalan workers opportunities. The maquila only pays enough for beans and tortillas. You lose your whole day being exploited, the pay is so low. . . .

READING AND DISCUSSION QUESTIONS

1. What convinced Carolina Sic and her compañeras to unionize?

2. According to Sic, how did the companies in Guatemala typically respond to strikes and other forms of labor organizing? What happened in her union's case?

3. What examples of employer abuse does Sic describe?

4. How did Sic's coworkers, family, and friends react to her involvement in organizing against unfair labor practices?

DOCUMENT 33-5

AL GORE

On Solving the Climate Crisis

September 18, 2006

Former U.S. vice president Al Gore has become almost synonymous with the movement to end global warming. Awarded the Nobel Peace Prize in 2007 for his efforts — which included the Oscar-winning documentary An Inconvenient Truth *— Gore has tirelessly campaigned worldwide to end practices that hasten the dangerous degradation of the earth's natural cooling systems. In a 2006 speech at New York University, he denied claims made by business and political leaders that the problem of global warming is*

Al Gore, Speech at New York University School of Law, September 18, 2006.

insurmountable and offered a viable strategy to counter it. He also alluded to — and countered — the less popular argument that global warming is a fabrication or part of a natural ecological process.

A few days ago, scientists announced alarming new evidence of the rapid melting of the perennial ice of the north polar cap, continuing a trend of the past several years that now confronts us with the prospect that human activities, if unchecked in the next decade, could destroy one of the earth's principle mechanisms for cooling itself. Another group of scientists presented evidence that human activities are responsible for the dramatic warming of sea surface temperatures in the areas of the ocean where hurricanes form. A few weeks earlier, new information from yet another team showed dramatic increases in the burning of forests throughout the American West, a trend that has increased decade by decade, as warmer temperatures have dried out soils and vegetation. All these findings come at the end of a summer with record-breaking temperatures and the hottest twelve-month period ever measured in the U.S., with persistent drought in vast areas of our country. *Scientific American* introduces the lead article in its special issue this month with the following sentence: "The debate on global warming is over."

Many scientists are now warning that we are moving closer to several "tipping points" that could — within as little as 10 years — make it impossible for us to avoid irretrievable damage to the planet's habitability for human civilization. In this regard, just a few weeks ago, another group of scientists reported on the unexpectedly rapid increases in the release of carbon and methane emissions from frozen tundra in Siberia, now beginning to thaw because of human-caused increases in global temperature. The scientists tell us that the tundra in danger of thawing contains an amount of additional global warming pollution that is equal to the total amount that is already in the earth's atmosphere. Similarly, earlier this year, yet another team of scientists reported that the previous twelve months saw 32 glacial earthquakes on Greenland between 4.6 and 5.1 on the Richter scale — a disturbing sign that a massive destabilization may now be underway deep within the second largest accumulation of ice on the planet, enough ice to raise sea level 20 feet worldwide if it broke up and slipped into the sea. Each passing day brings yet more evidence that we are now facing a planetary emergency — a climate crisis that demands immediate action to sharply reduce carbon dioxide emissions worldwide in order to turn down the earth's thermostat and avert catastrophe.

The serious debate over the climate crisis has now moved on to the question of how we can craft emergency solutions in order to avoid this catastrophic damage.

This debate over solutions has been slow to start in earnest not only because some of our leaders still find it more convenient to deny the reality of the crisis, but also because the hard truth for the rest of us is that the maximum that seems politically feasible still falls far short of the minimum that would be effective in solving the crisis. This no-man's land — or no-politician zone — falling between the farthest reaches of political feasibility and the first beginnings of truly effective change is the area that I would like to explore in my speech today. . . .

My purpose is not to present a comprehensive and detailed blue-print — for that is a task for our democracy as a whole — but rather to try to shine some light on a pathway through this terra incognita [unknown land] that lies between where we are and where we need to go. Because, if we acknowledge candidly that what we need to do is beyond the limits of our current political capacities, that really is just another way of saying that we have to urgently expand the limits of what is politically possible.

I have no doubt that we can do precisely that, because having served almost three decades in elected office, I believe I know one thing about America's political system that some of the pessimists do not: it shares something in common with the climate system; it can appear to move only at a slow pace, but it can also cross a tipping point beyond which it can move with lightning speed. Just as a single tumbling rock can trigger a massive landslide, America has sometimes experienced sudden avalanches of political change that had their beginnings with what first seemed like small changes.

Two weeks ago, Democrats and Republicans joined together in our largest state, California, to pass legally binding sharp reductions in CO_2 emissions. Two hundred ninety-five American cities have now independently "ratified" and embraced CO_2 reductions called for in the Kyoto Treaty.[8] Eighty-five conservative evangelical ministers publicly broke with the Bush-Cheney administration to call for bold action to solve the climate

---

[8] **Kyoto Treaty**: A 1995 agreement produced by the UN Conference on Climate Change in Kyoto, Japan, under which signatory countries vowed to reduce their emissions of greenhouse gases between 2008 and 2012, and agreed to instruments to measure compliance. The treaty was ratified by 141 nations and took effect in 2005; however, President George W. Bush pulled the United States from the agreement in 2001.

crisis. Business leaders in both political parties have taken significant steps to position their companies as leaders in this struggle and have adopted a policy that not only reduces CO_2 but makes their companies zero carbon companies. Many of them have discovered a way to increase profits and productivity by eliminating their contributions to global warming pollution.

Many Americans are now seeing a bright light shining from the far side of this no-man's land that illuminates not sacrifice and danger, but instead a vision of a bright future that is better for our country in every way — a future with better jobs, a cleaner environment, a more secure nation, and a safer world.

After all, many Americans are tired of borrowing huge amounts of money from China to buy huge amounts of oil from the Persian Gulf to make huge amounts of pollution that destroys the planet's climate. Increasingly, Americans believe that we have to change every part of that pattern.

When I visit port cities like Seattle, New Orleans, or Baltimore, I find massive ships, running low in the water, heavily burdened with foreign cargo or foreign oil arriving by the thousands. These same cargo ships and tankers depart riding high with only ballast water to keep them from rolling over. One-way trade is destructive to our economic future. We send money, electronically, in the opposite direction. But, we can change this by inventing and manufacturing new solutions to stop global warming right here in America. I still believe in good old-fashioned American ingenuity. We need to fill those ships with new products and technologies that we create to turn down the global thermostat. Working together, we can create jobs and stop global warming. But we must begin by winning the first key battle — against inertia and the fear of change. . . .

Our children have a right to hold us to a higher standard when their future — indeed the future of all human civilization — is hanging in the balance. They deserve better than the spectacle of censorship of the best scientific evidence about the truth of our situation and harassment of honest scientists who are trying to warn us about the looming catastrophe. They deserve better than politicians who sit on their hands and do nothing to confront the greatest challenge that humankind has ever faced — even as the danger bears down on us. . . .

So, what would a responsible approach to the climate crisis look like if we had one in America?

Well, first of all, we should start by immediately freezing CO_2 emissions and then beginning sharp reductions. Merely engaging in high-minded debates about theoretical future reductions while continuing to steadily increase emissions represents a self-delusional and reckless approach. In some ways, that approach is worse than doing nothing at all, because it lulls the gullible into thinking that something is actually being done when in fact it is not.

An immediate freeze has the virtue of being clear, simple, and easy to understand. It can attract support across partisan lines as a logical starting point for the more difficult work that lies ahead. . . .

A responsible approach to solving this crisis would also involve joining the rest of the global economy in playing by the rules of the world treaty that reduces global warming pollution by authorizing the trading of emissions within a global cap.

At present, the global system for carbon emissions trading is embodied in the Kyoto Treaty. It drives reductions in CO_2 and helps many countries that are a part of the treaty to find the most efficient ways to meet their targets for reductions. . . .

The absence of the United States from the treaty means that 25 percent of the world economy is now missing. It is like filling a bucket with a large hole in the bottom. When the United States eventually joins the rest of the world community in making this system operate well, the global market for carbon emissions will become a highly efficient closed system and every corporate board of directors on earth will have a fiduciary duty to manage and reduce CO_2 emissions in order to protect shareholder value.

Many American businesses that operate in other countries already have to abide by the Kyoto Treaty anyway, and unsurprisingly, they are the companies that have been most eager to adopt these new principles here at home as well. The United States and Australia are the only two countries in the developed world that have not yet ratified the Kyoto Treaty. Since the Treaty has been so demonized in America's internal debate, it is difficult to imagine the current Senate finding a way to ratify it. But the United States should immediately join the discussion that is now under way on the new tougher treaty that will soon be completed. We should plan to accelerate its adoption and phase it in more quickly than is presently planned.

Third, a responsible approach to solutions would avoid the mistake of trying to find a single magic "silver bullet" and recognize that the answer will involve what Bill McKibben has called "silver-buckshot" — numerous important solutions, all of which are hard, but no one of which is by itself the full answer for our problem. . . .

Over the next year, I intend to convene an ongoing broad-based discussion of solutions that will involve leaders from government, science, business, labor, agriculture, grass-roots activists, faith communities, and others.

I am convinced that it is possible to build an effective consensus in the United States and in the world at large on the most effective approaches to solve the climate crisis. . . .

First, dramatic improvements in the efficiency with which we generate, transport, and use energy will almost certainly prove to be the single biggest source of sharp reductions in global warming pollution. Because pollution has been systematically ignored in the old rules of America's marketplace, there are lots of relatively easy ways to use new and more efficient options to cheaply eliminate it. Since pollution is, after all, waste, business and industry usually become more productive and efficient when they systematically go about reducing pollution. After all, many of the technologies on which we depend are actually so old that they are inherently far less efficient than newer technologies that we haven't started using. One of the best examples is the internal combustion engine. When scientists calculate the energy content in BTUs of each gallon of gasoline used in a typical car, and then measure the amounts wasted in the car's routine operation, they find that an incredible 90% of that energy is completely wasted. . . .

To take another example, many older factories use obsolete processes that generate prodigious amounts of waste heat that actually has tremendous economic value. By redesigning their processes and capturing all of that waste, they can eliminate huge amounts of global warming pollution while saving billions of dollars at the same time. . . .

We worry today that terrorists might try to inflict great damage on America's energy infrastructure by attacking a single vulnerable part of the oil distribution or electricity distribution network. So . . . we should develop a distributed electricity and liquid fuels distribution network that is less dependent on large coal-fired generating plants and vulnerable oil ports and refineries.

Small windmills and photovoltaic solar cells distributed widely throughout the electricity grid would sharply reduce CO_2 emissions and at the same time increase our energy security. Likewise, widely dispersed ethanol and biodiesel production facilities would shift our transportation fuel stocks to renewable forms of energy while making us less dependent on and vulnerable to disruptions in the supply of expensive crude oil from the Persian Gulf, Venezuela, and Nigeria, all of which are extremely unreliable sources upon which to base our future economic vitality. It would also make us less vulnerable to the impact of a category 5 hurricane hitting coastal refineries or to a terrorist attack on ports or key parts of our current energy infrastructure. . . .

A second group of building blocks to solve the climate crisis involves America's transportation infrastructure. We could further increase the value and efficiency of a distributed energy network by retooling our failing auto giants — GM and Ford — to require and assist them in switching to the manufacture of flex-fuel, plug-in, hybrid vehicles. The owners of such vehicles would have the ability to use electricity as a principle source of power and to supplement it by switching from gasoline to ethanol or biodiesel. . . .

This shift would also offer the hope of saving tens of thousands of good jobs in American companies that are presently fighting a losing battle selling cars and trucks that are less efficient than the ones made by their competitors in countries where they were forced to reduce their pollution and thus become more efficient. . . .

Our current ridiculous dependence on oil endangers not only our national security, but also our economic security. Anyone who believes that the international market for oil is a "free market" is seriously deluded. It has many characteristics of a free market, but it is also subject to periodic manipulation by the small group of nations controlling the largest recoverable reserves, sometimes in concert with companies that have great influence over the global production, refining, and distribution network.

It is extremely important for us to be clear among ourselves that these periodic efforts to manipulate price and supply have not one but two objectives. They naturally seek to maximize profits. But even more significantly, they seek to manipulate our political will. Every time we come close to recognizing the wisdom of developing our own independent sources of renewable fuels, they seek to dissipate our sense of urgency and derail our effort to become less dependent. That is what is happening at this very moment. . . .

Several important building blocks for America's role in solving the climate crisis can be found in new approaches to agriculture. As pointed out by the "25 by 25" movement (aimed at securing 25 percent of America's power and transportation fuels from agricultural sources by the year 2025) we can revitalize the farm economy by shifting its mission from a focus on food, feed, and fiber to a focus on food, feed, fiber, fuel, and ecosystem services. We can restore the health of depleted soils by encouraging and rewarding the growing of fuel source crops like switchgrass and saw-grass, using no-till cultivation, and scientific crop rotation. We should also reward farmers for planting more trees and sequestering more carbon. . . .

Similarly, we should take bold steps to stop deforestation and extend the harvest cycle on timber to optimize the carbon sequestration that is most powerful and most efficient with older trees. On a worldwide basis, 2 and 1/2 trillion tons of the 10 trillion tons of CO_2 emitted each year come from burning forests. So, better management of forests is one of the single most important strategies for solving the climate crisis.

Biomass — whether in the form of trees, switchgrass, or other sources — is one of the most important forms of renewable energy. And renewable sources make up one of the most promising building blocks for reducing carbon pollution.

Wind energy is already fully competitive as a mainstream source of electricity and will continue to grow in prominence and profitability. . . .

The rapid urbanization of the world's population is leading to the prospective development of more new urban buildings in the next 35 years than have been constructed in all previous human history. This startling trend represents a tremendous opportunity for sharp reductions in global warming pollution through the use of intelligent architecture and design and stringent standards. . . .

The most important set of problems by that must be solved in charting solutions for the climate crisis have to do with coal, one of the dirtiest sources of energy that produces far more CO_2 for each unit of energy output than oil or gas. Yet, coal is found in abundance in the United States, China, and many other places. Because the pollution from the burning of coal is currently excluded from the market calculations of what it costs, coal is presently the cheapest source of abundant energy. And its relative role is growing rapidly day by day.

Fortunately, there may be a way to capture the CO_2 produced as coal is burned and sequester it safely to prevent it from adding to the climate crisis. It is not easy. This technique, known as carbon capture and sequestration (CCS), is expensive and most users of coal have resisted the investments necessary to use it. However, when the cost of *not* using it is calculated, it becomes obvious that CCS will play a significant and growing role as one of the major building blocks of a solution to the climate crisis. . . .

Global warming pollution, indeed all pollution, is now described by economists as an "externality." This absurd label means, in essence: we don't [need] to keep track of this stuff so let's pretend it doesn't exist.

And sure enough, when it's not recognized in the marketplace, it does make it much easier for government, business, and all the rest of us to pretend that it doesn't exist. But what we're pretending doesn't exist is the stuff that is destroying the habitability of the planet. We put 70 million tons of it into the atmosphere every 24 hours and the amount is increasing day by day. . . .

Many of our leading businesses are already making dramatic changes to reduce their global warming pollution. General Electric, Dupont, Cinergy, Caterpillar, and Wal-Mart are among the many who are providing leadership for the business community in helping us devise a solution for this crisis.

Leaders among unions — particularly the steel workers — have also added momentum to this growing movement.

Hunters and fishermen are also now adding their voices to the call for a solution to the crisis. In a recent poll, 86 percent of licensed hunters and anglers said that we have a moral obligation to stop global warming to protect our children's future.

And, young people — as they did during the Civil Rights Revolution — are confronting their elders with insistent questions about the morality of not moving swiftly to make these needed changes.

Moreover, the American religious community — including a group of 85 conservative evangelicals and especially the U.S. Conference of Catholic Bishops — has made an extraordinary contribution to this entire enterprise. . . . Individual faith groups have offered their own distinctive views. And yet — uniquely in religious life at this moment and even historically — they have established common ground and resolve across tenacious differences. . . .

Individual Americans of all ages are becoming a part of a movement, asking what they can do as individuals and what they can do as consumers and as citizens and voters. Many individuals and businesses have decided to take an approach known as "Zero Carbon." They are reducing their CO_2 as much as possible and then offsetting the rest with reductions elsewhere, including by the planting of trees. . . . This is not a political issue. This is a moral issue. It affects the survival of human civilization. It is not a question of left vs. right; it is a question of right vs. wrong. Put simply, it is wrong to destroy the habitability of our planet and ruin the prospects of every generation that follows ours. . . . By rising to meet the climate crisis, we will find the vision and moral authority to see them not as political problems but as moral imperatives. . . .

READING AND DISCUSSION QUESTIONS

1. According to Al Gore, why have solutions to the global environmental crisis been lacking?

2. What steps does Gore outline for ending the climate crisis?

3. How does Gore link oil dependence and U.S. national security?

4. What different groups have united behind this single cause and how have they come together?

COMPARATIVE QUESTIONS

1. How do George Bush and Al Gore define America's role and its relationship to the rest of the world in handling the political and environmental crises at hand?

2. Compare Tarabishi's and bin Laden's reactions to the impact of globalization on the Arab world.

3. How do Bush and bin Laden imagine the role of other countries and people in their very different missions?

4. In what ways does Carolina Sic's experience of globalization resonate (or conflict with) Tarabishi's theories?

5. How does Sic's story compare to the concerns of and demands made by feminist protesters in the United States in the 1960s (Document 31-4)?

6. What differences do you see in bin Laden's discussion of Muslims and Jews and the experiences of the soccer players described in Document 32-5?

Acknowledgments *(continued from p. iv)*

CHAPTER 15

15-1. Bartolomé de Las Casas, excerpt from *Brief Account of the Devastation of the Indies* (1542), *The Devastation of the Indies: A Brief Account*, translated by Herma Briffault (New York: A Continuum Book, Seabury Press 1974): 37–44, 51–52. Copyright © 1974 by Seabury Press. Reprinted by permission.

15-2. Zheng He, *Stele Inscription*. From *China and Africa in the Middle Ages*, translated by David Morison. Copyright © 1972. Reprinted with the permission of Taylor & Francis Ltd.

15-4. Bernardino de Sahagún, excerpt from *General History of the Things of New Spain* in *We People Here: Nahuatl Accounts of the Conquest of Mexico*, edited and translated by James Lockhart. Copyright © 1993. Reprinted with the permission of James Lockhart.

15-5. Matteo Ricci, excerpt from *China in the Sixteenth Century*, translated by Louis J. Gallagher, S. J. Copyright © 1942, 1953. Renewed © 1970 by Louis J. Gallagher, S. J. Used by permission of Random House, Inc.

CHAPTER 16

16-1. Louis XIV, from *Mémoires for the Instruction of the Dauphin*, translated and edited by Paul Sonnino. Copyright © 1970 by The Free Press. Reprinted with the permission of The Free Press, a Division of Simon & Schuster, Inc. All rights reserved.

16-2. Jacques-Benigne Bossuet, "On Divine Right." Excerpt from *Politics Drawn from the Very Words of Holy Scripture*, translated and edited by Patrick Riley. Copyright © 1990 by Cambridge University Press. Reprinted with the permission of Cambridge University Press.

16-4. Peter the Great, "Edicts and Decrees: Imposing Western Style on the Russians." Excerpts from *Peter the Great*, by Jay Oliva, p. 50. Prentice-Hall, 1970. *Peter the Great*, vol. 2, pp. 176–177. "Decree on the New Calendar (1699), from *Life and Thought in Old Russia*, translated by Marthe Blinoff, pp. 49–50. Copyright © 1961 by The Pennsylvania State University. Reprinted with the permission of Penn State Press. Excerpts from *A Source Book for Russian History from Early Times to 1917*, vol. 2, by George Vernadsky et al., pp. 347, 329, 357. Copyright © 1972. Reprinted by permission of Yale University Press.

CHAPTER 17

17-1. Galileo Galilei, from a "Letter to the Grand Duchess Christina." From *Discoveries and Opinions of Galileo*, translated by Stillman Drake. Copyright © 1957 by Stillman Drake. Used by permission of Doubleday, a division of Random House, Inc.

17-4. Voltaire (Francois-Marie Arouet), from "Of Universal Tolerance" and "Prayer to God." From *Les Philosophes*, edited by Norman L. Torrey, translated by Norman L. Torrey. Copyright © 1960 by Norman L. Torrey. Used by permission of G. P. Putnam's, a division of Penguin Group (USA), Inc.

17-5. Immanuel Kant, "What Is Enlightenment?" From *Introduction to Contemporary Civilization in the West* by Peter Guy, translator. Copyright © 1954 by Columbia University Press. Reprinted with the permission of the publisher.

CHAPTER 18

18-1. Nzinga Mbemba (Alfonso I), from "Letters to the King of Portugal." From *The African Past: Chronicles from Antiquity to Modern Times* (Boston: Little, Brown and Company, 1964). Copyright © 1964 by Basil Davidson. Reprinted with the permission of Curtis Brown, Ltd.

18-2. Leo Africanus, "A Description of Timbuktu." From "The Description of Africa," in *Reading About the World*, Volume 2, Third Edition. Translated by Paul Brians, written by Paul Brians et al., published by Harcourt Brace College Custom Books. Reprinted with the permission of the translator.

18-3. James Barbot, "A Voyage to New Calabar River." From *Collections of Voyages and Travels*, Third Edition, edited by Awnsham Churchill and John Churchill (London: H. Lintor, 1744–1747), Volume 5, p. 459. Modernized by A. J. Andrea. Reprinted with the permission of Alfred J. Andrea.

CHAPTER 20

20-1. Zhang-Han, "On Strange Tales" and "On Merchants." From "The Merchant Network in 16th Century China" by Timothy Brooks. Published in the *Journal of the Economic and Social History of the Orient XXIV* (May 1981): 186–208. Reprinted with the permission of E. J. Brill.

20-2. Kaibara Ekiken and Kaibara Tōken, "Common Sense Teachings for Japanese Children and Greater Learning for Women." From *Japan: A Documentary History*. (Armonk, NY: M. E. Sharpe, 1997): 258–261. Copyright © 1997 by David J. Lu. Reprinted with the permission of the author.

20-3. Mitsui Takafusa, "Some Observations on Merchants." From "Some Observations on Merchants," a translation of Mitsui Takafusa's "Choni Koken Roku," edited and translated by E. S. Crawcoeur. Published in *Transactions of the Asiatic Society of Japan*, Third Series, Volume 8. Reprinted with the permission of The Asiatic Society of Japan.

CHAPTER 23

23-2. Heinrich von Treitschke, excerpts from *History of Germany in the Nineteenth Century and Historical and Political Writings* from *Documents of German History*, edited and annotated by Louis L. Snyder. Copyright © 1958 by Rutgers University Press. Reprinted by permission of Rutgers University Press.

23-3. Leo Pinsker, from *Auto-Emancipation*: "The Case for a Jewish Homeland." Excerpt from *Auto-Emanicpation: An Appeal to His People, by a Russian Jew*, translated by Dr. D. S. Blondheim (Masada Youth Organization of America, 1939). Copyright © 1939. Reprinted with the permission of The Zionest Organization of America.

23-4. Theodor Herzl, excerpt from *The Jews' State*, edited and translated by Henk Overberg (Jason Aronson, Inc., 1977): 123, 129, 130, 134, 135, 139, 140, 144–146, 148, 149, 196. Copyright © 1977. Reprinted with the permission of Jason Aronson, Inc./Rowman & Littlefield Publishing Group.

CHAPTER 24

24-2. "An Ottoman Government Decree on the 'Modern' Citizen," excerpt from *Ottoman Government Decree Issued to the Amir of Shamr, His Excellency Firhan Pasha*, June 19, 1870. Ottoman archives of Directorate General of State Archives at the Prime

Ministry. Mosul: Tapu Tahrir, 1869–1872. Translated by Akram Khater. Reprinted with Permission of Akram Khater.

24-3. Ndansi Kumalo, "On the British Incursion in Zimbabwe." Excerpt from "His Story," from *Ten Africans*, edited by Margery Perham. Copyright 1936 by Faber and Faber Ltd. Reprinted with permission.

CHAPTER 25

25-1. Lin Zexu, from a "Letter to Queen Victoria." From *China in Transition 1517–1911*, edited by Zen Kuofan and Dun J. Li (Van Nostrand, 1969): 64–67. Reprinted with the permission of John Wiley & Sons, Inc.

25-4. Sun Yat-sen, "On The Three People's Principles and the Future of the Chinese People" From *Prescriptions for Saving China: Selected Writings of Sun Yat-sen*, edited by Julie Lee Wei, Ramon H. Myers, and Donald G. Gillin. Translation copyright © 1994 by the Board of Trustees of Leland Stanford Junior University. Reprinted with permission.

25-5. The Black Dragon Society, "Anniversary Statement." From *Sources of Japanese Traditions*, Volume 2, by William Theodore de Bary and Donald Keene. Copyright © 1963 by Columbia University Press. Reprinted by permission of the publisher.

CHAPTER 26

26-1. Don Manuel Valdivieso y Carrion, "A Spanish Colonist Protests the Marriage of His Daughter to Don Teodoro Jaramillo, a Person of Lower Social Standing." Quito, 1784–1785. Excerpts from *Colonial Lives: Documents in Latin American History, 1550–1850*, edited by Richard Boyer and Geoffrey Spurling. Copyright © 2000 Oxford University Press, Inc. Reprinted with permission of Oxford University Press, Ltd.

26-4. José Carlos Maríategui, excerpt from "The Problem of the Indian," from *Seven Interpretive Essays on Peruvian Reality*: "On the Indian and Land" by Jose Carlos Mariategui, translated by Majority Urquidi, pp. 22–25. Copyright © 1971. Reprinted by permission of University of Texas Press.

CHAPTER 27

27-1. Henry S. Clapham, from *Mud and Khaki: Memoirs of an Incomplete Soldier.* Copyright © 1930 by Henry S. Clapham, pp. 141–153. Reprinted with the permission of Hutchinson Publishing Group Ltd.

CHAPTER 28

28-5. Hu Shi, "The Chinese Attitude Toward Modern Civilization of the West." Excerpt from *Modern China: From Mandarin to Commissar*. Copyright © 1978 by Dun J. Li. Reprinted with the permission of Scribner, a division of Simon & Schuster, Inc.

CHAPTER 29

29-3. Adolf Hitler, excerpts from *Mein Kampf* by Adolf Hitler, translated by Ralph Manheim. Copyright © 1943. Renewed 1971 by Houghton Mifflin Company. Reprinted by permission of Houghton Mifflin Harcourt Publishing Company and the Random House Group, Ltd. All rights reserved.

29-4. Sigmund Freud, excerpts from *Civilization and Its Discontents* by Sigmund Freud, translated by James Strachey. Copyright 1961 by James Strachey, renewed by

33-2. George Tarabishi, "A Remarkable Discussion of Globalization and Its Impact on Arab Culture: Globalization as a Matter of Conflict." From *al-Bahrain al-Thaqafia*, October 2000. Translated by Akram Khater. Reprinted with permission Akram Khater.

33-4. Carolina Sic, from an "Interview with Women United for Worker Justice." Excerpt from an interview in *Pushing Back: Women Workers Speak Out On Free Trade*, Washington: STITCH, 2004. Reprinted by permission.

33-4. Al Gore, "On Solving the Climate Crisis." From a speech at New York University School of Law, September 18, 2006. Reprinted with permission.